T0327005

Ukrainian Economic History
Interpretive Essays

HARVARD UKRAINIAN RESEARCH INSTITUTE
HARVARD SERIES IN UKRAINIAN STUDIES

Editorial Board

George G. Grabowicz, *Editor-in-Chief*

Robert A. De Lossa, *Managing Editor*

Michael S. Flier
Lubomyr Hajda
Edward L. Keenan
Roman Szporluk

Dzvinka S. Dobrianska, *Administrative Assistant*

Cambridge, Massachusetts

Ukrainian Economic History

Interpretive Essays

I. S. Koropeckyj, Editor

Distributed by Harvard University Press
for the
Harvard Ukrainian Research Institute

Publication of this volume was made possible through the generous support of Thomas Yarema, major benefactor of the Ukrainian Studies Fund at Harvard University.

© 1991 by the President and Fellows of Harvard College
All rights reserved

Second Printing, 1994
ISBN 0-916458-35-0 (cl.)
ISBN 0-916458-63-6 (pb.)
Library of Congress Catalog Number 90-50460

Cover Design: *Designworks, Inc.*
Typesetting: *Chiron, Inc.*
Printed on Acid-Free Paper in the United States of America
by *Thomson-Shore, Inc.*

The Harvard Ukrainian Research Institute was established in 1973 as an integral part of Harvard University. It supports research associates and visiting scholars who are engaged in projects concerned with all aspects of Ukrainian studies. The Institute also works in close cooperation with the Committee on Ukrainian Studies, which supervises and coordinates the teaching of Ukrainian history, language, and literature at Harvard University.

Contents

Preface

Western studies of the economy of the USSR have been concerned primarily with problems pertaining to the Soviet Union as a whole. Almost no attention has been paid to the economic problems of the constituent parts of the union. The objective of the quinquennial conferences at the Harvard Ukrainian Research Institute has been to remedy this situation to a certain degree by studying various aspects of the economy of one of the most important Soviet republics, the Ukraine. Thus, the First Conference, which took place in 1975, was devoted to an analysis of current conditions in the Ukrainian economy; its proceedings were published under the title, *The Ukraine within the USSR: An Economic Balance Sheet* (New York, 1977). The subject of the Second Conference in 1981 was the development of economics in the Ukraine; its proceedings appeared as *Selected Contributions of Ukrainian Scholars to Economics* (Cambridge, Mass., 1984). The Third Conference in 1985 dealt with the history of the Ukrainian economy from the time of Kievan Rus' to the outbreak of World War I. The Fourth Conference, scheduled for 1990, will be devoted to an analysis of the Ukrainian economy since the early 1970s and to projections of economic trends for the beginning of the twenty-first century.

The present volume contains the papers presented at the 1985 conference, except for the chapters by Robert E. Jones and myself which were added to round out the proceedings. It is a pleasure to acknowledge the generous assistance of Holland Hunter throughout this entire project on Ukrainian economics, including his remarks at the last conference's dinner. I am grateful to Frank Sysyn for help with the organization of the conference and Orest Subtelny for help with the preparation of a historical chronology. I would also like to express my gratitude to the Ukrainian Studies Fund for financial support in organizing the conference. Finally, I would like to thank Sophia Koropeckyj for translating one of the chapters and for her manifold help in editing this book.

I.S.K.

Chronology of Historical Events
in the Ukraine prior to World War I

I. Kievan Rus' and the Period
until the End of the Sixteenth Century

Early 9th c.	Beginning of Kievan Rus'
882	Prince Oleg's conquest of Kiev, which becomes capital of the Riurik dynasty
907	Prince Oleg's commercial treaty with Byzantium
2nd half of 10th c.	Expansion of the Kievan Rus' state
988	Christianity is accepted from Byzantium
1018–31	Galicia under the Cracow Principality's rule
End of 11th c.	Transcarpathia incorporated into Hungary
11th–12th c.	Composition of the *Pravda Rus'skaia*
1150s–60s	Expansion of the Galician Principality toward South-East (Black Sea)
1169	Destruction of Kiev by Prince Andrei Bogoliubskii of Rostov-Suzdal'
1199	Consolidation of Galicia and Volhynia into an autonomous principality under Prince Roman
1214–19	Galicia under Hungarian rule
1230s–40s	Consolidation of the Grand Duchy of Lithuania
1240	Conquest of Kiev by Tatars
Early 1250s	Founding of the city of Lviv
1253	Crowning of Prince Danylo as king of Galicia and Volhynia by Pope Innocent IV

1264	Prince (King) Lev I unites Transcarpathia with Galicia
1339	Sanok, the first city to be granted Magdeburg Law
1340	Volhynia incorporated into the Grand Duchy of Lithuania after the death of King Iurii II (Boleslav Troidenovych)
1348	Incorporation of Galicia and part of Volhynia into Poland
mid-14th c.	Bukovyna incorporated into the Moldavian Principality
1360s	Incorporation of Kiev, Chernihiv, Pereiaslav, and Podillia provinces into Lithuania
1372–78	Galicia, under Prince Volodyslav Opil's'kyi's rule, becomes semi-autonomous entity under Hungary
1378–87	Galicia under Hungary's rule
1385	Personal union between Poland and Lithuania
1387	Incorporation of Galicia and Kholm and Belz provinces into Poland
1450	Abolition of the Volhynian Principality
1471	Abolition of the Kievan Principality
1475	Crimea's Tatar Khanate (organized in 1443) becomes the vassal of Turkey
1st half of 16th c.	Bukovyna (within the Moldavian Principality) under Turkey's sovereignty
1505	Peasants (under Polish rule) forbidden to leave villages without lord's permission
1514	Chernihiv, Starodub, Novhorod Sivers'kyi, and Putyvl' regions incorporated into the Grand Duchy of Muscovy
1529, 1566, 1588	Introduction of Statutes in the Grand Duchy of Lithuania
Mid-16th c.	Organization of Zaporozhian Sich and growth of Cossackdom; colonization of Dnieper Basin
1557	Voloky Ustav—regulation of peasants' rights and obligations

1569	Union between Poland and Lithuania at Lublin and transfer of Kiev, Volhynia, and Bratslav provinces from Lithuanian to Polish administration
1574	First printed book in the Ukraine, in Lviv
1596	Union of a part of the Kiev Metropolitan's Orthodox Church with the Catholic Church in Brest
End of 16th c.	Rise of Orthodox Church brotherhoods in various cities

II. The Seventeenth and Eighteenth Centuries

1st half of 17th c.	Settlement of East (Sloboda) Ukraine
1618	Polish rule of Chernihiv and Sivers'k provinces
1632	Founding of Kiev Mohyla Academy
1648	Uprising led by Bohdan Khmel'nyts'kyi
1648	Establishment of Cossack regimental administrative division
1649	Organization of the Hetman State (Bratslav, Kiev, and Chernihiv provinces)
1654	Agreement between the Ukraine and Muscovy in Pereiaslav
1658	Proposed confederation of the Ukraine (under Ivan Vyhovs'kyi), Lithuania, and Poland in Hadiach
1661	Founding of Jesuit Academy in Lviv
1667	Treaty between Poland and Russia in Andrusiv: the Left Bank and the city of Kiev within Russian interests and the Right Bank under Poland
1668	Right- and Left-Bank Ukraine under the rule of Petro Doroshenko for a short period
1672	The Right Bank annexed by Turkey from Poland as a result of treaty in Buchach
1686	Treaty at Bakhchesarai returns Right Bank from Turkey to Poland and the region between the Dnieper and Buh rivers becomes no man's land

1702–04	Semen Palii's uprising on the Right Bank
1709	Battle at Poltava
1718, 1720	Founding of first manufactories in the Ukraine: tobacco in Okhtyrka and woolen textiles in Putyvl'
1754	Abolition of custom duties between Russia and the Ukraine
1764–83	Gradual abolition of the office of Hetman
1768	Haidamak uprising on the Right Bank
1772	Annexation of Galicia by Austria from Poland (first partition of Poland-Lithuania)
1775	Annexation of Bukovyna by Austria from Turkey
1775	Destruction of the Zaporozhian Sich
2nd half of 18th c.	Settlement of Southern Ukraine
1774–83	Incorporation of Crimea into the Russian Empire
1783	Introduction of general serfdom in the former Hetmanate
1792	Settlement of Zaporozhian Cossacks in the Kuban' region
1793, 1795	Incorporation of the Right Bank, Volhynia, Polissia, and Pidliashshia into the Russian Empire (second and third partitions of Poland)
1796	Opening of the first coal mine in Lysychans'k
1798	Publication of the first literary work in the modern Ukrainian language in Russian-ruled Ukraine
End of 18th c.	Founding of Black Sea ports (Kherson, Mykolaiv, Odessa)

III. The Nineteenth Century

1800	Opening of the first foundry in Luhans'k
1805	Founding of Kharkiv University
1809–15	Ternopil' province under Russia's rule
1812	Western and Eastern Galicia become a province of Austria

1817	Founding of Lviv University
Beginning of 19th c.	Expansion of Black Sea trade
1824	Opening of the first sugar mill in Troshchyn (Cherkasy region)
1834	Founding of Kiev University
1835	Abolition of Magdeburg Law in Kiev (last city in Russian-ruled Ukraine to lose it)
1837	Publication of the first literary work in the modern Ukrainian language in Western Ukraine
1846–47	Activity of Cyril-Methodius Brotherhood
1840s	Activity of Taras Shevchenko and development of modern national consciousness
1848	Abolition of serfdom in Austria-Hungary
1848	"Zoria Halytska"—the first Ukrainian-language daily newspaper
1849	Bukovyna becomes crown province of Austria
1860s	Beginning of oil industry in Western Ukraine
1861	Abolition of serfdom in the Russian Empire
1861	Construction of the first railroad line (Lviv–Peremyshl')
1863, 1876	Valuev and Ems decrees directed against the Ukrainian language and culture
1865	Founding of Odessa University
Last third of 19th c.	Cooperative movement in Western Ukraine
Last third of 19th c.	Expansion of heavy industry in Donbas
1867	Transcarpathian Ukraine becomes a part of Hungary within Austria-Hungary
1875	Founding of Chernivtsi University
1881	Development of iron ore production center in Kryvyi Rih

CHAPTER ONE

Periodization of Ukrainian Economic History

I. S. Koropeckyj

Introduction

The purpose of this study is to discuss the problem of the periodization of the millennium-long history of the Ukrainian economy. This economy at times constituted the national economy of an independent Ukrainian state and at other times was an economic region within other countries. Moreover, the Ukraine's economy was sometimes divided between two or more foreign states. There have not been many economies of this type in the world. An analogue would be the Italian economy, which experienced a similar history to that of the Ukrainian economy, but which, of course, has been a united national economy of an independent state for over a century. Economies which remain regions within foreign states, such as the Ukrainian economy within the USSR, have by and large been neglected in economic literature. It is true that recently considerable attention has been paid to the study of individual regions within national economies, including those inhabited by various ethnic groups. But these studies mostly focus on interregional inequality rather than on historical development.

For the most part, historico-economic studies have dealt with the economies of states with a history of continuous political independence. The term "national economy" is applied to such economies. Ukrainian history does not show such continuity. The Ukraine, which was not always known by this name, was a political independent state during three distinct periods: that of Kievan Rus' (ninth to mid-fourteenth century), the Hetman state (mid-seventeenth to mid-eighteenth century), and briefly at the end of the First World War. At other times, the Ukraine was incorporated either into one or a combination of the empires of Poland, Russia, and Austria-Hungary. During the periods when the Ukraine lacked independence, its lands were usually organized into separate administrative units mainly because of their ethnic distinctiveness. The status of the Ukraine as a region has stood in the way, to a certain degree, of complete integration of the Ukrainian economy into the national economy of these empires.

Regardless of the formal political status of the Ukraine, the fact remains that the Ukrainian nation lived compactly on more or less the same "national territory" for over a period of a thousand years. Certain regions, such as the middle and northern Right Bank of the Dnieper River, the northern Left Bank, Galicia, and Volhynia, were settled by Ukrainians from the earliest times. Other regions— Transcarpathian Ukraine, Bukovyna, the rest of the Left Bank, the eastern region (Sloboda Ukraine), the southern region, and the Kuban'—were settled by Ukrainians at various times later on. Since the political boundaries of the present-day Ukrainian SSR include the bulk of these lands, the republic's territory may be assumed to be Ukrainian "national territory." Whatever the political status of their land may have been, the people had to carry on economic activity on this territory in order to survive. Therefore, this economy can rightly be considered the national economy of the Ukrainian nation.

The Ukrainian economy, like any other, has undergone enormous change during the period of more than a thousand years. In order to understand this historical process, it is worthwhile to divide it into specific stages. This chapter investigates the problem of the periodization of Ukrainian economic history up to the 1917 Revolution. Part 1 is devoted to a survey of problems related to the periodization of economic history in general. In Part 2 two available periodization schemes of Ukrainian economic history are analyzed. A proposal for an alternative periodization is presented in Part 3 and its usefulness is tested in Part 4 using two economic variables, foreign trade and monetary circulation.

Finally, like the histories of other nations, Ukrainian history has a number of blank spots, unexplained relationships, and controversial issues. The objective of this chapter is not to contribute to the solution of these problems. In order to discuss the periodization of

Ukrainian economic history, we shall utilize those interpretations which have been generally accepted, but not necessarily completely agreed upon, by historians.

1. Problems of Historico-Economic Periodization

There are basically two approaches toward dividing economic history into defined periods. The Polish economist Witold Kula labels them "realistic" and "conventional."[1] According to the realistic approach, to which Marxists subscribe, periodization criteria have to be sought in the subject under investigation. In other words, economic periodization should be based on economic criteria which should, in turn, be used to identify breaks in the underlying variables and thus determine successive periods. The adherents of the conventional approach argue that, in view of the continuity of important variables, the empirical identification of breaks is quite difficult. But since periodization is necessary, even if only for didactic purposes, it cannot be but imperfect and pragmatic. Often events external to the economy have to serve as bench marks. However, such a methodology can still be considered realistic, as opposed to pragmatic conventionalism, as long as specific economic phenomena, which are found in a period chosen in this way, do not significantly overlap with the preceding or succeeding periods.[2]

Studies on periodization have a long tradition in the field of economic history.[3] They were particularly popular in nineteenth-century Germany, where several economists and historians proposed classifications of economic development into stages using a variety of criteria for this purpose.[4] However, these constructs ignore the fact

[1] Witold Kula, *Problemy i metody historii gospodarczej* (Warsaw, 1963), p. 173.

[2] Ibid., p. 188.

[3] For an enumeration of various stage theories from ancient times on, see N. S. B. Gras, "Stages in Economic History," *Journal of Economic and Business History* 2, no. 3 (May 1930): 397–98. Among the most recent, the theory by W. W. Rostow is probably the best known. See his *The Stages of Economic Growth, A Non-Communist Manifesto*, 2d ed. (Cambridge, 1971).

[4] Among the German theories, those by Friedrich List, Bruno Hilderbrand, Karl Bücher, Werner Sombart, and, of course, Karl Marx are best known. For a recent discussion of the theories, see Bert F. Hoselitz, "Theories of Stages of Economic Growth," in Bert F. Hoselitz, ed., *Theories of Economic Growth* (Glencoe, N.Y., 1960); Elias H. Tuma, *European Economic History* (New York, 1970), chap. 3.

that economic life is a continuous process: "There is no hiatus in economic development, but always a constant tide of progress and change, in which the new blend[s] almost imperceptibly with the old."[5] Therefore, a stage does not represent a period in which the relevant variables are unchangeable; rather, what one can say is that "an economic stage is a socially competitive condition in which a new method or institution first rivals, then threatens, and finally out-distances an old one."[6] Not being able to identify a break in economic variables in order to delineate a particular stage, these scholars had to rely on discrete developments of non-economic institutions or on external events. As a result, the various stage theories are not useful for the study of purely economic factors responsible for the transition from one stage to another[7] or for economic development in general. A researcher interested in the historical development of an economic variable—for example, the extension of markets or exchange—does not need to refer to the stage framework at all.[8]

These theories suffer from an additional and very important shortcoming: the inability to integrate economic development with the development of social institutions. Without such integration economic development cannot be fully understood. This synthesis was achieved by Karl Marx, who was the first to unify sociology and economics into a theory intended to explain the immanent evolution of economic processes.[9] In fact, according to Joseph Schumpeter, this achievement justifies Marx's claim to greatness as an economic analyst.[10]

The Marxian theory of historical materialism deserves our attention because, as will be subsequently shown, it serves as the basis for one of the two available periodizations of Ukrainian economic history. According to Marxian theory, there are two dynamic forces in history: forces of production and relations of production. Both concepts are quite broad. Forces of production comprise: the existing organization

---

[5] Herbert Heaton, "Criteria of Periodization in Economic History," *Journal of Economic and Business History* 14, no. 3 (September 1955): 267.

[6] Gras, "Stages in Economic History," p. 397.

[7] Hoselitz, "Theories of Stages of Economic Growth," p. 234.

[8] Cf. John Hicks, *A Theory of Economic History* (London, 1976), p. 7.

[9] Joseph A. Schumpeter, *History of Economic Analysis* (New York, 1961), p. 441.

[10] Idem.

of production, rationality, technology, science, and, most importantly, man. Relations of production refer to social conditions and principles of distribution. The existing political, cultural, religious, and juridical institutions are called the superstructure. The development of the forces of production precedes changes in all aspects of social life. The process takes place through changes in the relationships between broad social groups (classes), which are defined by the ownership of the means of production and the distribution of national income between them. Class relations, which are antagonistic in character, are the agents of historical change. Marx classified human history into the following five stages or, as they are commonly referred to, socioeconomic formations: primeval communism, slaveholding, feudalism, capitalism, and socialism.[11]

In recent times, modern Marxists have offered modifications or revisions of this orthodox materialistic explanation of history. Three such variants deserve our attention. While adhering to the claim that the forces of production are ultimately bound to overcome the obstacles presented by the prevailing relations of production, Paul Baran and Eric Hobsbawm deny that the dynamics and characteristics of these variables are the same in all situations.[12] There is a multitude of possibilities for the relationships between them. These authors explain this as follows:

> The struggle between the forces of production and the relations of production proceeds unevenly. Dramatic conquests are less frequent than long periods of siege in which victories remain elusive, imperfect, and impermanent. Different countries display different patterns which depend on their size, location, the strength and cohesion of their ruling classes, the courage, determination and leadership of the under-privileged; on the measure of foreign influence and support of which both or either is exposed; on the pervasiveness and power of the dom-

[11] Cf. Karl Marx, *A Contribution to the Critique of Political Economy* (New York, 1970), pp. 20–21.

[12] Paul Baran and Eric Hobsbawm, "The Stages of Economic Growth: A Review," *Kyklos*, 1961, no. 2. The relationship between the forces of production and the relations of production in the less developed countries of today is quite different from that found in countries with a history of "classical" development, such as England or France. See Kula, *Problemy i metody*, p. 189.

inant ideologies (e.g. religion). Moreover, the course taken by this struggle and its outcome differs greatly from period to period.[13]

Therefore, no scheme of historical development with a specified number of stages, be it five or seven or three, can accommodate all concrete situations. The history of individual countries can best be explained by empirical investigations of their specific economic and political developments on the basis of some theoretical assumptions.[14]

For Kula, the claim that Marxian theory is capable of integrating economic and social developments is of great importance as applied to historical periodization. This characteristic allows the historian flexibility in the choice of variables needed for the construction of developmental stages.[15] If an economic variable, because of its continuity, cannot serve as the basis for periodization, discrete institutional changes can be used instead. Of course, this flexibility is possible given the assumption that institutional changes reflect the preceding changes in the forces of production which are difficult to identify.[16]

In these approaches modern Marxists continue to adhere to the premise of the primacy of economic changes vis-à-vis social change throughout all stages of historical development. Most recently, Roger Gottlieb has rejected such an approach, referring to it as a ''hard'' form of Marxian theory, especially with respect to feudalism.[17] He argues that under feudalism economic and social aspects are not yet emancipated from each other and change in society is thus a function of change in both aspects and not just in economics.[18] Furthermore, the ''hard'' theory cannot explain the transition from feudalism to

[13] Baran and Hobsbawm, ''Stages of Economic Growth,'' p. 239.

[14] Ibid., p. 240.

[15] Kula, *Problemy i metody*, pp. 188ff.

[16] Ibid., pp. 187–88.

[17] See Roger S. Gottlieb, ''Feudalism and Historical Materialism: a Critique and a Synthesis,'' *Science and Society* 47, no. 1 (Spring 1984). In this article Gottlieb also discusses the views on this problem of Maurice Dobb, Rodney Hilton, Robert Brenner, Guy Bois, Perry Anderson, and Immanuel Wallerstein. Gottlieb's views are shared by Samir Amin, ''Modes of Production, History and Unequal Development,'' *Science and Society* 49, no. 2 (Summer 1985), especially p. 197.

[18] It is a general proposition that economic activities become less differentiated from other human activities the further one goes into the past. Cf. Hicks, *A Theory of Economic History*, p. 1.

capitalism.[19] Instead, Gottlieb offers the "soft" form of Marxian historical materialism. Thus, he confines the primacy of economic over social change to capitalist formation only. Under feudalism, according to him, class relations are determined not only by the structure of the expropriation of economic surplus, but also by historically specific political conditions. These relations are affected by actions of the antagonistic classes involved and also by such forces as the world trade network (colonialism, imperialism). In effect, social life and historical changes under feudalism are an indeterminate outcome of political struggles rather than a determinate outcome of economic forces alone.[20]

The periodization of the economic history of a nation based on a theoretical model is no doubt attractive. For a historian such as Fernand Braudel, it is even imperative, as when he writes: "Economic history is comprehensible only within a succession of systems, whose model must be constructed by the historian as exactly as possible— ideally in its whole development, from its first emergence to its maturity and its end."[21] However, it is, as a rule, very difficult to determine empirically the borderline between the end of one stage and the beginning of another on the basis of economic activities. Further, non-Marxian historians have difficulty accepting the Marxian insistence on the specific relationship between economic and social variables, so they are unwilling to rely on social variables for economic periodization. Therefore, a pragmatic approach predominates in the applied work on the periodization of economic history in the West. Salient political events are usually selected as breaking points between two periods, e.g., the Great Revolution in France or the Civil War in the United States. When a work encompasses the economic history of an entire continent, periodization is simplified even further; important variables are discussed by centuries (e.g., 900–1500, 1500–1700, 1700–1914, 1920–1970).[22]

---

[19] Gottlieb, "Feudalism and Historical Materialism," p. 35.

[20] Ibid., p. 4.

[21] See his "Presentation" to Witold Kula, *An Economic Theory of the Feudal System: Towards a Model of the Polish Economy, 1500–1800* (London, 1976), p. 7.

[22] Cf. Carlo M. Cipolla, ed., *The Fontana Economic History of Europe*, vols. 1–4 (London, 1972–1973).

2. Available Schemes for the Periodization
of Ukrainian Economic History

The problem of the periodization of Ukrainian history seems to be quite perplexing. It has been satisfactorily solved neither with respect to economic history nor with respect to the general history of the Ukraine.[23] Before submitting a new proposal, let us first consider how Ukrainian economic history has been periodized in the existing literature. There exist two proposals: one by Kostiantyn Voblyi dating from 1919; the other in a recent collective work on Ukrainian economic history.

Voblyi divides the economic history of the Ukraine before the Revolution into four stages:[24] up to the mid-fifteenth century; from the end of the sixteenth century to the end of the eighteenth century; from the end of the eighteenth century until the emancipation of the peasants in 1861; and from the emancipation until the outbreak of World War I. Voblyi uses economic criteria, such as the composition and direction of foreign trade and its influence on the structure of Ukrainian economy and social conditions, in defining the various stages. Although he does not state it explicitly, Voblyi uses events extraneous to economics as bench marks, since the economic variables underlying his periodization are continuous and do not exhibit salient breaks.

Specifically, the first stage is characterized by the importance for the Ukrainian economy of transit trade between Scandinavia and Byzantium. The Ukraine exported forest products and imported primarily luxury goods. Voblyi sees the occupation of Constantinople by the Turks in 1453 and the closing of the Black Sea to Italian merchants as events marking the end of this stage. According to Voblyi, the second stage begins with the Union of Lublin of 1569 when Volhynia and the Right Bank were included in the Baltic trade via the Vistula River and in trade with Germany via the overland route. During this time, forest products were gradually replaced by grain and livestock as the main exports. The third stage begins at the end of the

---

[23] See "Round Table Discussion," in Ivan L. Rudnytsky, ed., *Rethinking Ukrainian History* (Edmonton, Alberta, 1981).

[24] See K. G. Voblyi, *Ekonomicheskaia geografiia Ukrainy* (Kiev, 1919), pp. 149–69.

eighteenth century with the incorporation of Volhynia and the Right Bank into the Russian Tsardom; the Left Bank and eastern Ukraine had already fallen under its influence by the mid-seventeenth century. This stage is characterized by the settlement of eastern and southern Ukraine and by the gaining of access to the Black Sea. The *chumak* trade (using oxen-driven wagons) between the hinterland and the Black Sea littoral and the beginnings of grain exports through the Black Sea ports are significant features of this stage. Finally, the emancipation marks the beginning of the fourth stage, the stage of industrialization and intensification of agricultural exports through the Black Sea.

While Voblyi's periodization scheme appears reasonable, the following three deficiencies make it difficult to accept. For one, the proposal is quite superficial. One gets the impression that it was added as an afterthought in the last section of Voblyi's book on economic geography. It is very likely that a scholar of Voblyi's stature considered this presentation an exploratory step to be followed by a more substantial work on the subject. Furthermore, Voblyi failed to reconcile the changes in economic criteria with the non-economic events used as bench marks. For example, the hiatus of one-and-a-half centuries between the first and second stages remains unexplained. The shift of the economic gravity point from Kiev and the Dnieper River to Halych and Volodymyr (and later to Lviv) and the Dniester River began substantially earlier than at the time of the Lublin union. If one considers the expansion of the sugar industry as the beginning of Ukrainian industrialization, then the latter occurred about thirty years earlier than the emancipation. On the other hand, if this beginning is identified with the rise of coal mining and ferrous metallurgy, then industrialization began about ten to twenty years after the emancipation. Finally, the omission of Galicia (and also of Transcarpathian Ukraine and Bukovyna) from consideration makes the understanding of Ukrainian economic development difficult, especially during the late period of Kievan Rus' when this region played a key role among the principalities.

The other periodization proposal, more substantial than that of Voblyi, is presented in *Istoriia narodnoho hospodarstva Ukrains'koi RSR. Ekonomika dosotsialistychnykh formatsii*, edited by T. I. Dereviankin (Kiev, 1983).[25] This is an important publication because it is the only work, written by a team of specialists, that treats Ukrainian economic history until 1917 comprehensively and on an advanced level. Other economic histories are either incomplete[26] or intended for classroom use.[27]

In this book, the pre-revolutionary economic history of the territory of the present-day Ukrainian SSR is divided into eight chapters, each devoted to a stage of economic development. The chapters are titled as follows: 1) The economic history of Ukrainian lands during the primeval communistic system and the inception of class society; 2) The economic development of the early feudal Old Rus' state— Kievan Rus' (9th – 12th centuries); 3) The economic condition of the Ukrainian lands during the period of feudal fragmentation of Rus' (12th – 15th centuries); 4) The development of the Ukraine's economy during the period of late feudalism (16th – 17th centuries); 5) The Ukraine's economic development during the conditions of disintegration of the feudal-serf economic system and the development of capitalist conditions (18th century); 6) The Ukraine's economy during the period of disintegration and crisis of the feudal-serf system and the continuing growth of capitalist conditions (the first half of the 19th century); 7) The economic development of the Ukraine during the age of capitalism (the 60s – 90s of the 19th century); 8) The Ukraine's economy during the age of imperialism (the beginning of the 20th century).

[25] This is the first volume of the three-volume work. See also my review of this volume, *Slavic Review* 45, no. 1 (Spring 1986). The remaining two volumes (in three parts, published in 1984, 1985, and 1987) are devoted to Ukrainian economic history after the 1917 Revolution.

[26] For example, D. I. Bahalii, *Narys istorii Ukrainy na sotsial'no-ekonomichnomu grunti*, vol. 1 (n.p., 1928), covers the history up to the fifteenth century; M. Ie. Slabchenko, in his works: *Hospodarstvo Het'manshchyny, XVII – XVIII stolittiv* (Odessa, 1923), *Zemlevladenie i formy sel'skogo khoziaistva* (Odessa, 1922), *Sud'by fabriki i promyshlennosti* (Odessa, 1922), *Ocherki torgovli i torgovogo kapitalizma* (Odessa, 1923), covers the seventeenth and eighteenth centuries only; Oleksander Ohloblyn, *A History of Ukrainian Industry*, Harvard Series in Ukrainian Studies, vol. 12 (Munich, 1971) covers the development of Ukrainian industry between the first half of the eighteenth century and the second third of the nineteenth century.

[27] V. O. Holobuts'kyi, *Ekonomichna istoriia Ukrains'koi RSR* (Kiev, 1970).

The contributors do not pay much attention to the stages of development which appear in the headings of their chapters. In their analysis of social and economic conditions they hardly make use of the concepts usually associated with such stages as feudalism and capitalism. True, the terms "feudalism" and "capitalism" are occasionally mentioned, but the connotation is primarily a negative one. In the official ideology of the USSR, both formations imply the exploitation of one group of people by another, poverty and enserfment (under feudalism) and unemployment and income inequality (under capitalism). In general, the authors go about their business of presenting Ukrainian economic history within the time frame of the particular chapters in a straightforward and chronological manner. Nevertheless, two characteristics of the periodization of Ukrainian economic history to be found in this work are worth mentioning. First, the periodization of Ukrainian economic history is patterned exactly on the periodization of Russian economic history.[28] Second, it is rigidly based on the orthodox (Gottlieb's "hard") version of Marxian theory. As will be shown, however, periodization based on these considerations is inappropriate for an analysis of Ukrainian economic history.

With respect to the first point, it does not make sense to use the same periodization for both Ukrainian and Russian economies as their paths of development have often diverged. The Ukrainian economy was completely separated from the economy of Muscovy/Russia during the period from the mid-thirteenth to the late seventeenth century and in some regions until the end of the eighteenth century. Substantial parts of the Ukraine, such as Galicia and Transcarpathian Ukraine, were never a part of the Russian state until World War II when they were incorporated into the USSR. But even with respect to the very early period, between the ninth and mid-thirteenth century, it is hardly justifiable to give the same label to the development stage of all regions composing the state of Kievan Rus'. The vast distances, lack of transportation and communication networks among the regions, extreme differences in climatic and resource conditions, and the particular geographical settings made the economies of principalities like Halych, Novgorod, or Iaroslavl' substantially different from one another.

---

[28] Cf. P. I. Liashchenko, *Istoriia narodnogo khoziaistva SSSR* vols. 1 and 2 (Moscow, 1948); P. O. Khromov, *Ekonomicheskoe razvitie Rossii* (Moscow, 1967).

Most of the Ukraine was incorporated into the Russian Empire at the end of the eighteenth century. Of course, the regions of the newly formed empire were not all at the same level of economic development at that time. As Oleksander Ohloblyn, the foremost specialist of this period of Ukrainian history, states,

> It is inadmissible to treat the history of Eastern Europe, and particularly of the f[ormer] Russian Empire as a single entity. One cannot proceed on the basis of the current political boundaries of a given economy. They developed during the course of history, and if the existing scheme happens to coincide with the reality in a given period, it all the same fails to explain the essential details and—most importantly—the historical evolution of existing forms and relationships.[29]

But there is no reason to assume that all regions of the newly created USSR (the time during which the preceding passage was written) were at the same level of economic development. Soviet historians argue that the all-Russian market was created during the 1760s,[30] a few decades before the annexation of the Right Bank and Volhynia. Although the bulk of the Ukrainian economy was part of this market until World War I, this condition was insufficient to ensure the same rate of growth for the Ukraine and for all other regions of the vast empire during this period. Historical experience and the differential growth of the various regions of the empire after political integration suggest that assigning the same developmental stage to all of them is far too general and obscures specific characteristics of the particular regions.

Another objection to the Soviet periodization is the classification of five out of eight stages of Ukrainian economic history, covering a period of about a thousand years, as feudal. It is highly inappropriate, on empirical grounds, to apply the same term to the Ukrainian economy in both the ninth and the nineteenth centuries. The analogy of the Ukrainian experience to that of feudalism in Western Europe between the fifth and fifteenth centuries is also inappropriate. Western

[29] Ohloblyn, *A History of Ukrainian Industry*, pt. 3, p. 17.

[30] The 1760s are considered the precise period. For a discussion of this problem, see Samuel H. Baron, "The Transition from Feudalism to Capitalism in Russia: A Major Soviet Historical Controversy," *American Historical Review* 77, no. 3 (June 1972): 725–27.

European feudalism, also referred to as the Middle Ages, was characterized by very slow change in social institutions and almost no technological and economic progress. On the other hand, during the one thousand years of so-called feudalism in the Ukraine, especially during the second half of this period, there occurred significant changes in technology, progress in education, discovery of new trade routes, and various social and political upheavals in world history. Thus, the term feudal, even with various qualifications, can hardly be applied to this long period in Ukrainian economic history.

Can the concept of feudalism be applied to any of these sub-periods in Ukrainian economic history? First, this concept has to be clarified because there is a difference between the definition usually accepted in the West and the Soviet definition. According to George Vernadsky, the outstanding specialist on this issue in the West, the concept of feudalism comprises the following three aspects: political—the mediatization of the supreme political authority, a hierarchy of rulers, and the reciprocity of personal contracts; economic—a manorial economy, restrictions on the legal status of peasants, and the distinction between the right of use and the right of ownership of landed estates; the feudal nexus—the control of land by a vassal on the condition of service to his seignior.[31] As Ivan Rudnytsky writes, "Feudalism may perhaps be best understood as a syndrome, a coming together of several interrelated socioeconomic, political, judicial, and cultural traits."[32] On the other hand, for Soviet historians, feudalism means a social formation under which pre-capitalist rent is extracted from peasants by princes and manorial lords using non-economic pressure.[33] The Soviet concept of this socioeconomic formation is simpler than the Western concept and thus leaves room for various interpretations.

The problem of feudalism in Eastern Europe was of no particular interest to scholars before the 1917 Revolution. However, in Soviet historiography, the argument put forth is that Eastern European nations, in the spirit of official ideology, like other nations, advanced through stages of development, as specified by Marx. With respect to feudalism, Soviet historians during the 1920s and 1930s claimed that

---

[31] George Vernadsky, *Kievan Russia* (New Haven, 1948), p. 165.

[32] See the entry by I. L. Rudnytsky, "Feudalism," in Volodymyr Kubijovyč, ed., *Encyclopedia of Ukraine*, vol. 1 (Toronto, 1984), p. 879.

[33] *Sovetskaia istoricheskaia entsiklopediia*, vol. 15 (Moscow, 1974), p. 20.

this socioeconomic formation prevailed as early as the period of Kievan Rus'. In the post-Stalin era, several conferences, symposia, and publications were devoted to this problem.[34] While the recent Soviet historians, on the basis of new research, were able to deviate from the Marxian scheme by arguing that Eastern Slavs, like the Germanic peoples, skipped the slaveholding stage, they were not permitted to deny the existence of feudalism. However, having accepted its existence, these historians could not agree as to the meaning, periodization, and typology of this developmental stage.[35] A Western scholar summarized the discussion as follows:

> The basic dilemma, however, remains and it became even sharper as a result of open discussion: there is an absolute necessity for the Party to adjust new scholarly insights at least minimally in accordance with the Marxian theorems, which were developed on the basis of historical knowledge arrived at during the nineteenth century. . . . [But] the generally agreed upon rejection of schematic dogmatism, the demand for an argument based on the sources, and the further creative development of the heritage of Marxist classicists cannot obscure the fact that for most Soviet historians this creative development still amounts to the simple insurance for their hypotheses by the use of quotations from Lenin.[36]

It is rather difficult not to have some doubts concerning the honesty of Soviet historians in this respect.

Such eminent historians as Mykhailo Hrushevs'kyi, Dmytro Bahalii, and George Vernadsky[37] belong to the group of those who question the applicability of feudalism to Kievan Rus'. On economic grounds, Vernadsky makes the following objections.[38] Although the manor economy expanded, it was not the foundation of the economy. In addition to great estates, there existed a large number of small

---

[34] For a review of these discussions, see Carsten Goehrke, "Zum gegenwärtigen Stand der Feudalismusdiskussion in der Sowjetunion," *Jahrbücher für Geschichte Osteuropas* 22, no. 2 (1974).

[35] Ibid., pp. 235–43.

[36] Ibid., p. 244.

[37] Mykhailo Hrushevs'kyi, *Istoriia Ukrainy-Rusy*, vol. 3 (1905; reprint, New York, 1954), chap. 3; Bahalii, *Narys istorii*, chap. 8; George Vernadsky, "Feudalism in Russia," *Speculum* 14, no. 3 (July 1939), also his *Kievan Russia*, pp. 163–73.

[38] Vernadsky, *Kievan Russia*, pp. 166–70.

landholdings. The large estates were not only of the manorial type, but also resembled the ancient latifundia. Land was privately owned and could be traded. The authority of the manorial lord was less extensive than in the West and he was subject to law like other people. The cultivators of the land had various kinds of legal status: completely free, free with various kinds of restrictions, serfs, and slaves. Because of the importance of foreign trade, a money economy was relatively well developed in all of economic life. Many of Vernadsky's arguments have been recently confirmed by the research of Soviet historians.[39]

However, if Kievan Rus' was not, at least until the mid-twelfth century, a feudal state, how would one define its socioeconomic system? According to Vernadsky, Kievan Rus' came into being on the Pontic steppes, replacing the Khazar kaganate. The Khazars were primarily involved in commerce with the Northern, Oriental, and Mediterranean regions. In addition to this legacy, another component of the economy of Kievan Rus' was the agriculture of the Slavic tribes, long settled in this territory. Finally, the social and economic institutions were formed under the strong influence of the slave capitalism of ancient Rome that was introduced via Byzantium. As a result, Vernadsky argues that "Kievan capitalism may be called commercial par excellence."[40]

Feudalistic tendencies, particularly with respect to the manorial economy, became more pronounced at the end of the twelfth century in the entire Kievan state. Increased attention in economic life to agriculture was related to the decline in foreign trade caused by persistent

[39] E.g., I. Ia. Froianov, *Kievskaia Rus'*, 2 vols. (Leningrad, 1974, 1980). He claims, for example, that the wealth of princes and boyars was associated with hunting and the ownership of livestock and not with agriculture (pp. 56–59) and also with gold, silver, furs, silk, and wines to be obtained through the plunder of foreign lands (p. 88); peasants' tribute to princes and boyars was not feudal rent but a tax in kind (pp. 64–79); if an expansion of landholdings was taking place, it was not through the takeover of peasant lands but through the increased cultivation of idle lands (pp. 95–96); small holdings by peasants, members of the *obshchina*, rather than large landholdings prevailed in agriculture (p. 99); agricultural workers were either slaves or free or semi-free people (vol. 2, pt. 3); there was no manorial economy (the mainstay of feudalism) because large estates were weakly developed and feudal relations were nonexistent (vol. 2, pt. 3).

[40] Vernadsky, *Kievan Russia*, pp. 170–72.

raids of the Polovtsians along the Dnieper trade route as well as to the decline of Byzantium as a trading center following its occupation by the crusaders in 1204.[41] Feudalism in all its aspects—economic, political, and social—became especially strong in Galicia, where it was reinforced by Romano-Germanic influences coming from the West through neighboring Poland and Hungary.[42] Non-Soviet historians agree that full-fledged feudalism existed on the Ukrainian lands (excluding Galicia and Volhynia) from the mid-fifteenth century up to the time of the Union of Lublin in 1569—i.e., the period when they were part of the Grand Duchy of Lithuania.[43]

In the aftermath of the Lublin union, practically all of the Ukraine became part of the Polish-Lithuanian Commonwealth and remained in the Commonwealth until the Khmel'nyts'kyi uprising of 1648. Kula, who studied the economic system of the Commonwealth, characterizes it as a feudal system on the basis of the Soviet definition.[44] Its main characteristics were: large-scale estates of the nobility surrounded by small peasant plots; economic and juridical dependence of peasants on their landlords and their obligation to provide services, mainly corvée; low agricultural productivity; large-scale estates producing grains primarily for export to Western Europe through the Baltic ports; the importation of consumer goods, mostly for the nobility.[45] Without providing an explanation, Kula considers this system to be the prevalent one throughout the Commonwealth, including Galicia and Volhynia, but not in the Dnieper Ukraine.[46] If Kula's system, without the political nexus, can be called feudalism at all, it was, according to Braudel, feudalism of a specific kind, not applicable to other times and other countries.[47] Politically, the Commonwealth, with its electoral monarchy and its parliament of nobles was not a

---

[41] Bahalii, *Narys istorii*, p. 317.

[42] Vernadsky, "Feudalism in Russia," pp. 310–11.

[43] Ibid., pp. 314–15. Vernadsky refers to this part of the Ukraine as "Lithuanian Russia."

[44] See Kula, *An Economic Theory of the Feudal System.*

[45] Ibid., p. 9.

[46] Ibid., p. 27. It is most likely that Kula excludes the Dnieper Ukraine because of its location along the rivers which flow to the Black Sea, while his system refers to the basin of the Vistula, including the Ukrainian sections of such rivers as the San and the Buh.

[47] Ibid., p. 7.

feudal state but an aristocratic republic.[48] With regard to the Dnieper Ukraine and its magnates' latifundia, it would be more appropriate to refer to this system as a plantation economy.[49]

The Khmel'nyts'kyi uprising culminated in the establishment of the Hetman state. This political entity, which was centered mainly in the Left-Bank Ukraine, lasted only about a century. Notwithstanding a continuously diminishing autonomy, it brought about significant economic and social changes. Most of the Polish landlords were expelled and their estates were distributed among peasants and Cossacks. In some instances the estates were also owned by the church. On the whole, however, small landowners predominated. A contemporary historian detects the beginnings of petty bourgeois tendencies in such agricultural conditions.[50] At the same time, one can also observe the disintegration of the old system in the commercialization of agriculture brought about by the intensification of grain exports to Western Europe and in the expansion of manufactory production (potash, iron ore, glass, some food processing).[51] The expanding share of the non-agricultural sector within the Ukrainian economy can be estimated by looking at the proportion of the urban population within the total population which reflects a growing number of artisans and merchants.[52]

In terms of social differentiation, the following estates can be distinguished:[53] Cossack officers (often owners of estates formerly held by the nobility); rank-and-file Cossacks who were small and middle-sized agricultural entrepreneurs, subject to military service; urban dwellers, frequently subject to Magdeburg Law; Orthodox churchmen;

[48] Vernadsky, "Feudalism in Russia," p. 315.

[49] Rudnytsky, "Feudalism," p. 880.

[50] Mykhailo Braichevs'kyi, "Pryiednannia chy voziednannia," in *Shyroke more Ukrainy*, Dokumenty samvydavu Ukrainy (Paris, 1972), p. 286.

[51] Ibid., p. 287.

[52] The share of the urban population in the total population during the period under discussion has been recently estimated at 46 percent. See O. Kompan, *Mista Ukrainy v druhii polovyni XVII st.* (Kiev, 1963), p. 73. In this context "urban" means a settlement with a population anywhere from a few hundred up to five or six thousand people (p. 57). According to the 1640 survey, the average population of a town in Volhynia province amounted to 1,045 people and in Podillia province to 417 people (pp. 62, 65).

[53] Rudnytsky, "Feudalism," p. 880.

and peasants who were small-scale landowners. There was no slavery or serfdom.

Similar socioeconomic and urbanization trends prevailed in the Western European countries at that time. These trends would become the foundation for the industrial revolution, market economies, and political democracy.[54] One can speculate that the course of history would have been similar in the Ukraine if the Tsarist Empire had not abolished the Hetmanate. The absorption of the Ukraine by Russia, however, not only aborted this process, but actually reversed it. A recent historian calls this tsarist action "the restoration of feudalism, moreover, in its most cruel, most brutal, and almost Asiatic form."[55]

The changes in agricultural conditions brought about by the Khmel'nyts'kyi movement lasted only about a quarter of a century in the Right-Bank Ukraine. Soon this region once again became part of Poland, as were the Ukrainian lands of Galicia and Volhynia already. The type of economic system described by Kula began to disintegrate there only at the end of the eighteenth century as a result of Poland's partitions and of various economic factors. The following factors deserve to be mentioned: a drop in the interest rate; the attractiveness of non-agricultural investment; the emergence of commodities and labor markets; a drastic decline in grain exports; as well as the Industrial Revolution in the West; the Continental Blockade, and the Napoleonic Wars.[56]

The partitioning of Poland (1772) turned Galicia over to Austria (later Austria-Hungary), of which it remained a part, together with Transcarpathian Ukraine and Bukovyna, until the First World War. The economic development of these Ukrainian lands, marked by the emancipation of peasants in 1848, came about very slowly. Despite some urbanization and industrialization, especially at the turn of the century, they remained economically the least developed provinces of the Danube Empire. Nevertheless, their socioeconomic stage was not feudalistic in the accepted sense of the word.

Upon the abolition of the Hetmanate and the incorporation of the Right Bank and Volhynia into the Russian Empire (1793, 1795), the socioeconomic conditions of these Ukrainian lands can be sum-

---

[54] Cf. Gottlieb, "Feudalism and Historical Materialism," p. 33.
[55] Braichevs'kyi, "Pryiednannia chy voziednannia," p. 299.
[56] Kula, *An Economic Theory of the Feudal System*, p. 185.

marized as follows. The large estates were hereditarily owned by Polish, Russian, and Ukrainian (descendants of the Cossack officers) landlords. Semi-free and subsequently enserfed peasants owned small plots of land and were obliged to provide corvée or quitrent to the landlords. The non-agricultural sector was poorly developed. Some manufacturing enterprises were organized, especially during the first half of the eighteenth century, mostly as a result of the initiative of the Russian government. Although the initial purpose for establishing manufacturing enterprises was to satisfy government demand for various products (textiles, potash), with time these enterprises became part of the Ukrainian economy through the hiring of local labor, the buying of raw materials, and the selling of part of the output in local markets.[57] The empire's labor market was rudimentary and the middle class insignificant. The tsar exercised unlimited political power, whereas citizens had none. Under these circumstances, there was indeed cruel exploitation of the peasantry by parasitic nobility, but to call these conditions feudal is hardly justifiable.

This system lasted, in legal terms, until the emancipation of the peasants in 1861. But signs of the approaching new era could be observed earlier. As previously mentioned, Soviet historians, after a prolonged debate, seem to have reached the conclusion that the beginnings of capitalism, marked by the extension of the labor market and the growth of industrialization, can be dated back to the 1760s.[58] Subsequent economic progress proceeded unevenly throughout the vast empire. It was particularly vigorous in the Ukraine. The commercialization of agriculture, especially in southern Ukraine, the rapid growth of food processing industries, particularly, sugar mills and liquor distilleries in the 1830s, and the development of heavy industry in the Donbas and the Lower Dnieper region during the last one-third of the century put the Ukrainian economy ahead of that of the empire's other regions. From the Ukraine's point of view, the construction of the railroad network during the second half of the nineteenth century was of crucial importance. The railroads now linked, and thus integrated, the Right Bank, which until then had been in the Polish-German sphere of interest, and the Left Bank, which had been under Russia's economic influence, with the southern region and the Ukrainian ports

[57] Ohloblyn, *A History of Ukrainian Industry*, pt. 1, pp. 209 – 16.
[58] Cf. Baron, "The Transition from Feudalism."

on the Black Sea and the Sea of Azov. Therefore, it is correct to say that the modern national, and one may say "capitalist," economy of the Ukraine, albeit without the Western Ukraine, emerged at this time. The Ukrainian regions shared common interests which at times differed from those of the rest of the empire.[59]

In summary, it seems that both periodization schemes of the Ukrainian economic history—that of Voblyi and the one advanced in Dereviankin's volume—are not satisfactory. The weaknesses of Voblyi's proposal are its preliminary nature and the failure to reconcile changes in economic criteria with the historical events used as bench marks. The structural shortcomings of the volume edited by Dereviankin are even more serious. The application of the periodization of Russian history to Ukrainian economic development obscures the specificity of the latter. By the same token, the Marxian scheme is not appropriate for an analysis of the periodization of Ukrainian economic history, particularly with regard to the characterization of almost a thousand years of its history as a feudal stage.

3. A Proposal for the Periodization of Ukrainian Economic History

It would be preferable to base the periodization of Ukrainian economic history on economic criteria, or on a combination of economic and social variables, as in the Marxian scheme. But as we saw earlier, empirical stage construction based on purely economic indicators is difficult because of the continuity of such indicators. By the same token, establishing Marxian relationships between economic and non-economic factors remains elusive in practice. Thus, events extraneous to economics, as a rule political events, have to be used for this purpose. Such an approach is most appropriate for the study of the Ukrainian economy because there is probably no other economy in the world which has experienced as many political changes and been as strongly influenced by them.

---

[59] Cf. Oleksander Ohloblyn, "Ukrainian Economics in Scholarly and Public Thought in the 19th–20th Centuries," *The Annals of the Ukrainian Academy of Arts and Sciences in the U. S.*, vol. 13 (1973–1977).

Only a few of the many significant political events that occurred throughout the Ukraine's history affected its entire territory; most of them affected only particular regions. Moreover, these events were of varying significance for economic development. In order to make the proposed periodization workable, only the most important events which affected the core of the Ukrainian lands and their economic development ought to be considered as bench marks. In my opinion, two such events stand out in Ukrainian history: the Mongol invasion in the mid-thirteenth century and the Pereiaslav Treaty of 1654. As a result, we have the following three periods:

I. Mid-ninth to the mid-thirteenth century—Kievan Rus';

II. Mid-thirteenth to the end of the eighteenth century—Galician-Volhynian Principality and, subsequently, the entire Ukraine under Poland, the Grand Duchy of Lithuania, and the Polish-Lithuanian Commonwealth (except for the Left Bank and eastern Ukraine from the second half of the seventeenth century);

III. Mid-seventeenth century to World War I—the Hetman state and eastern Ukraine and, from the end of the eighteenth century, the entire Ukraine (except for Western Ukraine—Galicia, Transcarpathian Ukraine, and Bukovyna—under Austria-Hungary).

Depending on the research objectives, other scholars may use different historical events for the periodization.

Before discussing the reasons for choosing the particular bench mark events, an explanation of the proposed periodization is in order. Although Mongol rule extended to the Galician-Volhynian Principality, it was relatively weak and intermittent there. The orientation of the principality toward Poland and Lithuania was already evident when other lands of the former Kievan Rus' were still firmly under Tatar domination. For this reason, the last century of the principality's existence is included in the second period. The autonomy of the Hetman state, although diminishing, lasted for almost a century. Nevertheless, the Hetman state is included in the third period, that of Russian domination, because of successful tsarist efforts to subvert Cossack independence immediately following the Pereiaslav Treaty.

This periodization, however, has two serious drawbacks. First, two areas of the Ukraine, one under the Polish-Lithuanian Commonwealth and the other under Russia, must be analyzed separately from the period between the second half of the seventeenth century and the end of the eighteenth century. Such separate treatment is also required for the nineteenth and the beginning of the twentieth centuries, when the bulk of the Ukraine was part of the Tsarist Empire while Western Ukraine was part of Austria-Hungary. In both cases, the economic orientation and the social institutions were quite different so that a joint analysis of the relevant regions would not be meaningful. Second, because of the focus on the Ukrainian heartland, the proposed scheme pays little attention to the economic history of such former borderlands as Transcarpathian Ukraine and Bukovyna, and to more recently colonized regions such as eastern Ukraine, southern Ukraine, and the Kuban' region. This is the price which has to be paid for the simplicity of the scheme.[60]

The primary reason for the choice of these events for the proposed periodization is their impact on the geographical orientation of the Ukrainian economy. This orientation, in terms of international trade links and the susceptibility to the adoption of technological and social progress from a particular cultural area (in the broadest sense of the word), significantly influenced the structure and efficiency of the economy. During the first period, the economy of Kievan Rus' was dependent on extensive commerce with many countries of the world due to its location at the crossroads of European and Asiatic trade. During the second period, following the Mongol invasion, the Ukrainian lands were gradually drawn into the Western European market. The Khmel'nyts'kyi war of liberation, ending with the Pereiaslav Treaty, at the beginning of the third period, gave the tsarist government an opportunity to draw the Ukrainian economy into its sphere of interest. It appears that in the second half of the eighteenth century, starting with the settlement of the southern Ukraine, a new trend began to assert itself—namely, an orientation toward the Black Sea and the sea routes toward the markets of Western and Southern

---

[60] A historian, in an attempt to make the periodization of Ukrainian history comprehensive and inclusive of all regions and comparable to that in Western Europe, proposed to utilize such general concepts as antiquity, Middle Ages, and Modern Times. See Rudnytsky in "Round Table," pp. 238–39.

Europe.[61] This trend was reinforced during the second half of the nineteenth century when the railroad network linked the Black Sea littoral with the Ukrainian hinterland. It was interrupted by the outbreak of World War I and subsequent developments.

It is important to emphasize that the Ukraine's geographical orientation during each of these three periods affected not only foreign trade and economic life in general but all aspects of social life, such as politics, religion, law, and culture. During the first period, Byzantium and the Near East were the major influences on the Ukraine; during the second period, it was the occidental influence coming through Poland that became dominant, and during the third period, Russia held sway. Each of these three cultures was reflected in specific social institutions, which, in turn, proved to be either more or less conducive to economic life.

Thus, with each change in the political status of the Ukraine, its economy had to adjust to new conditions of foreign trade and to new social institutions. With respect to trade, Ivan Dzhydzhora, an analyst of the post-Poltava Petrine policies in the Ukraine, wrote:

> From a purely formal point of view, the meaning of the discussed regulations would only amount to a radical change in the trade routes, i.e., a ban on the old routes and the compulsory use of the new ones and, of course, the concurrent change in markets; however, and more importantly, these measures tended to include the Ukrainian trade in the sphere of unfamiliar conditions which were related to Russian commercial interests . . .one can say that such a radical and, at the same time, artificial change in trade routes (because it was not caused by the genuine requirements of the Ukrainian trade) could not have other than a negative effect on this trade . . . .[62] [The Ukrainian merchant] was forced to abandon the old ways, established commercial relations with the markets with which he was linked until now also with credit rela-

---

[61] Ohloblyn, *A History of Ukrainian Industry*, pt. 3, p. 39; Voblyi, *Ekonomicheskaia geografiia*, pp. 165–66.

[62] Ivan Dzhydzhora, "Ekonomichna polityka rosiis'koho pravytel'stva suproty Ukrainy v 1710–1730 rr.," *Zapysky Naukovoho Tovarystva im. Shevchenka* 101 (1911): 87.

tions, and instead had to travel to the Russian ports where everything had to be built up anew.[63]

Similar considerations also apply to politically related changes in trade patterns during other periods of Ukrainian history.

Political changes were, of course, accompanied by institutional changes in the Ukraine. When the Ukraine regained its independence under Khmel'nyts'kyi it had to develop many of its own institutions to replace those which had existed under Polish rule. When the Ukraine was annexed by other states, as was the case after the Mongol invasion and the Battle of Poltava (1709), the institutions of the conquerors were imposed on the Ukrainian economy. These institutions were developed gradually according to the needs of these countries and were suitable for their economies. They were not necessarily appropriate for the Ukrainian economy, which, nevertheless, had to accept them.

Finally, political developments repeatedly led to the partition of Ukrainian lands. As a result, individual regions had to function under different social institutions, which, in turn, exerted differential effects on economic life. This led to the uneven development of the separate Ukrainian regions. Furthermore, historically developed interrelations were severed by these partitions. Thus their economies were compelled to establish alternative relations. All these factors had a detrimental effect on Ukrainian economic development.

It would be too simple to assume that all these changes in the economic and social conditions took place during the bench mark years. As was noted at the beginning of this chapter, social variables are continuous and do not exhibit radical breaks, as is the case with political developments. Political events may not be useful for delineating qualitatively different socioeconomic stages, but they have a clear expository function.

The Mongol invasion and the Pereiaslav Treaty were selected as turning points in Ukrainian economic development not by generalizing a large number of variables but rather on the basis of an overall understanding of Ukrainian history. While the choice may appear logical, its validity has to be tested on some representative variables. If the selected variables exhibit discernable changes with respect to the

---

[63] Ibid., p. 89.

geographic orientation of the Ukrainian economy around the time of these two events, the validity of our choice will be enhanced. In the following section, the behavior of foreign trade and monetary circulation will be investigated with such a purpose in mind. These variables were selected because foreign trade is tantamount to foreign economic relations and monetary circulation is one of the most important economic institutions.

4. Foreign Trade and Monetary Circulation: Case Studies

Several historians have argued that foreign trade played an extraordinarily important role in the life of Kievan Rus', primarily because of its geographical location.[64] Active participants in this trade were not only merchants but also state leaders. Princes and boyars collected tribute from their subjects; the large revenues enabled them to satisfy their needs and to export the surplus. In return, luxury products were imported. The princes were also involved in the slave trade. Trade was particularly extensive with Byzantium and to a lesser extent with the East and the countries of Central and Western Europe. Trade with European countries was transacted primarily through Galicia.[65] The regions contiguous to the Dnieper River served as a transit route between Scandinavia and Byzantium.[66]

The Mongol invasion significantly affected the geographical distribution of this trade. Commercial relations of the Dnieper regions with Byzantium declined, and, instead, trade with such eastern countries as Persia, Afghanistan, and India became more intensive. Particularly important, however, was the shift of the center of economic activity and political power, from Kiev to Halych and Volodymyr in Volhynia and subsequently to Lviv. The Dniester replaced the Dnieper as the main trade artery linking the Ukrainian lands with the Black Sea. Galician merchants conducted trade through the Black Sea ports not only with Byzantium, but also with various Italian and French cities. Trade with Moldavia, Hungary, Poland, and Germany increased during this

---

[64] V. O. Kliuchevskii, *Sochineniia*, vol. 1 (Moscow, 1956), pp. 153–62; Bahalii, *Narys istorii*, pp. 277–94; T. I. Dereviankin et al., eds., *Istoriia narodnoho hospodarstva Ukrains'koi RSR*, vol. 1 (Kiev, 1983), p. 82.

[65] Bahalii, *Narys istorii*, pp. 385–86.

[66] Dereviankin et al., *Istoriia narodnoho hospodarstva*, pp. 82–83.

period as well.[67] An important event was the Battle of Grunwald (Tannenberg) in 1410. The Polish-Lithuanian victory over the Teutonic order won access to the Baltic Sea for these nations, including their Ukrainian possessions. Consequently, the export of grain to Western Europe became attractive. Pressure was exerted to ensure extensive cultivation of grain, primarily in the Ukrainian regions along the rivers that flow to the Vistula and then on to the Baltic Sea. As can be seen, the fall of the Kievan state brought about, on the one hand, a shift to the west of the north-south axis of Ukrainian foreign trade and, on the other, reorientaion of this trade toward Western European countries. Both of these trends drew the Ukrainian economy into the orbit of European economic relations.

Ukrainian trade with the West through Poland, the Baltic ports, and the Silesian route was disrupted by the Khmel'nyts'kyi uprising.[68] It was resumed in the last third of the seventeenth century in that part of the Ukraine which remained under Poland. After the annexation of the Right Bank and Volhynia by Russia, a struggle for these markets, especially with regard to textile products, took place among Polish, Prussian, and Russian industries.[69] Up to the partition, and for a short period thereafter, these markets were dominated by Polish and German producers. However, after the unsuccessful Polish uprising of 1830, the Russian government substantially increased the tariffs on Polish and German textiles. This measure facilitated a moderate development of the local Ukrainian textile industry. The abolition of customs borders and thus, of tariffs, between the Polish Kingdom and the Russian Empire in 1850 enabled Polish industry to regain its markets in the Right Bank and Volhynia. As a result of this integrative measure by the tsarist government, consumer demand in these regions for textiles and other products was satisfied primarily by producers from the Polish Kingdom and the Moscow region. Understandably, this tariff policy led to a reduction of the Ukraine's economic relations with Germany and other European countries.

The foreign trade of the Hetman state was subjected to a somewhat different fate after the Pereiaslav Treaty. The trade links of this newly established political entity as well as those of the entire Left Bank

---

[67] Bahalii, *Narys istorii*, pp. 363, 364.

[68] Dereviankin et al., *Istoriia narodnoho hospodarstva*, p. 156.

[69] Ohloblyn, *A History of Ukrainian Industry*, pt. 3, chap. 2.

with the West were gradually loosened by the tsarist government and reoriented toward the Russian markets.[70] The integration of these regions into the Russian economy was intensified, as will be shown below, following the Battle of Poltava. After the incorporation of the territory of southern Ukraine was completed during the second half of the eighteenth century, the struggle for markets by the Russian industry, especially by the textile industry, was expanded into this region. The protectionist tariffs of 1822 served to cut off Ukrainian trade from the world markets.[71] By mid-century, the Ukraine (the Right and Left Banks, and the south) was securely within the sphere of influence of the Russian economy with a concomitant reduction in the Ukraine's economic relations with other countries.[72]

It might be interesting to look more closely at some of the measures taken by Peter I and his successors. 1) In addition to the customary 2 percent tariff *ad valorem* on exports and imports (*evekta* and *indukta*, respectively), a new tariff was imposed which varied anywhere from 3 to 37 percent, depending on the product.[73] 2) Certain products could be exported only through the Russian ports of Archangel and St. Petersburg and, later on, Riga and Azov.[74] Subsequently this regulation was reduced to apply to a few products only. 3) Certain products could be imported only through St. Petersburg from where they were resold to other parts of the empire, including the Ukraine.[75] 4) To protect Russian producers, certain commodities (woolen textiles, needles) could not be imported at all.[76] 5) Ukrainian merchants were not given adequate protection by the Russian government while on business trips abroad[77] and an insufficient amount of money and provisions was allocated for this purpose.[78] 6) Certain consumer goods (tobacco, vodka) could not be exported to Russia at all

---

[70] Dereviankin et al., *Istoriia narodnoho hospodarstva*, p. 151.

[71] Ohloblyn, *A History of Ukrainian Industry*, pt. 3, pp. 39ff.

[72] Ibid., pp. 41–45.

[73] Dzhydzhora, "Ekonomichna polityka," vol. 101 (1911), p. 99.

[74] Ibid., vol. 101 (1911), p. 84; vol. 98 (1910), p. 63.

[75] Ibid., vol. 101 (1911), p. 91.

[76] Ibid., vol. 101 (1911), pp. 90–91.

[77] Ibid., vol. 101 (1911), pp. 68ff.

[78] Ibid., vol. 103 (1911), pp. 66–67.

for a number of years.[79] While this regulation was rescinded in 1727, a high tariff was imposed on both products.[80] 7) Trade with the Zaporozhian lands, and trade with the Crimea via Zaporizhzhia, were strictly forbidden.[81] 8) The Russian government and some of its high officials (e.g., Prince Menshikov) could avail themselves of the exclusive right in specific regions to buy certain products (hemp, oxen) for export—goods for which they paid less than the market price.[82]

These measures reflected the mercantilist policy of the Russian rulers; they were intended to attain the following objectives: point 1, to increase the state revenues; points 2 and 3, to further the development of Russian ports; points 4 and 5, to protect the domestic economy, especially manufacturing, from foreign competition. Points 6, 7, and 8 were politically motivated.

It is important to draw attention to the ambiguous attitude of the Russian government toward the Ukraine during the period under discussion. With respect to some policy measures (points 1–5), this newly acquired province was treated like any other province; whenever necessary, its interests had to be subordinated, irrespective of the costs, to the interests of the entire empire. But other policies (points 6–8), were specifically designed as measures against the Ukraine. The restriction on exports of Ukrainian tobacco and vodka to Russia was introduced not only to promote such industries in Russia, but also to prevent the outflow of preferred money (gold and silver) from Russia to the Ukraine.[83] The ban on trade with Zaporizhzhia was enacted in retaliation of its military support of Mazepa. By the same token, the economic power of such individuals as Menshikov in the Ukraine came in the aftermath of the Battle of Poltava whereupon the estates of the defeated were distributed to the tsar's chief lieutenants.

This ambiguity ended in 1754, when the last vestiges of Ukrainian economic autonomy were eliminated: the customs borders between the Ukraine and Russia were abolished. From that time on Ukrainian trade became subject to the laws of the empire and its institutions and,

[79] Ibid., vol. 98 (1910), p. 64.
[80] Ibid., vol. 103 (1911), p. 78.
[81] Ibid., vol. 101 (1911), p. 99.
[82] Ibid., vol. 103 (1911), pp. 57–58, 60.
[83] Ibid., vol. 101 (1911), pp. 87–88.

thus, was drawn into the Russian market at the expense of trade with other countries.

As was alluded to earlier, political events led to changes not only in the economy, but also, and with lasting consequences, in the social life of the country. Ohloblyn describes the effect of one such event, the annexation of southern Ukraine, as follows:

> The secure position of Russian capitalism in the Ukrainian market is, of course, to a great extent due to the fact that Russian commercial capital gradually penetrates deeper into the Ukrainian economy, sinks into the Ukraine, grows into the local economic conditions and relations and, on its part, modifies them. Russian commercial colonies and centers are an old phenomenon in the Ukraine; they first appeared in the second half of the seventeenth century. In the next century, especially during its second half, in connection with the opening of Black Sea trade routes, Russian merchants became peculiarly "Ukrainified," firmly maintaining their ethnic-cultural distinctiveness but aggressively seizing local commerce and industry by using their economic influence and penetrating local community life by using their cultural influence. . . Whereas in the Ukrainian cities the old colonies of Russian merchants consolidated their position by means of a long and stubborn struggle with the local Ukrainian merchants, in southern Ukraine the Russian merchant either filled an empty place or had to deal with the competition of foreign (Greek and Armenian) merchants. . . The contribution of Russian merchants to the development of industrial capitalism in the Ukraine is unquestionable. However, the dominance of the Russian merchants in the Ukraine, especially in the south and along its trade routes, paved the way for Russian capitalism in the Ukraine, in the process, ruining local economic life, destroying local economic centers, and subordinating them to Russia.[84]

Let us now turn to the topic of monetary circulation. Coins of various kinds have been found on Ukrainian territory dating from prehistoric times. During the existence of the Kievan state, Sassanid drachmas, Arab dirhams, Western European dinars, and other coins were all in circulation.[85] Moreover, Kievan princes, starting with Volodimer the Great at the end of the tenth century, issued their own

---

[84] Ohloblyn, *A History of Ukrainian Industry*, pt. 3, pp. 45–46.

[85] M. F. Kotliar, *Hroshovyi obih na terytorii Ukrainy doby feodalizmu* (Kiev, 1971), chap. 1.

coins. The issuing of Kievan coins may be ascribed not so much to economic and fiscal needs, but rather,

> This measure was a kind of declaration of the sovereignty of the young Rus' state. The minting of its own coins was, certainly, an attempt to legitimize the power of the Christian prince and, at the same time, a means of protecting it from Byzantium's ideological aggression.[86]

Of greater economic importance was the Kievan *grivny*, issued by various princes from about the eleventh century. This currency served as the main means of payment in Kievan Rus' during the twelfth and up to the middle of the thirteenth centuries.[87]

The Tatar invasion in the mid-thirteenth century undermined the economic life of Kievan Rus', including the monetary sector. The accumulation of money needed to promote commerce was no longer possible to the same extent as in the preceding period. In the Western Ukraine, to which the focus of economic life now shifted, the decrease in the supply of Kievan currency was supplemented by a variety of coins of such diverse origin as Czech, Tatar, Lithuanian, Polish, Hungarian, Italian, Moldavian, and Genoa-Crimean.[88] Some coins were also minted in Lviv.[89] Gradually, however, Polish coins in Galicia and Lithuanian coins in other Ukrainian lands drove out the other currencies. Following the Lublin union, Polish currency became dominant in the entire Polish-Lithuanian Commonwealth. Subsequently, in the sixteenth century an inflow of silver talers, the most common currency in Western Europe, can be observed in the Ukraine.[90] All these developments indicate a deterioration of Ukrainian economic ties with the East and the South and a gradual integration into Western European markets.

The Khmel'nyts'kyi war of liberation and its aftermath also had significant effects upon the monetary circulation in the Ukraine. Although a wide variety of coins were in circulation during the period of the uprising, Polish currency was the dominant one. But as early as

---

[86] Ibid., p. 34.

[87] Ibid., pp. 51–52.

[88] Ibid., pp. 63–64.

[89] Ibid., pp. 70, 73. It is necessary to mention that coins were also minted in Kiev during the second half of the fourteenth century despite its occupation by the Tatars.

[90] Ibid., p. 92.

the Pereiaslav Treaty, Tsar Aleksei began to introduce a common currency for both the Ukraine and Russia as a means of integrating the two economies. The Soviet Ukrainian scholar Mykola Kotliar, on whose work this section of the chapter is based, referring to the work of another Soviet historian,[91] writes about this financial measure of the tsar as follows:

> [The reform] is considered in the extensive literature as a dishonest, if not fraudulent, undertaking by the Russian tsar, induced by financial difficulties stemming from the war with Poland. Studying the coin and documentary sources, I. G. Spasskii showed a direct relationship of the mentioned reform [by Tsar Aleksei] to the reunion of the Ukraine with Russia, with the desire by the Russian government to introduce a monetary system linking both parties. Certainly, the Ukrainian money market prior to the reunion was weakly linked with the Russian market.[92]

It is obvious that economic integration, as reflected in a common currency, went hand in hand with political integration from the very beginning.

From a purely monetary point of view, the measure taken by the Moscow government was probably beneficial to the Ukrainian economy. It replaced a large number of diverse coins by a single Russian currency and thus contributed to the lessening of uncertainty in the monetary sphere. However, the transitional period seems to have been prolonged. The inflow of Western European currencies into the Left-Bank Ukraine during the post-Pereiaslav period slowed down somewhat, but the supply of Russian currency was insufficient. As a result, monetary conditions, in terms of the supply of money needed for business transactions, worsened.[93]

Russian currency virtually drove out all other currencies from the Hetman Ukraine after the 1700–1704 monetary reforms of Peter I.[94] Subsequently, southern Ukraine, the Right Bank, and Volhynia were

---

[91] See I. G. Spasskii, ''Denezhnoe khoziaistvo Russkogo gosudarstva v seredine XVII v. i reformy 1654–1663 gg.,'' in *Arkheograficheskii ezhegodnik za 1959 g.* (Moscow, 1960).

[92] Kotliar, *Hroshovyi obih*, pp. 114–15.

[93] Ibid., p. 130.

[94] Dereviankin et al., *Istoriia narodnoho hospodarstva*, p. 208.

incorporated into the empire and thus joined its monetary and rudimentary credit systems, under which they remained until the 1917 revolution. Galicia, Transcarpathian Ukraine, and Bukovyna became part of Austria-Hungary's monetary and credit systems, under which they remained until 1918. These monetary developments were accompanied by economic dislocations of varying degree, firmly attaching in the process the two separate parts of the Ukraine into two different economic orbits, that of Tsarist Russia and that of Central-Western Europe.

The preceding discussion shows that foreign trade and monetary circulation series exhibited pronounced changes in their trends as a result of the Mongol invasion and the Pereiaslav Treaty. One can assume that other important economic variables, not discussed here because of space limitations, behaved similarly. The changes in these variables support the hypothesis that the two selected events were crucial turning points in Ukrainian history and thus can serve as bench marks in a broad and preliminary periodization of the economic history of the Ukraine.

Part I: Kievan Rus'

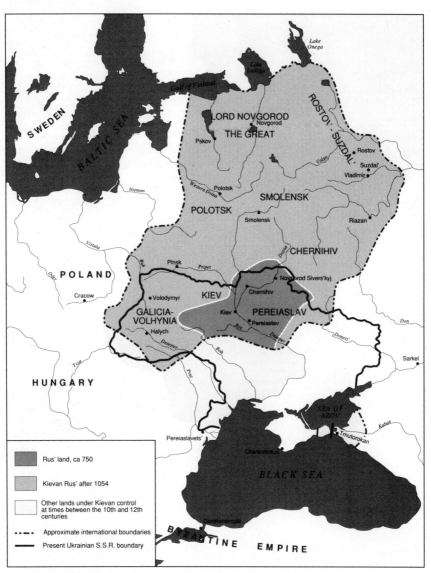

Kievan Rus' in the Eleventh Century
(based on map in: Paul Robert Magocsi, *Ukraine: A Historical Atlas*, 3rd rev. ed. [Toronto, 1987]; reprinted with permission from author)

The Economy of Kievan Rus':
Evidence from the Pravda Rus'skaia

Daniel H. Kaiser

No single source can provide complete documentation on the economy of Kievan Rus'. Archaeological, numismatic, and literary sources all provide their own insights into Rus' economic history, and only in combination can they present a reasonably complete picture. But one particularly useful form of written source is the law; in many contexts the law simultaneously reflects and regulates the society that constructs it. To be sure, there are great dangers in judging a society by its law, which often depicts the aims, rather than the realities, of a given polity. The law of traditional societies, however, conforms closely to social consensus and, therefore, provides vivid insight into social organization.[1]

The *Pravda Rus'skaia* is one example of the law of a traditional society. There are, of course, advantages and disadvantages for the scholar. On the one hand, the *Pravda* is certainly not comprehensive or rationally developed, and as a result does not fully depict Rus' society. As the following discussion illustrates, many aspects of Kievan economy and society receive almost no attention in the code, despite the importance we know them to have had. On the other hand, however, the simplicity and casuistic character of the *Pravda Rus'skaia* make the institutions it describes almost transparent, and bring Rus' society vividly to life.

---

[1] See Michael Barkun, "Conflict Resolution Through Implicit Mediation," *Journal of Conflict Resolution* 8 (1964):124; and Lawrence M. Friedman, *The Legal System: A Social Science Perspective* (New York, 1975), p. 4.

The *Pravda Rus'skaia* survives in three basic redactions: Short, Expanded, and Abbreviated. While controversy about the editorial history of the *Pravda* remains, most scholars agree that the Abbreviated redaction was probably composed sometime after the fourteenth century, and derived from the two earlier redactions. The Short redaction contains but forty-two articles, and achieved its present form sometime late in the eleventh century. The Expanded *Pravda*, which built upon the Short version but also introduced many additional norms, contains fully 121 articles. Like its older parallel and source, the Expanded redaction comprises several constituent parts, all of which were joined by the end of the twelfth or early in the thirteenth century.[2]

Both of the main redactions of the *Pravda Rus'skaia* devoted attention to the economy. As might be expected, the Short *Pravda* has less to say on these matters, while the Expanded *Pravda* contains several sections expressly devoted to commerce, slavery, and indentured labor. But first place in both redactions belongs to agriculture.

Agriculture

The *Pravda Rus'skaia* shows agriculture to have been important, since it devotes considerable attention to the various branches of agriculture. To judge from the contents, livestock-raising was most important, and the most valued animal seems to have been the horse. Of course, especially for the steppe settlements of the southern principalities, the horse was vital to military and transport needs. The chronicles point out that the struggles against the Pechenegs, Polovtsians, and other steppe nomads required the accumulation of considerable cavalry detachments.[3] But it appears that the horse was important not

---

[2] For an introduction to the *Pravda Rus'skaia*, its composition and text history, see Daniel H. Kaiser, *The Growth of the Law in Medieval Russia* (Princeton, 1980), pp. 41–47.

[3] The Pechenegs and Polovtsians troubled Kiev and the surrounding settlements almost annually. See, for example, the account under the years 997 and 1068 in *Polnoe sobranie russkikh letopisei* (St. Petersburg and Moscow, 1846–), 1:127–29, 167–71; 2:112–14, 156–61. As some of the chronicle accounts point out, ordinary free men, in addition to the prince's retinue, also supplied horses for military campaigns. For a fuller discussion of the evidence, see I. Ia. Froianov, *Kievskaia Rus'. Ocherki sotsial'no-politicheskoi istorii* (Leningrad, 1980), pp. 198–200.

only for military campaigns. Wherever possible, the horse served as a draft animal, particularly for farming operations where a heavy plow was in use.[4] And finally, in times of great duress horses also represented a meat source. The archaeological data confirm that, while never having constituted a very important percentage of consumed meat, the horse, nevertheless, was occasionally eaten.[5] Despite the fact that Rus' knew a significant variety of horse breeds, the *Pravda Rus'skaia* makes no attempt to distinguish among the different horses. To be sure, the prince's horse was more valuable than another man's, but there is no mention of any of the steppe horses that had already become popular in Rus'. The Short *Pravda* refers only to horse (*kon'*) and mare (*kobyla*), while the Expanded *Pravda* adds only mention of foal and stallion (*zherebets*).[6]

To judge from the excavations, cattle provided the main source of meat in the Kievan diet. Swine and sheep also were important, and the *Pravda Rus'skaia* confirms the significance of these animals.[7] The Short *Pravda* includes cattle, oxen, swine, sheep (including both rams and lambs), and goats in the list of animals whose theft brought the owner composition. The Expanded *Pravda* identifies the same animals, only bringing more thoroughness to the list. A suckling pig, milk cow, and a two-year-old heifer appear along with the other

[4] I. I. Liapushkin, *Gorodishche Novotroitskoe, Materialy i issledovaniia po arkheologii SSSR* 74 (1958):215; V. P. Levashova, "Sel'skoe khoziaistvo," in *Ocherki po istorii russkoi derevni X–XIII vv., Trudy gosudarstvennogo istoricheskogo muzeia* 32 (1956): 31–35, 83.

[5] O. M. Prykhodniuk, *Sloviany na Podilli (VI–VII st. n. e.)* (Kiev, 1975), p. 52; O. V. Sukhobokov, *Slaviane Dneprovskogo Levoberezh'ia* (Kiev, 1975), pp. 104–105.

[6] Short PR, 28; Expanded PR, 45. Also see Short PR, 12, 13, 21, 31; Expanded PR, 84. All citations to the *Pravda Rus'skaia* are from the Academy copy of the Short *Pravda* (abbreviated here to Short PR) and the Trinity copy of the Expanded *Pravda* (abbreviated here to Expanded PR). Article division corresponds to that introduced in *Pravda russkaia*, 3 vols. (Moscow and Leningrad, 1940–1963).

[7] Prykhodniuk, *Sloviany*, p. 52; N. H. Timchenko, "Sviis'ki tvaryny z davnorus'koho mista Chuchyna," *Arkheolohiia*, 1972, no. 6, pp. 96–102; Sukhobokov, *Slaviane*, p. 105; E. A. Goriunov, *Rannie etapy istorii slavian Dneprovskogo Levoberezh'ia* (Leningrad, 1981), pp. 34–35; V. V. Sedov, *Sel'skie poseleniia tsentral'nykh raionov Smolenskoi zemli (VIII–XV vv.), Materialy i issledovaniia po arkheologii SSSR* 92 (1960):74–75; and Levashova, "Sel'skoe khoziaistvo," pp. 76–84.

animals. Both redactions affix a cash value to the animals, and the values remain constant in the two lists, providing a useful index of their relative value (see Table 2.1).[8]

TABLE 2.1

Relative Value of Livestock According to the *Pravda Rus'skaia*
(in *grivny*)

Horses

3.00	Prince's horse
2.00	Horse
1.20	Mare
1.00	Stallion (not yet broken)
0.30	Foal

Cattle

0.80	Cow
0.60	Three-year-old
0.50	Two-year-old
0.10	Calf

Others

0.10	Sheep
0.05	Ram
0.05	Lamb
0.10	Swine
0.05	Suckling pig
0.10	Goat

Not surprisingly, the horse was the most valued animal in the Kievan economy, with cattle following immediately thereafter. Smaller animals were in less demand, perhaps the only surprise being the relative position of swine which, according to some accounts, were highly prized as a food source in Kiev.[9] Evidently, at least in wealthier

[8] Short PR, 21, 31, 40; Expanded PR, 42, 45.

[9] P. N. Tret'iakov, "Sel'skoe khoziaistvo i promysly," in *Istoriia kul'tury drevnei Rusi*, vol. 1 (Moscow and Leningrad, 1948–51), p. 55. Excavations of some com-

estates, livestock was sheltered in barns, since both redactions provide for a case when animals might be stolen from the barn.[10] And the *Pravda* also protects hay, evidently the most important source of livestock food supply.[11]

Kievan farmers also raised poultry. Both redactions of the *Pravda Rus'skaia* protect from theft and damage chickens, ducks, geese, swans, and cranes.[12] Furthermore, the bloodwite collector could expect to collect a portion of his provisions in poultry; in addition to other goods, the law allotted him two chickens a day. Presumably, then, Kievans raised birds both for their meat and eggs, which together with milk and cheese, held an important place in the diet.[13]

Despite the importance that other sources attribute to grain farming in Kievan Rus', the subject receives scant attention from the law. The Short *Pravda*, for example, makes but a single reference to plowland borders, and the Expanded redaction repeats that measure.[14] But whether the land was owned or not the texts do not say. The Short *Pravda* makes no allusion whatsoever to landed property; the Expanded *Pravda* proves only somewhat more helpful by including a separate codex on succession and inheritance.[15] By these provisions, it would appear that both a peasant freeman and a boyar could own (and alienate) landed property. Both, for example, might pass on their estates to their children; in the absence of surviving children, the code asserts, the estate escheated to the prince.[16] Throughout, the code employs the neutral term *zadnitsa* to refer to "estate," but while the term *might* include land, it need not, and neither in the Short nor the Expanded redactions is there evidence to suppose that the compilers

---

munities reveal far greater percentage of swine bones than any other. See I. I. Liapushkin, *Gorodishche Novotroitskoe*, p. 215.

[10] Short PR, 21, 31, 38; Expanded PR, 40, 41.

[11] Short PR, 39; Expanded PR, 82.

[12] Short PR, 36, 42; Expanded PR, 9, 81.

[13] Short PR, 42; Expanded PR, 9.

[14] Short PR, 34; Expanded PR, 72, 109. For a discussion on land tenure in Rus', see F. J. M. Feldbrugge, "The Law of Land Tenure in Kievan Russia," in William E. Butler, ed., *Russian Law: Historical and Political Perspectives* (Leyden, 1977), pp. 1–28.

[15] Expanded PR, 90–95, 98–106, 108.

[16] Expanded PR, 90–91.

had land in mind.[17] Indeed, the most detailed provisions govern the income a guardian might receive from his wards' property that he administered during their minority. But several times the text identifies the property as movable goods (*tovar*), and compares it with the increase gained from slaves and livestock who reproduced during the term of guardianship.[18] If, therefore, land ownership had legal standing, the *Pravda Rus'skaia* does little to confirm that status. And beyond the reference to domestic residences (*dom*), also identified in the inheritance provisions of the Expanded *Pravda*, the codes pay no attention to agricultural land.[19]

The *Pravda Rus'skaia* does, however, identify and protect agricultural products. The Expanded *Pravda*, for example, protects grain from theft, imposing on thieves a substantial monetary penalty. The same article also mentions threshing floors and storage pits—essential components of grain-raising agriculture.[20] Specific grains are mentioned only in articles detailing provisioning requirements for the bloodwite collector, who was entitled to malt, millet, bread, peas, and feed (probably oats) for his horses.[21] The town builder also received oats for his horses, as well as bread, millet and malt for himself; the bridge builder could eat as much as he wished and his horse was given four measures of oats each week during which there was work.[22]

As the provisions lists make clear, Kievan farmers did raise grain. Furthermore, numerous sites now excavated by Soviet archaeologists have confirmed the presence of millet (particularly in the southern regions), rye (particularly in the northern regions), wheat, oats, and various other grains.[23] But at the same time some grains that

---

[17] See I. I. Sreznevskii, *Materialy dlia slovaria drevnerusskogo iazyka*, 3 vols. (St. Petersburg, 1893–1903; reprint, Moscow, 1958), 1:910.

[18] Expanded PR, 99.

[19] Expanded PR, 100, 102.

[20] Expanded PR, 43. As V. I. Dovzhenok points out, some late copies of the Pravda (Obolensk II and Museum II) also include specific mention of rye, oats and barley (*Zemlerobstvo drevn'oi Rusi do seredyny XIII st.* [Kiev, 1961], pp. 134–35), but the earliest copies do not contain these references. See *Pravda russkaia*, vol. 1, pp. 353–54, 379–80.

[21] Short PR, 42; Expanded PR, 9. On oats as feed, see Expanded PR, 74.

[22] Expanded PR, 96–97. Compare Short PR, 43.

[23] Sukhobokov, *Slaviane*, pp. 87–89; Levashova, "Sel'skoe khoziaistvo," pp. 50–60; Dovzhensk, *Zemlerobotovo*, pp. 129–40.

archaeologists have determined to have been important to Rus' agriculture are not mentioned in the *Pravda Rus'skaia* at all. Various digs have unearthed seeds of rye, buckwheat, flax, and varieties of wheat among materials of the eleventh and twelfth centuries;[24] neither version of *Pravda Rus'skaia* mentions any of those grains at all.

Farming implements also rate slight attention. A single article in the Expanded *Pravda* mentions a plow (*pluh*) and harrow (*borona*) that a lord might lend to his indentured laborer.[25] Otherwise, these tools do not appear in the codes even among the inventory of farm goods, the theft of which obliged the thief to make restitution. The omission is curious, since the archaeological evidence for various plows and harrows from an early time in Rus' is plentiful. Even at that, the greatest quantity of evidence pertains not to the *pluh*, evidently a fairly heavy plow that required significant draft labor, but to rather simpler implements that antedated the light plow (*sokha*) of a later time. Other tools—sickle, scythe, and mattock, for example— survive in great quantities from the period around the eleventh century, but neither redaction of the *Pravda Rus'skaia* makes any reference to what were clearly important instruments of grain agriculture.[26]

It is also noteworthy that while the compilers considered the theft of livestock at market, they made no provision for grain theft at market. Only theft from the threshing floor or storage pit entered the list of recognized crimes, thereby suggesting little commerce in grain in Kievan Rus'.[27] Of course, it is possible that much of grain agriculture was subsistence; according to the *Pravda Rus'skaia*, even the bloodwite collector was to be paid in kind while he was on his rounds.[28] But the well-documented emergence of Kievan towns, with their attendant craft industries, indicates that there must have been a

[24] Tret'iakov, "Sel'skoe khoziaistvo," p. 63.

[25] Expanded PR, 57.

[26] O. M. Prykhodniuk, *Arkheolohichni pamiatky serednioho prydniprovia VI–IX st. n. e.* (Kiev, 1980), pp. 60–62, 86; Iu. A. Krasnov, "Ralo iz Tokarevskogo torfianika," *Kratkie soobshcheniia Instituta arkheologii* 164 (1981):58–65; Tret'iakov, "Sel'skoe khoziaistvo," pp. 52–60; A. D. Gorskii, "Sel'skoe khoziaistvo i promysly," in *Ocherki russkoi kul'tury XIII–XV vv.*, vol. 1 (Moscow, 1969), pp. 64–84 (which includes much material from before the thirteenth century); Dovzhenok, *Zemlerobotovo*, pp. 53–99.

[27] Expanded PR, 37, 43.

[28] Short PR, 42; Expanded PR, 9.

noticeable grain trade as well. And in times of famine and hardship, as the chroniclers pointed out, grain prices escalated dramatically.[29] The *Pravda Rus'skaia*, however, gives the theme short shrift.

Hunting and fishing also received attention in the *Pravda*, because undoubtedly they both contributed significantly to the food supply of Rus'.[30] Certainly the location of any settlement played a large role in deciding exactly how important these occupations might be. In general, both hunting and fishing seem to have grown in importance the further north one went. But even in settlements with the most developed farming, the auxiliary food occupations played their role. Again archaeologists have determined which animals were most popular for hunters. Bones left at the sites indicate that in addition to domestic animals consumed for food, wild game also played an important role in the diet. In various settlements of the Left-Bank Ukraine, for example, the percentage of wild game varied from 19 to 63 percent of the animals identified from the discarded bones.[31]

The *Pravda* itself says rather little about which animals were hunted. As other sources make clear, Rus' hunters chased game not only for food, but also for pelts. The Expanded *Pravda* identifies only one animal hunted for its pelt—the beaver—despite the fact that many other animals also figured in the fur trade.[32] Of course, pelts played a larger role in the northern Rus' lands, yet even in the south, rabbit, squirrel, and fox seem to have been important to local trade.[33] None of these animals, however, appears in the *Pravda Rus'skaia*.

[29] Dovzhenok, *Zemlerobotovo*, pp. 175–83. For a survey of hunger crises in Rus' and their effect on grain prices, see V. T. Pashuto, "Golodnye gody v Drevnei Rusi," in *Ezhegodnik po agrarnoi istorii vostochnoi Evropy za 1962 g.* (Minsk, 1964), pp. 61–94.

[30] V. A. Mal'm "Promysly drevnerusskoi derevni," in *Ocherki russkoi kul'tury X–XIII vv.*, *Trudy gosudarstvennogo istoricheskogo muzeia* 32 (1956):106–129; A. V. Kuza, "Rybolovstvo u vostochnykh slavian vo vtoroi polovine I tysiacheletiia n. e.," in *Drevnie slaviane i ikh sosedi, Materialy i issledovaniia po arkheologii SSSR* 176 (1970): 132–37; Tret'iakov, "Sel'skoe khoziaistvo," pp. 72–76; Prykhodniuk, *Sloviany*, p. 53.

[31] Sukhobokov, *Slaviane*, p. 104.

[32] Expanded PR, 69.

[33] Tret'iakov, "Sel'skoe khoziaistvo," p. 73.

Birds too helped enrich Rus' hunters' larders. The net snare (*pereves*), developed for bird hunting, enjoyed special protection in the Expanded *Pravda*.[34] Both redactions of the *Pravda* also protected hawks and falcons with a three-*grivna* payment; the provisions are not, however, identical.[35] From the Short *Pravda* it is not clear whether the birds were themselves used in the hunt or, as in the Expanded redaction, simply captured in a snare. There were other means of capturing game, and the list of weapons archaeologists have so far discovered is extensive.[36] The Short *Pravda*, however, mentions none of them, with the exception of a hunting dog, valued at three *grivny*, like the hawk and falcon.[37] Otherwise, the codes specify no protection for the instruments by which Rus' hunters carried on their work.

Neither redaction says much about fishing. By the Short *Pravda*'s reckoning, the bloodwite collector could receive part of his provisions in fish if he made his rounds during Lent; otherwise fish are not recalled in either code.[38] Both redactions do prescribe financial penalties for boat theft, but the Expanded *Pravda* again provides more detail, distinguishing among different kinds of boats: a sea-going boat was valued at three *grivny*, a high-sided boat at two *grivny*, a river boat at one *grivna*, and a dugout canoe at only twenty *kuny* (0.4 *grivny*).[39] The greater detail suggests a more extensive boat trade, and, by extension, a more vigorous fishing industry in later Rus' history. Evidently the dugout canoe was a very usual and inexpensive possession; the Expanded *Pravda* rates a swan, crane, goose, and duck as more valuable than a dugout.[40]

---

[34] Expanded PR, 80. See Tret'iakov, "Sel'skoe khoziaistvo," pp. 73–75, and Mal'm, "Promysly," pp. 112–13.

[35] Short PR, 37; Expanded PR, 81.

[36] Mal'm, "Promysly," pp. 108–12. For a more detailed description of various weapons, although mainly for military purposes, see A. N. Kirpichnikov, *Drev-nerusskoe oruzhie*, 2 pts., *Arkheologiia SSSR. Svod arkheologicheskikh istochnikov*, vyp. E, 1–36 (1966).

[37] Short PR, 37.

[38] Short PR, 42.

[39] Short PR, 35; Expanded PR, 79.

[40] Compare with Expanded PR, 81. On the early history of Rus' boating, see V. V. Mavrodin, *Russkoe morekhodstvo na iuzhnykh moriakh* (Symferopil', 1955).

Despite the reticence that characterizes the *Pravda Rus'skaia*'s discussion of fishing, other evidence make clear that, at least in some places, fishing was very important. Numerous iron fishhooks and spears survive, together with floats, sinkers, and other equipment peripheral to fishing. And archaeology too has shown, again by examining bones and fish scales, that fishing served at least as a food supplement in many settlements and in some was even a cottage industry. Pike was important almost everywhere, and perch, bream, carp, and other species appear often in excavations.[41] To the *Pravda Rus'skaia*, however, neither fishing implements nor the fish themselves warranted special attention.

Apiculture too figured in the Kievan economy and honey and wax were evidently among the most important trading commodities.[42] Nevertheless, the *Pravda Rus'skaia* makes no mention whatsoever of wax and only one reference to honey.[43] The codes illustrate, however, the value that apiculture had in Rus'. The Short *Pravda*, in the single article devoted to beekeeping, rates the prince's beehive as more precious than an ox, horse, or cow, and equal to a hunting dog, hawk, or falcon (three *grivny*).[44] The Expanded *Pravda* mentions beehives in five articles. An empty hive had relatively little value (0.1 *grivny*), while honey was twice as valuable (0.2 *grivny*). But the bees themselves or a hive with bees was clearly worth far more; stealing or destroying the bees or the hive obliged the perpetrator to pay a three-*grivna* fine.[45] By the time that the Expanded *Pravda* received its final configuration, cases concerning beehives ranked high on the list of concerns involving the prince's men, just after homicides, and well above matters involving slave manumission.[46]

Commerce and Credit

Contrary to what one might expect, given archaeological and other sources of information about Rus' trade, the Short redaction of *Pravda*

[41] See Kuza, "Rybolovstvo," pp. 132–37, and Mal'm, "Promysly," pp. 116–29.
[42] Mal'm, "Promysly," pp. 129–38. Compare with Gorskii, "Sel'skoe khoziaistvo," pp. 130–37.
[43] Expanded PR, 76.
[44] Expanded PR, 32. Also see Short PR, 28, 37.
[45] Expanded PR, 71, 72, 75.
[46] Expanded PR, 107, 109.

Rus'skaia devotes very little attention to commerce. Only one article examines credit claims, and the context provides scant evidence to suppose that credit operations were extensive or even commercial. The provision merely stipulates that a person who sought repayment of money owed him was to pursue his claim at an investigation before twelve men who evidently decided the legitimacy of his claim.[47]

The Expanded redaction includes a similar regulation; unlike the Short *Pravda*, however, the revised text makes clear that commerce is the subject:

> If some *merchant* gives [another] *merchant* money for local or foreign trade, then the merchant is not to take the money before witnesses; he needs no witnesses, but he himself is to take an oath if he shall deny [that he received any such money].[48]

A subsequent article also establishes beyond any doubt that the law covered commercial credit, in this instance between local and out-of-town merchants:

> If someone be greatly indebted and a merchant from another town or a foreigner having arrived, and, not knowing [about the man's indebtedness], leaves goods with him, and [the debtor] refuses to give the merchant his money, and the first creditors begin to object, not giving him money; then lead the debtor to the market square, and sell him [into slavery] and return the money [realized by the sale of the debtor] to the first merchant, and give the local creditors what remains [from the sale], divided among them; if the money be the prince's, then first the prince is to take his money and divide the rest; if someone took [too] much interest, then he is not to take anything [from the debtor].[49]

The special nature of this article, which amounts to a description of bankruptcy proceedings, makes clear that it arose from an instance observed in life, thereby providing indisputable evidence of commercial credit. Likewise, these provisions confirm the practice of foreign and out-of-town trade, and the necessary credit operations they

---

[47] Short PR, 15.
[48] Expanded PR, 48 (emphasis is mine—DK).
[49] Expanded PR, 55.

required; local banking in Rus' involved not only the merchants, but even the prince himself.

Apparently, at an earlier time the law showed little concern for banking and credit. Not only does the Short *Pravda* contain no specific reference to commercial credit, but it also makes no allusion to credit rates. By contrast, the Expanded *Pravda* includes a whole complex of regulations governing interest rates. Article 50 formally permitted any interest rate that the contracting parties agreed upon. And Article 52 constitutes but a small amplification of the old norms, prescribing witnesses for loans of more than three *grivny*. Article 51 also permitted any agreed-upon interest rate for short-term loans, but simultaneously established an interest cap for loans of longer duration: "... if the money [remains on loan] for up to one year, then they give him his money back at a third [i.e., at 50 percent interest] and the monthly interest is annulled."

It was, evidently, Volodimer Monomakh who was concerned about exorbitant interest rates, and the Expanded *Pravda Rus'skaia* attributes to him the attempt to set limits on interest exacted for loans.[50] According to Article 53, Monomakh gathered his counselors at Berestovo to enact a reform of the law on credit. It was clearly the prince's initiative, therefore, that changed Rus' law:

> They [Monomakh and his counselors] established interest rates of up to 50 percent if [the creditor] collects [his principal] before the third payment; if someone takes his interest twice, then he is to take the principal; if he takes his interest three times, then he is not [entitled] to take his principal.

In other words, each interest payment represented one-half the sum loaned. The merchant who collected two interest payments might still retrieve the principal. By contrast, the merchant who had already collected three interest payments had realized 150 percent against the sum he had loaned and, therefore, had already obtained his principal and a 50 percent return on the loan.[51] Monomakh, whom we know

---

[50] The chronicles do not record the gathering, but for a reconstruction of the conference, see *Pamiatniki russkogo prava*, vol. 1 (Moscow, 1952), p. 162.

[51] On the calculation of interest, see ibid., vol. 1, pp. 160–63; *Rossiiskoe zakonodatel'stvo X–XX vekov*, vol. 1 (Moscow, 1984), pp. 100–101; V. O. Klu-

from other sources to have been a man of scruples, judged that creditors required no greater income from their loans.[52]

But, as noted above, not all regulations of the *Pravda Rus'skaia* are fully consistent with one another. For example, in an addendum to the Monomakh regulations, the *Pravda Rus'skaia* introduces one instance of interest-taking that diverges somewhat from the principles just described: "If someone takes ten *kuny* per year on a [principal of] one *grivna*, then this is not disallowed." Presumably the law has in view the usual (rather than the silver) *grivna* which in the Expanded *Pravda* equalled 50 *kuny*. On small loans, the law permitted an interest rate of 20 percent.[53] Another, although vaguer, regulation confirms that by the twelfth century Rus' society recognized interest ceilings. Creditors who took "too much interest" were not entitled to anything realized from the sale of bankrupts.[54]

These regulations are troublesome to interpret, and, probably because they entered the code from particular instances that arose in real life, also present some apparent contradictions. But at the same time they prove conclusively the operation of commercial credit—both for local and international trade.

Not all Rus' commercial law concerned interest. The Short *Pravda* has nothing to say about storage contracts, for example, but the Expanded redaction does establish the means for the party who stored someone's goods to purge himself of an accusation of theft.[55] Likewise, the Expanded redaction examines the case of merchants who, quite independent of their own actions, lost someone's goods. A merchant who was shipwrecked, or who lost someone's property by fire or by an act of war could escape immediate sale into slavery, "for the misfortune is from God, and [the merchant] is not to blame." But merchants were liable for acts of carelessness or neglect that led to property loss. Drunkenness, gambling, and "foolishness" [*v bezum'i*]

---

chevskii, *Sochineniia*, vol. 1 (Moscow, 1956), p. 248. For a summary of other views, see *Pravda Rus'skaia*, vol. 2, pp. 417–24.

[52] See "Pouchenie Vladimira Monomakha," in *Pamiatniki literatury Drevnei Rusi XI–nachalo XII veka* (Moscow, 1978), pp. 392–412.

[53] Expanded PR, 53.

[54] Expanded PR, 55.

[55] Expanded PR, 49.

could permit creditors to sell the merchant into slavery.[56]

Again, the norms point to a commercial market in which storage contracts and transportation agreements had real importance. But these same measures suggest that commerce was not yet very highly developed. When, for example, a merchant who stored someone's goods could relieve himself of responsibility merely by affirming that he was not guilty of theft or carelessness, we may suspect that commercial relations were not yet very highly developed. In this instance, the law relied upon smaller communities where the actors were known both to one another and to the larger jural community. But when a man of Chernihiv vouchsafed the goods of a Baltic merchant, the community confidence present in smaller, less fragmented environments no longer held. Evidently, then, the Expanded *Pravda* describes a commercial economy in transition.[57]

The law codes provide little specific evidence of active crafts or trades. Metalworking, pottery, woodworking, and other crafts had a long history in Rus', but, all the same, the *Pravda Rus'skaia* takes no notice of them.[58] The codes identify only the craftsmen and tradesmen who carried out public service. Both redactions of the *Pravda* specify compensation for the bridge builders,[59] and the Expanded *Pravda* also defines compensation for town builders.[60] That other crafts existed can be shown only by reference to the metal, wood, and pottery vessels that the *Pravda* occasionally identifies.[61]

Labor

In contrast to some other aspects of the economy, about which the *Pravda Rus'skaia* is strangely reticent, both redactions include a

---

[56] Expanded PR, 54.

[57] Very clearly, as archaeology demonstrates, there was substantial trade, but that reality seems little evident from the law. Compare the provisions of the *Pravda Rus'skaia* with the Smolensk treaties with the Baltic merchants (*Pamiatniki russkogo prava*, vol. 2, pp. 57–75).

[58] The *Pravda Rus'skaia* does protect slave craftsmen and craftswomen, but what crafts they practiced the text does not make clear (Expanded PR, 15).

[59] Short PR, 43; Expanded PR, 97.

[60] Expanded PR, 96.

[61] Short PR, 3, 4, 9, 13, 18; Expanded PR, 23–26, 30, 34, 35, 37. For a fuller description of craft industries, see B. A. Rybakov, *Remeslo Drevnei Rusi* (Moscow, 1948).

wealth of information on labor, especially slavery. The Short *Pravda* specifically refers to slavery in six of its forty-two articles, while the Expanded *Pravda* identifies slavery in twenty-seven of its 121 articles, including a separate codex of twelve articles (Arts. 110–121). Clearly slavery was an institution central to the Rus' economy.[62]

By the law's definition, there were three forms of slavery in Rus': purchase; marriage to a female slave without stipulating the man's freedom; and accepting the position of estate overseer without having stipulated contractually the man's freedom.[63] In practice, as other articles make clear, a man could also become a slave by default on contractual obligations. For example, a merchant who by his own fault was unable to repay his creditors might be sold into slavery to help the creditors recoup their investments.[64] Likewise, an indentured laborer who fled to escape his obligation might, upon recapture, be converted into a full slave.[65] And finally, some men and women fell into slavery by their own choice, effecting what amounts to self-sale. A man who could not repay his debt within one year could be converted into a slave, or sold to someone else as a slave.[66]

What kind of labor did slaves in Rus' perform? The Short *Pravda* provides few clues; almost all the provisions that appear in the older redaction only detail procedures and compensation appropriate to slave theft.[67] The bulk of the slave workforce must have fulfilled undifferentiated labor, similar, perhaps, to that of free peasants, since the *Pravda* seems to rank slaves with peasants.[68] There was also specialized slave labor, although perhaps only in the prince's own house-

---

[62] For a comprehensive, although sometimes tendentious, discussion of slavery in Kievan Rus', see A. A. Zimin, *Kholopy na Rusi* (Moscow, 1973). E. I. Kolycheva presents an excellent discussion of slave occupations in a later time, but often in the context of their origins in Rus': *Kholopstvo i krepostnichestvo (konets XV–XVI v.)* (Moscow, 1971).

[63] Expanded PR, 110.

[64] Expanded PR, 54–55.

[65] Expanded PR, 56.

[66] Expanded PR, 111. This measure resembles the later Muscovite institution of limited service contract slavery (*kabal'noe kholopstvo*). See V. M. Paneiakh, *Kabal'noe kholopstvo na Rusi v XVI veke* (Leningrad, 1967); Richard Hellie, *Slavery in Russia 1450–1725* (Chicago, 1982), esp. pp. 49–56.

[67] Short PR, 11, 16, 17, 27, 29.

[68] Short PR, 26; Expanded PR, 16.

hold. The Short *Pravda* knows slave wet nurses, for example, and it is probable that the tutor (*kormilichits*) was also a slave, as the parallel regulation in the Expanded *Pravda* suggests.[69] Almost certainly the prince's field supervisor and plowland supervisor were also slaves, since the law protected their lives with exactly the same compensation that the wet nurses and tutors merited.[70]

Slaves evidently could and did engage in commerce in Rus'. The *Pravda Rus'skaia* points out that slaves who contracted debts in the course of trade at the market square were not personally liable; their lords were to answer for them.[71] Slaves, then, did conduct business, but they remained their lords' property; the homicide of a slave did not oblige the killer to pay the bloodwite, but only compensation to the slaveowner who had thereby suffered a property loss.[72] Some slaveowners evidently did emancipate their slaves, since the Expanded *Pravda* established fees for oaths administered in connection with slave manumissions.[73] Perhaps some of those freedmen subsequently continued to pursue commerce.

Additional evidence for the proliferation of slavery comes from other measures of the Expanded *Pravda*. Apparently slaves were known to commit theft and assault.[74] Of course, slave theft merited attention,[75] but the Expanded *Pravda* goes on to indicate other social and economic relationships that slaves had. As in other slave societies, in Rus' too slavewomen came to bear the children of their masters and other freemen.[76] Some slaves even provided testimony (although there were substantial limits on its use).[77] In short, slavery was pervasive and was a most important labor source in Kievan Rus'.

A second variety of unfree labor was indenture. The Short redaction of the *Pravda Rus'skaia* makes no mention of indentured labor; there is only a single reference to contract laborers (*riadovnitsi*), who

---

[69] Expanded PR, 17.

[70] Short PR, 24.

[71] Expanded PR, 117, 119–121.

[72] Expanded PR, 89.

[73] Expanded PR, 109.

[74] Expanded PR, 46, 63, 120–121; Short PR, 17 and Expanded PR, 65, respectively.

[75] Expanded PR, 32, 38.

[76] Expanded PR, 98.

[77] Expanded PR, 66. Cf. Expanded PR, 85.

may well have been the predecessors of indentured laborers.[78] But the Expanded redaction includes a special complex of articles devoted to the indentured laborer, the *zakup*.[79] As noted above, when an indentured laborer fled, the law permitted his lord to convert him into a full slave.[80] The indentured man also bore responsibility for his lord's property if, as a result of negligence, he damaged or lost it. For example, were he to damage his lord's horse because he did not direct it properly in the field, or did not secure it properly when he returned it to the barn, he had to recompense his lord for the damage.[81] In that way, then, the *Pravda Rus'skaia* treated him as a subject of the law, able to bear legal responsibility.

He was also free to travel, even to the prince's court where he might, like any other recognized subject, appeal for justice against an oppressive lord.[82] Indeed, a lord was not to abuse his indentured laborer or the laborer's property; should the laborer suffer loss as a result, his lord was to make recompense and pay an additional sum for the offense.[83] The law did permit lords to beat their indentured laborers "for cause," but capricious beatings were not allowed, and the man's lord was to make "the same payment for beating the indentured laborer as if he had beaten a free man."[84] Nor might a lord try to sell his laborer as if he were a slave; should he do so, the indentured laborer was free of all debts to his lord and, furthermore, the lord was to pay a twelve-*grivna* fine.[85] Or, to put the measure differently, an indentured laborer was not his lord's chattel. Indeed, the *Pravda Rus'skaia* even cited an instance in which the *zakup* might loan money to his lord, rather than the reverse; to be sure, the *Pravda* regarded such a transaction as illegitimate, decreeing that the laborer was to

[78] Short PR, 25.

[79] Expanded PR, 56–62, 64. There is substantial disagreement over the meaning of *zakup*. For a recent, reasonable discussion, see I. Ia. Froianov, *Kievskaia Rus'. Ocherki sotsial'no-ekonomicheskoi istorii* (Leningrad, 1974), pp. 126–36. Froianov points out that one Rus' bookman translated the Greek term *hemidoulos* with *zakup*, making him a "semi-slave."

[80] Expanded PR, 56.

[81] Expanded PR, 58.

[82] Expanded PR, 56.

[83] Expanded PR, 59.

[84] Expanded PR, 62.

[85] Expanded PR, 61.

receive back the original loan.[86] But almost certainly the situation had arisen in practice, affirming the distinctive status that the indentured laborer held in Rus' society.

In other respects, however, the *zakup* did resemble the slave. If, for example, the indentured man stole someone else's property, it was his lord who answered for him, just as a slaveowner answered for his slave. The text goes on to add that the lord was then free to convert the man immediately into a full slave, either making him his own slave or selling him to someone else, once the lord had made recompense for what was stolen.[87] The indentured laborer, then, occupied a station somewhat higher than the slave, but somewhat short of an ordinary freeman.

Despite the law's preoccupation with slavery and indentured labor, almost certainly the great bulk of the labor of Rus' society belonged to free peasants, who receive little attention in either redaction of the *Pravda Rus'skaia*. A peasant (*smerd*) is identified only once in the Short *Pravda*, in a measure that nearly equates his life with that of a male slave.[88] The Expanded *Pravda* includes but two mentions of peasants. By one provision, the law enjoined peasants from torturing other peasants;[89] by another, the law specified that peasants' estates escheated to the prince, presumably if there were no surviving sons, since the law did provide a portion at least for unmarried daughters.[90] Otherwise, the law took little cognizance of what must have been the basic labor reserve.

The prince's court was filled with many other persons, such as bailiffs and members of the prince's personal guard, who executed specialized tasks.[91] The law also recognized hired military help, such as the Vikings or other foreign residents.[92] Those individuals who served in the prince's court or estates as steward, collector of fines, overseer,

---

[86] Expanded PR, 60.

[87] Expanded PR, 64.

[88] Short PR, 26. The meaning of *smerd* has generated much debate, which I need not reproduce here. To be sure, the text is less specific than we might wish to make clear exactly what the law has in mind.

[89] Expanded PR, 78.

[90] Expanded PR, 90.

[91] Short PR, 1; Expanded PR, 1.

[92] Short PR, 10; Expanded PR, 18.

and the prince's senior stablemaster[93] were free men in the prince's service, as the bloodwites make clear (80 *grivny*). Others who served the prince were the guard, bloodwite collector, cook, groom, and page.[94] Their lives were not so valuable before the law, but, nevertheless, the *Pravda* assigned them bloodwites far higher than that of most slaves.

In one sense, the prince's servitors supplied labor for the Rus' economy, particularly in the collection of the prince's revenue or by hunting and gathering. Presumably, some part of the capital that these men helped the prince to accumulate found its way as invested funds into the commercial economy. But at the same time much of their labor was not productive; the stablemaster, bloodwite collector, and others contributed to what we might call (with exaggeration) the service sector. And, just as services were relatively undeveloped, so too service-sector labor played a relatively unimportant role in the Rus' economy.

Conclusions

The *Pravda Rus'skaia*, then, by itself does not depict in full the various operations of the Kievan economy, so that we cannot with confidence use the law as an exclusive source for economic history. Nevertheless, the Short and Expanded redactions do provide valuable information about economic development over time. In the first place, it is important to observe that the Expanded *Pravda*, the later of the two basic redactions, devotes substantially more space to the economy than did the earlier, Short redaction. Presumably that attention was a function of the growing importance of the various branches of the economy that the law served. Furthermore, as noted above, many of the regulations of the Expanded *Pravda* almost certainly represent actual cases that arose in Rus' and then entered the code as laws.[95] The laws dealing with credit and interest limits, for example, surely arose from actual experience in the late eleventh or early twelfth cen-

---

[93] Short PR, 19–20, 22, 23, 33; Expanded PR, 12.

[94] Short PR, 33, 41–42; Expanded PR, 11.

[95] For example, Short PR, 23: "And for the senior stablemaster [who is murdered] while [he is] with the herds [pay] 80 *grivny*, as Iziaslav established when the residents of Dorohobuzh killed his stablemaster." Other regulations carry a similar specificity.

turies. Clearly the economy of that time experienced growth and new
conflicts which demanded novel responses from the law.

Secondly, some important aspects of the economy are left untreated
in the law; there are, for example, few regulations governing free
labor; crafts and trades that we know to have flourished nevertheless
received no attention. Certainly the *Pravda*'s silence cannot be taken
as a denial of these institutions. As the auxiliary evidence demonstrates, the law simply did not recognize economic relations that in
fact did exist. This is not surprising. A careful, comprehensive examination shows that the *Pravda Rus'skaia* was not created to serve a
highly differentiated society, nor did it come into being to serve
exclusively economic interests. The increasing attention allotted to
economic concerns argues not so much for intensified economic
activity as for increasing social heterogeneity that itself demanded
warranties stronger than a man's word alone.

At the same time, the limited evidence that the *Pravda* does contain
suggests that the economy underlying Rus' society was undergoing
dramatic change at the time the Expanded *Pravda* was compiled.
Some economic relations, already important in the Short *Pravda*,
found greater amplification in the Expanded *Pravda*. Slavery, for
example, was clearly a significant institution even in Iaroslav's time.
Half a century later, it gained still more attention from the law. Other
economic interests, totally unknown to the Short *Pravda*, received
elaborate regulation in the Expanded *Pravda*. As instances cited here
prove, the Short *Pravda*'s silence cannot argue that indentured labor,
for example, did not exist at an earlier time. But the amplitude of provisions in the Expanded *Pravda* indicates clearly that by the twelfth
century the old consensual norms no longer sufficed. Only positive
law was sufficient to deal with the difficulties that practice had
revealed. Similarly, regulations governing interest rates, storage
agreements, and other commercial contracts all received detailed
explication in the Expanded *Pravda*, while none was even mentioned
in the Short *Pravda*.

In other words, the expansion of commercial law in the late
eleventh and early twelfth centuries suggests not so much an abrupt
change in the economy of Rus' as a significant change in the society
that the law serviced. Disagreement and social conflict had evidently
arisen over sources of labor, so that slavery and indentured labor
received extended treatment in the *Pravda Rus'skaia*. At the same

time, other sectors of the economy seem to have changed little in the interval between the two codes. Agriculture, for example, although treated in more detail in the later redaction, nevertheless did not command an exhaustive consideration. In the Rus' hinterland consensus had not yet broken down.

CHAPTER THREE

Aspects of the Nomadic Factor in the Economic Development of Kievan Rus'

Peter B. Golden

"... and why, O *druzhyna*, do you give no thought that when the smerd begins to plough, the Cuman [*Polovchyn*], having come will shoot him down with an arrow. He will take his horse and riding into his village, will seize his wife and children and all his property..."[1]

The theme of the ruin of the Rus' land by nomadic depredations, so graphically illustrated by the comments of Volodimer Monomakh (reigned 1113–1125) made at the congress of Dolobs'k in 1103, is a commonplace in the Old Rus' chronicles whose clerical authors took every occasion to excoriate the *poganye*. It is a theme that has often been repeated by later generations of Ukrainian and Russian scholars and has received considerable attention in Soviet scholarship as well. It is not our task to survey the extensive Ukrainian and Russian literature on the nomads of medieval Eastern Europe. Elements of such a much-needed survey have been carried out admirably by the late R. M. Mavrodina in her regrettably brief study, *Kievskaia Rus' i kochevniki*.[2] Nonetheless, a few words on the subject may be in order

[1] *Polnoe sobranie russkikh letopisei* (henceforth *PSRL*), 33 vols. (St. Petersburg, Petrograd, Leningrad, 1941–1977), 1:277.

[2] R. M. Mavrodina, *Kievskaia Rus' i kochevniki (Pechengi, Torki, Polovtsy)* (Leningrad, 1983) and her "Rus' i kochevniki," in V. V. Mavrodin et al., eds., *Sovetskaia istoriografiia Kievskoi Rusi* (Leningrad, 1973), pp. 210–21.

so that the themes treated in this paper may be set in a proper context. Early nineteenth-century Eastern Slavic historians tended to ascribe to the nomads a largely negative role in the history of Rus'.[3] S. M. Solov'ëv viewed nomadic-sedentary relations as confrontation of forest and steppe, Europe against Asia.[4] V. O. Kliuchevskii, elaborating further on this theme, claimed that whole territories were stripped of (Slavic) population fleeing the ferocious nomadic onslaughts. Rus', he argues, was driven from the Dnieper with concomitant dislocations in its economy.[5] Similar themes of destruction and retardation of political, social, and economic development because of the ravages of the wild steppe hordes are sounded by other nineteenth- and early twentieth-century historians.[6] Thus Mykhailo Hrushevs'kyi, continuing Solov'ëv's earlier themes, portrayed the Slavo-nomadic confrontation as a struggle to colonize the fertile steppe lands in which the nomads did much to push back the steady Slavic southward advance.[7] Like his predecessors he ignored the fact that the steppes were the centuries-old preserve of the nomads.

The forest versus steppe thesis was sharply attacked by M. N. Pokrovskii representing the new, Soviet, Marxist scholarship. While not underestimating the destructive effects of nomadic incursions (to

[3] Mavrodina, *Kievskaia Rus'*, pp. 11–13. A. A. Kunik in his "Istoricheskie materialy i razyskaniia, 2: O Torkskikh Pechenegakh i Polovtsakh po mad'iarskim istochnikam," *Uchënye Zapiski Imp. Akademii Nauk po pervomu i tret'emu otdeleniiu* 3 (1855):714, for example, concluded that the steppe-dwellers "will never occupy a lofty position in world history, but in the same way as the natural sciences subject to observation and scrupulous research the lower imperfect organisms in relation to the most perfect ones, so too historians for a variety of reasons must, in the future, pay more attention to these lower orders of humanity especially with respect to an evaluation of the history of Russia. . . ."

[4] S. M. Solov'ëv, *Istoriia Rossii s drevneishikh vremën* (reprint, Moscow, 1959), vol. 1, pp. 616–47; Mavrodina, *Kievskaia Rus'*, pp. 15–17.

[5] V. O. Kliuchevskii, *Kurs russkoi istorii* (reprint, Moscow, 1956), vol. 1, pp. 279–83.

[6] Cf. N. I. Kostomarov, P. V. Golubovskii, N. Ia. Aristov, P. N. Miliukov, G. V. Plekhanov (the founder of Russian Marxist historiography), N. A. Rozhkov et al. Only a few scholars (such as M. D. Zatyrkevich and P. Burachkov) saw anything positive in the meeting of Eastern Slav and Nomad; see Mavrodina, *Kievskaia Rus'*, pp. 17–19, 21–23, 30–31, 34, 36, 38.

[7] M. S. Hrushevs'kyi, *Istoriia Ukraïny-Rusy* (Lviv, 1904–1922), vol. 1, pp. 203ff.; vol. 2, pp. 505–506, 530, 533.

which he ascribed the decline of Rus''s lively urban civilization and ruralization of the economy), Pokrovskii suggested that the role of the nomads in the enervation of Rus' was matched by the destruction caused by princely strife. Attacking the racism underlying the earlier visions of the nomads as some malevolent Asiatic force, he saw the nomads as having a positive cultural impact on Rus'.[8] In B. D. Grekov's revival of the older but now less harshly articulated "patriotic" portrait of the nomads, Rus' not only successfully fended off the steppe predators but was able to assimilate sizable groups of them.[9] A return to still more strident tones is seen in recent Soviet scholarship. Thus V. T. Pashuto points to the "rapacity" of the "early feudal" nomadic aristocracy leading to the destruction of Rus' during the Polovtsian era.[10] V. V. Kargalov paints a bleak canvas of "huge masses of fertile chernozem torn from Rus'" and "transformed into pasturages" by rapacious nomads who killed or carried off the population into slavery. The survivors "fled northward to the protection of the forests."[11]

---

[8] M. N. Pokrovskii, *Russkaia istoriia s drevneishikh vremën*, 7th ed. (Moscow, 1924), vol. 1, pp. 94, 111–15, and his *Ocherki istorii russkoi kul'tury* (Petrograd, 1923), p. 46. Closely akin to Pokrovskii on this issue was V. A. Parkhomenko in his "Sledy polovetskogo eposa v letopisiakh," *Problemy istochnikovedeniia*, vol. 3 (Moscow-Leningrad, 1940), p. 391; Mavrodina, *Kievskaia Rus'*, pp. 48–50, 52–53.

[9] B. D. Grekov, *Kievskaia Rus'* in his *Izbrannye sochineniia* (Moscow, 1957, 1959), vol. 2, pp. 373–75. Cf. also the measured tones employed by Grekov and A. Ia. Iakubovskii in their *Zolotaia orda i eë padenie* (Moscow, 1950), pp. 28–29, 31–32.

[10] V. T. Pashuto, "Ob osobennosti struktury Drevnerusskogo gosudarstva" in A. P. Novosel'tsev, V. T. Pashuto et al., eds., *Drevnerusskoe gosudarstvo i ego mezhdunarodnoe znachenie* (Moscow, 1965), p. 98. Pashuto also notes, seemingly without making any connection, that Rus' raids into the steppe were a source of silver, gold, tribute, slaves, cattle, etc. (pp. 99–100).

[11] V. V. Kargalov, *Vneshnepoliticheskie faktory razvitiia feodal'noi Rusi* (Moscow, 1967), p. 57. In an earlier article, "Polovetskie nabegi na Rus'," *Voprosy istorii*, 1965, no. 3, p. 68, Kargalov writes of the "waves" of nomadic hordes that "rolled over the agricultural settlements of the Slavs. Towns and villages on the southern border of Rus' went up in smoke... The eternally billowing nomadic storm cut off Rus' from the centers of world trade ... Rus''s war with the steppes lasted for centuries; it was an unbroken and exhausting one." A more moderate note is sounded by I. M. Shekera, *Kyïvs'ka Rus' XI st. u mizhnarodnykh vidnosynakh* (Kiev, 1967) who notes (p. 50) that the Pecheneg threat "was not decisive for the political and economic life of Rus'," (p. 99) "The continual threat of attack of the Pechenegs, to a certain

Western scholarship, little concerned with early Rus', has often uncritically incorporated some aspects of this thesis into general works. For example, Jerome Blum blames the activity of the nomads for the faltering of the Rus' economy in the twelfth century, citing the "unprecedented frequency and violence" of Polovtsian raids. Blum notes, however, that it was the First Crusade and a subsequent shifting of trade routes that dealt a mortal blow to Kiev's preeminence in the eastern trade.[12] Richard Pipes writes that, facing "nomad harrassment as an inescapable fact of life," the Slav colonists in the chernozem were forced to withdraw because of Pecheneg and Polovtsian raids that had "made life unbearable."[13]

In reality, Rus'-nomadic relations were far more intricate than the various national historical schools would have us believe.[14] Recent

---

degree, impeded the normal social-economic growth of the Kievan state," and (p. 122) "The attacks of the nomads, without doubt, to a considerable extent, undermined the productive forces of the Kievan state but they could not by much hold back much less halt the development of Rus'."

[12] J. Blum, *Lord and Peasant in Russia from the Ninth to the Nineteenth Century* (Princeton, 1961; reprint, New York, 1964), p. 57. See also G. Vernadsky, *Kievan Russia* (New Haven, 1948), p. 118.

[13] R. Pipes, *Russia under the Old Regime* (New York, 1974), pp. 37, 54.

[14] An attempt at a more critical appraisal was made by D. A. Rasovskii in a series of occasionally flawed but still useful articles: cf. "O roli chërnykh klobukov v istorii drevnei Rusi," *Seminarium Kondakevianum* (henceforth *SK*), 1 (1927):93–109; "Pechenegi, torki i berendei na Rusi i v Ugrii," *SK* 6 (1933):1–66; "Polovtsy," *SK* 7 (1935), 8 (1936), 9 (1937), 10 (1938), 11 (1940). "Rus i kochevniki v epokhu Sviatogo Vladimira," *Vladimirskii Sbornik v Pamiat' 950-letiia kreshcheniia Rusi* (Belgrad, 1938), pp. 149–54; "Rus', Chërnye Klobuki i Polovtsy v XIIv.," *Sbornik v Pamet' na Prof. Petr Nikov* [Izvestiia na Bulgarskoto Istorichesko Druzhestvo, vols. 16–18] (Sofia, 1940), pp. 369–78.

Taking a number of cues from Rasovskii, L. N. Gumilëv in his *Poiski vymyshlennogo tsarstva* (Moscow, 1970), pp. 311–12, put forward several controversial and provocative statements. He declared that the long-held generalization about the struggle between sedentary Rus' and the steppe was an "exaggeration." Quite correctly, as we shall see, he noted that the steppe was hardly a political monolith. Moreover, with the internal unification brought about (or restored) by Volodimer Monomakh, Rus', in effect, brought the steppes under its control and integrated the Polovtsians into the Rus' political system. Indeed, he states, "from the fall of the Khazar Kaganate in 965 until the founding of the Golden Horde in 1241, there was no unified steppe grouping and there was no danger to the Russian land from the steppe." These views, which he never really substantiated, were harshly attacked by B. A. Rybakov

scholarship has demonstrated that these relations covered a broad spectrum of interaction in the political, economic, social, and cultural spheres.[15] Omeljan Pritsak, for example, has concluded that the Polovtsians ''orientalized'' Slavic Kievan Rus' and that ''contrary to the impression one gets from the Chronicles that the Polovtsian danger was the basic problem of Rus' history between 1055 and 1240, the objective historian will have to stress that there was no such Polovtsian danger at all. The Polovtsians never aimed to occupy even a part of a frontier Rus' principality. . . .''[16]

In order to understand this relationship and assess properly the nomadic impact on the economic development of Rus' (about which there are so many opposing views), we will have to examine the larger question of how nomads and sedentary societies interact.[17] Such an assessment is not easily carried out for it requires an analysis of both societies. Our task is further complicated by the fragmentary nature of our sources and the consequent diversity of scholarly opinion about specific events and broad trends. Having sketched a brief (and undoubtedly idiosyncratic) overview of Rus' political, social, and economic evolution, a similarly rapid survey of the nomadic peoples whose activities most directly affected Rus' will be presented. We may then turn to an examination of nomadism as an economic system, for it is this factor—above all the strengths and weaknesses of pastoral production—that has largely determined the nature of the nomad's interaction with his sedentary neighbors.

---

in ''O preodolenii samoobmana,'' *Voprosy istorii*, 1971, no. 3, reprinted in *Iz istorii kul' tury Drevnei Rusi* (Moscow, 1984), pp. 132 – 38.

[15] Cf. O. Pritsak, ''The Pečenegs, a Case of Social and Economic Transformation,'' *Archivum Eurasiae Medii Aevi* (henceforth *AEMA*), 1 (1975):211 – 35 and his ''The Polovcians and Rus','' *AEMA* 2 (1982):321 – 80; P. B. Golden, ''The *Polovci Dikii*,'' *Harvard Ukrainian Studies* (henceforth *HUS*), 3/4 (1979 – 1980):296 – 309 and his ''Cumanica I: The Qipčaqs in Georgia,'' *AEMA* 4 (1984):45 – 87.

[16] Pritsak, ''The Polovcians and Rus','' p. 380.

[17] There is a growing body of literature dealing with this phenomenon in Eurasia, the Near and Middle East, and Africa. With regard to the themes most pertinent to our study, I would single out A. M. Khazanov's *Nomads and the Outside World* (Cambridge, 1984), and S. A. Pletnëva's *Kochevniki srednevekovia* (Moscow, 1982).

Kievan Rus'

Without venturing too deeply into the quagmire of the origins and formation of the Rus' people and state,[18] I think it has been reasonably well established that the early Rus', when they first appear in western Eurasia, were a kind of polyethnic "company" of trader/merchant-mercenaries. Organized into a "militarized trade diaspora"—a trading-military "community of merchants living among aliens in associated networks. . .found on every continent and back through time to the very beginnings of urban life. . ."—they, in time, would establish "new bonds of solidarity. . .between the diaspora traders and members of the host society."[19] In the ninth century, they were probably not the only such "company" operating in northwestern Eurasia engaged in the gathering of furs and slaves for sale in both Byzantine and Islamic metropolises and the West. According to the ninth-century "Book of the Routes and Kingdoms," by the Irano-Muslim intelligence official, Ibn Khurdādbeh, they largely supplanted the Rādhānīya, a similar, Jewish "trading diaspora."[20]

The Rus', of Scandinavian origin but having rapidly incorporated other ethnic elements as well, were regarded by our Muslim sources as a "tribe" or "kind" (*jins*) of the Ṣaqāliba (Gr. Σκλάβος "Slav"), a term used to designate the "ruddy-faced, fair-haired and blue-eyed peoples of the North."[21] Early steppe influences are apparent in the

[18] Among the most recent works treating this topic, we may cite V. V. Mavrodin, *Proiskhozhdenie russkogo naroda* (Leningrad, 1978); O. Pritsak, *The Origin of Rus'*, vol. 1 (Cambridge, Mass., 1981), which promises a new and much expanded vision of this tangled historical process; and, B. A. Rybakov, *Kievskaia Rus' i russkie kniazhestva* (Moscow, 1982).

[19] P. D. Curtin, *Cross-Cultural Trade in World History* (Cambridge, 1984), pp. 2 – 3, 46.

[20] Ibn Khurdādbeh, *Kitāb al-Masālik wa'l-Mamālik*, ed., M. J. de Goeje (Leiden, 1889), p. 154; J. Brønsted, *The Vikings*, trans. K. Skov (Baltimore, 1965), pp. 267 – 69; I. Boba, *Nomads, Northmen and Slavs* (The Hague and Wiesbaden, 1967), pp. 108 – 109; P. H. Sawyer, *Kings and Vikings: Scandinavia and Europe AD 700 – 1100* (London and New York, 1982), pp. 75, 121 – 22; O. Pritsak, "An Arabic Text on the Trade Route of the Corporation Ar-Rūs in the Second Half of the Ninth Century," *Folia Orientalia* (henceforth *FO*), 12 (1970):242 – 57; P. B. Golden, "The Question of the Rus' Qağanate," *AEMA* 2 (1982):89 – 91.

[21] Ibn Khurdādbeh, ed. M. J. de Goeje, p. 154; Fr. Westberg, "K analizu vostochnykh istochnikov o Vostochnoi Evrope," *Zhurnal Ministerstva Narodnogo*

institution of the Rus' "Kaganate" (*Chacanus* of the *Rhos/Khāqān Rūs*; Turk. *Qaghan* "Emperor") recorded in ninth- and tenth-century Western[22] and Muslim accounts as well as later Rus' sources.[23] This institution, so important in the early stages of Rus' state formation, was of Khazar (and, ultimately, of Imperial Türk) origin.[24] Pritsak has suggested that elements of the empire-building ideology of the nomads, premised on the concept of a *pax* and the *Männerbünde* came to the Scandinavian bands in the East Slavic lands via the Alano-As.[25] A dynasty with blood ties to the Khazar ruling house, as is implied in the very notion of a Rus' "Kagan," could only have served to reinforce these influences.

One must be careful, however, not to overemphasize these elements in the evolution of the Rus' state to the exclusion of "native" Slavic developments. The Rus' and other Varangian groupings in Eastern Europe were composite entities containing Slavic, Finnic, and other elements. The Slavic tribal groupings were themselves evolving into larger, more complex political organisms.[26] It is hard to envision the rapid political development of Rus' without such well-prepared groundwork. One of the factors contributing to this rapid growth of tribal confederations and later of the state, it is argued, was the need

---

Prosveshcheniia 13 (January, 1908):369; Pritsak, "An Arabic Text," p. 249.

[22] *Annales de Saint-Bertin*, ed. F. Grat et al. (Paris, 1964), p. 30.

[23] See Golden, "Rus' Qağanate," pp. 81–82 for full references to the sources. Cf. also A. V. Riasanovsky, "The Embassy of 838 Revisited: Some Comments in Connection with a 'Normanist' Source on Early Russian History," *Jahrbücher für Geschichte Osteuropas* 10, no. 1 (1962); P. Smirnov, *Volz'kyi shliakh i starodavni Rusi* (Kiev, 1928), pp. 118ff. Ibn Faḍlān (ca. 921–922) describes this Rus' kagan as a sacral king on the Khazar model; see Ibn Faḍlān, *Risāla*, ed. S. ad-Dahhār (Damascus, 1379/1959), pp. 165–66.

[24] For an approach somewhat different from Golden, "Rus' Qağanate," pp. 83–97, see N. Golb and O. Pritsak, *Khazarian Hebrew Documents of the Tenth Century* (Ithaca, N.Y., 1982), p. 64.

[25] Pritsak, *Origin of Rus'*, vol. 1, pp. 86, 197, 294.

[26] This is especially underscored in the works of Rybakov (cf. his *Kievskaia Rus' i russkie kniazhestva*, pp. 258, 284–86, 298ff), while at the same time "external" factors are either completely rejected as playing any substantive role (the Khazars) or considerably downplayed (the Varangians); see also T. I. Dereviankin et al., eds., *Istoriia narodnoho hospodarstva Ukraïns'koï RSR*, vol. 1 (Kiev, 1983), p. 54.

for organization and defense against the nomads and others.[27] With the unification of most of the East Slavic confederations, traditionally ascribed to the 880s (but perhaps to be dated to ca. 930 as Pritsak has suggested),[28] the Rus' state, with its capital in Kiev but containing a number of urban centers, grew by extending its tribute-collecting and juridical authority. This authority, however, was spread from several sources simultaneously. Thus, a unitary state, but one subdivided into principalities (following old, tribal confederational lines) developed. As members of the large princely clan who ruled Rus', the Rurikids demanded and frequently fought for their own patrimonies, the concept of a unitary state gave way, especially after 1132, to that of a federation of sovereign or near sovereign princely states nominally united under a "senior" prince residing in Kiev. Unity, such as there was, was largely in facing a common foe (the Polovtsians),[29] and even here the threat was not always perceived as such by all the Rurikids. It is not our task, however, to trace the dreary details of inter-princely feuding and intrigues to possess Kiev, the symbol of a unity about which few of the participants evinced any real concern.

The circumstances surrounding the origins of Rus' statehood and its evolution have given rise to a long-standing debate over the relative importance of trade versus agriculture in the economy of Kievan Rus'. At present, agriculture is assigned the leading role as it was, without doubt, the predominant occupation of the majority of the population. The picture given is that, despite pressure from the nomads and the demands of a growing population, agriculture made continual advancements due to the expansion of the two- and three-field systems and technological improvements. Increases in productivity are attributed to the peasant small-holders and not the feudal estates.[30] This

---

[27] B. A. Rybakov, *"Slovo o polku Igoreve" i ego sovremenniki* (Moscow, 1971), p. 162.

[28] Golb and Pritsak, *Khazarian Hebrew Documents*, pp. 64–69.

[29] A. N. Nasonov, *"Russkaia zemlia" i obrazovanie territorii drevnerusskogo gosudarstva* (Moscow, 1951), pp. 216–19; P. P. Tolochko, *Kiev i kievskaia zemlia XII–XIII vekov* (Kiev, 1980), pp. 9, 14, 114, 189; Rybakov, *Kievskaia Rus' i russkie kniazhestva*, pp. 464, 469–78, 572–78.

[30] Dereviankin et al., *Istoriia narodnoho hospodarstva*, pp. 58, 61, 64–65, 69, 75, 83, 87–88, 90–92; Blum, *Lord and Peasant*, p. 21. The *Istoriia narodnoho hospodarstva*, p. 83 gives the following formulation: "However, despite the large volume of foreign trade it did not play an important role in the economy of the country

glowing picture of steady improvement in productive capacities is, seemingly, contradicted by the often repeated claim that the pre-Chinggisid nomadic incursions disrupted the economy and brought about the decline of Kievan Rus'.[31] Such may have been the case in border zones such as the exposed Pereiaslav Principality, but such a cause and effect relationship has not been established for other regions.

Where circumstances permitted, peasant agriculture was augmented by livestock-raising, apiculture, hunting, and fishing. There were also growing cottage handicraft and large-scale handicraft industries. The latter was located in the towns and was, by the mid-twelfth century, market-oriented. The nobility tended to live in the towns and cities and most peasant villages were located near urban areas.[32] Thus possibilities existed for the rural population to be drawn into the larger net of urban markets and thence even into international markets. Handicraft production also did not undergo any decline in the twelfth – thirteenth centuries,[33] the period during which Polovtsian incursions were supposed to have most seriously disrupted or retarded economic growth. In fact, new centers were appearing and Kievan artistic influences were spreading.[34]

The most hotly debated issue has been the nature, extent and influence of trade on Kievan political, social, and economic development. There is general agreement that Kievan Rus', lying astride the

---

because it did not draw the main producer of feudal society—the peasant—into commercial, monetary relations. The articles which were exported to foreign markets were taken from the peasants in the form of rent (not goods). Moreover, these articles were mainly the products of industry, not agriculture, the principal field of the economy of Old Rus'."

[31] Rybakov, *Kievskaia Rus' i russkie kniazhestva*, p. 480, however, speaks of the creation of major economic regions, the movement towards the integration of town and country and other "progressive phenomena" which were cut short by the *Mongol invasions*.

[32] Dereviankin et al., *Istoriia narodnoho hospodarstva*, pp. 76, 79 – 81; Rybakov, *Kievskaia Rus' i russkie kniazhestva*, pp. 433 – 36; P. Bushkovitch, "Towns and Castles in Kievan Rus': Boyar Residences and Landownership in the Eleventh and Twelfth Centuries," *Russian History* 7, no. 3 (1980):258 – 60.

[33] B. A. Rybakov, *Remeslo Drevnei Rusi* (Moscow, 1948), p. 521.

[34] Tolochko, *Kiev i kievskaia zemlia*, pp. 46 – 47; F. D. Gurevich, "K istorii kul'turnykh sviazei drevnerusskikh gorodov Poneman'ia s kievskoi zemlëi," *Kul'tura srednevekovoi Rusi* (Leningrad, 1974), pp. 22, 24.

major arteries of international trade, was deeply involved in this commerce both as a middleman and as a producer and exporter of highly prized commodities (furs, slaves, honey, wax, flax, and various handicrafts). The two most lucrative articles of trade were furs and slaves. The chief actors in this trade were, probably, the princes (one must remember the mercantile origins of the Rus' ruling elite, the Rurikids) and a class of foreign and native merchants. In time, the Rus' merchant company, originally "nomads of the seas" and rivers,[35] had been transformed into landholders each concerned with securing his own patrimony, a principle established at the Liubech congress in 1097. Nonetheless, they were the class that had the means (and traditions) to engage in foreign trade and the affluence to consume luxury goods.[36] Foreign imports, however, were not exclusively of the luxury variety. Some goods were aimed at the larger population and as such are attested archaeologically.

Particularly important in Rus' commercial relations were the ties with the Orient. Eastern Slavic trade contacts with Byzantium, Sassanid Iran, and its successor state the Arabian Caliphate (especially under the 'Abbāssids who came to power in 750), were long-standing. The 'Abbāssids, like their contemporaries in China, were anxious to promote international commerce.[37]

The dating of this eastern trade, like so much else, is open to dispute. There is no doubt, however, that it became significant after after 750, following the Arab-Khazar wars for domination of the Caucasus. I will leave to the numismatists to comment on the still incomplete testimony of the coins that has figured so largely in our understanding of this trade. But, it should be noted briefly that in the ninth and tenth centuries there is a large influx of Muslim silver coins, or dirhams, from the Near East, North Africa, Central Asia, and Volga Bulgaria, which then drops off precipitously in the eleventh century (to be replaced, it would appear, to some degree, by western silver).[38]

---

[35] Pritsak, *Origin of Rus'*, vol. 1, pp. 10ff.

[36] *PSRL* 1:256–57; Shekera, *Kyïvs'ka Rus'*, p. 16.

[37] Curtin, *Cross-Cultural Trade*, p. 91.

[38] Tolochko, *Kiev i kievskaia zemlia*, p. 64, notes a rise in the entry of silver in the twelfth–thirteenth centuries rather than a decline, coming mainly from Germany. There exists an extensive literature on the Islamic coins in Rus'. Here we may cite V. L. Ianin, *Denezhno-vesovye sistemy russkogo srednevekov'ia, Domongol'skii period* (Moscow, 1956), which has references to earlier works, and the recent studies

The older theory of P. G. Liubomirov[39] and others that Rus''s eastern trade came to a virtual halt in the eleventh century has been convincingly challenged by M. V. Fekhner (among others) in an article dealing with finds of Near Eastern beads imported into Rus' during this period. Fekhner notes that the beads follow the same dispersal pattern as the dirhams and that the zenith of this trade was reached in the eleventh century, just when the eastern trade is supposed to have fallen into desuetude. The importation of beads comes to an end in the twelfth century and Fekhner, falling back on the older theories, attributes the cessation of this trade to the disruptions caused by the Seljuks and Polovtsians.[40] One wonders, however, why the Seljuks and Polovtsians, both of whom had completed their major territorial conquests in the eleventh century, would have disrupted this trade at this juncture? Thomas S. Noonan, sampling a number of imports (silks, metalwares), concluded that although there were fluctuations, trade, largely carried out through the Volga Bulgars, did not decline.[41] Rus'

---

of T. S. Noonan: "Medieval Islamic Copper Coins from European Russia and Surrounding Regions," *American Oriental Society* 94, no. 4 (1974):448–53; "When Did Dirhams First Reach the Ukraine?," *HUS* 2, no. 1 (March 1978):26–40; "When and How Did Dirhams First Reach Russia?," *Cahiers du monde russe et soviètique* 21, nos. 3–4 (1980):401–469; "Monetary Circulation in Early Medieval Rus': A Study of Volga Bulgar Dirham Finds," *Russian History* 7, no. 3 (1981):294–311; "A Ninth-Century Dirham Hoard From Devitsa in Southern Russia," *American Numismatic Society Museum Notes* (1982):185–209.

[39] P. G. Liubomirov, "Torgovye sviazi Rusi s Vostokom v VIII–IX vv.," *Zapiski Saratovskogo Universiteta* 1, no. 3 (1923).

[40] M. V. Fekhner, "Nekotorye svedeniia arkheologii po istorii russkovostochnykh ekonomicheskikh sviazei do serediny XIII v.," *Mezhdunarodnye sviazi Rossii do XVIII v.* (Moscow, 1961), pp. 46, 51–54.

[41] T. S. Noonan, "Russia's Eastern Trade, 1150–1350: The Archaeological Evidence," *AEMA* 3 (1983):201–60; see also his "Suzdalia's Eastern Trade in the Century Before the Mongol Conquest," *Cahiers du monde russe et soviètique* 19, no. 4 (1978):371–84; cf. also Iu. A. Limonov, "Iz istorii vostochnoi torgovli Vladimiro-Suzdal'skogo kniazhestva," *Mezhdunarodnye sviazi Rossii do XVIII v.* (Moscow, 1961), pp. 55–63. Tolochko, *Kiev i kievskaia zemlia*, pp. 61–64, has suggested that the diminution in the flow of foreign coins into Rus' does not necessarily imply a decline in commercial ties. Rather, it may point to trade in goods for goods. He cites as evidence for this the number of Kievan lead seals found in neighboring areas and notes that precious metals still were entering Rus' in the form of ingots. On the Volga Bulgar trade, see J. Martin, "Trade on the Volga: The Commercial Relations of Bulgar with Central Asia and Iran in the Eleventh–Twelfth Centuries," *International*

merchants were active in Sughdaq in the Crimea as well.[42] The latter, it might be noted, was the principal port of the Polovtsians. Much of this eastern trade went through Khazaria (up to ca. 965) and, subsequently, via Volga Bulgar intermediaries. These one-time nomadic, but now sedentary, states did much to protect and foster commerce. Indeed, trade was an important part of their economies and the greatest threats to them came not from the steppe but from Rus', which destroyed Khazaria and from the late eleventh to the thirteenth century challenged Bulgar commercial supremacy on the Volga as well. Thus, it was not the east-west routes, which were well-guarded, but the north-south routes that proved most vulnerable to attacks by the nomads, for these were the routes in which they had less of a commercial stake. This route, the "Route from the Varangians to the Greeks" (probably the later route of the "Grechniki"), was still in use in the twelfth century when it occasionally required, as it always had centuries earlier, special defense measures on the part of the Kievan ruler. By that time there were other southbound routes (e.g. the overland Solianyi route to the Crimea and the Zaloznyi route to the Sea of Azov).[43]

The earliest notices of the Muslim authors on the Rus' associate them with the trade in furs and slaves. Ibn Khurdādbeh describes their routes to Byzantium, Khazaria, and Baghdad whither they brought beaver, black fox pelts, and swords.[44] Ibn Rustah notes that "they have no landed property ['aqār] nor villages nor ploughed fields, but rather their profession is the trade in sable, grey squirrel and other furs."[45] Moreover, "the Rūs raid the Ṣaqāliba, travelling by boat until they come to them. They take them captive and go to Kazarān and Bulgār. They sell them (there). They have no ploughed fields, but eat what is brought from the land of the Ṣaqāliba."[46] The volume of the fur trade (much of which went to Khwārizm, Transoxiana, and Iran)

Journal of Turkish Studies (henceforth *IJTS*), 1/2 (1980):85–97.

[42] A. P. Novosel'tsev and V. T. Pashuto, "Vneshniaia torgovlia Drevnei Rusi (do serediny XIII v.)," *Istoriia SSSR* 3 (1967):107–108.

[43] On these routes, see Shekera, *Kyïvs'ka Rus'*, pp. 36–44; Tolochko, *Kiev i kievskaia zemlia*, pp. 58–60.

[44] Ibn Khurdādbeh, ed. M. J. de Goeje, p. 154.

[45] Ibn Rustah, *Kitāb al-'Alāq al-Nafīsah*, ed. M. J. de Goeje (Leiden, 1892), p. 145.

[46] Ibid. This notice is repeated by Gardīzī; see A. P. Martinez, "Gardīzī's Two Chapters on the Turks," *AEMA* 2 (1982):167.

was high and very profitable.[47] With the collapse of the Khazar Kaganate, Volga Bulgaria came to dominate much of the fur trade, especially the eastern Central Asian market. The Rus' began to challenge the Bulgar hold only in the late eleventh century, a source of conflict between the two until the Mongol conquests.[48]

The other major article of trade was that of slaves, in especial demand in the Islamic world. The major sources of these slaves were Africa, Slavic Eastern Europe, and Turkic Central Asia. The Turks were largely used as *ghulāms* or *mamlūks*, a special group of military slaves which in time came to dominate politics of the caliphate.[49] An increase in the number of Turkic and Slavic slaves is observed in the tenth century.[50] The Rus', as we know from the Muslim accounts (Ibn Rustah, Gardīzī), were deeply involved in this human traffic, the volume of which by the late tenth century was so great that a glut (at least in Central Asia) appears to have developed.[51] Among the products most closely associated with Rus'-Byzantine trade in the era of Ol'ga and Sviatoslav (d. 972) were slaves (*cheliad'*), furs, and honey.[52] The *Gesta Hungarorum* cites among the gifts given to the

[47] E. Ashtor, *A Social and Economic History of the Near East in the Middle Ages* (Berkeley, 1976), p. 148.

[48] A. Bennigsen, "Contributions à l'étude du commerce des fourrures russes," *Cahiers du monde russe et soviètique* 19, no. 4 (1978):394, 396. See also in the same issue, J. Martin, "The Land of Darkness and the Golden Horde: The Fur Trade Under the Mongols, Thirteenth – Fourteenth Centuries," p. 403. The hostilities were largely the result of movements by the recently established Rostov-Suzdal' princes to take over the upper Volga trade. Prior to the late eleventh century, the Rus' of Novgorod had been an important supplier of furs. Now, the Bulgars shifted their trade away from the bellicose Rus' and towards the Finno-Ugric peoples of the North, the Ves' and Iugra; see J. Martin, "Trade on the Volga," pp. 91ff.

[49] On Islamic military slavery, see the differing views of M. A. Shaban, *Islamic History, A New Interpretation,* vol. 2, *A.D. 750 – 1055 (A.H. 132 – 448)* (Cambridge, 1976), pp. 63ff.; P. Crone, *Slaves on Horseback: The Evolution of the Islamic Polity* (Cambridge, 1980); D. Pipes, *Slave Soldiers of Islam: The Genesis of a Military System* (New Haven, 1981).

[50] Ashtor, *Social and Economic History,* p. 106.

[51] Al-Muqaddasī, *Aḥsan at-Taqāsim fī Ma'rīfat al-Aqālīm,* ed. M. J. de Goeje (Leiden, 1906), p. 340, cites the prices of 70 – 100 dirhams for male slaves and 20 – 30 dirhams for females "if they are Turks."

[52] *PSRL* 1:62, 67. Shekera, *Kyïvs'ka Rus',* pp. 27 – 28 has advanced the thesis that the importance of Rus' slave-trade has been exaggerated, but has not offered any convincing argumentation. The *Istoriia narodnoho hospodarstva,* p. 82, however, con-

"Dux Almus," the semi-legendary chieftain who led the Hungarian migration through Eastern Slavic lands, by the "duces Ruthenorum, scilicet de Kyeu et Sudul [= Suzdal'—PBG]" were "centum pueros cumanos," as well as camels, furs, etc.[53] Clearly, the Rus' slave net extended to the steppes as well. As we shall see, it was a regular feature of the Rus' raids against the Polovtsians.

Other important items of export were the products of apiculture, which were collected in the princely tribute, and, later, the finished products of the Rus' handicraft industry (textiles, jewelry, glasswork, armor, and weapons), as well as agricultural products (a trade with roots deep in antiquity). Imports included silks, cottons and other textiles, arms, armor, art, church articles, jewelry, metalwares, spices, fruits, musk, aloe, camphor, preserved fish and meats, livestock and horses (from the nomads), and, on occasion, grain (from Volga Bulgaria).[54] Finally, we should note that the Rus', although active in all areas of production/gathering of goods for trade and pursuing a vigorous mercantile policy, also exploited, like their neighbors the Khazars, Bulgars, and Byzantines, the transit trade, taking 10 percent of the goods passing through their lands.[55] Rus''s position as a mid-

---

siders the Rus' slave-trade to have been highly developed, on a par with the fur trade. Bennigsen, "Contributions," p. 385, says that in the pre-Mongol period, the slave trade on the Volga was almost entirely in Rus' hands. A. N. Kurat's claim (*Peçenek tarihi* [Istanbul, 1037], p. 68) that the Rus' sold slaves to the Pechenegs seems less well-grounded.

[53] *Scriptores rerum Hungaricarum*, vol. 1, ed. E. Szentpétery (Budapest, 1937), p. 46. Hungarian sources often anachronistically applied the ethnonym *Kun/Cumanus-Comanus* to earlier nomadic peoples; see Gy. Németh, *A honfoglaló magyarság kialakulása* (Budapest, 1930), pp. 223, 235. In this instance, the anonymous author was probably describing circumstances of his own time, ca. late twelfth–early thirteenth century; see P. Hajdu, Gy. Kristó, A. Róna-Tas, *Bevezetés a magyar őstörténet kutatásanak forrásaiba*, 1, no. 2 (Budapest, 1976, 1977), pp. 187–89.

[54] Dereviankin et al., *Istoriia narodnoho hospodarstva*, pp. 82–83; Shekera, *Kyïvs'ka Rus'*, pp. 21–24, 28–31. On the silk imports, see M. V. Fekhner, "Nekotorye dannye o vneshnikh sviaziakh Kieva v XII v.," *Kul'tura srednevekovoi Rusi* (Leningrad, 1974), pp. 67, 69.

[55] Ibn Rustah, ed. M. J. de Goeje, p. 141; cf. also the comments of T. Lewicki, *Źródła arabskie do dziejów Słowiańszczyzny* (Wrocław, Warsaw, Cracow, 1956, 1969, 1977), vol. 1, pp. 131–32; vol. 2, pt. 2, p. 90.

dleman between Central Europe, the East, and Scandinavia and the Southeast thus proved to be very lucrative.

The Rus' society we have sketched here held a number of attractions for the nomads. It was a source of grains and other agricultural products which the nomads, as we shall see, needed and for which they were willing to trade or raid. The involvement of Rus' in international commerce, an area in which the nomads' interest was no less lively, also drew them. For example, the role of the nomads in the fur trade is well-attested and of long standing. Jordanes (sixth century) remarks that the Onoghurs are "noted because the commerce in marten skins comes from them."[56] The Volga Bulgars, whose tribal union included Onoghuric elements, later played a vital role in this trade. The Inner Asian Ting-ling nomads were also noted by Chinese sources as being involved in the fur trade.[57] The fur route, itself of considerable antiquity, going back to the period of Iranian domination of the steppe, was in many respects the analogue of the Silk Route and as such attracted the nomads not so much as hunters or trappers but as commercial agents or intermediaries.[58] Finally, there was Rus' itself. In the last stage of Kievan Rus' political development, the period of "feudal fragmentation," the nomads were drawn into and able to profit from Rus' internecine strife. They were brought right into the heart of the Rus' political system. Thus, although nomads and sedentary societies in western Eurasia occupied, unlike their counterparts in the Near and Middle East, different ecological niches, there were, nonetheless, many areas of contact. Before discussing these points of contact between the Kievan Rus' state and the various nomadic peoples, we must first provide some biographical data about the latter.

---

[56] Jordanes, *Getica:* Iordan, *O proiskhozhdenii i deianiiakh getov*, ed. E. Ch. Skrzhinskaia (Moscow, 1960), Latin text, p. 136: "Hunuguri autem hinc sunt noti, quia ab ipsis pellium murinarum venit commercium"; Russ. trans. p. 72. See also H. W. Haussig, *Die Geschichte Zentralasiens und der Seidenstrasse in vorislamischer Zeit* (Darmstadt, 1983), p. 154.

[57] W. Eberhard, *Çin'in şimal komşuları* (Ankara, 1942), p. 71; Németh, *A honfoglaló*, pp. 115–16. The Ting-ling are associated with the *T'ieh-le*, a large Turkic tribal union that included Oghuric groups and the Uyghurs; see K. Czeglédy, *Nomád népek vándorlása Napkelettől Napnyugatig* (Budapest, 1969), pp. 17–18.

[58] L. Ligeti, "Az uráli magyar őshaza," in L. Ligeti, ed., *A magyarság őstörténete* (Budapest, 1943), pp. 54ff.

The Political Organization of the Nomads of Western Eurasia

Primitive society has been characterized as being based primarily on the kinship system which, together with custom, serves as the means of achieving societal cohesion. It is, theoretically, an egalitarian society in which there is little in the way of formal "government," or any of the institutions usually associated with it: monarchy, tax-collection, standing armies, an organized priesthood. There is little evidence of social stratification or the division of labor. Possessing no governmental administrative structure worthy of note, other than village or lineage headman, such a society may drive off another such grouping but not truly conquer (i.e., subjugate) and rule them, just as they do not, in that sense, rule themselves. Religious concepts are largely concerned with magic and its techniques, shamanism. The link between this society and the sophisticated polities of archaic civilizations (Ancient Egypt, Mesopotamia, etc.) has been termed, recently, "complex society," which itself may be divided into three stages: "chieftainship, early monarchy and complex monarchy." The revolutionary change brought about by this form of political organization was to develop forms of social cohesions other than that of the kinship system. This was the state. In its advanced form, "complex society" developed: a monarchy (with centralizing tendencies), a state apparatus (bureaucrats, tax-collectors), a priestly hierarchy with attendent religious ideologies, and a socially differentiated population.[59] In terms of political organization, the nomadic societies of Eurasia could and did oscillate between various forms of primitive and complex society. In some instances, they moved considerably beyond to create empires spanning much of Eurasia. When these empires collapsed, the nomads reverted to their "natural" state, an advanced form of primitive or early complex society in which kinship (real and fictitious), custom, and the exigencies of the nomadic economy were the basic sources of social cohesion.

---

[59] On "Complex Society," see E. Sagan, *At the Dawn of Tyranny: The Origins of Individualism, Political Oppression and the State* (New York, 1985), pp. xvi – xxi where these definitions are elucidated and the concept of "Complex Society" is introduced. See also M. H. Fried, *The Evolution of Political Society* (New York, 1967) who discusses egalitarian, rank, stratified, and state society.

The nomadic neighbors of Rus' never presented a monolith in terms of political, social and economic development. With the exception of the Khazar Kaganate and Volga Bulgaria, they (i.e., the Pechenegs, Oghuz/Torki, and Polovtsians), for the most part, practiced various forms of extensive pastoral nomadism. Khazaria and Volga Bulgaria, however, were semi-nomadic societies which were in the process of becoming sedentary. In Khazaria this process never reached fruition as the state was destroyed by the Rus' before this could occur. In Volga Bulgaria, this process was well-advanced as trade and agriculture came to dominate its economy, although nomadic traditions remained strong. An intermediate stage may be seen in the *Chernii Kloboutsi*, a composite of tribal fragments organized by the Kievan princes as a borderguard against other nomads.

Paradoxically, in the pre-Chinggisid era, the Rus' state encountered early in its history the most organized of these nomadic societies—the Khazar Kaganate. The latter was an offspring and successor state of the Türk Kaganate (mid-sixth – mid-eighth century), from which it began to delineate itself ca. 650. Its "heroic age," the period in which a nomadic polity tests the defenses of its sedentary neighbors and attempts to establish its hegemony over its immediate neighbors in the steppes, came to a close by the late eighth century. Thus, in the formative years of Rus' development Khazaria was an established power whose most aggressive impulses had already been spent. It was presided over by a sacral king, the *Qaghan* and a sub-king (*Qaghan-beg, Shad, Yilig*) who carried out the daily administration of the realm. Its administrative apparatus (drawn from the royal clan, subject tribal rulers and appointees) ruled over a polyglot (Turkic, Iranian, Finno-Ugric, Slavic, and Caucasian) population of nomads, agriculturalists and hunter-gatherers. It derived considerable revenue from international trade and the tribute collected from subject peoples. Sometime around the year 800, the Khazar ruling groups and elements of their tribal union converted to Judaism abandoning (to varying degrees) the Tengri religion of their Türk forebears. The majority of the urban population (much of which was of foreign origin) was Muslim. Central Asian Iranians seem to have been particularly prominent in the urban commercial class. Christianity also had numerous adherents, while the Jews and Judaizing groups, according to Muslim sources, constituted the smallest of the three world religions. With the conversion to Judaism as a quasi-state religion, writing in Hebrew was added to the already existing Turkic runic scripts employed in Khazaria.[60] In brief, the Khazar state (which at its zenith extended into the Eastern Slavic lands in the west, controlled Volga Bulgaria in the north, bordered on the Khwārizmshāh state in the east and the Caucasus Mountains in the south) possessed all the attributes of an advanced, complex society or archaic empire. It had an ordered and regular government with an appropriate imperial ideology,[61] a system of tax-collection, the means to achieve external goals and internal security and a more or less fixed territory. On the whole, this was not true of its successors in the Ponto-Caspian steppes.

Typical of the latter were the Pechenegs. They were associated with the T'ieh-le, a huge Turkic tribal confederation under Türk domination noted in the Chinese sources and appear to have been in "K'ang-kiu" (the Tashkent-Samarqand region) and perhaps further east. Included in their midst were the Kangar/Kängäräs, a tribal subgrouping which may have contained urbanized, commercial elements.[62] Conflict with the Oghuz in the late eighth century and

---

[60] On the Khazars, see A. Zajączkowski, *Ze studiów nad zagadnieniem chazarskim* (Cracow, 1947); D. M. Dunlop, *The History of the Jewish Khazars* (Princeton, 1954); M. I. Artamonov, *Istoriia Khazar* (Leningrad, 1962); T. Nagrodzka-Majchrzyk, "Chazarowie" in E. Tryjarski et al., *Hunowie europejscy, Protobułgarzy, Chazarowie, Pieczyngowie* (Wrocław, Warsaw, Cracow, 1975); P. B. Golden, *Khazar Studies*, 2 vols. (Budapest, 1980); N. Golb and O. Pritsak, *Khazarian Hebrew Documents of the Tenth Century* (Ithaca, N.Y., 1982); and D. Ludwig, *Struktur und Gesellschaft des Chazaren-Reiches im Licht der schriftlichen Quellen* (Münster, 1982).

The Khazar conversion is most recently discussed in O. Pritsak, "The Khazar Kingdom's Conversion to Judaism," *HUS* 2, no. 3 (September 1978); in the Golb, Pritsak work, *Khazarian Hebrew Documents*; and by P. B. Golden, "Khazaria and Judaism," *AEMA* 3 (1983). On runiform scripts in Khazaria, see Gy. Németh, "The Runiform Inscriptions from Nagy-Szent-Miklós and the Runiform Scripts of Eastern Europe," *Acta Linguistica Hungarica* 21 (1971):1–51; S. G. Kliashtornyi, "Khazarskaia nadpis' na amfore s gorodishcha Maiaki," *Sovetskaia Arkheologiia* 1 (1979):270–75.

[61] See P. B. Golden, "Imperial Ideology and the Sources of Political Unity Amongst the Pre-Činggisid Nomads of Western Eurasia," *AEMA* 2 (1982):58–61, 73.

[62] On Pecheneg origins, see Pritsak, "The Pečenegs" *AEMA* 1 (1975):211–17; E. Tryjarski, "Pieczyngowie" in E. Tryjarski et al., *Hunowie europejscy*, pp. 494, 503–506; S. G. Kliashtornyi, *Drevnetiurkskie runicheskie pamiatniki kak istochnik po istorii Srednei Azii* (Moscow, 1964), pp. 156–79.

thereafter (reported in a Tibetan rendering of an Uyghur report and preserved in Oghuz legends) drove them westward to the Yayïq/Ural-Volga mesopotamia.[63] Continuing Oghuz and Khazar pressure brought them into the Ukrainian steppes whence they expelled the Hungarian tribal union from two successive habitats, Levedia and Etelköz. By 915, when they made their first formal entry in the Rus' chronicles, they had already been on the scene for several decades.[64]

Despite the report of Abu'l-Fidā (d. 1331), basing himself on the notice of Abu Sa'īd (d. 1286) about "Bajanākiyya, capital of the Khāqān of the Bajanāk" located to the east of "Qāmān" (Cuman),[65] it seems very unlikely that a Pecheneg Kaganate ever existed. This was no more than a learned conjecture by analogy with earlier Turkic state-formations by authors far removed in time and location from the Pechenegs. Even later Pecheneg history, such as we know it, indicates a loosely held tribal union in which there was little evidence of the growth of central authority. Earlier Pecheneg political organization, as outlined for us by the Byzantine emperor Constantine Porphyrogenitus,[66] seems equally devoid of monarchic centralization. "Pechenegia," then, was not a state but rather a loosely held tribal union. The absence of a strong central authority, however, in no way hindered the development of a strong economy. Gardīzī (mid-eleventh century) writes that these "Pechenegs are the possessors of (great) wealth (for)

---

[63] J. Bacot, "Reconnaissance en Haute Asie septentrionale par cinq envoyés Ouighours au VIIIe siècle," *Journal Asiatique* 244 (1956):146–47; L. Ligeti, "A propos du 'Rapport sur les rois demeurant dans le nord,'" *Études tibetaines dédiées à la memoire de Marcelle Lalou* (Paris, 1971), pp. 170, 176; P. B. Golden, "The Migrations of the Oğuz," *Archivum Ottomanicum* 4 (1972):56–59; Golden, "Imperial Ideology," p. 64.

[64] *PSRL* 1:42. On the Hungarian migrations, see I. Fodor, *Verecke híres útján...* (Budapest, 1975), pp. 158ff., 177–94, 202ff.; Ligeti, *A magyarság őstörténete*, pp. 100–153; Tryjarski, "Pieczyngowie," pp. 510–16; Pritsak, "The Pečenegs," pp. 217–18.

[65] Abu'l-Fidā, *Taqwīm al-Buldān: Geographie de Aboulfeda*, ed. M. Reinaud, M. Bon Mackin de Slane (Paris, 1840), p. 205.

[66] Constantine Porphyrogenitus, *De administrando imperio*, ed. Gy. Moravcsik, trans. R. Jenkins [Corpus Fontium Historiae Byzantinae, 1] (Dumbarton Oaks, Washington, D.C., 1967), pp. 166–70; S. A. Pletnëva, "Pechenegi, torki i polovtsy v iuzhnorusskikh stepiakh," *Materialy i issledovaniia po arkheologii SSSR* 62, no. 1 (1958):192–93; Pritsak, "The Pečenegs," pp. 218–21; Tryjarski, "Pieczyngowie," pp. 568–69; Kurat, *Peçenek tarihi*, p. 59.

they are possessors of abundant horses and sheep. They have many gold and silver vessels. They have many weapons. They have silver belts.'' He also notes that they were deeply involved in slave-raiding and the slave trade.[67]

The Oghuz tribal union (along with the Rus' one of the primary causes of the Pecheneg migrations in the eleventh century) had roots much more intimately associated with the Türk Kaganate as the Rus' designation *Tork* (= *Törk/Türk*) and the title of their headman, *yabghu*, indicate.[68] They entered the borderlands of Islamic Central Asia in the latter part of the eighth century, expelling the Pechenegs and testing the martial qualities of the Muslims. The ''Oghuz Yabghu State,'' in reality an unstable tribal union in the early stages of complex society, found itself under continual pressure from more powerful neighbors (the Ghaznawids, Qarakhanids and Kimäks). Oghuz mercenaries took service with the Ghaznawids, Qarakhanids and Khazaria. In time, Islam began to gain converts among them, engendering still further internal strife, but now giving it a religious patina. Out of this chaotic mass of nomads, the Seljuk movement emerged in the late tenth century. Forced out of Central Asia, the Seljuks went on to win an empire in the Near and Middle East. Under Polovtsian and then Rus' pressure, the Western Oghuz/Torks were pushed into and then out of the Pontic steppe zone.[69]

The genesis of the Polovtsian tribal union, which appears in our sources under a variety of designations, constitutes one of the most complex questions in Eurasian history: *Polovtsi* (Rus'), *Qifjāq*, *Qibjāq*, *Qipchāq* (Arabic, Persian), *Qivch'aq-i* (Georgian), *Khbshakh*, *Khartesh* (Armenian), *Kun* (Hungarian), Κόμανοι, Κούμανοι,

---

[67] Martinez, ''Gardīzī's Two chapters,'' pp. 151–52.

[68] In the Old Türk system, *yabghu* was one of the highest titles, just below that of *Qaghan*; see Kliashtornyi, *Drevnetiurk, runichesk, pamiatniki*, p. 111; F. László, ''A kagán és családja,'' *Kőrösi Csoma Archivum* 3 (1940):31; Maḥmūd al-Kāshgharī, *Dīwān Lughat at-Turk*, ed. Türk Dil Kurumu (Ankara, 1941), p. 458; O. Pritsak, ''Von den Karluk zu den Karachaniden,'' *Zeitschrift der Deutschen Morgenländischen Gesellschaft* 101 (1951):273–74 and his ''Der Untergang des Reiches des oġuzischen Yabġu,'' *60. doğum yili müna-sebetiyle Fuad Köprülü Armağanı*, ed. H. Eren et al. (İstanbul, 1953), p. 403.

[69] Golden, ''Migrations of the Oġuz,'' pp. 45–84.

Comani, Cumani (Greek, Latin), Falwen (German).[70] They also appear to have been part of the Türk Kaganate and like their contemporaries retained only a few of the organizational features of that state. After the Türk collapse, they are found in the Kimäk confederation which, in the eleventh century, came to be led by the Qun/Quman who had been propelled westward in a series of migrations originating in Inner Asia.[71] Masters of the Eurasian steppes by the mid-eleventh century, the Polovtsians were divided into a number of subconfederations, each with its own ruling, charismatic clan. In Rus', they sometimes came to be distinguished by geographical (e.g., the "Lukomorian Polovtsians") or political referents (e.g., the "Wild Polovtsians"). The easternmost groupings, the immediate neighbors of the Khwārizmshāh state, were also called Qanglï.[72] Rarely able to mount a coordinated, sustained effort against Rus', Polovtsian political development never moved beyond that of the tribal union, i.e., the early stages of complex society. It was only in the twilight of Polovtsian history, in the late twelfth–early thirteenth century, that one of the charismatic clans, the Sharuqanids, long-standing foes of Rus' who had acquired some political sophistication and intimate knowledge of the internal workings of sedentary states in service to the Georgian crown, under Könchäk and his son Iurgi (George) attempted to forge a strong central authority. This much-delayed

[70] See J. Marquart, Über das Volkstum der Komanen in W. Bang, J. Marquart, Osttürkische Dialektstudien, Abhandlungen der königlichen Gesellschaft der Wissenschaften zu Göttingen, philologisch-historische Klasse, N. F., 13 (1914); Pritsak, "The Polovcians and Rus'," pp. 321–35.

[71] On the Kimäk, see B. E. Kumekov, Gosudarstvo kimakov IX–XI vv. po arabskim istochnikam (Alma-Ata, 1972).

[72] For listings of the Polovtsian (Qïpchaq) tribes, see among others, Ad-Dimishqī, Nukhbat ad-Dahr fī 'Ajā'ib al-Barr wa'l-Baḥr, ed. A. Mehren (1866; reprint, Leipzig, 1923), p. 264 and similar listings in an-Nuwayrī and Ibn Khaldūn. On the groupings in Rus', see G. A. Fëdorov-Davydov, Kochevniki Vostochnoi Evropy pod vlast'iu zolotoordynskikh khanov (Moscow, 1966), pp. 222–27; O. Pritsak, "Non-'Wild' Polovcians," To Honor Roman Jakobson (The Hague and Paris, 1967), pp. 1615–1623 and his "Polovcians and Rus'," pp. 342–67; Golden, "The Polovci Dikii," pp. 296–309; and N. A. Baskakov, "Imena polovtsev i nazvaniia polovetskikh plemën v russkikh letopisiakh," A. T. Kaidarov et al., eds., Tiurkskaia onomastika (Alma-Ata, 1984), pp. 48–77. On the Qanglï, see A. T. Kaidarov, "K istoriko-lingvisticheskoi kharakteristike etnonima kangly/qangly," in Kaidarov et al., eds., Tiurkskaia onomastika, pp. 34–47.

Polovtsian movement towards statehood collapsed with Iurgi's death at the Battle of Kalka.[73]

The principal point of this brief survey is that the nomadic polities which the Kievan Rus' state faced for much of its history *were not organized states*. The Khazar Kaganate, a declining empire, was the one true exception and this state was destroyed by the Rus'. Volga Bulgaria, a trade-oriented state on a more modest scale, although a keen commercial competitor, never constituted a threat to Rus' or to its economic interests. On the contrary, Rus' aggressively challenged it and made encroachments on its spheres of activity. For the nomads to have threatened, in any serious and fundamental way, a large and powerful sedentary state, such as Rus', required a well-organized tightly disciplined tribal union already well-advanced on the road to statehood. This the Mongols convincingly demonstrated, organizing in the process most of the nomads of Eurasia. Their immediate predecessors, the Western Oghuz/Torks, Pechenegs and Polovtsians, were either unwilling or unable to do this. To understand why, we must turn to the internal workings of the nomadic economy and societal development.

Nomadic Society

As was noted earlier, the nomads of Eurasia, unlike their Near and Middle Eastern counterparts, occupied, for the most part, different ecological habitats from that of their sedentary neighbors.[74] The closest points of contact were the Slavic colonies advancing into the chernozem steppe lands. Even here, however, although some of these regions suffered from frequent nomadic raiding, contact was not as extensive as in the Near and Middle East where nomad and agriculturalist might, in whole or in part, share the same land. Except for the chernozem, much of the nomads' land was of marginal or little use to agriculturalists. Thus, conflict between sedentary and nomadic societies developed not so much over possession of certain lands as access to the products of those lands. Nomadism, although a highly

---

[73] *PSRL* 1:504; Pletněva, "Pechenegi, torki i polovtsy," pp. 222–24; Fëdorov-Davydov, *Kochevniki*, pp. 222–23.

[74] A. M. Khazanov, "The Early State Among the Eurasian Nomads," *Oikumene* 4 (1983):267.

profitable economic system, sometimes producing greater monetary wealth than agriculture, is, unlike the latter, not autarkic. Unable to produce certain foodstuffs (grains, vegetables) in sufficient quantities to meet its needs (many nomads practice a limited agriculture), it must gain access to these goods.[75] Moreover, the specialization required of extensive pastoral nomadism tends to limit or prevent the development of other forms of economic endeavor. As a consequence, nomadism is a highly unstable, precarious system, subject to great fluctuations. Overproduction can place explosive pressures on nomadic societies necessitating an increase in pasture land. This, in turn, usually entails wars of conquest. Added to this are the uncertainties of weather and disease which can decimate herds. The prudent nomad does not place all his wealth in livestock. Indeed, too much "success," i.e., a large-scale increase in livestock, can lead to congestion and the break-up of nomadic communities.[76] Nomadism, then, requires a very fine balance of forces. Nomads, unless they are willing to face Malthusian retribution, are forced to keep population in accord with herd size. The latter, in turn, was determined by pasturage. Agricultural society, capable of much greater and varied production of foodstuffs and requiring more labor, can support a larger population.[77] Hence, the nomads were usually outnumbered. Their mobility and martial skills honed by their lifestyle more than compensated for manpower shortcomings. Nomadic society was hard on those who did not meet its harsh requirements. Poor nomads who lost their herds were ultimately compelled to "sedentarize" (usually in the

[75] J. M. Smith, Jr., "Turanian Nomadism," *Iranian Studies* 11 (1978):60; Khazanov, *Nomads*, pp. 46, 50, 69, 70, 81, 83; F. Braudel, *Civilization and Capitalism*, 1, *The Structure of Everyday Life*, trans. S. Reynolds (New York, 1979), p. 104; W. Irons, *The Yomut Turkmen* (Ann Arbor, 1975), pp. 11, 22, 35; M. D. Sahlins, *Tribesmen* (Englewood Cliffs, N.J., 1968), p. 35.

[76] Khazanov, *Nomads*, pp. 69–72, 74–76, 78–79, 81. Ibn Faḍlān, ed. ad-Dahhār, p. 106, mentions that he has seen Oghuz who "possess 10,000 horses (*dābba*) and 100,000 head of sheep." This undoubtedly exaggerated figure could have been true only of the very rich. Nomadic herd sizes necessary to support a family vary with the local ecology. Modern researchers place it minimally at 60–100 sheep, horses, and cattle; cf. F. Barth, *Nomads of South Persia* (Boston, 1961), pp. 16–17; Smith, "Turanian Nomadism," p. 62.

[77] Irons, *Yomut Turkmen*, p. 150; Khazanov, *Nomads*, pp. 71–72 and his *Sotsial'naia istoriia skifov* (Moscow, 1975), p 76; Smith, "Turanian Nomadism," p. 62.

qïshlaqs "winter camps" or embryonic towns).[78] This was a natural means of population control. But, even these "sedentarized" nomads, when their economic situation permitted, reverted to a nomadic life. Surplus livestock, on the other hand, could be sold off or bartered for equally portable wealth (gold, silver, jewelry).

There were various means of assuring ready access to the products of agricultural society: sedentariness, often brought about by some more powerful sedentary state or the consequence of a forced migration into an area incapable of sustaining nomadism for all or most of the tribe (in some instances, e.g., the Hungarians, the aristocracy maintained a form of semi-nomadism while the mass of nomadic herders became sedentary);[79] acceptance of the overlordship of a sedentary state which usually entailed the granting of trading privileges or allowances; the conquest of sedentary territories and the establishment of tax/tributary relationships with sedentary peoples; and, trade and/or predation.[80]

The themes of trade and predation take us to the very heart of Rus'-nomadic relations. As has been noted, nomadic societies had a greater need for trade than their sedentary "trading partners." The nomadic disadvantages in this arrangement were usually offset by their military superiority.[81] Indeed, nomads often fought just for the

---

[78] Barth, *Nomads of South Persia*, pp. 108–109; Khazanov, *Sotsial'naia istoriia*, pp. 149–50. Sedentarization through wealth also occurred. Patricia Crone in her *Slaves on Horses*, p. 19 argues that the Eurasian steppes and the important horse economy that developed there (the horse being in the nature of "cash cattle") mitigated against sedentarization through impoverishment. Poor nomads could be carried economically by kinsmen and fellow tribesmen as shepherds. Modern research, however, has indicated that this was usually the last stage before abandoning nomadism altogether. Most Soviet publications argue for the sedentarization of the poor nomads in Eastern Europe and adduce some archaeological evidence for it, cf. S. A. Pletnëva, *Ot kochevii k gorodam* (Moscow, 1967). The debate about social differentiation within nomadic societies is far from settled.

[79] On the question of Hungarian semi-nomadism, see A. Bartha, *Hungarian Society in the Ninth and Tenth Centuries* (Budapest, 1975), pp. 54ff., 86ff.; Gy. Györffy, *István Király és műve*, 2d ed. (Budapest, 1983), pp. 397ff. On settlement patterns, see Gy. Györffy, "Système des résidences d'hiver et d'été chez les nomades et les chefs hongrois du Xe siècle," *AEMA* 1 (1975):45–153.

[80] Khazanov, "The Early State," pp. 270–71 and his *Nomads*, pp. 198–227.

[81] Sahlins, *Tribesmen*, pp. 35–36; T. Barfield, "The Hsiung-nu Imperial Confederation: Organization and Foreign Policy," *Journal of Asian Studies* 41, no. 1

right to trade and became quite adept at commerce. Nomadic animal husbandry, as modern scholarship suggests, can be good training for "commercial life."[82]

Although in some instances a genuine economic symbiosis between nomad and sedentary groups developed, more often than not the relationship was the result of various military, political, and economic configurations in which the stronger dominated the weaker.[83] The flip side of trade for the nomad was predation. When unable to trade or when raiding was more cost effective, the latter was preferable. Raids were aimed at several targets: newly harvested crops, people (to be ransomed or sold into slavery outside of nomadic society where few slaves were kept), gold, silver, and other valuables that could be retained or traded. Raids were also a vehicle for political, social, and economic advancement. Impoverished herdsmen and even "sedentarized" ex-nomads would recoup their losses.[84] The raids could be very destructive, frequently employing deliberate terror to make the sedentary populations more willing "partners" in the redistribution of goods.[85] The nomads raided one another as well (the *barïmta/baranta/barïntï*), driving off people and cattle.[86] For the

---

(1981):57; Barth, *Nomads of South Persia*, pp. 9 – 10; G. E. Markov, *Kochevniki Azii* (Moscow, 1976), pp. 37, 40, 42; Khazanov, *Nomads*, pp. 202 – 206, 209, 211 – 12.

[82] D. G. Bates, *Nomads and Farmers: A Study of the Yörük of Southeastern Turkey* (Ann Arbor, 1973), p. 26.

[83] Khazanov, *Nomads*, pp. 35 – 37.

[84] Pletněva, *Kochevniki*, pp. 38, 147, 189; D. Sinor, "Horse and Pasture in Inner Asian History," *Oriens Extremus* 19, no. 2 (1972):177; O. Lattimore, "Herdsmen, Farmers, Urban Culture," *Pastoral Production and Society*, ed. L'équipe ecologie et anthropologie des sociétés pastorales (Cambridge and Paris, 1979), pp. 483 – 84; R. Lindner, *Nomads and Ottomans in Medieval Anatolia* [= Indiana University, Uralic and Altaic Series, 144] (Bloomington, 1983), p. 11; T. S. Noonan, "Russia, the Near East and the Steppe in the Early Medieval Period: An Examination of the Sassanid and Byzantine Finds from the Kama-Urals Area," *AEMA* 2 (1982):275 – 81.

[85] Barfield, "Hsiung-nu," pp. 54 – 55. Villehardouin (F. T. Marzials, ed., *Memoirs of the Crusades by Villehardouin and De Joinville* [reprint, New York, 1958], p. 111) describes a Polovtsian attack of 1206: "So the Cumans seized the cattle of the land and took captive men, women and children and destroyed the cities and castles and caused such ruin and desolation that never has man heard tell of greater."

[86] E. V. Sevortian, *Ėtimologicheskii slovar' tiurkskikh iazykov* (Moscow, 1974, 1978, 1980), vol. 2, pp. 73 – 83; L. Krader, *Social Organization of the Mongol-Turkic Pastoral Nomads* [= Indiana University, Uralic and Altaic Series, 20] (The Hague, 1963), pp. 155 – 57, 355ff.

nomad, then, raiding and trading were merely two aspects of the same process, i.e., the acquisitum of needed goods or goods that could be used to obtain needed goods.

Another means of gaining additional income and access to desired goods was mercenary soldiering. Nomadic war bands frequently took service with sedentary rulers for specific military operations or as long-term "allies." In the latter instance, marital alliances were often used to strengthen these ties. Many Rus' princely houses had close family ties with the Polovtsian ruling houses. The "legalities" of the relationship could vary, but the ends were, from the nomads' stand-point, the same. Pecheneg bands, for example, had a contractual rela-tionship with the Byzantine Khersonites according to which they received, in return for services performed, "a pre-arranged remunera-tion . . . in the form of pieces of purple cloth, ribbons, loosely woven cloths, gold brocade, pepper, scarlet or 'Parthian' leather and other commodities which they require." Similar arrangements were made with the Pechenegs living near Bulgaria, whom, by contract, Byzan-tium would use against the Rus', Bulgarians, and Hungarians.[87] Pecheneg and especially Polovtsian bands were regularly involved in Rus' internecine strife as the allies of one or another princely faction. Their aim was not to undermine Rus' defenses with a view to later conquest, but simply to have the opportunity to raid and pillage. When the more astute Rus' statesmen limited or curtailed these possi-bilities, their "support" often disappeared. The annals of Rus'-Polovtsian relations are filled with many such examples.[88] Individual nomads took service with Rus' princes, often rising to responsible and sensitive posts.[89] Nomad "hirelings" were brought in not only to aid in intra-Rus' feuds, but also for specific military campaigns abroad. Thus, as early as 944, Igor' hired a band of Pechenegs for a raid on the Byzantine Empire.[90] The ill-fated Vasil'ko Rostislavich of Terebovlia, who had earlier led a Polovtsian force against Poland ca. 1097, was contemplating the conquest of that land using a band of Pechenegs,

---

[87] Constantine Porphyrogenitus, *De administrando imperio*, pp. 52–57.

[88] Kargalov, *Vneshnepoliticheskie faktory*, pp. 48–49; Rybakov, *Kievskaia Rus' i russkie kniazhestva*, p. 512.

[89] V. T. Pashuto, "Ob osobennosti struktury," pp. 105, 109.

[90] *PSRL* 1:45.

Torks, and Berendei to augment his own troops.[91] In the Rus' raid on
Sharvān, ca. 569 (late 1173–early 1174), the Rus' marauders were
joined by "Alans and Khazars" (used here anachronistically for the
Polovtisans).[92] From the time of their early encounters with the
Hsiung-nu, their "barbarian," nomadic, northern neighbors, it was
clear to the Chinese that warfare was the "business" of the nomads.
It was for them a "natural occupation."[93] Indeed, in the Middle Ages,
many entered the Islamic military as professional soldiers, *ghulāms*.[94]

Nomadic state-building, as with others, has been associated with
war and conquest.[95] Modern scholarship, however, has suggested that
the nomads, rather then being the aggressors in this process, may have
been responding to pressures on them generated by more powerful,
expansionist, sedentary neighbors.[96] Nomadic society, primarily concerned with its herds, pasturage, and access to goods, had little
inherent interest in permanent conquests of fixed territories. This was
all the more true because its own habitat, although often stable for
long periods of time, was neither permanent nor fixed. V. V. Barthold
depicted this society as essentially anarchic, one which only begrudg-
ingly relinquished some of its freedom to charismatic "empire build-

[91] *PSRL* 1:266.

[92] V. Minorsky, "Khāqānī and Andronicus Comnenus," *Bulletin of the School of
Oriental and African Studies* 11 (1943–1946):558–59.

[93] D. Sinor, "Inner Asian Warriors," *Journal of the American Oriental Society*
101, no. 2 (1981):134–35.

[94] Smith, "Turanian Nomadism," p. 65. See also fn. 49 for the recent literature on
the *ghulām* institution. The translation of *ghulām* or *mamlūk* as "slave soldier" while
technically correct, does not fully render the political and social complexities of this
institution. The *ghulām* forces (which were found in Christian Georgia as well) were
trained, professional soldiers and administrators who could acquire enormous political
power and influence. They had many of the attributes of a *comitatus* and, especially
in 'Abbāsid caliphal history, of a pretorian guard which made and unmade rulers. In
several instances, these Turkic ghulāms formed their own states, e.g., the Ghaznawid
state in Afghanistan and the Mamlūk state in Egypt.

[95] L. Krader, *Formation of the State* (Englewood Cliffs, N.J., 1968), pp. 44–45,
49–50; M. Claessen, P. Skalník eds., *The Early State* (The Hague, Paris, New York,
1978), p. 13.

[96] O. Lattimore, *The Inner Asian Frontiers of China* (New York, 1940, 1951;
reprint, Boston, 1962), pp. 62–63; Pritsak, *Origin of Rus'*, vol. 1, p. 13; Barfield,
"Hsiung-nu," pp. 46–47.

ers.''[97] Although outwardly egalitarian, differences in wealth and social standing did exist. They were masked, to some degree, by the bonds of kinship, real and fictitious. Nomads on the lower rungs of the economic ladder were willing candidates for the *comitatus* of the "empire-builders." This explosive force could be channeled outwards in the form of raids and conquests. These internal tensions and the needs of self-defense gave rise to organizations, military in nature, in which the embryo of the nomadic state, always present, could mature to full statehood. But, there was an inherent contradiction in this process. The nomadic "empire-builder," once elevated to the lofty heights of the Kaganate, was frequently at odds with his erstwhile fellow-tribesmen and now reluctant subjects, a status many of them never accepted. They resisted the social differentiation engendered or furthered by state-formation. To counteract the normally centrifugal tendencies of the tribesmen, powerful ideologies stressing the heavenly mandate, charisma, and sanctity of the kagan were created.[98] Lacking a fixed territory and viewing the historical process as essentially cyclical (like the growth and reduction in herd size), rather than evolving towards some more highly developed structure, personal ties and elaborate genealogical structures (a sophisticated development from the kinship system of primitive society) together with the prospects of a steady influx of booty from raiding or conquest, were important sources of unity in the quickly organized steppe "empires."

Pritsak has suggested that the nomadic empires created by the most successful of these charismatic warlords were, in essence, brought into being by "professional empire-builders" rooted in urban civilizations. Attracted by the lucrative profits of international trade which crossed their lands and lured by the riches of the cities created by the international merchants operating in the imperial, sedentary states ringing the southern tier of the Eurasian steppe, China, Iran, Byzantium, the nomadic "empire-builder," perhaps guided by the merchant, created a "pax" to guarantee the safe passage of this trade and to secure his

---

[97] W. Barthold, *Zwölf Vorlesungen über die Geschichte der Türken Mittelasiens* (1932–1935; reprint, Hildesheim, 1962), p. 11; F. László, "Die Tokuz-Oguz und die Kök Türken," *Bibliotheca Orientalis Hungarica* 5 (1942–1944):103–109.

[98] Golden, "Imperial Ideology," pp. 42–52.

share of it.[99] Thus, he argues, it is the merchant, cooperating with the "charismatic" clans of the steppe, who is the driving force in the creation of the nomadic empire. However one views the process, there is general agreement that some kind of outside catalyst is an essential element in pushing nomadic societies into more complex forms of political organization.

Aside from the widespread nomadic violence that tended to accompany the nomads' entry into a new territory or the creation of a conquest state, extraordinary violence on a massive scale was *not* typical of nomadic-sedentary relations in western Eurasia. Of course, there were exceptions (e.g., the tale of the Avar mistreatment of the Slavs), but, on the whole, the Rus' sources stress the peaceful nature of the initial encounters with the Pechenegs and Polovtsians. Recently, Patricia Crone has argued that the nomadic polities of western Eurasia were less conquest-prone because the Caucasus Mountains and the Danube protected sedentary society and the region's spaciousness "deflated" the pressure for conquest. Thus, the tribal "states" of the Ponto-Caspian steppes were much more loosely organized, consisting of "a layer of tribal rulers . . . spread thinly over a local population of pastoralists and hunters; military organization was usually restricted to a royal bodyguard and an army of nobles." These polities derived their "resources" from tribute and trade revenues.[100] Crone has somewhat overstated the case. The Danube and Caucasus were hardly impenetrable barriers. Both Balkan and Transcaucasian realms were raided. Moreover, the Khazar and Mongol military organizations (the only nomadic states in the western steppe zone; we exclude Volga Bulgaria from the *lisostep*) do not really correspond to the pattern she describes; those of the Pechenegs, Torks, and Polovtsians even less so. As we have seen, the latter three were not tightly organized states permanently oriented towards war and conquest. They were not states at all.

To some extent, this lack of political development may have been conditioned by the region they inhabited which was ideally suited for pastoral nomadism or semi-nomadism. Here, the nomad was in his natural element. Equally important, the catalysts necessary to propel the nomads beyond the tribal union stage of political organization,

[99] Pritsak, *Origin of Rus'*, vol. 1, pp. 15–17.
[100] Crone, *Slaves on Horseback*, p. 20.

towards statehood (i.e., weaker states to be conquered, stronger states
to defend against) were not there. Byzantium and Georgia never
directly threatened them, preferring to use surrogates (other steppe
peoples or mountaineers) to counter the danger from that direction.
Hungary, itself of nomadic origin and the frequent recipient of
nomadic refugees from the Pontic steppes, possessed no such ambitious eastern policy, having been driven from the region by the
Pechenegs. The Balkan states were even less capable of such action.
Bulgaria, for example, also of Inner Asian nomadic origin, was even
ruled in the late twelfth–fourteenth centuries by dynasties of Inner
Asian, nomadic origin (cf. the Asenids, Terterids, Shishmanids).
Muslim rule in the Caucasus was fragmented and the Khwārizmshāh
state, living in an uneasy symbiosis with the nomads, thought largely
in terms of conquests within the Islamic orbit. The most immediate
western and northwestern neighbor of the nomads, Rus', had the
potential to hurt them seriously as was demonstrated on a number of
occasions. But, Rus' never developed this potential into a consistent
policy; in part because the Rus' princes were not completely in agreement on such a policy (the lands of many were largely unaffected by
nomadic raiding). When, in the course of the twelfth century, Rus'
itself dissolved in internecine strife, the prospects for such a policy
became even more remote.

Rus' and the Nomads

With the preceding as background, we may now begin to analyze, in a
more concrete fasion, Rus'-nomadic relations to determine in what
ways these relations influenced Rus' economic growth. The *Povest'*
vremennykh let, in an introductory passage, lists the nomadic invaders
of the Slavic lands up to the tenth century: "the *Bolgare* who settled
on the Danube and were oppressors (*naselnitsi*) of the Slavs," the
Ougri Belii, the *Obri* (Avars) who inflicted cruelties on the Duleby,
the Pechenegs, and the *Ougri Chernii*. Interestingly, the Khazars,
except as a geographical referent, the equivalent of the learned *Skuf*
("Scythia"), are absent from this list.[101] They were, of course, the
neighboring superpower, resident in the region long before the establishment of the Rus' state. Khazaria, at various times, collected trib-

[101] *PSRL* 1:11–12.

ute from some of the Eastern Slavic tribes, the core of the future Rus'
state (the Polianians, Severians, Viatichians, and Radimichians) in the
form of swords, furs, and coins.[102] Slavs and Rus' had easy access to
the trade emporia of the Khazar-controlled Volga where a special judi-
ciary to adjudicate their disputes was established. Thus, it was under
Khazar auspices that the remarkable trade of the early Rus' state with
the Orient was carried out.[103]

Khazaria, by virtue of its geo-political situation, serving as
Byzantium's first line of defense against steppe disturbances, extended
this protective umbrella to Rus' as well. In al-Mas'ūdī's time (ca.
930s), the Khazars were still more or less guarding the lower Volga
and blocking Oghuz winter raids,[104] although in other respects this
ability to check the nomads was coming into question.[105] Khazar
power grew demonstrably weaker during the tenth century due to the
steady pressure of other nomads, the instabilities inherent in the semi-
nomadic state Khazaria had become and a shift in the balance of trade
in favor of Volga Bulgaria. The latter was closer to Transoxiana with
which the bulk of this eastern trade was conducted (the influx of
newly discovered Afghan silver greatly enriched Transoxiana) and
had made bold, open moves to embrace Islam, establishing direct contact with the Caliphate (cf. the mission described by Ibn Faḍlān in
921–922). Thus, although still able to control some of the Oghuz, the

[102] *PSRL* 1:17, 19, 24, 65. A. N. Nasonov in his *"Russkaia zemlia,"* p. 41 con-
cluded that the contours of the "Rus' land" took shape under the auspices of fading
Khazar power in the latter part of the ninth century and consisted of those Eastern
Slavic tribes that had been under Khazar overlordship: the Polianians, Severians,
Radimichians, and perhaps part of the Ulychians and Viatichians.

[103] T. S. Noonan, "What Does Historical Numismatics Suggest About the History of
Khazaria in the Ninth Century?," *AEMA* 3 (1983):265–70.

[104] al-Mas'ūdī, *Murūj adh-Dhahab wa Ma'ādin al-Jawhar*, ed. C. Pellat (Beirut,
1966–), vol. 1, p. 213; al-Iṣṭakhrī, *Kitāb Masālik al-Mamālik*, ed. M. J. de Goeje
(Leiden, 1927²), p. 220.

[105] al-Mas'ūdī, *Murūj*, vol. 1, p. 218. The Pechenegs had been causing trouble since
the ninth century. The *Ḥudūd al-'Ālam*, trans. V. Minorsky (London, 1937), p. 160
notes that the "Inner Bulghār are at war with all the Rūs but carry on commerce with
all those who live around them." It is unclear whether these Bulgars were the Danubian or Pontic (*Bolgare chernii*) groupings. Kurat, *Peçenek tarihi*, pp. 22–23, suggests that Khazar preoccupation with the Pechenegs allowed the Rus' state to form.
Rybakov, *Kievskaia Rus' i russkie kniazhestva*, pp. 257–58, in an overly "patriotic"
spirit, completely downplays and occasionally distorts the role of the Khazars.

Khazars were obliged to permit the Rus' to stage a series of raids on Muslim Caspian coastal holdings in the early tenth century.[106]

It was this backdrop of growing Rus'-Khazar tensions over the Volga trade and its exploitation that set the stage for the dramatic denouement of 965. In the face of growing Rus' pressure, Joseph, the Khazar ruler, wrote to the Jewish courtier in Muslim Spain, Ḥasdai b. Shaprut: "I war with them [the Rus']. If I left them (in peace) for one hour, they would destroy the entire land of the Ishmaelites up to Bagdad."[107] In a series of campaigns, Sviatoslav the Conqueror took control over the Viatichian lands (ca. 964, 966), a region which, judging from the heavy concentration of Arab dirhams found there, must have been heavily involved in the eastern trade. In 965, and perhaps again in 967, he attacked and plundered the major Khazar cities of the lower Volga and North Caucasus, including the Khazar capital.[108] The Rus' acted in concert with the Oghuz, former Khazar vassals.[109] It is still unclear whether this attack was simply an expedition for booty or for conquest, i.e., a well-thought-out plan to control the lower Volga trade routes. Sviatoslav may have hoped for the latter, but was prevented from settling in by his Oghuz allies and the Khwārizmians who claimed this area as their sphere of influence. That Sviatoslav had hoped to dominate one or another major trade artery may be conjectured from his conduct in the Balkans. In his famous speech to his mother recorded in the *Povest' vremennykh let* (s.a. 969), he clearly states his preference for Pereiaslavets' over Kiev as the "center of my

[106] For the most recent discussion of the Rus' Caspian raids, see Pritsak's reconstruction in Golb, Pritsak, *Khazarian Hebrew Documents*, pp. 139–42.

[107] P. K. Kokovtsov, *Evreisko-khazarskaia perepiska v X veke* (Leningrad, 1932), pp. 139–42.

[108] *PSRL* 1:64–65; Ibn Ḥawqal, *Kitāb Ṣūrat al-'Arḍ*, ed. J. H. Kramers (Leiden and Leipzig, 1938–1939), vol. 1, p. 15; vol. 2, pp. 392–93. On the dating see T. M. Kalinina, "Svedeniia Ibn Khaukalia o pokhodakh Rusi vremën Sviatoslava" in V. T. Pashuto, ed., *Drevneishie gosudarstva na territorii SSSR 1975* (Moscow, 1976), pp. 90–101. On the varying interpretations, see A. N. Sakharov, *Diplomatiia Sviatoslava* (Moscow, 1972), pp. 44–48, 75, 95–107, 204–205; Artamonov, *Istoriia Khazar*, pp. 427–30.

[109] Ibn Miskawaih, *Tajārub al-Umam*, ed. H. F. Amedroz (Oxford, 1920), vol. 2, p. 209; Ibn al-Athīr, *Al-Kāmil fī t-Ta'rīkh*, ed. C. J. Tornberg (Leiden, 1851–1876; reprint, with differing pagination, Beirut, 1965–1966), vol. 8, p. 565; Golden, "Migrations of the Oğuz," pp. 78–80; Pritsak, *Origin of Rus'*, vol. 1, p. 446.

land where all (trade) goods come together.''[110] The lower Volga trade routes apparently came under an Oghuz-Volga Bulgar condominium as we learn from the twelfth-century Spanish Arab traveller Abu Ḥāmid al-Gharnaṭī.[111] Clearly, Sviatoslav's activities did not bring about an end of the Volga-eastern trade.[112] It did, however, create a new situation in the region. Khazaria, for centuries a barrier to nomadic incursions, now dissolved. The Oghuz-Volga Bulgar synarchy that subsequently developed on the lower Volga was never as effective as that of the Khazars, for the latter had fostered trade and protected its arteries well beyond the Volga delta, e.g., the Pontic steppes. The latter was now dominated by the Pechenegs who, while interested in trade, as all nomads, did not have as sophisticated an appreciation of the measures needed to promote it. Moreover, as mortal enemies of the Oghuz, little cooperation could be expected. It must be emphasized, nonetheless, that trade continued.

The Khazar collapse also opened further steppe areas to Slavic colonization. Thus, Sarkel (Bela Vezha), the Khazar fortress built with Byzantine assistance in 838 as part of a larger defense system, was now settled by Slavs.[113] Such encroachments would not remain uncontested by the nomads.

The end of the Khazar era brought to a close one phase of Rus' history. The Khazars, with their strong commercial interests and as guardians of the steppe approaches to Eastern Europe (a role undertaken for self-protection), had provided an orientation and a setting for economic development. This setting emphasized trade and as such was a strong attraction to the early Rus' and other, internationally oriented, trading companies and merchant bands. Thus, the Rus' state underwent its formative years in an environment of extensive commercial relations with Byzantium and the Orient. The organization of the state which evolved, in part out of the requirements of tribute

---

[110] *PSRL* 1:67.

[111] *Abū Ḥāmid al-Granadino y su relación de viaje por tierras eurasiáticas*, ed. and trans. C. E. Dubler (Madrid, 1953), p. 5.

[112] Noonan, "Suzdalia's Eastern Trade," pp. 371–73.

[113] Golden, *Khazar Studies*, vol. 1, pp. 67–69, 76–77, 239–43; M. I. Artamonov, "Sarkel-Belaia Vezha," *Materialy i issledovaniia po arkheologii SSSR* 62, no. 1 (1958):82–83; V. D. Beletskii, "Zhilishche Sarkela-Beloi Vezhy," *Materialy i issledovaniia po arkheologii SSSR* 75, no. 2 (1959):132–34.

collection (*poliud'e*) that was used to provide the wherewithal for participation in this trade, was, obviously, not uninfluenced by these factors. The presence of a Rus' kagan, whose popular and official memory was still alive and employed for ideological purposes in the age of Iaroslav the Wise (reigned 1018 – 1054)[114] and beyond, testifies to the importance of this commercial, political, and cultural orientation. Clearly, the princes and great merchants enriched themselves from this trade. Ibn Faḍlān's description of the Rus' women bedecked in jewelry, gold, and silver worth thousands of dirhams[115] probably referred only to the women of the well-to-do. Nonetheless, the growth of the Rus' economy was undoubtedly spurred on by production for this vast foreign market.

The Pecheneg movement, ca. 900, into the Pontic region (largely due to Oghuz pressure) was not a war of conquest directed against Rus', but rather a migration of defeated nomads seeking a new territory. In the process, they drove out a group of weaker nomads, the Hungarians.[116] Sedentary society felt little immediate effect.

The first Pecheneg-Rus' encounter, in 915, was largely for the purpose of arranging a peace so that the Pechenegs, now Byzantine "allies," could attack Bulgaria.[117] With a declining Khazaria, Constantinople had come to rely increasingly on the Pechenegs as their agents in the steppe. Constantine Porphyrogenitus, in the *De administrando imperio* (ca. 950), a foreign policy handbook for his sons, emphasizes that the Rus' can be prevented from waging war away from their home territories by the threat of a Pecheneg attack. Similar pressure could be exerted on the Bulgarians and Hungarians.[118] The first Rus'-Pecheneg military encounter took place in 920 and as the

---

[114] Cf. references in the *Slovo o zakone i blagodati* of the Metropolitan Ilarion, *Des Metropoliten Ilarion Lobrede auf Vladimir den Heiligen und Glaubensbekenntnis*, ed. L. Müller (Wiesbaden, 1962), pp. 37, 100, 103, 129, 143; cf. also the graffiti of the Cathedral of St. Sophia in Kiev, S. A. Vysotskii, "Drevnerusskie graffiti Sofii Kievskoi," *Numizmatika i Épigrafika* 3 (1962):157 – 58: *"Spasi, Gospodi, kagana nashego."* References are also found in the *Slovo o polku Igoreve*, ed. D. S. Likhachëv (Moscow, 1982), p. 143.

[115] Ibn Faḍlān, ed. ad-Dahhār, p. 150.

[116] L. M. Rutkivs'ka, "Stepovi kochivnyky ta Kyïvs'ka Rus' IX–X st.," *Ukraïns'kyi istorychnyi zhurnal*, 1965, no. 2, p. 90.

[117] *PSRL* 1:42; Kurat, *Peçenek tarihi*, p. 86.

[118] Constantine Porphyrogenitus, *De administrando imperio*, pp. 50 – 53.

Rus' annals laconically note, "Igor' made war on the Pechenegs."[119]
It would appear that it was Rus' that initiated the hostilities, perhaps
in response to Pecheneg raiding, probing of the border defenses, or
simply out of a desire to take booty from the nomads. When next
mentioned, twenty-four years later, the Pechenegs were "hired" by
Igor' (who nonetheless took hostages from them to ensure their good
conduct) for his 944 campaign against Byzantium.[120] As we have
noted, such mercenary soldiering was a normal part of the nomadic
economy. Subsequently, they would be brought in as "allies" (in
essence as mercenaries) in Rus' internecine strife.

The first Pecheneg attack on Rus' came only in 968, more than half
a century after their appearance in the Rus' annals. In this instance,
they were, most probably, brought in by Byzantium to divert Sviatoslav from the Balkans where he was menacing imperial holdings.
This episode, in which the Pechenegs besieged Kiev, is also instructive with regard to Rus'-Pecheneg social relations. In the course of
the siege, a Rus' youth was able to sneak through the Pecheneg lines
because of his fluency in their tongue.[121] Such language proficiency
bespeaks close commercial and cultural ties. The account itself has
epic or folkloric elements as well as a political message, the main
focus of which was to castigate Sviatoslav for neglecting Kiev while
demonstrating the heroism of the voevoda Pretich and the chivalry of
the Pecheneg "prince." This episode and the hostilities of 971 and
972, which ended with the death of Sviatoslav in a Pecheneg
ambush,[122] were part of the Pecheneg-Byzantine "entente" (with
appropriate payments) according to which the Pechenegs safeguarded
imperial interests in the steppe and its adjoining regions. There was
no attempt to conquer Rus', merely to force it to abandon its Balkan
policy and punish Sviatoslav.

Thereafter, a much more intense period of Pecheneg-Rus' interaction begins. In the ensuing struggle for the Kievan throne, one of the
contenders, Iaropolk, is advised to "flee to the Pechenegs and bring

[119] *PSRL* 1:43.
[120] *PSRL* 1:45.
[121] *PSRL* 1:65–66.
[122] *PSRL* 1:72, 73.

back an army,"[123] a theme that would be often repeated and one that is not presented here as a novel concept. Volodimer the Great (978–1015), who ultimately succeeded to the throne, sought to reunify the realm and establish the central authority of Kiev. His own servile origins (his mother was a concubine of Sviatoslav and he was derogatorily referred to as *robichich'*, "son of a slave") may have lent a special urgency to this policy. Some overarching focus of unity had to be found. In his choices Volodimer succeeded brilliantly. He chose religion (culminating in the Christianization of Rus' one decade after his coming to power) which brought him a Byzantine princess to shore up his legitimacy, and the "threat" of a foreign foe—the Pechenegs. Although "patriotic" modern historians speak of waves of Pecheneg attacks in the 980s as the *casus belli* for Volodimer's military response, the Rus' annals take note only s.a. 988 of this, the first clash with the Pechenegs since the death of Sviatoslav. The Rus'-Pecheneg "war" is discussed there in connection with Volodimer's program of massive military and urban construction to wall in the Kievan land's southern approach. Volodimer, closing a "window of vulnerability," brought in population from the north (Slovenians, Krivichians, Chuds, and Viatichians) to settle the newly founded towns and garrisons. Indeed, it may have been this dramatic buildup and extension of Rus' military might in the borderlands that provoked the conflict with the Pechenegs.[124] At the same time, Volodimer was allied with the Oghuz (as the joint Rus'-Oghuz attack on Volga Bulgaria in 985 indicates),[125] the mortal foes of the Pechenegs. The Rus' accounts of the "war" are fragmentary and have a strong epic or folkloric quality (e.g., the David and Goliath-like confrontation between a

---

[123] *PSRL* 1:78.

[124] *PSRL* 1:121; see Shekera, *Kyïvs'ka Rus'*, p. 48 on Volodimer's defense system. Shekera also makes the rather extravagant claim that Rus', absorbing these "shocks," was sparing Europe and finally that the war may have been connected with the Christianization of Rus' as the Pechenegs were converting to Islam (Shekera, ibid., 49). This is far-fetched indeed. Pecheneg Islamization, in any sizable numbers, occurred only in the early eleventh century. Moreover, Christianity, Manichaeism and other religions were known among them; see Pritsak, "The Pečenegs," p. 230; Kurat, *Peçenek tarihi*, pp. 52, 97–99.

[125] *PSRL* 1:84. This campaign, according to Shekera (*Mizhnarodni zv'iazky Kyïvs'koï Rusi* [Kiev, 1963], p. 109), was to prevent the Bulgar takeover of the Volga trade route.

Rus' youth and the Pecheneg champion, the hoodwinking of the Pechenegs by the besieged inhabitants of Belgorod).[126] The pace of warfare slackened after 997[127] and peace negotiations were conducted in 1006–1007 by the Christian missionary Bruno of Querfurth on behalf of Rus'.[128]

At the time of his death, Volodimer had sent his son Boris to fend off Pecheneg raiders who proved to be very elusive. Indeed, the whole episode may well have been part of the larger internal struggle between Volodimer and his sons that was beginning to surface. In the contest for the throne that followed, Sviatopolk the Damned (1015–1019) had Pecheneg allies, but was decisively defeated by Iaroslav on the Al'ta in 1019.[129]

The Pechenegs, probably due to Oghuz and Rus' pressures, now largely busied themselves with affairs in the Byzantine Balkan borderlands.[130] It was only after the death of Mstislav Volodimerovich, Iaroslav's co-ruler (in the East), and while Iaroslav, who had devoted many resources to strengthening the steppe fortification line and expansion in that region, was in Novgorod, that the Pechenegs again attempted to move on Kiev. They were disastrously defeated at the site on which the Cathedral of St. Sophia, raised in commemoration of this victory, now stands.[131] Driven from the steppe zone south of Kiev and increasingly drawn into Byzantine Balkan affairs, the Pechenegs were destroyed there in 1091 by the Byzantines and their Polovtsian allies.[132]

---

[126] *PSRL* 1:122–24, 127–29.

[127] In the year 1000, Volodar led a force of Pechenegs against Kiev (*PSRL* 9:68), but this was rather an example of Rus' factional strife.

[128] Shekera, *Kyïvs'ka Rus'*, pp. 79–80.

[129] *PSRL* 1:130, 141–42, 144; Shekera, *Kyïvs'ka Rus'*, pp. 90–93, 99–108.

[130] The Rus', presumably under Mstislav, were also active in the Caucasus during this period. In 1029, a campaign was conducted against the As (*PSRL* 9:79). In 1030 and 1031, according to the *Ta'rīkh al-Bāb*, see V. F. Minorsky, *Studies in Caucasian History* [London, 1953] [Arabic text, pp. 11, 12; Eng. trans. p. 17]), there were Rus' expeditions against Sharvān.

[131] *PSRL* 1:150–51.

[132] See V. G. Vasil'evskii, *Vizantiia i Pechenegi*, vol. 1 of his *Trudy* (St. Petersburg, 1908) on the fate of the Pechenegs in this region.

Pecheneg-Rus' economic relations focused on mutually beneficial trade. The Pechenegs traded their horses, cattle, and sheep, as Constantine Porphyrogenitus tells us, directly to the Rus'. He cites this as one of the reasons that the Rus' sought peaceful relations with the Pechenegs since "none of the aforesaid animals is found in Russia."[133] Although one may question the complete accuracy of this statement, there can be no doubt that the Pechenegs traded surplus livestock for agricultural products and manufactures. Al-Mas'ūdī reports that merchants from Khazaria, Bāb al-Abwāb Darband, Alania, and elsewhere came to their country.[134] Gardīzī, however, notes that the trade routes through Pechenegia are "desolate and disagreeable," through "wooded lands" in which the merchant can "go astray."[135]

Despite (or perhaps because of) the difficulties of these routes, the Pechenegs were keenly interested in trade. The southerly routes connecting them with the Crimea were very important and they greatly profited from their relationship with the Greeks of Kherson.[136] Judging from the account of the Rus' water-borne caravans that set out from Kiev down the Dnieper, in their *monoxyla*, to Constantinople, it seems quite probable that the Pechenegs were capable of and had ample opportunity to close off or seriously hinder trade on this route.[137] The question is, however, did they want to and did they actually do so regularly? Certainly, robbing the trade caravans (which involved a certain element of risk) might have been more profitable in the short run, but inevitably it would have drawn a strong military response or a shift in the route. As trade was essential to their economy, it seems unlikely that they were anxious to disrupt this trade for long periods of time. The fact that they could do so does not necessarily mean that they did so. Actually, when one surveys the 121-year recorded history (915–1036) of Rus'-Pecheneg relations, there are relatively few periods of real warfare which would have endangered that route. The warfare that took place was associated largely with the bellicose Sviatoslav whose activities may well have been detrimental

---

[133] Constantine Porphyrogenitus, *De administrando imperio*, pp. 48–51.

[134] al-Mas'ūdī, *Murūj*, vol. 1, p. 237.

[135] Martinez, "Gardīzī's Two Chapters," p. 152.

[136] Constantine Porphyrogenitus, *De administrando imperio*, pp. 52–53. For the routes, see Tryjarski, "Pieczyngowie," p. 542.

[137] Constantine Porphyrogenitus, *De administrando imperio*, chap. 9.

to Pecheneg trading interests (as well as Byzantine policy) and with the "activist" Volodimer the Great who used the Pechenegs as a focus for his unification policy and initiated an aggressive policy of fortification construction on the borders and beyond.

Pecheneg remnants, which could still prove to be annoying raiders, now dispersed in Danubian Europe. In Hungary, as later in Rus', they were transformed into borderguard units.[138] The Pecheneg Ukrainian habitat was now occupied by the Oghuz who were themselves propelled westward by Polovtsian pressure. We cannot pinpoint the exact time of arrival of the Oghuz (the *Torki* of Rus' sources) in the Pontic steppes, but it must have taken place ca. 1036–1050. One-time Rus' allies, the Torks entered into hostilities with Rus' in 1054, the same year in which the Polovtsians made their first appearance in the Rus' chronicles. The two events are hardly coincidental. Vsevolod of Pereiaslav, the most exposed of the Rus' principalities, defeated them in a winter campaign at Voiin'. The Polovtsians then appeared and Vsevolod made peace with them and "they returned whence they came."[139] In 1060, in what Hrushevs'kyi mistakenly termed the "first aggression" of Rus' against a steppe people,[140] the joint Rus' forces delivered a smashing blow to the hapless Torks. They fled in panic to the relative safety of the Byzantine Balkan borderzone with many perishing from cold, hunger, and disease.[141] In 1064, they were defeated by Byzantium and in 1068 again routed in Hungary. Some remained here and entered Byzantine service. Others returned to the central Pontic steppes where they took service with Rus', continuing a tradition of soldiering that many Oghuz had followed in Central Asia. These Torks, together with Pecheneg fragments and other lesser groupings, such as the Berendei, became the borderguard units for the Kievan princes, especially in the Ros' river region where their town, Torchesk, developed and in other strategic positions guarding the southern frontiers. By the 1140s, they were officially termed the *Chernii Kloboutsi* "Black Cowls," a calque from a Turkic term (*Qara*

---

[138] P. Diaconu, *Les Petchénègues au Bas-Danube* (Bucharest, 1970), p. 134. On the Pecheneg borderguard units in Hungary, see H. Göckenjan, *Hilfsvölker und Grenzwächter in mittelalterlichen Ungarn* (Wiesbaden, 1972).

[139] *PSRL* 1:162; *PSRL* 2:151.

[140] Hrushevs'kyi, *Istoriia*, vol. 2, p. 55.

[141] *PSRL* 1:163; *PSRL* 2:152.

Qalpaq? Qara Papax?)[142] which may have denoted "vassal border-guard."

The defeat and flight of the Torks removed the buffer zone between the Rus' and the Polovtsians. The effect was quickly felt. In 1061, a Polovtsian war band under "Sokal"[143] staged a winter raid and defeated Vsevolod who was attempting to end their depredations.[144] Limitations of space will not permit a detailed analysis here of Polovtsian-Rus' military-political history. Nonetheless, the broad contours of these relations can be outlined. First, we must note that the Polovtsians were not engaged in a war to conquer Rus'. The territories they occupied were well suited to pastoral nomadism. They had points of contact with sedentary states. Khwārizm (east), Georgia (south), Rus' (north), Hungary (west), Byzantium and the Balkan states (southeast). As required by the exigencies of the nomadic economy, they traded and raided with all of them. The raiding, undoubtedly troublesome and occasionally very destructive, appears to have resulted in population displacements in the most exposed borderzones of Rus'. However, the thesis that Polovtsian raiding caused a large-scale Slavic exodus to the northeast and southwest has often been stated but never actually documented.

Similarly, the claim that Polovtsian predations severely interrupted economic life has not been substantiated. Agriculture in the borderzone was, of course, affected. Harvests were stolen. But this did not affect agriculture elsewhere which appears to have flourished. Moreover, the population of the frontier principality of Pereiaslav, the most vulnerable to Polovtsian raids, seems to have suffered as much from the impositions of its own *posadnyky* and other officials as from the Polovtsians.[145] The claim is often voiced that Polovtsian raiding destroyed or severely curtailed the Rus' eastern trade and in particular

---

[142] Rashīd al-Dīn, *Jāmi' at-Tavārīkh*, vol. 2, pt. 1, ed. A. A. Alizade (Moscow and Baku, 1957, 1965, 1980), pp. 162–63 notes the *qaum-i siyāh kulāhān* "the tribe of the Black Hats." See also Rasovskii, "O roli Chërnykh Klobukov," pp. 93–109; idem, "Pechenegi, torki i berendei," pp. 1–66; and S. A. Pletnëva, *Drevnosti Chërnykh Klobukov*, [= Arkheologia SSSR, svod arkheologicheskikh materialov, vyp. E1–19] (Moscow, 1973).

[143] In Turkish, *Saqal* means "beard." See Sir G. Clauson, *An Etymological Dictionary of the Pre-Thirteenth Century Turkish* (Oxford, 1972), pp. 808–809.

[144] *PSRL* 1:163; *PSRL* 2:152.

[145] *PSRL* 2:215; Nasonov, *"Russkaia zemlia,"* pp. 67–68.

that of Kiev, leading to the decline of the latter.[146] The Rus' chronicles, actually, record very few incidents of such disruptions. One of the few such notices, that of the 1168 gathering of the princes to keep open the "Grech'skii put'" and the Solianyi and Zaloznyi routes,[147] is treated as the exception, not the rule. Even more revealing is the notice, s.a. 1185 of the Rus' victory over the Polovtsian khan Könchäk (Turk. "trousers"; Rus', *Konchak*)[148] in which the latter planned to bring in a Khwārizmian military specialist in "Greek fire" and siege equipment in an operation to capture and burn Rus' cities. This was a truly exceptional episode of warfare. The Rus', however, were forewarned by merchants returning from the Polovtsian camps![149] In short, trade continued even during the worst of hostilities. The eastern trade, especially the Volga trade, was not disrupted. The Polovtsians were the ultimate overlords of this trade in which Oghuz and Bulgar agents were more directly involved (especially in Saqsin) and the all-important port of Sughdaq in the Crimea. The latter was an important conduit for Rus' goods (grain, furs, flax, slaves) to Trabzon and beyond. The Polovtsians functioned here as middlemen and took a tax for their "services" and "protection." There was an extensive trade between the Polovtsian land and Rus', which the nomads were anxious to foster and promote.[150] Merchants from Transcaucasia had no difficulty in reaching Rus' and the Polovtsian land. The Georgians, it would appear, even maintained or could put together a special system of relay posts (not unlike the later Mongol *jam*) to assure rapid travel to this region, as is illustrated in the journey of the Tbilisi merchant Zankan Zorababeli, ca. 1185, to the city of the Polovtsian khan Sevinch, to bring back to Georgia Iurii, son of Andrei Bogoliubskii, as bridegroom to T'amar, Queen of Georgia.[151] Finally, we may note that Khwārizm, the leading mercantile power of Muslim Central Asia with

---

[146] Kargalov, *Vneshnepoliticheskie faktory*, p. 58; Shekera, *Kyïvs'ka Rus'*, p. 39.

[147] *PSRL* 2:538.

[148] K. Grønbech, *Komanisches Wörterbuch* (Copenhagen, 1942), p. 151.

[149] *PSRL* 2:634–35.

[150] Grekov, Iakubovskii, *Zolotaia orda i eë padenie*, pp. 23–25, 27, 29, 31.

[151] *K'art'lis C'xovreba*, vol. 2, ed. S. Qaukhch'ishvili (Tbilisi, 1959), pp. 36–37. On Transcaucasian Muslim merchants, see al-Idrīsī, *Kitāb Nuzhat al-Mushtāq fī Ikhtirāq al-Afāq: Opus Geographicum*, ed. A. Bombaci et al. (Leiden, Naples, Rome, 1970–1978), fasc. viii, p. 917: "Muslim merchants from Arminiyya reach Kūyāba (Kiev)."

an extensive caravan trade through nomad territory and close ties to the Volga commerce was surrounded by Eastern Polovtsian (Qïpchaq-Qanglï) tribes. As in Rus', the Eastern Polovtsians (often the same groups active in eastern Rus') were deeply enmeshed in Khwārizmian affairs. There is no evidence that this trade suffered any systematic or serious disruptions from the nomads. The same may be said of Rus'. Whatever decline took place in Kiev was due to shifts in trade patterns following the First Crusade. Kiev's role as a middle-man between East and West was consequently reduced. A Soviet scholar (P. P. Tolochko) has recently made the following points: trade was important to Kiev and it remained a major center of international trade and certainly one of the principal commercial centers of Rus', according to written and archaeological data, until the early thirteenth century. The basic trade routes continued to function. Moreover, the real economic strength of the now badly fragmented Rus' state was agriculture,[152] which was affected only in frontier areas (the majority of Polovtsian attacks were directed against Pereiaslav and the Ros' region).[153] Tolochko, basing himself on archaeological materials, further notes that during the period of feudal fragmentation, the twelfth–thirteenth centuries, there was a growth of productive forces rather than a loss of communications between the increasingly auto-nomous principalities as local trade strengthened and united various regions. "Despite the continual pressure of the Polovtsians on the southern Rus' border, all the basic trade routes along which the trade of Rus' was carried out in the twelfth–thirteenth centuries continued to function."[154]

The Rus' and Polovtsians established a kind of symbiosis. To some extent this was based on mutual weakness. The nomads, as we have noted, were in what was for them ideal territory. There was abundant pasturage, easy access to the goods of sedentary society and the opportunity to supplement their income by mercenary soldiering. There was little impetus for them to change the status quo. A period

[152] Tolochko, *Kiev i kievskaia zemlia*, pp. 39–40, 58, 60.

[153] Kargalov, *Vneshnepoliticheskie faktory*, p. 57 cites the data but fails to draw the proper conclusions. Of the forty-six major campaigns of the Polovtsians, nineteen were directed against Pereiaslav and twelve against the Ros' region, see P. Golubovskii, *Pechenegi, torki i polovtsy do nashestvii tatar* (Kiev, 1884), p. 83.

[154] Tolochko, *Kiev i kievskaia zemlia*, pp. 197–98.

of testing, typical of the nomadic *Landnahme*, took place ca. 1061–1120. The nomads, who were not well organized, probed the Rus' defenses. This was a Rus', however, that was undergoing change. It was a Rus' in which central power was weakening. Rus', despite its internal troubles, was able, eventually, to rally under Volodimer Monomakh (d. 1125), who inflicted a number of resounding defeats on the nomads in a nasty war that even witnessed the murder, by Monomakh, of Polovtsian ambassadors. One major, Eastern Polovtsian horde took refuge in Georgia whither it was invited in 1118 by Davit' Aghmashenebeli, the son-in-law of its khan Äträk.[155] Once again, the nomads had served as a convenient focal point for a policy of unification. Rus', however, was unable to follow up on this victory as the centrifugal forces at work within its own body politic resurfaced with renewed vigor. After the death of Mstislav (1132), Monomakh's capable son, Rus' ceased to be anything but a nominally unitary country. Faced with an ''opponent'' which had the military strength to inflict serious damage on them, but which had become almost as loosely organized as themselves, the nomads, who normally needed a strong outside catalyst to move them along the road to tighter organization and statehood (in which instance they might have seriously threatened Rus'), felt no such pressure. The result was a stasis punctuated by relatively brief flare-ups between different factions of the Rus' and Polovtsians. Each raided the other, the Polovtsians often being invited in by their Rus' kinsmen or ''allies'' to fight other kinsmen. The Rus' chronicles, in discussing those occasions when more or less united Rus' forces raided deep into Polovtsian lands, speak glowingly of the numbers of slaves, horses, cattle, and sheep captured and of the Rus' hostages freed.[156] It may well be that Rus' expeditions provided enough of a jolt to keep the Polovtsians off-balance. Indeed, whatever successes the nomads enjoyed were largely the result of Rus' internal divisions, as Tatishchev long ago observed.[157] As was noted earlier, it was only in the late twelfth–early thirteenth century, under the Sharuqanid Könchäk (whose hatred for Rus' was another

---

[155] Golden, ''Cumanica I: The Qipčaqs in Georgia,'' *AEMA* 4 (1984): 45–87.

[156] V. G. Liaskoronskii, *Russkie pokhody v stepi v udel'no-vechevoe vremia* (St. Petersburg, 1907), pp. 94–95.

[157] V. N. Tatishchev, *Istoriia rossiiskaia*, vol. 1 (Moscow and Leningrad, 1962–1968), pp. 271–74.

epic theme in the chronicles and has survived in folklore; he was the son of Äträk.) and his son Iurgi (a name indicating that he had been baptized at some point, perhaps in Georgia), that an attempt was made to unite the Polovtsian tribes. It never reached fruition, proved insufficient to stop the real threat of the Mongols and died with Iurgi Konchakovich at Kalka.

The Rus', whether by design or instinct, began to integrate the Polovtsian political elite into their own ranks through a series of inter-marriages and "alliances." The latter were, in reality, a modified form of mercenary soldiering cemented by marital ties. Equally close politico-marital ties were established with Georgia, the Khwārizmshāh state and later Hungary,[158] indicating that the Polovtsians were not passive players in this sophisticated diplomatic game. Unlike their predecessors, the Pechenegs, and Torks, the Polovtsians secured for themselves an important niche in the political structure of the sur-rounding sedentary states. This was certainly a factor in their survival; for unlike their predecessors (the Khazars, Pechenegs, and Turks), they did not succumb to the military power of the Rus'. In the period from ca. 900–1240, it was the nomad, not the sedentary, who was the military and political loser. Defeated repeatedly and limited in terms of economic growth (without abandoning nomadism), the nomad, as occasional predator, could be an annoyance but was hardly a scourge. Whatever inadequacies or problems developed in the Rus' economy, they were primarily the result of internal Rus' forces (e.g., the ongoing intra-princely strife) and the operation of larger, interna-tional, economic forces.

---

[158] On martial ties, see N. A. Baskakov, "Polovetskie otbleski v 'Slove o polku Igoreve'," *Ural-Altaische Jahrbücher* 48 (1976):17–18; Rybakov, *"Slovo o polku Igoreve" i ego sovremenniki*, pp. 121–23; Pritsak, "Polovcians and Rus'," p. 378. On Khwārizmian-Qıpchaq ties, see I. Kafesoğlu, *Harezmşahlar devleti tarihi* (Ankara, 1956), pp. 37–42; al-Jūzjānī, *Ṭabaqāt-i Nāṣirī*, ed. 'Abd al-Ḥayy Ḥabībī (Kabul, 1342–1343; 1963–1964), vol. 1, pp. 300, 313; Ibn Khaldūn, *Ta'rīkh Ibn Khaldūn al musammā bi-Kitāb al-'Ibar wa Dīwān al-Mubtadā* (Beirut, 1971), vol. 5, p. 235.

CHAPTER FOUR

The Flourishing of Kiev's International and Domestic Trade, ca. 1100 – ca. 1240

Thomas S. Noonan

Introduction

Kiev's role in the commerce of the pre-Mongol era merits study for several important reasons. First, Kiev was the "mother of Rus' cities,"[1] the first capital of a historical East Slavic state and the foremost center of the Rus' principalities until the Mongol conquest of 1240. In fact, the city was so prominent in early Rus' history that its name is often taken to describe the entire period from ca. 850 to 1240, i.e., Kievan or Kievskaia Rus'. While Kiev's importance at this time is unquestioned, there is no general agreement on why and how it became the capital of the earliest Rus' state or to what extent Kiev still maintained its preeminence on the eve of the Mongol conquest. However, many scholars have maintained that Kiev's significance during the pre-Mongol era was closely connected with its role in the foreign and domestic commerce of Rus'. The rise of Kiev, for example, is believed to have been greatly facilitated by its key location along the famous Varangian-Greek route to Constantinople. As the famous Russian historian Vasilii Kliuchevskii argued so persuasively, Kiev became the center of the early Rus' state because it could control

---

[1] *Povest' vremennykh let*, vol. 1, ed. V. P. Adrianova-Peretts (Moscow and Leningrad, 1950), p. 20, (s.a. 882); *The Russian Primary Chronicle, Laurentian Text*, trans. and ed. Samuel H. Cross and Olgerd P. Sherbowitz-Wetzor (Cambridge, Mass., 1953), p. 61, (s.a. 882).

the lucrative Rus' trade with Byzantium.[2] Similarly, Kiev's supposed decline prior to the Mongol conquest has often been attributed to the disruption of its trade with the south in the twelfth and early thirteenth centuries. As Nicholas Riasanovsky has noted, in summarizing the reasons advanced to explain Kiev's alleged decline, some historians have argued that Kiev perished primarily because its trade with Byzantium and the Orient was adversely affected by a series of events which took place starting in the eleventh century.[3] In short, there exists a fairly widespread belief that Kiev's premier position in Rus' was due, in large part, to its active commerce with the south and that the decline of this trade was one of the major reasons for the city's loss of power and prestige in the century or so before the Mongol conquest. The traditional view, at least in pre-revolutionary Russia and the West, has thus been that Kiev's place as the political, economic, social, religious, and cultural center of Rus' between ca. 850 and 1240 was very closely connected with its commerce and especially its trade with Byzantium and the Black Sea.[4]

As the above comments suggest, Kiev's commerce was significant not only for Kiev itself but also for all of Rus'. Kiev was clearly the greatest commercial center in Rus' during the pre-Mongol era, rivaled only by the growth of Novgorod and its Baltic trade. Consequently, in order to understand the economic history of Kievan Rus' and the place of commerce in this history, it is necessary to examine in depth both the international and domestic trade of Kiev. And, without becoming doctrinaire Marxists, we can acknowledge that the Rus' economy in general and its commerce in particular played a major role in the overall history of Rus' during the pre-Mongol era. Any serious study of Kievan Rus' must thus take into account the lively commerce of its capital city.

Finally, there is no doubt that Kiev was one of the major commercial centers of medieval western Eurasia between ca. 900 and 1240. One cannot properly appreciate the economic relationships within this

[2] V. O. Kluchevsky, *A History of Russia*, vol. 1 (reprint, New York, 1960), pp. 69–73.

[3] Nicholas V. Riasanovsky, *A History of Russia*, 4th ed. (New York and Oxford, 1984), p. 41.

[4] Soviet historians, while recognizing the importance of Kiev's foreign trade, tend to link the city's history in the pre-Mongol era more with internal developments.

larger region unless Kiev's role in the foreign and domestic trade of
Rus' is taken into account. In short, an examination of the commerce
of Central and Eastern Europe, Byzantium, the Baltic, the Caucasus,
the Near East, and Central Asia during the period 900–1240 requires
that consideration be given to the role of Kiev in the trade of this time.

Despite the unquestioned importance of Kiev's commerce for the
history of Kiev, of Rus', and of western Eurasia, we lack a
comprehensive, up-to-date study of this commerce during the pre-
Mongol era. There are many general works about Kiev, the Rus'
economy, and pre-Mongol Rus' which touch upon this topic. There
are also studies of various trade goods as well as the trade of specific
areas which discuss Kiev's commerce, if only briefly. But, there is no
recent, detailed study devoted to Kiev's commerce in the pre-Mongol
era which attempts to integrate all the available data and which re-
examines some of the older hypotheses regarding this commerce.
Existing studies of Kiev's commerce also suffer from several problems. Many are simply out-of-date and do not reflect the vast amount
of new data which has become available over the past two decades or
so. Even M. K. Karger's monumental two-volume work on early
Kiev,[5] which only appeared a quarter-century ago, is already being
supplanted by the studies of a new generation of specialists on pre-
Mongol Kiev.[6]

In addition, historians tend to focus upon written sources and thus
do not always fully utilize the vast archaeological and numismatic
data. Numismatists do not always put the evidence of coin hoards and
finds into a historical context. And, archaeologists all too often adopt
a highly selective and superficial approach to the written sources.
Obviously, we cannot expect a single scholar to be a specialist on all
aspects of all the various sources. But, we can ask that a study of
Kiev's commerce in the pre-Mongol era should try to incorporate in a
critical fashion as much of the extant evidence as possible. The different types of evidence (e.g., written sources, archaeology, numismatics, etc.) are not isolated, water-tight compartments; rather, they all

---

[5] M. K. Karger, *Drevnii Kiev. Ocherki po istorii material'noi kul'tury drevnerusskogo goroda*, 2 vols. (Moscow and Leningrad, 1958–1961).

[6] See, for example, *Novoe v arkheologii Kieva* (Kiev, 1981); S. R. Kilievych
(Kilievich), *Detinets Kieva IX–pervoi poloviny XIII vekov. Po materialam arkheologicheskikh issledovanii* (Kiev, 1982); and P. P. Tolochko, *Drevnii Kiev* (Kiev, 1983).

reflect, if only imperfectly, a single historical reality. Consequently, we must try to integrate the insights from all the various disciplines into a more perfect vision of the past.

Many works dealing with Kiev's commerce attempt to create a composite, static picture based on evidence from a rather lengthy time span. While such a composite picture has some value, it tends to ignore or distort the many changes which Kiev's trade experienced over the course of four centuries. In fact, we can say that one of the most important tasks in the study of Kiev's trade is to determine when, why, and how changes took place and to describe the evolution of this commerce. The way in which Kievan commerce changed thus needs far more attention than it has received in the past.

In sum, we do not now possess a comprehensive analysis of Kiev's commerce in the pre-Mongol era which integrates all of the available evidence into a dynamic model that illuminates how and why this trade evolved over four centuries. This essay does *not* pretend in any way to constitute such a comprehensive study. I make no claims to having examined, much less understood, all the evidence concerning Kievan trade nor do I wish to convey the impression that I have systematically examined all the possible ways to evaluate this trade. This essay does attempt to suggest some of the approaches and contours which such a work might find useful. At a minimum, this essay seeks to stimulate discussion and even controversy about how we can better conceptualize, analyze, and periodize Kiev's pre-Mongol trade.

Originally, it was my intention to cover the entire pre-Mongol era in this essay. However, it soon became clear that it would be impossible to explore all of the important aspects of Kiev's trade between ca. 850 and 1240 in the space allotted for this essay. Consequently, I have focused upon the twelfth and first part of the thirteenth century because it is precisely for this time that the traditional picture of Kiev's trade needs the greatest revision. It is my hope to expand upon this highly abbreviated account of Kiev's pre-twelfth-century commerce in another study.

Kiev's Trade Before Ca. 1100: An Overview

The history of Kiev's trade in the pre-Mongol era is normally divided, either explicitly or implicitly, into two major periods. The first period, encompassing the ninth and tenth centuries, is often seen as a time of expansion and growth when Kiev established an active foreign trade with the Islamic world and especially Byzantium. While not always so labeled, this period is usually seen as the time when Kiev's trade flourished and seemingly reached its zenith. The second period is commonly dated to the twelfth and first-half of the thirteenth century. Due to such factors as constant Polovtsian attacks against the southern Rus' lands, the growing political and economic weakness of Byzantium, Italy's expanding Near Eastern trade, the alleged demise of Rus' trade with the Orient, and the transformation of several other Rus' principalities into major political and economic rivals of Kiev, this period is considered a time of decline in Kiev's trade, a decline which was paralleled by Kiev's loss of political power following the death of Grand Prince Volodimer Monomakh in 1125. The eleventh century does not fall clearly into either period and thus becomes, by default, a transitional time whose earlier years are grouped with the first period while its later years are attached to the second period. Thus, the traditional picture of Kiev's trade usually depicts a time of growth in the ninth, tenth, and early eleventh centuries followed by a period of decline and stagnation which began in the late eleventh century and lasted up to the time of the Mongol conquest of Kiev in 1240.

This essay will attempt to demonstrate that the traditional conceptualization of Kiev's trade needs drastic revision. A careful analysis of the written, numismatic, and archaeological sources suggests that Kiev's international and domestic commerce followed a vey different evolutionary pattern in the pre-Mongol era. This commerce can best be divided into three periods. The first period dates to the tenth and early eleventh centuries. There is no conclusive evidence to show that Kiev's trade with either Byzantium or the Islamic world was anything more than sporadic in the ninth century. Kievan commerce really began in the early tenth century and its focus was Byzantium. There was some trade between Kiev and the Orient during the tenth and early eleventh centuries but the extent of this commerce has probably been greatly exaggerated. The central and northwestern regions of Rus' were far more involved than Kiev in the Islamic trade. Kiev's trade with Byzantium during the tenth century was based almost entirely on the primitive exploitation of the tributary population of the Dnieper basin by the self-appointed Rus' princes of Kiev and their henchmen in other towns. This trade can be compared with that of modern-day mafiosi who extort money, using force or the threat of force, from small shopkeepers and then invest their ill-gotten gains in

what is called legitimate business. The Rus' princes and their retinues, systematically stole the furs, wax, and even bodies of the subjects they had conquered and then exchanged them in Constantinople
for luxury goods otherwise unavailable in Rus'. The process by which
the Rus' rulers exchanged with Byzantium the raw materials extorted
from their unwilling subjects is usually referred to as trade or commerce. In fact, it is nothing more than a variety of colonial exploitation although in this case the colonial rulers, i.e., the Rus' princes and
their retinues eventually became assimilated into local society (like
the Spanish in South America rather than the British in India). However, since terms like colonialism and imperialism have such a variety
of connotations and thus might easily be misunderstood, the first
period in Kiev's pre-Mongol trade can best be labeled one of primitive
exploitation.

In the late tenth and early eleventh centuries, major changes took
place in the trading patterns of Eastern Europe. These changes were
precipitated by developments in the Orient, most notably the so-called
"silver crisis," over which Kiev and Rus' had no control. At this
time, when some traditional markets were severely disrupted and new
commercial relationships were forged, Kiev's trade might have
declined sharply or even collapsed. Whether consciously or by
accident, Kiev adapted to the new environment and created a highly
developed and sophisticated system of commerce. This is not to say
that the old practice of primitive exploitation ceased. Extortion of
furs, wax, honey, and other goods by the Rus' princes and their
officials continued although it was now routinized and increasingly
dignified as the tax legally owed to a ruler by his subjects. No one
will deny that the products collected by such taxes or tributes did not
remain important items in Kiev's trade. But, this continuity is
overshadowed by the fundamental changes that started to take place in
Kiev's trade during the eleventh century. Thus, the second period in
Kiev's pre-Mongol commerce dates to the eleventh century and can be
called a period of transition.

Perhaps the most significant development of the transitional period
was Kiev's emergence as a major industrial center. This development
can be seen graphically in the following table on handicraft workshops
in pre-Mongol Kiev, drawn from P. P. Tolochko's recent monograph.[7]

---

[7] Tolochko, *Drevnii Kiev*, p. 139.

TABLE 4.1

Pre-Mongol Craft Production in Kiev

Workshop	*Date*	*Location*
1. Kiln for baking plinths	X cen.	vul. Volodymyrs'ka, No. 2
2. Stonecutting workshop	X cen.	vul. Volodymyrs'ka, No. 2
3. Jewelry workshop—for making decorative plaques	X cen.	vul. Verkhnii Val
4. Pottery workshop	X – XI cen.	slopes of Starokyivs'ka hora
5. Blacksmith workshop	X – XI cen.	slopes of Starokyivs'ka hora
6. Blacksmith workshop	X – XI cen.	vul. Volos'ka
7. Blacksmith workshop	X – XI cen.	vul. Mezhyhirs'ka, No. 42
8. Kiln for baking lime	XI cen.	vul. Irynyns'ka, No. 3 – 5
9. Pottery kiln	XI cen.	St. Sophia Cathedral
10. Glassmaking workshop	XI – XII cen.	vul. Reitars'ka, No. 33
11. Blacksmith workshop	XI – XII cen.	former Mykhailivs'ko-Zolotoverkhyi Monastery
12. Two bone-cutting workshops	XI – XIII cen.	Zamkova hora
13. Three jewelry workshops	XI – XIII cen.	Zamkova hora
14. Amber jewelry workshop	XI – XIII cen.	vul. Iaroslavs'ka, No. 43
15. Blacksmith and perhaps jewelry workshops	XI – XIII cen.	vul. Volos'ka, No. 20
16. Glassmaking workshop	XI – XIII cen.	vul. Volodymyrs'ka, No. 2
17. Enameling workshop	XII cen.	
18. Blacksmith workshop	XII cen.	hora Dytynka
19. Two jewelry workshops	XII – XIII cen.	vul. Volodymyrs'ka, No. 2
20. Bone-cutting workshop	XII – XIII cen.	vul. Volodymyrs'ka, No. 2
21. Workshop for making bronze goods	XII – XIII cen.	vul. Volodymyrs'ka, No. 2
22. Forges for jewelry	XII – XIII cen.	vul. Volodymyrs'ka, No. 7 – 9
23. Glassmaking workshop	XII – XIII cen.	former Mykhailivs'ko-Zolotoverkhyi Monastery
24. Glassmaking workshop	XII – XIII cen.	vul. Konstantynivs'ka, No. 6
25. Workshop for making slate spindle whorls	XII – XIII cen.	vul. Verkhnii Val
26. Amber jewelry workshop	XII – XIII cen.	vul. Zelins'koho, No. 2
27. "Dwelling of the blacksmith"	XII – XIII cen.	vul. B. Zhytomyrs'ka, No. 4
28. Blacksmith workshop	XII – XIII cen.	vul. Verkhnii Val
29. The "artist's" workshop		former Mykhailivs'ko-Zolotoverkhyi Monastery

30. Glassmaking workshop   vul. Volodymyrs'ka
31. Workshop for dressing hides   Podil

The chronological distribution of these workshops is shown in the following table.

TABLE 4.2

Chronological Distribution of Pre-Mongol Workshops in Kiev

Date	Number	Type
Tenth Century	3	baking plinths, stonecutting, jewelry-decorative plaques
Tenth-Eleventh Centuries	4	pottery, blacksmith (3)
Eleventh Century	2	baking lime, pottery
Eleventh-Twelfth Centuries	2	glassmaking, blacksmith
Eleventh-Thirteenth Centuries	9	bone-cutting (2), jewelry (4), amber jewelry, blacksmith, glassmaking
Twelfth Century	2	enameling, blacksmith
Twelfth-Thirteenth Centuries	11	jewelry (2), bone-cutting, bronze goods, jewelry, glassmaking (2), slate spindle whorls, amber jewelry, blacksmith (2)
Undated	3	"artist's" workshop, glassmaking, dressing hides

Several conclusions emerge from this data. First, only three of the thirty-three dated workshops (9 percent) date exclusively to the tenth century. Seventeen workshops (52 percent) were probably in operation during the eleventh century. Of these seventeen, four apparently started in the tenth century, but thirteen, or 39 percent, of all workshops probably began to function in the eleventh century. Thirteen, or 39 percent, of all workshops were begun in the twelfth and thirteenth centuries. However, of these thirteen, only three constitute new crafts not represented in earlier workshops (enameling, bronzeware production, slate spindle whorls). In other words, only 23 percent of the new workshops established in the twelfth and thirteenth centuries were for previously unknown crafts. This analysis suggests that the eleventh century was a crucial period in the development of handicraft production in Kiev. Most of the known and dated workshops appear to have been established at this time and they produced most of the types of goods made in pre-Mongol Kiev. Furthermore, the existence of two eleventh-century workshops for the production of glass demonstrates quite clearly that Kiev craftsmen were also becoming more sophisticated. In short, one can say that the eleventh century brought a major development in Kiev's craft production. More craftsmen now began to produce a greater number and variety of goods, including some, like glass, which required completely new technologies borrowed from abroad.

In examining the archaeological evidence of Kiev's pre-Mongol craft production, several factors should be remembered. First, these thirty-six workshops come from that relatively small part of medieval Kiev which has been excavated. Consequently, this is a minimal figure which shall grow as the annual digs in Kiev continue. In 1983, for example, a new bonecutting workshop was uncovered at No. 16 vul. Volos'ka in the Podil section.[8] Second, the number of workshops in Tolochko's list may already be a very conservative figure. He lists, for instance, five workshops for glassmaking. However, a recent review of archaeological excavations in Kiev specifically indicates that evidence of glass production has been found at eight sites in Kiev.[9] Finally, Tolochko's list is based entirely on archaeological data. He does not utilize any of the written sources that point to the existence of a larger number of crafts in Kievan Rus'.[10] These considerations all suggest that the number of workshops that existed in pre-Mongol Kiev was far greater and perhaps far more diverse than the thirty-six in Tolochko's list. As research on handicraft production in Kiev continues, the list of workshops will undoubtedly increase. But, for the time being, Tolochko's list represents a good sample of pre-Mongol craft production in Kiev. And, this sample clearly demonstrates that the eleventh century witnessed a "great leap forward" in the production of Kiev's artisans.

There are probably many reasons to account for this marked development in Kiev's craft production. One factor must surely have been the growing affluence of Kiev. By the eleventh century, there existed a significant number of princes, princely officials, boyars,

---

[8] M. A. Sahaidak (Sagaidak), "Raskopki v Kieve," *Arkheologicheskie otkrytiia 1983 goda* (Moscow, 1985), pp. 351–52.

[9] *Novoe v arkheologii Kieva*, p. 318.

[10] See M. Tikhomirov, *The Towns of Ancient Rus* (Moscow, 1959), pp. 72–95.

important clerics, and merchants who had become wealthy primarily from the primitive exploitation of the natives and the related commerce with Constantinople. We can also assume that the tastes of these elites had become much more refined by the eleventh century, especially after the conversion to Orthodoxy with its concomitant intensification of relations with Byzantium. The more sophisticated, Byzantine-influenced ruling elites which emerged in Kiev after the conversion were unquestionably far different in their tastes from the old Rus' princes and their retinues. These ruling elites had greater wealth and sophistication than their predecessors.

Related to this greater wealth and sophistication was what has been called the sedentarization of the ruling elites. In the tenth century, the Rus' princes and their retinues spent a good part of each year traveling through the Rus' land in order to collect tribute. During the second half of the tenth century, these annual extortion trips gradually gave way to the local collection of tribute by princely officials and relatives. Thus, the Kievan elite spent more time either in Kiev or in the cities they governed for Kiev's Grand Prince. It is reasonable to believe that as the sedentarization of the ruling elites set in, these elites became more interested in creating the good life at home. Thus, the days of spartan campaigning, epitomized by Grand Prince Sviatoslav (the Conqueror), gave way to a period when luxuries and material comfort were more appreciated and desired.

The combination of affluence, Byzantine-inspired refinement, and sedentarization produced in Kiev a demand for various goods, many of which could be termed luxury goods. The ruling elites of Kiev wanted and could afford such things as fine pottery, expensive glass, silks, and fancy jewelry. Consequently, a number of new and more sophisticated crafts began to appear in Kiev to satisfy this demand. Some crafts, like the silk trade, could not be introduced into Kiev for a variety of reasons, but others could be developed there if the appropriate skilled craftsmen from Byzantium or the Near East were invited to Kiev. Once these foreign craftsmen began to work in Kiev, catering to the needs of the Kievan ruling classes, it was not long before native Kiev craftsmen began to learn the secrets of these foreign specialists and supply the demands of the Kiev market. In fact, these craftsmen probably became so skilled in certain of these crafts that they gradually began to win a larger share of the market from foreign imports. Finally, Kiev craftsmen and merchants soon discovered that a large market existed for their goods in other Rus' towns. In order to satisfy both the growing Rus' demand and the needs of Kiev, Kiev's craftsmen must certainly have changed their orientation from custom production for the few to mass production for the Rus' market. Thus, by the twelfth century, the craftsmen of Kiev were able to supply a large quantity of fairly sophisticated products to numerous towns throughout Rus'.

The transitional era in Kiev's pre-Mongol commerce is characterized by the transformation of Kiev into an advanced center of craft production. This transformation did not mean that the old system was abandoned. At most, tribute was converted into taxes which were collected in a more orderly but no less exploitative fashion. The extortion of furs, wax, and honey from the peasantry did not cease and prisoners of war, bankrupt debtors, and other unfortunates were still sold into slavery. But, despite all this, a new and growing sector of craft production became part of Kiev's commerce. Kiev's trade became more diverse and the era of primitive exploitation gave way to a period when Kiev produced manufactured goods and sold raw materials.

While Kiev became a major industrial center supplying the Rus' market, its foreign trade, especially with Byzantium and the Black Sea, continued to prosper during the eleventh century. Byzantine sources provide contradictory reports about the reasons for the 1043 Rus' expedition against Constantinople. Some sources, however, link this expedition with an attack upon Rus' merchants in Constantinople in which a Rus' noble was killed.[11] Without excluding other factors or insisting upon a mono-causal explanation, we can nevertheless conclude that the events of 1043 clearly demonstrate that Rus' merchants continued to frequent Constantinople and that their trade there was still of the greatest importance to the princes of Kiev.

---

[11] Cedrenus, *Historiarum Compendium*, 2 vols, ed. J. Bekker (Bonn, 1838–1839), 2:551, cited by Cross in *The Russian Primary Chronicle*, p. 260, fn. 175; John Scylitzes, *Synopsis Historiarum*, ed. I. Thurn (Berlin, 1973), p. 430. For good recent studies of the 1043 Rus' raid and the role of Rus' trade with Constantinople, see J. Shepard, "Why Did the Russians Attack Byzantium in 1043?," *Byzantinisch-Neugriechischen Jahrbücher* 22 (1979):147–212, and A. Poppe, "La dernière expédition russe contre Constantinople," *Byzantinoslavica* 32 (1971):1–29, 233–68.

In 1084, *Grechniki* and their goods were captured at Oleshshia in the Dnieper estuary by one of the lesser Rus' princes.[12] These *Grechniki* were merchants on their way to Greece, apparently from Kiev.[13] Thus, the traditional Kiev-Byzantine trade was still flourishing at the end of the eleventh century. Furthermore, the events of 1084 demonstrated that the Grand Prince of Kiev retained a very keen interest in his city's Byzantine trade and would take immediate action to defuse any threat to it.[14] Finally, the events of 1084 strongly suggest that Rus' merchants still made regular use of the islands in the Dnieper estuary on their voyages to and from Constantinople. In fact, excavations at one of these islands, namely Berezan', have uncovered evidence of many temporary dwellings from the tenth–twelfth centuries. Apparently, these were the dwellings of merchants who wintered on the island while on their way to and from Constantinople as well as the homes of fishermen.[15]

In the lives of the monks of the Kievan Caves Monastery (Pechers'ka Lavra), we learn that "numerous merchants, Greeks and Abkhazians" traveled to Kiev from Constantinople at the time when Nikon (d. 1088) was abbot of the monastery.[16] This report constitutes yet another confirmation of Kiev's trade with Constantinople in the eleventh century and it is one of the few sources which specifically states that Greek merchants from Constantinople visited Kiev.

[12] *Povest' vremennykh let*, p. 135, (s.a. 1084); *The Russian Primary Chronicle*, p. 168, (s.a. 1084).

[13] Cross in *The Russian Primary Chronicle*, p. 273, fn. 261; *Slovar' russkogo iazyka, XII–XVII vv.*, vol. 4 (Moscow, 1977), p. 132, defines *Grechnik* as "a merchant conducting trade along the route from the Varangians to the Greeks." Also see Tikhomirov, *Towns of Ancient Rus*, pp. 129–30, and *The Nikonian Chronicle*, vol. 1, *From the Beginning to the Year 1132*, ed. Serge A. Zenkovsky, trans. Serge A. and Betty Jean Zenkovsky (Princeton, 1984), p. 185, fn. 114.

[14] Upon hearing of the seizure of the Grechniki and their wares, Grand Prince Vsevolod of Kiev immediately got in touch with the offending prince David, had him brought to Kiev, and then awarded him the town of Dorohobuzh in order to keep him occupied elsewhere.

[15] K. S. Gorbunova, "O kharaktere srednevekogo poseleniia na ostrove Berezan'," in *Problemy arkheologii*, vol. 2, *Sbornik statei v pamiat' professora M. I. Artamonova* (Leningrad, 1978), pp. 170–73.

[16] There is an English translation of this excerpt from the *Kievan Crypt Paterikon* in Serge A. Zenkovsky, ed., *Medieval Russia's Epics, Chronicles, and Tales*, rev. ed. (New York, 1974), p. 139.

Finally, another eleventh-century Byzantine source, the "Miracle of St. Nicholas," mentions a special market in Constantinople where Rus' merchants regularly went to sell slaves.[17] Rus' merchants still brought their slaves to Constantinople for sale in the eleventh century, just as they had in the tenth century.

Archaeological data reinforce these varied written sources which testify to an active trade between Kiev and Byzantium in the eleventh century. For example, shards of amphorae used to transport wine and olive oil are found throughout Rus' in large quantities from the eleventh century until the Mongol conquest of 1240. Most of these amphorae were made in the Byzantine centers of the northern Black Sea, primarily in the Crimea, from whence they were shipped up the Dnieper to Kiev. From Kiev, these amphorae were then sent to numerous towns in the middle and upper Dnieper as well as to many more distant Rus' centers in the north. In addition to producing and selling its own goods throughout Rus', Kiev served as the major distribution point to which imported goods such as wine and oil were brought from the Black Sea and then reshipped to large parts of Rus'. Kiev emerged as the chief middleman in a complex international and domestic commerce which involved sending goods to the south to pay for wine and oil imports and then exchanging these imports for goods offered by numerous Rus' towns and villages.

In sum, several major conclusions can be drawn about Kiev's international and domestic trade during the eleventh century period of transition. Kiev's foreign commerce with Byzantium continued to flourish and in certain respects, e.g., wine and oil imports, even grew. The primitive exploitation of the Rus' peasantry apparently provided the furs, wax, and slaves which formed the basic Rus' exports. At the same time, the eleventh century was a period of transition due to the emergence of Kiev as a major industrial center whose products began to reach all parts of Rus' in growing quantities. While the primitive exploitation of the peasantry still played an important role in Kiev's commerce, Kiev was slowly transformed into the industrial and

---

[17] "Chudesa sv. Nikolaia," in *Pamiatniki obshchestva liubitelei drevnei pis'mennosti*, ed. Archimandrite Leonid, 72 (1888):85, quoted in A. P. Novosel'tsev and V. T. Pashuto, "Vneshniaia torgovlia Drevnei Rusi (do serediny XIII v.)," *Istoriia SSSR*, 1967, no. 3, p. 83, fn. 10. The citation to this same passage in Shepard, "Why Did the Russians Attack," p. 154, fn. 4, is somewhat different.

commercial center of Rus', the center for a complex and expanding trade which extended throughout Rus' and even abroad. Real trade involving manufactured goods gradually developed, whereas in the tenth century Kiev's commerce had consisted entirely of selling expropriated raw materials and people to foreigners. In any event, there is no evidence that Kiev's trade began to decline during the eleventh century. On the contrary, its commerce and especially its internal trade grew steadily.

Kiev's International and Domestic Trade, Ca. 1100 – 1240

The third period in Kiev's pre-Mongol trade dates to the twelfth and first half of the thirteenth centuries. This was a time, contrary to the traditional view, when both Kiev's international and domestic trade flourished. However, as indicated above, the most outstanding feature of this period was clearly the spectacular growth of Kiev's industrial production which resulted in massive exports of Kiev's manufactured goods throughout Rus'. Consequently, this section will begin with an examination of Kiev's expanding domestic commerce.

A. *Kiev's Domestic Trade*

Earlier, in looking at the transitional period, we reproduced listings of Kiev handicraft workshops of the pre-Mongol era (Tables 4.1 and 4.2). These tables demonstrate that the sharp growth in Kiev's handicraft production which began in the eleventh century continued in the period between ca. 1100 and 1240. During this time, thirteen of thirty-three dated workshops, or 39 percent of the total, began operation. However, these figures by themselves provide very little idea of the massive exports of Kiev's goods to the rest of Rus' which was now taking place. To gain a better picture of these exports we must examine the excavations from the numerous towns and villages in Rus' where significant amounts of Kiev's products now began to appear. Space and other limitations do not allow us to consider all the pertinent data from all the excavations of pre-Mongol Rus' towns. But, there have been a goodly number of recent, comprehensive studies of the excavations from the upper Dnieper region and modern Belorussia. If we add to these studies the pertinent works on selected sites in northern and southern Rus', we then possess a fairly large number of sites located throughout Rus'. An analysis of this sample provides a good idea of the extent of Kiev's exports to the other parts of Rus'.

In examining this date, the best way to proceed is probably to focus on each type of product separately. Let us thus begin with the huge quantities of glassware made in Kiev which have been found throughout Rus'. The origins and development of glassmaking in Rus' have been carefully examined in a series of studies by Iu. L. Shchapova and other scholars.[18] These studies indicate that relatively large numbers of Near Eastern and Byzantine glass beads were imported into Rus' during the tenth century. By the first quarter of the eleventh century, the construction of various Christian churches in Kiev led to the establishment of the first glass workshops in the city. These earliest workshops produced glass beads and rings. Soon after they began to make glass vessels and window glass as well. About a century later, during the second quarter of the twelfth century, Kiev glassmakers began to produce bracelets. Thus, during the eleventh and early twelfth centuries Kiev became a producer of glass beads, glass rings, glassware, window glass, and glass bracelets.

The Byzantine masters invited to make the first glass in Kiev probably employed the traditional Byzantine sodium-potassium-silica (Na-K-Si) recipe. This recipe, however, was not adopted by the first Rus' glassmakers, perhaps because the Byzantines kept it secret. The original Rus' glassmakers apparently used a simple lead-silica (Pb-Si) recipe as well as a more complex potassium-lead-silica (K-Pb-Si) recipe. Thus, while the Rus' masters of Kiev adopted Byzantine technology in glassmaking, they employed very different recipes. During the eleventh century, some beads and rings were produced in Kiev using the Pb-Si recipe, whereas the K-Pb-Si recipe was used in other Kiev workshops for jewelry as well as for glassware and window glass. By the late eleventh century glass jewelry made from the Pb-Si recipe was rapidly disappearing from Kiev's workshops as the K-Pb-Si glass began to dominate the market. Around this same time, the Pb-Si recipe was adopted for glazed ceramics since there existed a fast

---

[18] The most important of these studies is Iu. L. Shchapova, *Steklo Kievskoi Rusi* (Moscow, 1972). For a more recent work which places Rus' glassmaking within a much broader chronological and geographical context, see Iu. L. Shchapova, *Ocherki istorii drevnego steklodeliia (po materialam Nila, Blizhnego Vostoka i Evropy)* (Moscow, 1983).

growing market for floor and wall tiles, mosaics, and *pysanky* or glazed ceramic eggs. The manufacture of glass bracelets using the K-Pb-Si recipe began in Kiev around 1125.

From the early eleventh century until the mid-twelfth century, Kiev enjoyed a monopoly over glass production in Rus'. The Kiev workshops were so skillful that they competed very successfully with foreign imports which consequently never captured a large share of the Rus' market. Around the mid-twelfth century, workshops producing bracelets of Pb-Si glass began to appear throughout Rus'. These so-called provincial workshops are noted in Novgorod from the mid-twelfth century, in Polatsk from the second half of the twelfth century, at Smolensk prior to the Mongol conquest, and possibly elsewhere. Nevertheless, huge quantities of glass bracelets made in Kiev using the traditional K-Pb-Si recipe continued to be imported into these towns.[19]

Kiev enjoyed a monopoly within Rus' in the production of glassware and window glass during the pre-Mongol era. Thus, such finds from Rus' made of K-Pb-Si glass can be attributed, with relative confidence, to Kiev's workshops. In fact, it has been suggested that glassware was produced in the workshops found in the Pechers'ka Lavra and the Podil.[20] Fragments of glass vessels made in Kiev have been reported in Vyshhorod, Chernihiv, Liubech, Vshchyzh, Raiky, Horods'k, and Iziaslav.[21] Thus, glassware from Kiev appeared in very modest quantities throughout the middle Dnieper region. During the second half of the twelfth century, Kiev's glassware also reached Novgorod and Navahrudak while Kiev's glassware is found in Turaŭ from the mid-twelfth century to the Mongol conquest.[22] A few fragments of Kiev's glassware have also been reported in other towns: Moscow, Slobodka, Tmutarakan', Smolensk, Vladimir-on-the-Kliaz'ma, Suzdal', Rostov, Polatsk, Pskov, Minsk, and Halych.[23] As of the early 1970s, some 1,000 fragments of glassware made in pre-Mongol Kiev had been found in various Rus' towns, with the largest

---

[19] This survey of glassmaking in Rus' is based primarily on Shchapova, *Steklo Kievskoi Rusi*, pp. 176–93.

[20] Ibid., pp. 33, 40.

[21] Ibid., pp. 34–37.

[22] Ibid., pp. 42–53.

[23] Ibid., p. 63.

concentrations coming from Novgorod (ca. 300 fragments), Turaŭ (ca. 200 fragments), and Navahrudak (ca. 300 fragments). Judging by those sites whose stratigraphy is well established, the export of Kiev's glassware throughout Rus' took place primarily in the twelfth century.

The production of glassware in Kiev was closely connected with a modest production of window glass. Kiev's window glass, made with the K-Pb-Si recipe, has been found in small quantities in Novgorod, Navahrudak, Chernihiv, Turaŭ, Vladimir, and Riazan'.[24] It is postulated that churches may have formed the largest market for both Rus' and Byzantine window glass.[25] Most of this Kiev window glass seems to have reached other Rus' towns in the twelfth and first half of the thirteenth centuries.

Large numbers of glass beads have been found in Rus' burial and habitation sites of the pre-Mongol period. Glass beads were apparently made in Kiev from the early eleventh century until 1240.[26] It is still not clear whether the Rus' production of beads at this time was concentrated in Kiev or whether other centers also began to make beads during the twelfth and early thirteenth centuries.[27] In any event, there are thousands of glass beads of various types from pre-Mongol sites and Shchapova's studies suggest that over half were probably made in Rus'[28] where the leading center of production was unquestionably Kiev. Based upon present knowledge, it would seem that the manufacture of these glass beads began in Kiev during the first half of the eleventh century and by the early twelfth century relatively large numbers were being produced for the Rus' market.[29] Glass beads made in Kiev are found in Novgorod as well as in burial mounds throughout the northern and central regions of Rus'.

Compared with glass beads and especially glass bracelets, relatively few glass rings have been found; most of those studied come from Novgorod and Beloozero, i.e., northern Rus'. Nevertheless, Shchapova's analysis suggests that glass rings were made in Kiev starting in the eleventh century and that Kiev exported its glass rings

[24] Ibid., p. 69.
[25] Ibid., pp. 70–72.
[26] Ibid., pp. 76–78, 95–96.
[27] Ibid., p. 75.
[28] Ibid., p. 87.
[29] Ibid., pp. 76–80, 94–96.

to Novgorod from the early eleventh century until the Mongol conquest with the high points (although modest quantitatively) coming in the 1070s, 1160s, and early thirteenth century.[30]

If glassware, glass rings, and window glass were all produced in small or modest quantities, then the manufacture of glass bracelets reached truly massive proportions in the pre-Mongol era. And, a very large part of these glass bracelets were made in Kiev. Glass bracelets made in Kiev's workshops have been found in Kiev itself and in Polatsk, Novgorod, Tserkovishcha (Voishchiny) near Smolensk, Smolensk, Liubech, Kostroma, Horods'k, Kolodiazhyn, Raiky, Old Riazan', Turaŭ, Pinsk, Vladimir-on-the Kliaz'ma, Iziaslav, Pirovo, Beloozero, Moscow, Drutsk, Minsk, Navahrudak and elsewhere.[31] Glass bracelets were without question the most popular jewelry of city inhabitants everywhere in Rus' during the immediate pre-Mongol era.

Shchapova has noted that when we combine all the finds of Kiev's glass bracelets from all these sites throughout Rus', it is then clear that glass bracelets were produced in Kiev during the pre-Mongol era in truly colossal quantities. In her study of Rus' glass bracelets, she examined over 30,000 glass bracelets from twenty-two Rus' towns and cities.[32] Although this sounds like a very large number of bracelets, it represents only a part of the glass bracelets produced in Rus'. The 5,226 Novgorod bracelets, for instance, were uncovered in the Nerevskii excavations which ended in the early 1960s. Thus, the Novgorod figures do not include any of the glass bracelets found in the subsequent annual excavations. A recent estimate is that over 7,500 fragments of glass bracelets have been found in excavations at Novgorod.[33] Shchapova examined only 252 bracelets from Polatsk. A slightly later study indicated that 792 glass bracelets had been found in just the upper castle region of old Polatsk.[34] The 1,776 glass bracelets from Smolensk all come from the 1957 excavations. Thus, all the numerous glass bracelets found in Smolensk before and after 1957 are omitted from this total. The 498 glass bracelets from old Riazan'

[30] Ibid., pp. 97–102, especially Fig. 18, p. 99.

[31] Ibid., pp. 108–74.

[32] Ibid., Table 30, p. 166.

[33] B. A. Kolchin and V. L. Ianin, eds., *Novgorodskii sbornik. 50 let raskopok Novgoroda* (Moscow, 1982), p. 85.

[34] G. V. Shtykhov, *Drevnii Polotsk, IX–XIII vv.* (Minsk, 1975), p. 95.

come almost entirely from the 1967 excavations. None of the many glass bracelets found in other years at Riazan' are represented in the 30,000 figure. The totals for Navahrudak show 520 glass bracelets. A recent study estimates that 2,500–3,000 glass bracelets were found there.[35] Only 100 glass bracelets are listed for Minsk while it has been estimated that around 1,100 fragments of glass bracelets had been found there.[36] Some 529 glass bracelets are noted for Turaŭ while a now somewhat dated study indicates that in just four years the excavations at Turaŭ uncovered over 1,600 fragments of glass bracelets.[37] The 192 glass bracelets shown from Pinsk under-represent the total number found there.[38] The number of fragments of glass bracelets from Beloozero should be 613 rather than the 326 listed.[39] Thus, the 30,000 aggregate figure for the glass bracelets from 22 Rus' towns reflects only a fraction of the true total of glass bracelets found in these towns.

In addition, significant numbers of glass bracelets have been uncovered during excavations in other Rus' towns. At Serensk in the Viatichian land, for example, some 8,120 fragments of glass bracelets have been found.[40] Around 670 fragments of glass bracelets were discovered at Slobodka, also in the Viatichian land.[41] Several hundred glass bracelet fragments had been excavated at Vitsebsk.[42] Over 300 fragments were found at Lukomil'[43] while at least several hundred glass bracelets have been reported from the excavations at Kopys'.[44] The 1965–1968 digs at Orsha uncovered almost 400 fragments of

[35] F. D. Gurevich, *Drevnii Novogrudok (posad-okol'nyi gorod)* (Leningrad, 1981), pp. 153–54.

[36] E. M. Zagorul'skii, *Vozniknovenie Minska* (Minsk, 1982), p. 228.

[37] P. F. Lysenko, *Goroda Turovskoi zemli* (Minsk, 1974), p. 60.

[38] Ibid., pp. 83–86.

[39] L. A. Golubeva, *Ves' i slaviane na Belom ozere X–XIII vv.* (Moscow, 1973), p. 183.

[40] T. N. Nikol'skaia, *Zemlia Viatichei: K istorii naseleniia basseina verkhnei i srednei Oki v IX–XIII vv.* (Moscow, 1981), p. 235.

[41] Ibid.

[42] G. V. Shtykhov, *Goroda Polotskoi zemli (IX–XIII vv.)* (Minsk, 1978), pp. 34–40.

[43] Ibid., p. 46.

[44] Ibid., pp. 93–95.

glass bracelets.[45] Several hundred fragments of glass bracelets were also reported from the excavations at Davyd-Haradok and Slutsk.[46] Glass bracelets have also appeared in excavations in southwestern Rus' towns. Massive finds of glass bracelets are reported, for instance, from Old Chernivtsi or Lenkivtsi in the upper Prut region while glass bracelets were also found in Vasyliv on the Dniester.[47] Finally, finds of glass bracelets have also showed up in excavations from Suzdal'.[48] Thus, there are literally thousands of fragments of glass bracelets from towns and cities all over Rus' which were not included in Shchapova's survey.

The above comments are not intended as criticism of Shchapova. She was simply unable to utilize many unpublished excavation reports in her study and it appears she could not always examine those materials which were published or found long ago. Furthermore, Shchapova's purpose was to obtain a random sample of bracelets from various towns in order to determine when, where, and how glass bracelets were made in medieval Rus', not to measure Kiev's exports throughout Rus' in the pre-Mongol era. In sum, her 30,000 total for glass bracelets was not intended to be misleading. Given all the glass bracelets found in the villages, towns, and cities from all parts of Rus', we are talking of a Rus' production which quite probably reached the hundreds of thousands, especially when we take into consideration the unexcavated parts of all these sites. Based on the excavations to date, we can probably say that at least 60,000 glass bracelets of Rus' manufacture have been found throughout Rus'.

The production of glass bracelets started in Kiev around 1125.[49] The tremendous demand throughout Rus' for these glass bracelets became evident very quickly and soon these bracelets were also being produced in other towns. By the mid-twelfth century glass bracelets were being made in Novgorod and by the second half of the twelfth

---

[45] Ibid., p. 98.

[46] Lysenko, *Goroda Turovskoi zemli*, pp. 138, 150.

[47] B. A. Timoshchuk, "Drevnerusskie goroda Severnoi Bukoviny," in *Drevnerusskie goroda* (Moscow, 1981), pp. 129, 133.

[48] M. V. Sedova and D. A. Belen'kaia, "Okol'nyi gorod Suzdalia," in ibid., pp. 103, 107.

[49] Shchapova, *Steklo Kievskoi Rusi*, p. 191.

century production had begun in Polatsk as well.[50] Glass bracelets were also produced at Tserkovishcha, a small town 15 km from Smolensk, as well as in Smolensk itself, starting around the mid-twelfth century.[51] Liubech also produced glass bracelets[52] as did Old Riazan'.[53] At Serensk, a workshop and other evidence of glassmaking has been uncovered.[54] Most of the Rus' glass produced outside of Kiev used a Pb-Si recipe although the traditional Kiev K-Pb-Si recipe was employed at Liubech in the 1130s and at Novgorod, Old Riazan', and Serensk starting around 1200. In the latter four sites, local K-Pb-Si glass is distinguished from that made in Kiev by the presence of small quantities of other elements.[55] In short, the demand for glass bracelets was so great in Rus' that, over the course of a century, some of Kiev's masters were lured or invited to a series of other cities where they initiated the manufacture of glass bracelets to satisfy local and regional demand. Nevertheless, as Shchapova notes, glass bracelets from Kiev are found at every one of the sites studied. The only question remaining is what percentage of the glass bracelets from a given city were imported from Kiev.[56]

In concluding our review of the admittedly incomplete evidence on Kiev's glass exports in the pre-Mongol era, it is instructive to survey all the finds of different types of Kiev glass from various towns. In evaluating this material, it should be emphasized that Kiev's glass production only began to reach significant levels in the late eleventh – early twelfth century and that it ceased abruptly with the Mongol conquest of 1240. Thus, the overwhelming majority of Kiev's glass exports to Rus' date from this third period in the city's trade.

[50] Ibid.

[51] Ibid., pp. 136, 141, 143.

[52] Ibid., p. 143.

[53] Ibid., p. 156.

[54] Nikol'skaia, *Zemlia Viatichei*, pp. 141, 237.

[55] V. M. Petegirich, "Iz istorii ekonomicheskikh i kul'turnykh sviazei Galitsko-Volynskoi Rusi v X – XIII vv. (Po arkheologicheskim dannym)," in *Slavianskie drevnosti: Etnogenez. Material'naia kul'tura drevnei Rusi. Sbornik nauchnykh trudov* (Kiev, 1980), p. 153.

[56] Shchapova, *Steklo Kievskoi Rusi*, p. 16.

Beloozero—Many of the 613 fragments of glass bracelets come from Kiev (or Novgorod?). Almost all the fragments of glassware (ca. 60) come from Kiev. There were also 892 glass beads and 52 glass rings, part of which were no doubt Kiev's exports.[57]

Borisov—A few fragments of Kiev's glassware were found here and at a nearby village. The glass bracelets from here (at least 59) also appear to have come from Kiev.[58]

Davyd-Haradok—Almost 200 fragments of glass bracelets, apparently imported from Kiev, were found here.[59]

Drutsk—Shchapova suggests that around 66 percent of the glass bracelets found here were brought from Kiev.[60]

Gorodilovok—Glass bracelets made in Kiev were found in this village near Navahrudak.[61]

Hrodna—Some glassware fragments and the glass bracelets found here apparently came from Kiev.[62]

Iziaslav—A few fragments of Kiev's glassware were found here. Most of the 10,000 fragments of glass bracelets from the excavations here seem to be from Kiev.[63]

Kopys'—Many of the several hundred glass bracelets found here seem to have been Kiev exports.[64]

Kostroma—As many as 85 percent of the small sample of glass bracelets from here which were studied appear to be from Kiev.[65]

Lenkivtsi—A window glass fragment and some of the many glass bracelets found here came from Kiev.[66] It has also been suggested that

---

[57] Golubeva, *Ves' i slaviane*, pp. 180–85.

[58] Shtykhov, *Goroda Polotskoi zemli*, pp. 101–102, 115; G. V. Shtykhov, "Kiev i goroda Polotskoi zemli," in *Kiev i zapadnye zemli Rusi v IX–XIII vv.* (Minsk, 1982),p. 61.

[59] Lysenko, *Goroda Turovskoi zemli*, pp. 138, 146.

[60] Shchapova, *Steklo Kievskoi Rusi*, p. 171.

[61] Ia. G. Zverugo, "Kiev i zemli Belorusskogo Poneman'ia," in *Kiev i zapadnye zemli Rusi*, p. 116.

[62] Zverugo, "Kiev i zemli Belorusskogo," pp. 116–18.

[63] Shchapova, *Steklo Kievskoi Rusi*, pp. 37, 160–64, 168.

[64] Shtykhov, "Kiev i goroda Polotskoi zemli," p. 61.

[65] Shchapova, *Steklo Kievskoi Rusi*, pp. 148–49.

[66] Timoshchuk, "Drevnerusskie goroda," pp. 126–29; Petegirich, "Iz istorii ekonomicheskikh," pp. 153–54.

most of the glass, including bracelets, found in Galicia and Volhynia, came from Kiev despite local glass production in Halych.[67]

Liubech—Some Kiev glassware was found here. While many of the glass bracelets found here were locally made, some did come from Kiev.[68]

Lukomil'—The glassware fragment and many of the glass bracelets from here apparently came from Kiev.[69]

Minsk—Over 95 percent of the some 1,100 glass bracelets from here were seemingly made in Kiev. The fragments of glass beads, glass rings, and glassware found here also seem to have been Kiev exports.[70]

Moscow—The glassware found here as well as 65 percent of the glass bracelets were apparently imports from Kiev.[71]

Novgorod—A significant percentage of the 1,397 glass beads found here were probably from Kiev. Glass rings from Kiev were imported from the early eleventh century until 1240. From the late eleventh century until the early thirteenth century, Kiev's imports of glassware were predominant here. Some of the window glass from Novgorod was made in Kiev. Of the some 5,200 glass bracelets found here, it is estimated that about 66 percent were Kiev's imports, 32 percent were locally made, and 2 percent came from Byzantium.[72]

Navahrudak—The 60 glassware fragments found here came from Kiev, as did a large percentage of the 141 glass beads. Around 300 fragments of Kiev window glass were found here. Some of the 140 glass rings probably came from Kiev. Most of the roughly 3,000 glass bracelets found here were apparently made in Kiev.[73]

---

[67] Petegirich, "Iz istorii ekonomicheskikh," pp. 153.

[68] Shchapova, *Steklo Kievskoi Rusi*, pp. 143–45.

[69] Shtykhov, *Goroda Polotskoi zemli*, pp. 44–50.

[70] Zagorul'skii, *Vozniknovenie Minska*, pp. 229–35, 284.

[71] Shchapova, *Steklo Kievskoi Rusi*, pp. 169–71; Nikol'skaia, *Zemlia Viatichei*, p. 283.

[72] E. A. Rybina, *Arkheologicheskie ocherki istorii Novgorodskoi torgovli X–XIV vv.* (Moscow, 1978), pp. 32–37; Shchapova, *Steklo Kievskoi Rusi*, pp. 43–44, 54, 78–79, 120–32.

[73] Gurevich, *Drevnii Novogrudok*, pp. 149–54.

Orsha—Many of the 400–500 glass bracelets from here were probably made in Kiev.[74]

Pinsk—The window glass and glassware found here came from Kiev. Many of the glass rings and glass beads apparently came from Kiev. Most of the several hundred glass bracelets were seemingly from Kiev.[75]

Polatsk—The 41 fragments of glassware, the window glass, and some of the glass beads and glass rings apparently came from Kiev. About 62 percent of the hundreds of glass bracelets from here were imports from Kiev while 37 percent were locally made.[76]

Riazan'—Of the thousands of glass bracelets found here, about 15–24 percent were locally made. The remaining 76–85 percent appear to have come from Kiev. Most of the glass beads and over half the glassware were apparently Kiev imports.[77]

Serensk—The glassware and window glass at Serensk were imported, apparently, in large part, from Kiev. While a local workshop probably made most of the 8,120 glass bracelets as well as many of the glass beads and rings, some of these glass products may have been imports from Kiev.[78]

Slobodka—The glassware fragments as well as most of the 670 glass bracelets and the 10 glass beads found here seemingly came from Kiev.[79]

Slonim—The few fragments of glassware as well as most of the glass bracelets from here seem to have been Kiev imports.[80]

Slutsk—Many if not most of the 146 glass bracelets, glass rings, glass beads, and glassware found here probably came from Kiev.[81]

Smolensk—Special analysis suggests that 52 percent of the thousands of glass bracelets found here came from Rus' workshops in Kiev

[74] Shtykhov, *Goroda Polotskoi zemli*, pp. 96–98.

[75] Lysenko, *Goroda Turovskoi zemli*, pp. 86, 111, 117.

[76] Shtykhov, *Drevnii Polotsk*, pp. 95–96, 104; Shtykhov, "Kiev i goroda Polotskoi zemli," pp. 61–62; Shchapova, *Steklo Kievskoi Rusi*, pp. 113–18.

[77] Iu. L. Shchapova, "Stekliannye izdeliia iz Staroi Riazani (po materialam raskopki 1966–1968 gg.)," in *Arkheologiia Riazanskoi zemli* (Moscow, 1974), pp. 77–90.

[78] Nikol'skaia, *Zemlia Viatichei*, p. 237.

[79] Ibid., pp. 237–38.

[80] Zverugo, "Kiev i zemli Belorusskogo," pp. 116–18.

[81] Lysenko, *Goroda Turovskoi zemli*, pp. 150, 190.

while another 7 percent were made by Greeks working in Kiev. About 30 percent of the bracelets, mostly from the thirteenth and early fourteenth centuries, were locally made.[82]

Suzdal'—Kiev glassware was found in several dwellings here.[83]

Turiisk—Some of the glass bracelets found here as well as the few fragments of glassware undoubtedly came from Kiev.[84]

Turaŭ—The 200 fragments of glassware from one year's digs as well as the window glass and most of the over 1,600 glass bracelets were all Kiev imports.[85]

Vladimir-on-the-Kliaz'ma—While the sample was very small, most of the glass bracelets found here apparently came from Kiev.[86]

Vaŭkavysk—The few fragments of glassware as well as 75 percent of the glass bracelets and most of the 100 glass beads and glass rings were apparently made in Kiev.[87]

Vyshhorod, Raiky, etc.—The glassware from these and other sites in the middle Dnieper as well as most of the glass bracelets seem to have been imports from Kiev.[88]

There is no doubt that from the early eleventh century until the Mongol conquest, Kiev's glassmakers produced a huge quantity of glass goods which formed the basis of an active trade with towns and cities in all parts of Rus'. Kiev, not Byzantium or the Near East, supplied the Rus' demand for glass between ca. 1100 and ca. 1240.

Along with glass production, pre-Mongol Rus' also witnessed the development of a glazed pottery industry. Using primarily the Pb-Si recipe, Rus' craftsmen produced various glazed vessels, glazed decorated tiles, and, perhaps best known, glazed ceramic eggs, or *pysanky*. Fortunately, the glazed ceramics found in Rus' during the

---

[82] L. V. Alekseev, *Smolenskaia zemlia v IX–XIII vv. Ocherki istorii Smolenshchiny i Vostochnoi Belorussii* (Moscow, 1980), pp. 91–92; Shchapova, *Steklo Kievskoi Rusi*, pp. 136–38.

[83] Sedova and Belen'kaia, "Okol'nyi gorod," pp. 98, 99, 103, 105, 107, 112.

[84] Zverugo, " Kiev i zemli Belorusskogo," pp. 116–18.

[85] Lysenko, *Goroda Turovskoi zemli*, p. 60; P. F. Lysenko, "Kiev i Turovskaia zemlia," in *Kiev i zapadnye zemli*, pp. 104–105; Shchapova, *Steklo Kievskoi Rusi*, pp. 52, 69, 158.

[86] Shchapova, *Steklo Kievskoi Rusi*, p. 160.

[87] Zverugo, "Kiev i zemli Belorusskogo," pp. 116–18.

[88] Shchapova, *Steklo Kievskoi Rusi*, pp. 34–36, 54, 168.

pre-Mongol era have been carefully studied by T. I. Makarova.[89] In addition to the imported Byzantine, Near Eastern, and Central Asian glazed pottery, Makarova has examined local Rus' production in some detail. Glazed ceramics were first made in Rus' during the late tenth – early eleventh century in connection with the construction of the first stone churches in Kiev, i.e., the Tithe Church and St. Sophia cathedral. Greek and Rus' masters were needed to produce, among other things, the glazed tiles used in these churches.[90] As a result, the use of glazed decorated tiles for masonry churches and palaces, as well as for the wooden homes of boyars, became established in Rus'.

Soon after the local manufacture of glazed tiles began, Rus' masters also started to produce glazed vessels and dishes. The earliest such vessels date to the eleventh century and were made of white clay pottery covered with green or yellow glaze or they were decorated with a painting beneath the glaze. These white clay glazed vessels of the late tenth – eleventh centuries have been uncovered at various sites in the middle Dnieper (Kiev, Pereiaslav-Khmel'nyts'kyi, Voin', Vyshhorod, Horods'k, Chernihiv, Liubech), at two northern Rus' towns (Novgorod, Beloozero), and in the region of the Dnieper rapids (Dniprovi porohy). The vessels and dishes are fairly homogeneous, suggesting one center of production, i.e., Kiev. However, it is possible that these white clay glazed vessels were produced elsewhere in Rus'.[91]

In the mid-eleventh century, glazed ceramic eggs or *pysanky* began to appear at various sites within Rus' and in adjacent lands. As of the mid-1960s, around 100 *pysanky* were known from Rus', Poland, and Scandinavia. Makarova studied the over 70 *pysanky* found in Rus' and divided them into two typological groups—those with and those without a metallic sheen on the surface. She concluded that there were at least two major centers in Rus' for the production of *pysanky*. The first center was probably Novgorod where the *pysanky* with the metallic sheen were apparently made between the mid-eleventh and

---

[89] T. I. Makarova, *Polivnaia posuda. Iz istorii keramicheskogo importa i proizvodstva Drevnei Rusi* [Arkheologiia SSSR. Svod arkheologicheskikh istochnikov, E1 – 38] (Moscow, 1967); idem, *Polivnaia keramika v Drevnei Rusi/Céramique vernissée de l'ancienne Russie* (Moscow, 1972).

[90] Makarova, *Polivnaia posuda*, pp. 36 – 37.

[91] Ibid., pp. 37 – 41, 47, 60 – 61, 66.

mid-twelfth century.[92] The second group of *pysanky*, those without a metallic sheen, are found in and around Kiev, in Liubech, in the Gochevskie burial mound, in Poltava oblast', in Mstsislaŭ, and at Belaia Vezha.[93] Consequently, it is believed that these *pysanky* were produced in Kiev, and possibly in other nearby towns, starting around the mid-eleventh century and continuing until the early thirteenth century.[94]

The glazed white clay pottery made in Kiev during the eleventh century was soon replaced by glazed vessels of everyday gray or grayish clay made in various centers. Such vessels have been found in at least thirty-five Rus' sites.[95] The production of these vessels is dated from the eleventh to thirteenth centuries. Makarova is inclined to see local production of this "everyday" gray glazed ware in Liubech, possibly Chernihiv, Slobodka, Vyshhorod, possibly Horods'k, the village of Polovets'kyi on the Ros' River, Pereiaslav-Khmel'nyts'kyi, possibly Mstsislaŭ, Navahrudak, Hrodna, possibly Pinsk, possibly Drutsk, Novgorod, Iziaslav, Riazan', and possibly in Suzdalia (Vladimir).[96] It remains to be seen whether the manufacture of gray glazed ware was, in fact, so widespread throughout Rus'. Nevertheless, it is also clear that large quantities of gray vessels covered with a transparent light yellowish, green, or dark greenish glaze were made in Kiev during the pre-Mongol era. These "everyday" glazed vessels have been found in rather large quantities at excavations of numerous sites throughout the city.[97] Since Kiev's glassware was exported throughout Rus' and glazed white clay ceramics made in Kiev were sent to other Rus' towns,[98] it is reasonable to believe that not

---

[92] Ibid., pp. 42–45.

[93] See the map of find spots in Makarova, *Polivnaia posuda*, p. 44, fig. 6.

[94] Ibid., pp. 44–46. The *pysanky* are also discussed in T. I. Makarova, "O proizvodstve pisanok na Rusi," in *Kul'tura Drevnei Rusi* (Moscow, 1966), pp. 141–45. Zverugo ("Kiev i zemli," p. 118) believes that the *pysanky* from Hrodna were made in Kiev. Petegirich ("Iz istorii ekonomicheskikh," p. 155) notes *pysanky* from Kiev which have been found at Zvenyhorod, Plisnes'k, Lenkivtsi, Tovste, and Cherven' in Galicia and Volhynia.

[95] Makarova, *Polivnaia posuda*, p. 47 and p. 48, fig. 8.

[96] Ibid., pp. 48–58.

[97] Ibid., pp. 51–52.

[98] According to Makarova (*Polivnaia posuda*, p. 48), 10 percent of the glazed pottery found at Liubech was glazed white ware made in Kiev.

insignificant quantities of various glazed gray vessels produced in Kiev ended up in other towns and villages of Rus'.

While Kiev's production of glazed tiles, glazed vessels, and *pysanky* never reached the levels of its glassware, and while it was apparently easier to begin production of glazed wares than glass elsewhere in Rus', the evidence available to us clearly indicates that Kiev emerged in the eleventh century as a major center exporting its glazed wares to many other towns and villages of Rus'. The Kiev craftsmen who first supplied glazed wares to local churches and secular dignitaries during the eleventh century soon found that they had a market for these goods elsewhere in Rus'.

As with glazed ware, the production in Kiev of inlaid enamel items as well as expensive jewelry decorated with niello, granulation, and filigree work was largely an offshoot of glassmaking. It is believed that Greek masters and their Rus' pupils first began to produce inlaid enamelware in Kiev by the mid-eleventh century as an outgrowth of the construction of the Cathedral of St. Sophia.[99] By the twelfth century, Rus' craftsmen were able to adorn a variety of exquisite items with inlaid enamel. During the twelfth and thirteenth centuries, when the use of inlaid enamel reached its height in Rus', the enamelers of Kiev produced princely diadems, regalia (*barmy*), medallions, special silver medallions (*kolts*), crosses, necklaces, and even bindings for valuable books (the so-called Mstislav Gospel) with decorations of inlaid enamel.[100] Several workshops of the pre-Mongol era where enamelware was made have been uncovered in Kiev.[101]

As with other crafts, the production of inlaid enamel items spread to other Rus' cities in the twelfth century. It is believed, for example, that enameling workshops appeared at this time in Riazan', Vladimir, Novgorod, Halych, and possibly elsewhere.[102] Unfortunately, the manufacture of inlaid enamelware in various Rus' centers has made it difficult to determine precisely where each such piece of enamel was made. Nevertheless, the origins and development of the inlaid enamel craft in Rus' are clearly linked with Kiev where, presumably, all of the

---

[99] T. I. Makarova, *Peregorodchatye emali Drevnei Rusi* (Moscow, 1975), pp. 94–95.

[100] *Istoriia Kieva*, vol. 1, *Drevnii i srednevekovyi Kiev* (Kiev, 1982), p. 93.

[101] *Novoe v arkheologii*, p. 312; *Istoriia Kieva*, p. 93.

[102] Makarova, *Peregorodchatye emali*, pp. 98–100; *Istoriia Kieva*, p. 93.

eleventh-century and much of the later objects adorned with inlaid enamel were made.[103] However, an analysis of the method by which human figures were clothed in pieces of inlaid enamel has suggested the existence of several distinct schools, e.g., the Kiev, Vladimir, Riazan', Novgorod, and other, unknown, schools.[104] Thus, it is to be hoped that in the future scholars may be able to determine where each of the almost 160 pieces of Rus' inlaid enamel known in the early 1970s was made.[105] At the present, we can only say that most of these pieces of Rus' inlaid enamel were produced by Kiev craftsmen for wealthy princely, boyar, and ecclesiastical clients. Since such expensive pieces were comparatively rare, they are not found throughout Rus' in numbers approaching glass bracelets or spindle whorls. There seems little doubt, however, that objects of inlaid enamel made in Kiev reached some lay and monastic lords in various parts of Rus'.[106]

Besides inlaid enamelware, Kiev's craftsmen produced a great variety of expensive metal jewelry in the pre-Mongol era: three-beaded earrings, bracelets, belt plaques, pendants, *kolts*, necklaces, medallions, etc. In 60 hoards from the upper city of Kiev alone, over 3,000 items of expensive jewelry have been found.[107] This jewelry was often decorated using such advanced techniques as granulation, filigree work, and niello.[108] As with other crafts, much of this production dates back to the eleventh century although both the quality and quantity of production grew markedly in the twelfth century. In the late twelfth – early thirteenth century, Kiev craftsmen mastered the technique of making imitation molds for gold and silver jewelry.[109] Finds analagous to those from Kiev have been uncovered in Beloozero, Voin', and Novgorod[110] while jewelry cast in Kiev imitation

---

[103] Makarova, *Peregorodchatye emali*, p. 97.

[104] Ibid., Table 1, p. 96.

[105] These 158 Rus' objects with inlaid enamel are described by Makarova, ibid., pp. 102–127.

[106] For Kiev's production of inlaid enamel, see also *Novoe v arkheologii*, pp. 350–51.

[107] *Istoriia Kieva*, p. 92.

[108] Ibid., pp. 93–95.

[109] Ibid., p. 93.

[110] *Novoe v arkheologii*, pp. 309–310.

molds has appeared throughout northern Rus'.[111] Unquestionably, Kiev was the leading center producing a large variety of expensive and increasingly sophisticated jewelry in ever larger quantities for the Rus' market during the pre-Mongol era, and most notably in the twelfth and first half of the thirteenth century.[112] Finds of Kiev jewelry have been reported recently from various sites in the Viatichian land (Serensk, Old Riazan', Slobodka, Pronsk, Moscow).[113] A Kiev three-beaded earring was also found at Borisov in the Polatsk land.[114] Thus, fine jewelry was another item manufactured in Kiev which was exported to other parts of Rus'.

The concentration on glassware, glazed ware, and fine jewelry could easily lead us to overlook the fact that Kiev was also the leading producer of religious goods in pre-Mongol Rus'. Many of the religious items made in Kiev were then exported throughout Rus'. This aspect of Kiev's trade is best exemplified by the cast bronze crosses-encolpia produced in Kiev from special molds.[115] These encolpia have been found throughout Rus': Serensk, Moscow, and Old Riazan' in the Viatichian land,[116] in Novgorod,[117] at Halych, Belz, Zvenyhorod, Lviv, and Dorohychyn in western Rus',[118] at Vasyliv on the Dniester,[119] at Drutsk, Minsk, Mstsislaŭ, Smolensk, Navahrudak, and Polatsk in modern Belorussia,[120] at Toropets in northwestern Rus',[121] and at various towns along the Nieman.[122] In other words, there is a growing body of evidence to show that Kiev's craftsmen developed an

---

[111] *Istoriia Kieva*, p. 92.

[112] See the overview of Kiev's jewelry and related craft production in *Novoe v arkheologii*, pp. 349–51.

[113] Nikol'skaia, *Zemlia Viatichei*, p. 285.

[114] Shtykhov, "Kiev i goroda Polotskoi zemli," p. 62.

[115] *Istoriia Kieva*, p. 92, where such a cross-encolpion is also illustrated.

[116] Nikol'skaia, *Zemlia Viatichei*, p. 285.

[117] M. V. Sedova, *Iuvelirnye izdeliia Drevnego Novgoroda (X–XV vv.)* (Moscow, 1981), pp. 57–61.

[118] Petegirich, "Iz istorii ekonomicheskikh," p. 154.

[119] Timoshchuk, "Drevnerusskie goroda," pp. 133–34.

[120] Shtykhov, "Kiev i goroda Polotskoi zemli," p. 62; idem., *Goroda Polotskoi zemli*, p. 115; Gurevich, *Drevnii Novogrudok*, pp. 152–54; Alekseev, *Smolenskaia zemlia*, pp. 88, 92; Zagorul'skii, *Vozniknovenie Minska*, pp. 225, 284.

[121] Alekseev, *Smolenskaia zemlia*, p. 88.

[122] Zverugo, "Kiev i zemli," p. 120.

active commerce supplying these crosses-encolpia to numerous towns throughout Rus'.

Excavations also suggest that Kiev's craftsmen made other religious items for export throughout Rus'. For example, church chandeliers and lamps with three tabs imported from Kiev were found in the Viatichian land[123] and along the Nieman.[124] Bronze icon lamps with three holes for hanging, made in Kiev, have been uncovered at Slobodka in the Viatichian land, at the Borodino fortified site near Smolensk, at Raikovets, and at Hrodna.[125] Stone crosses and icons made in Kiev were excavated at Minsk.[126] Stone icons from Kiev were also found at the Borodino site.[127] Slate crosses made in Kiev have been uncovered at Navahrudak.[128] Thus, the craftsmen of Kiev supplied a large variety of religious goods to numerous towns located throughout Rus'.

Large numbers of spindle whorls made of red or rose slate have been uncovered in the pre-Mongol strata of almost all Rus' towns as well as in neighboring lands. The red slate used to make these spindle whorls came from the area of Ovruch some 125 kilometers northwest of Kiev in modern Zhytomyr oblast'. Excavations at Ovruch found the remains of workshops where this local slate was made into spindle whorls and other objects.[129] Red slate was used as building material and for sarcophagi in various places in Kiev, e.g., the Cathedral of St. Sophia, the Church of St. Iryna, the Golden Gate. But, the absence of workshops for processing this slate in Kiev itself had created the impression that products of red Ovruch slate were not made in Kiev.[130] Recently, however, evidence pointing to the manufacture of red slate spindle whorls in Kiev has come to light. In 1975, for instance, the remains of a workshop where red slate spindle whorls were made was found in the Podil quarter of Kiev. As a result, we

---

[123] Nikol'skaia, *Zemlia Viatichei*, p. 285.

[124] Zverugo, "Kiev i zemli," p. 120.

[125] Nikol'skaia, *Zemlia Viatichei*, p. 164.

[126] Zagorul'skii, *Vozniknovenie Minska*, pp. 228, 284.

[127] Alekseev, *Smolenskaia zemlia*, p. 88.

[128] Gurevich, *Drevnii Novogrudok*, pp. 152, 154.

[129] For the Ovruch red slate spindle whorls, see B. A. Rybakov, *Remeslo Drevnei Rusi* (Moscow, 1948), pp. 188–202, where these workshops are noted on pp. 190–91.

[130] Ibid., p. 190.

must now reckon with the manufacture of these spindle whorls in Kiev itself.[131]

In fact, the problem becomes even more complex since recent digs also suggest that red slate spindle whorls were made elsewhere in Rus' besides Ovruch and Kiev. Unfortunately, we know of no way at present to determine at which center particular red slate spindle whorls were made. Thus, we can only assume that some of the many red slate spindle whorls found in every Rus' town probably came from Kiev. And, even if the percentage made in Kiev was relatively low, the finds of red slate spindle whorls are so numerous that it would suggest the existence of a very active craft production within Kiev geared to the larger Rus' market. In order to understand better the potential volume of red slate spindle whorl production in Kiev, let us briefly describe the finds from only a few sites within Rus'. From this small sample, we can project what the total production might have been.

At Beloozero, the 667 spindle whorls of Ovruch slate were distributed as follows:[132]

Tenth century	2
Late tenth – early eleventh century	32
Eleventh century	144
Twelfth century	219
First half of thirteenth century	161
Second half of thirteenth – fourteenth century	73

Around 2,000 slate spindle whorls were found in the excavations of the 1950s – early 1960s in Novgorod.[133] Summarizing the data from each of the twenty-eight strata, we can say that these spindle whorls appeared in the earliest stratum (953 – 972), that the number grew markedly in the late eleventh – early twelfth century, and remained relatively high until the Mongol conquest. Even though the Mongol conquest put an end to new production, older slate spindle whorls remained in circulation in ever declining numbers until the mid-fifteenth century. A recent count, which includes figures from excava-

[131] *Novoe v arkheologii*, pp. 330 – 32.

[132] Golubeva, *Ves' i slaviane*, p. 179.

[133] Rybina, *Arkheologicheskie ocherki*, pp. 24, 160 – 61.

tions conducted after the 1960s, puts the number of slate spindle whorls found in Novgorod at over 3,000.[134]

In just the upper castle part of Polatsk some 451 slate spindle whorls were uncovered.[135] Excavations at the small town of Volkovysk in the Neman region found 224 slate spindle whorls in strata of the early eleventh to fourteenth centuries.[136] Just the 1959 excavations at Minsk revealed 234 slate spindle whorls.[137] Digs at the small town of Lukomil' in the Polatsk land produced 222 slate spindle whorls.[138] Some 65 slate spindle whorls were found in excavations at Turaŭ,[139] while 74 such spindle whorls were reported from the digs at Pinsk.[140] Almost a hundred slate spindle whorls were found at Navahrudak.[141] Lesser numbers of spindle whorls made from Ovruch slate have turned up at almost every town in what is now Belorussia and adjacent regions.[142] Finds of Ovruch slate spindle whorls also occur throughout Galicia and Volhynia[143] as well as in Suzdalia.[144]

Even this very short and highly selective sampling makes it clear that hundreds of thousands of spindle whorls made from Ovruch slate were apparently produced in pre-Mongol Rus'. And, as recent excavations suggest, a significant portion of these slate spindle whorls were no doubt made in the workshops of Kiev and then exported throughout Rus' and even abroad.

For a long time it was believed that the amber found in medieval Rus' came almost entirely from the Baltic. Recently, however, E. A. Rybina has argued that amber from Kiev and the middle Dnieper

[134] Kolchin and Ianin, *Novgorodskii sbornik*, p. 81.
[135] Shtykhov, *Goroda Polotskoi zemli*, p. 114.
[136] Zverugo, "Kiev i zemli," p. 116.
[137] Shtykhov, *Goroda Polotskoi zemli*, p. 114.
[138] Ibid., pp. 46, 114.
[139] Lysenko, *Goroda Turovskoi zemli*, p. 41.
[140] Ibid., p. 86.
[141] Gurevich, *Drevnii Novogrudok*, p. 154, Table 21.
[142] Lysenko, *Goroda Turovskoi zemli*, reports thirty-seven from Slutsk (p. 150) while Shtykhov, *Goroda Polotskoi zemli*, notes lesser quantities at Zaslaŭ (pp. 85–87), Logoisk (p. 90), Braslaŭ (p. 58), Kukenois (p. 60), Barysaŭ (p. 101), Kopys' (pp. 94–95), Orsha (p. 97), and Vitsebsk (pp. 38–40).
[143] Petegirich, "Iz istorii ekonomicheskikh," p. 153.
[144] Sedova and Belen'kaia, "Okol'nyi gorod," pp. 98–99, 103, 112.

region was exported to Novgorod during the pre-Mongol era.[145] Rybina's thesis rests on two foundations. First, the distribution pattern of the amber found in the pre-Mongol strata of Novgorod is the same as that for other southern imports which were brought to Novgorod by the Dnieper route.[146] Therefore, Rybina concluded that amber was also imported by the Dnieper route to Novgorod. Second, there is definite evidence that amber deposits are located in the Kiev region as well as in Volhynia, around the Dnieper rapids, and in the former Poltava guberniia.[147] In addition, the authors of excavations at Belaia Vezha along the lower Don, at a site in the Volga Bulgar lands, and of several North Caucasian cemeteries all concluded that the amber from these various sites came from the Dnieper.[148] Rybina thus maintained that it was this indigenous Dnieper amber which was exported from Kiev to Novgorod from the tenth century until the time of the Mongol conquest.[149]

Rybina's thesis clearly merits serious attention. To resolve this issue, scientific analyses were undertaken in the hope they might settle conclusively the question of the source of Novgorod's amber in the pre-Mongol era. However, the infrared spectra of Baltic and Dnieper amber proved to be identical since they come from the very same amber province.[150] Thus, as R. L. Rozenfel'dt remarked, "by chemical composition, quality, and external appearance" it is impossible to distinguish between Baltic and Dnieper amber.[151] As a result, specialists have not been able to determine scientifically whether the amber from pre-Mongol sites came from the Baltic or the Dnieper.

While Rybina's two main arguments possess a certain attraction, I do not find them completely convincing. The similarity in the Novgorod distribution pattern of amber and other southern imports could be coincidental. A similar pattern does not necessarily mean a similar source. And, just because Kiev's pre-Mongol inhabitants had

---

[145] Rybina, *Arkheologicheskie ocherki*, pp. 38–45.
[146] Ibid., p. 41.
[147] Ibid., pp. 41–43.
[148] Ibid., pp. 43–44.
[149] Ibid., p. 44.
[150] Ibid., pp. 44–45.
[151] R. L. Rozenfel'dt, "Iantar' na Rusi (X–XIII vv.)," in *Problemy Sovetskoi arkheologii* (Moscow, 1978), p. 197.

potential local sources of amber does not demonstrate that they in fact used these sources to export thousands of amber pieces to Novgorod. It is also not clear why pre-Mongol Novgorod would import large quantities of amber from Kiev rather than the eastern Baltic, a traditional supplier of amber to northern Russia. In sum, Rybina's thesis about the export of Dnieper amber to Novgorod prior to 1240 needs further study.

It is pertinent to note here that Soviet archaeologists themselves seem uncertain about the source of the amber found in pre-Mongol Novgorod, Kiev, and other Rus' sites. Rozenfel'dt's special article on amber from pre-Mongol Rus' appeared in the same year as Rybina's book. In this article, Rozenfel'dt stated that the "overwhelming majority of amber objects in Rus' were made from Baltic amber." He then discussed the main routes by which amber was brought from the Baltic coasts to Rus' and how it was transported along these routes.[152] In sum, Rozenfel'dt acknowledged the similarity of Baltic and Dnieper amber but clearly implied that most of the amber in pre-Mongol Rus' originated in the Baltic. In addition, Rozenfel'dt mentioned the 1967 discovery of an early thirteenth-century amber workshop in Novgorod. He claimed that over 700 pieces of amber, "unquestionably of Baltic origin," were found in this workshop.[153] However, the source cited by Rozenfel'dt notes the over 700 pieces of unworked amber from the jewelry workshop but does not say anything about the origins of this amber.[154] I have attempted to clarify this issue by examining several recent studies pertaining to Novgorod, Novgorod's jewelry crafts, and the excavation in question but without much luck. One recent study does indicate, however, that over 3,000 amber pieces and over 900 amber objects had been found in the Novgorod excavations. This study mentioned two major accumulations: 1,151 amber pieces from the twelfth-century "residence of the artist" and over 800 pieces from a twelfth–early thirteenth-century residence of a merchant. Finally, this study simply repeats Rybina's

---

[152] Ibid., pp. 197–98.

[153] Ibid., p. 199.

[154] N. V. Ryndina and A. S. Khoroshev, "Raskopki v Novgorode," *Arkheologicheskie otkrytiia 1967 goda* (Moscow, 1968), p. 18.

thesis that amber in pre-Mongol Novgorod came from the Dnieper.[155] In short, we seem to lack a detailed study which would clarify the discrepancy between Rybina and Rozenfel'dt. The absence of such a study no doubt accounts for the ambivalence of the archaeologists excavating Kiev. They appear uncertain themselves whether the amber they have uncovered was of local origin or came from the Baltic.[156]

There are three possible solutions to the amber question. The traditional view that almost all amber came from the Baltic may be the correct one. Or, Rybina is right that Novgorod, and presumably other Rus' cities, imported amber from the middle Dnieper. Finally, there is a compromise solution. Lysenko, for example, notes many finds in Turaŭ of dark Dnieper amber as well as light Baltic amber.[157] In this last scenario, the amber found in pre-Mongol Rus' came from both the Dnieper and the Baltic.

In a certain sense, the source of the amber may not be that important. The most significant consideration may well be that Kiev was clearly a major center for producing items of amber during the pre-Mongol period. Using either local amber or imported Baltic amber, or both, Kiev's craftsmen fashioned a variety of amber beads, pendants, rings, crosses, and other goods. Four workshops where such amber products were made in the pre-Mongol era have been uncovered in Kiev, two in the upper city and two in the Podil.[158] We can safely assume that the amber objects made in these four workshops were intended both for the local market and for other Rus' towns and hamlets. The discovery of amber workshops in Vaŭkavysk, Novgorod, Beloozero, Old Riazan', Rostov, and Murom also points to considerable demand for objects of amber throughout Rus'.[159] Thus, Kiev's exports to the rest of Rus' unquestionably included a variety of finished amber objects.

---

[155] Kolchin and Ianin, *Novgorodskii sbornik*, pp. 85–86. B. A. Kolchin, A. S. Khoroshev, V. L. Ianin, *Usad'ba Novgorodskogo khudozhnika XII v.* (Moscow, 1981), p. 122, note the 1,151 amber pieces briefly without any analysis.

[156] *Novoe v arkheologii*, p. 334.

[157] Lysenko, *Goroda Turovskoi zemli*, p. 68.

[158] *Novoe v arkheologii*, pp. 333–34.

[159] Rozenfel'dt, "Iantar' na Rusi," pp. 199–200.

The above discussion of the exports of Kiev's craft production throughout Rus' is necessarily incomplete. It does not include all the different goods made in Kiev nor all the relevant finds from elsewhere in Rus'. However, even this brief overview leaves no doubt that in the twelfth and first half of the thirteenth century Kiev's trade with the rest of Rus' flourished and that this lively domestic commerce was based, to a great extent, upon the large number of various products made in the many workshops of the city.

B. *Kiev's International Trade*

Kiev's active commerce depended upon more than just the export of the goods made in its own workshops. Kiev was also a major middle-man in the diffusion of imported products to large parts of Rus'. Kiev's role as a key commercial intermediary is perhaps best seen by examining the wine and olive oil trade of pre-Mongol Rus'.

Excavations at Kiev and other Rus' towns have uncovered thousands of amphora shards. In general, these shards come from two basic types of amphorae. The first, usually made from red clay, was pear-shaped with a round bottom, short throat, and small bow-like handles. In Rus' such an amphora was called a *korchaga*. The second type, made from red and gray clay, was longer and thinner, had a narrow bottom and long throat, and was distinguished by high, arched handles.[160] At one time it was argued that some of these amphorae were made in Kiev. The reasons advanced for local production did not, however, convince all specialists on pre-Mongol Kiev.[161] But, recent studies of the chemical composition of red-clay and gray-clay amphorae found in Kiev points to two different centers of production. The gray-clay amphorae were exactly like the pottery made from local clay while the red-clay amphorae were completely different in their composition from Kievan pottery.[162] In any event, it is now univer-sally accepted that the red-clay amphorae found throughout Rus' were imports from Byzantium and the Black Sea and most probably from

---

[160] For illustrations of these two basic types see *Novoe v arkheologii*, fig. 160, p. 375, and A. L. Iakobson, *Keramika i keramicheskoe proizvodstvo srednevekovoi Tavriki* (Leningrad, 1979), fig. 68, p. 110 and fig. 69, p. 112.

[161] *Novoe v arkheologii*, pp. 286–87.

[162] Ibid., pp. 288–89.

such Byzantine centers in the northern Black Sea as the Crimea.[163]

The import of amphorae to Kiev from the Black Sea dates to the first half of the tenth century, if not earlier. A Byzantine amphora with the monogram of Emperor Constantine VIII (913–959) was found near Rzhyshchiv in Kiev oblast' while another amphora of the ninth–tenth century, probably from the Crimea, was uncovered in the Podil section of Kiev itself.[164] Shards of these imported "provincial Byzantine" amphorae, as well as an occasional whole amphora, have been found in large numbers from digs throughout Kiev: in the upper city, in the Podil section, in the Kopyriv Kinets, and in surrounding suburban regions. These amphorae appeared in Kiev between the tenth century and the mid-thirteenth century in growing intensity and are especially numerous in strata of the second half of the eleventh and twelfth centuries.[165] Recent excavations in Kiev have revealed more dwellings with large concentrations of amphora shards as well as regions with hundreds of these shards.[166] Moreover, each new year's excavations produce more reports of imported amphora shards from pre-Mongol Kiev.[167] Thus, there is no doubt that large numbers of amphorae were imported into Kiev from the northern Black Sea during the pre-Mongol era.

Amphorae were usually used to carry wine, olive oil, and other liquids. Consequently, the finds of numerous amphorae and amphora shards from the northern Black Sea in Kiev and other Rus' cities seem to be clear-cut evidence that large quantities of wine and olive oil were being shipped from the Black Sea to Rus'. However, many aspects of this trade are still uncertain. We do not know, for example, if all the amphorae were sent to Kiev with their liquid contents or whether this trade was in the hands of Black Sea or Rus' merchants.[168] In any event, unless future studies show otherwise, these amphorae

---

[163] Ibid., pp. 288, 373–74; Iakobson, *Keramika*, pp. 74–75, 109, 111–13; Rybina, *Arkheologicheskie ocherki*, p. 28.

[164] Iakobson, *Keramika*, pp. 74–75.

[165] *Novoe v arkheologii*, p. 373.

[166] Ibid.

[167] S. R. Kilievych (Kilievich), "Raskopki na territorii monastyrskogo dvora v Kieve," *Arkheologicheskie otkrytiia 1983 goda* (Moscow, 1985), p. 281, where two whole imported amphorae from a tenth-century dwelling are noted from the 1983 digs.

[168] *Novoe v arkheologii*, p. 374.

can be considered as evidence of imports of wine and olive oil from the Black Sea into Rus'.

Besides Kiev, these "provincial Byzantine" amphorae were imported into various other towns of the middle Dnieper. They have been found, for example, at Voin' south of Kiev,[169] at Vyshhorod,[170] in Pereiaslav-Khmel'nyts'kyi,[171] at Bakozhyna near Kiev,[172] and elsewhere in the middle Dnieper. These finds suggest that some wine and olive oil going to Kiev was exchanged along the way or that Kiev re-exported some of its wine and olive oil to towns in the middle Dnieper.

But, Kiev also re-exported a significant part of its imported wine and olive oil to many towns in modern Belorussia and northwestern Rus'. In a recent study, for instance, Gurevich noted the presence of shards of amphorae made in the northern Black Sea in numerous Belorussian towns between the eleventh and thirteenth centuries; these towns included Brest, Pinsk, Turaŭ, Slutsk, Slonim, Vaŭkavysk, Turiisk, Hrodna, Navahrudak, Gorodishche na Menks, Minsk, Zaslaŭ, Logoisk, Borisov, Lukomil', Polatsk, Vitsebsk, and Orsha.[173] At some of these towns only a relatively small number of shards have as yet been found. But, hundreds and even thousands of shards of "provincial Byzantine" amphorae have turned up in the excavations of many towns.

The data from a few of these sites is as follows: at Navahrudak, some 2,200–2,500 shards of Black Sea amphorae were found in strata of the twelfth–thirteenth centuries;[174] around 1,600 amphora shards were found at Vaŭkavysk;[175] at Turaŭ, 346 such amphora shards were found, of which 174 were in strata from the first half of the thirteenth

---

[169] Iakobson, *Keramika*, p. 111.

[170] Ibid., p. 113.

[171] Ibid.

[172] Ibid.

[173] F. D. Gurevich, "Sviazi drevnikh gorodov Belorussii s prichernomor'em i Sredizemnomor'em," *Drevnerusskoe gosudarstvo i slaviane* (Minsk, 1983), fig. 13 (map), p. 64. Also see Shtykhov, "Kiev i goroda Polotskoi zemli," p. 61; idem, *Goroda Polotskoi zemli*, p. 115.

[174] Gurevich, *Drevnii Novogrudok*, Table 21, p. 154; idem, "Sviazi drevnikh gorodov," p. 63.

[175] Zverugo, "Kiev i zemli," p. 120; Gurevich, "Sviazi drevnikh gorodov," p. 63.

century;[176] some 109 amphora shards were uncovered at Pinsk;[177] and, at Polatsk, 187 amphora shards and one crushed red-clay amphora were found.[178] This evidence leaves no doubt that a substantial part of the wine and olive oil imported into Kiev from the south was then shipped by the upper Dnieper to numerous cities and towns in what is now Belorussia. Judging from the strata in which these shards were found, the export of Black Sea wine and olive oil from Kiev to Belorussia continued up to the time of the Mongol conquest.

The wine and olive oil reaching Kiev from the Black Sea was also re-shipped to northwestern Rus'. Some 200 amphora shards were found at Novgorod during the excavations of the 1950s and early 1960s. These shards first appeared in strata of the late tenth century, gradually grew more numerous, reaching a high point in the twelfth century, and then disappeared with the Mongol conquest.[179] More recent figures indicate that in thirty years of excavations at Novgorod over 700 shards of imported amphorae have been collected.[180] In fact, in just one Novgorod residence excavated between 1973 and 1977, which dated to the second half of the twelfth and early thirteenth centuries, over 130 amphora shards were found.[181] There is no doubt that significant quantities of wine and olive oil from the Black Sea were reaching Novgorod via Kiev.

Novgorod was not the only town in northwestern Rus' to import wine and olive oil by way of Kiev. Almost five hundred shards of amphorae from the northern Black Sea were found in the digs at Beloozero. These shards were distributed, by percentages, as follows:[182]

Tenth Century	4%
Eleventh Century	46%
Twelfth Century	17%
Thirteenth Century	33%

---

[176] Lysenko, *Goroda Turovskoi zemli*, fig. 5, p. 44.
[177] Ibid., p. 86.
[178] Shtykhov, *Goroda Polotskoi zemli*, p. 115; idem, *Drevnii Polotsk*, pp. 87, 104.
[179] Rybina, *Arkheologicheskie ocherki*, p. 29.
[180] Kolchin, Khoroshev, Ianin, *Usad'ba Novgorodskogo khudozhnika*, p. 86.
[181] Ibid., pp. 86–88.
[182] Golubeva, *Ves' i slavanie*, p. 188.

These figures suggest that wine and olive oil were first imported into Beloozero in substantial quantities during the eléventh century. Following a decline in the twelfth century, the exports of wine and olive oil grew sharply during the first half of the thirteenth century.

In addition to amphorae, other vessels made in the northern Black Sea or southern Rus' and used to carry or preserve wine have turned up in modern Belorussia and northwestern Rus'. At Beloozero, for example, 14 shards of red-clay jugs like those made in Taman' were uncovered in strata of the eleventh century.[183] Small *korchagas* from Kiev and other south Rus' towns have been found at Kopys' and Drutsk in the Polatsk land. These jugs were used for table wine.[184] Thus, not only did Kiev re-export wine and olive oil from the Black Sea to the north but it also produced some of the containers used to store this wine.

In sum, there is no doubt that Kiev imported large quantities of wine and olive oil from the northern Black Sea starting in the eleventh century and then shipped a goodly portion of this wine and oil to numerous towns of Belorussia and northwestern Rus'.

Shards of red-clay Black Sea amphorae have turned up in other parts of Rus'. Such finds are reported, for instance, from Halych, Belz, Zvenyhorod, Lenkivtsi, and Vasyliv in western Rus'[185] as well as in Moscow, Serensk, Old Riazan', Pronsk, and Slobodka in eastern Rus'.[186] While some of these amphorae, including their contents, may have been shipped via Kiev and the Dnieper, it is far more likely that most were transported by other, more direct routes, e.g., by the Dniester, Southern Buh (Boh), and Prut to western Rus' and by the Don and Northern Donets' to eastern Rus'. But, here again, Kiev may also have supplied some of the vessels used to store the wine locally.[187] Hopefully, future research can determine the precise routes by which wine and olive oil from the Black Sea reached western and eastern

---

[183] Ibid.

[184] Shtykhov, "Kiev i goroda Polotskoi zemli," p. 61; idem, *Goroda Polotskoi zemli*, p. 115.

[185] Petegirich, "Iz istorii ekonomicheskikh," p. 156; Timoshchuk, "Drevnerusskie goroda," pp. 129, 133.

[186] Nikol'skaia, *Zemlia Viatichei*, p. 285.

[187] Petegirich, "Iz istorii ekonomicheskikh," p. 155, notes the shard of an amphora of the Kievan type found at Dorohobuzh.

Rus'. There seems little doubt, however, that Kiev was the key middleman in the flow of such products northward into Belorussia and northwestern Rus'.

Space does not permit us to elaborate on all the other southern products which reached Rus' towns by way of Kiev. But, as Gurevich has shown, a wide variety of goods from the eastern Mediterranean and the Black Sea was imported into what is now Belorussia during the pre-Mongol era: glass vessels and goblets, bracelets and other glass jewelry, silks, various religious items such as icons, boxwood combs, and walnuts. The main route for the transit of such goods to Belorussia was the Dnieper, i.e., they came by way of Kiev.[188] Thus, the archaeological evidence from excavations at numerous Rus' towns clearly demonstrates that Kiev was the major center for the transit trade between Rus' and the Mediterranean, Near Eastern, and Black Sea worlds during the pre-Mongol era. This trade was especially active during the twelfth and the first half of the thirteenth centuries. Kiev unquestionably occupied a key role in the international commerce of Rus' at this time.

Conclusions

To summarize, the following are some of the conclusions that can be drawn from the data presented in this study.

1. The handicraft production of Rus' and Kiev in particular have long been known. The study of these workshops began in the pre-revolutionary period and has been continued by Soviet scholars in such well known books as Rybakov's *Handicrafts of Ancient Rus'* (*Remeslo Drevnei Rusi*). Nevertheless, there has been a certain reluctance to accept the claims of Soviet archaeologists concerning the very diverse and highly developed state of handicraft production in pre-Mongol Rus'. It has seemed to most Western scholars, myself included, that our Soviet colleagues were exaggerating the level and extent of this handicraft production. Perhaps such an attitude arose from our absorption with written sources and corresponding neglect of the many towns literally being uncovered before our very eyes. In any event, the time has come to abandon such doubts. We might still

---

[188] Gurevich, "Sviazi drevnikh gorodov," pp. 63–66. The walnut shells found at Novgorod are examined in Rybina, *Arkheologicheskie ocherki*, p. 30.

question the views of Soviet colleagues on the role of the Vikings or the existence of feudalism in Kievan Rus', but they have been absolutely correct about the extent of handicraft production in pre-Mongol Rus'. If anything, new excavations have shown that even some Soviet specialists have not always appreciated the variety and volume of this production.

2. Soviet scholars have done an excellent job in examining craft production from specific sites as well as producing studies of certain crafts such as glassmaking and enamelware. They have not yet incorporated this research into a general reappraisal of Kiev's history and trade. Soviet scholars have noted the active internal trade of Rus' and they have emphasized the twelfth and first half of the thirteenth century. But they have not offered a new model of Kiev's trade to accommodate the growing body of archaeological evidence nor have they considered its implications for Kiev's history. The aim of this paper has been to begin to create such a new model and to suggest some of the historical ramifications.

3. The essence of the model advanced here is that the traditional prerevolutionary and Western view of Kiev's trade has been inaccurate. We have too long been mesmerized by a few superb tenth-century sources such as the Rus'-Byzantine trade treaties and the account of Constantine VII in *De administrando imperio*. There is little evidence that Kiev had any trade in the ninth century. Kiev's trade began in the tenth century but at that time it functioned as a mafioso extortion operation run by the princes. Kiev's true trade only started in the eleventh century and was sparked by the growing local demand for a variety of expensive and sophisticated goods by an increasingly sedentarized ruling class and a new ecclesiastical market. In this process, the Rus' conversion to Orthodoxy seems to have acted as a powerful catalyst in refining tastes, introducing new crafts and advanced methods, and creating markets. This local demand sparked the growing production of Kiev's workshops in the eleventh century, which led to a period in the twelfth century when both the quantity and quality of craft production in Kiev increased markedly. Kiev's commerce, driven in large part by this growing production, *expanded* as time went on. It did *not* peak in the tenth century and decline as the Mongol conquest approached.

4. The twelfth-century take-off era in Kiev's artisan production and trade was also characterized by a large-scale process of technology transfer within Rus'. Originally Greek masters had introduced such crafts as glassmaking, enameling, glazing, and the production of fine jewelry into Kiev during the late tenth and first half of the eleventh century. Now Rus' masters from Kiev as well as a few newly invited Greek masters spread these crafts to towns throughout Rus'. Kiev lost its monopoly over the production of "high-tech" products as its craftsmen began to set up shops elsewhere in Rus'.

5. The above picture of Kiev's flourishing trade after ca. 1100 casts new light on the city's political history at the time. All too often, scholars have emphasized the political decline of Kiev after the reign of Volodimer Monomakh (1113–1125). We have been told that Kiev clearly lost its pre-eminence after being sacked by Andrei Bogoliub-skii who added insult to injury by refusing to make Kiev his capital. Any doubters were reminded of the terrible 1203 sack of Kiev by the Rus' prince Rurik and his Polovtsian allies. When the fierce struggle among the Rus' princes to control Kiev is mentioned, Kiev is usually depicted as a "symbolic" prize sought after because of its past glory and prestige. After reviewing the evidence of Kiev's diverse production and prosperous trade, one is forced to dismiss such ideas. The Rus' princes fought so long and so hard for Kiev because of its wealth and not because of its symbolic importance. In her study of Rus' hoards of the pre-Mongol era, G. F. Korzukhina enumerated 111 hoards dated between the 1170s and 1240. Of these 111 hoards, 47 were deposited in Kiev itself, 12 were deposited in Kniazha Hora near Kiev, and 15 were deposited elsewhere in the former Kiev province.[189] In addition, some 270 silver and gold *grivny* or monetary ingots have been found at 41 different points in Kiev. These *grivny* from Kiev, which weigh 45 kg, constitute about one-third of all Rus' *grivny* of the twelfth–thirteenth century, whose total weight was 130 kg.[190] Kiev was not a declining city sought only for its former glory. Kiev in the century before the Mongol conquest was a wealthy,

---

[189] G. F. Korzukhina, *Russkie klady IX – XIII vv.* (Moscow and Leningrad, 1954), pp. 105–150, Map 5.

[190] *Novoe v arkheologii*, p. 367 and p. 369 for a map of Kiev showing their find spots.

prosperous city which was sacked and fiercely contested precisely because it was so rich and flourishing.

6. Kiev's active trade in the immediate pre-Mongol era was the result of a highly complex process. A variety of goods made in Kiev's workshops were exported throughout Rus'. In return, raw products such as Ovruch slate, possibly Baltic amber, and, most important of all, northern furs were sent to Kiev. Some of these furs were then exchanged for southern imports such as wine and olive oil, products which were also re-exported in part to the north to pay for the furs. In short, Kiev was the center of a highly developed international and domestic network through which imports and exports as well as raw materials and finished goods were transported to and from a large number of local markets in Eastern Europe.

7. This study, with its limits of time and space, has only touched upon the leading crafts of Kiev and the finds from a relatively few sites. We clearly need detailed and comprehensive studies of many specific products and towns. In addition, we need broader studies which seek to illuminate Kiev's trade in the light of the archaeological evidence.

8. Finally, the flourishing of Kiev's trade explains numerous isolated references to local as well as international trade in our written sources. When the future St. Theodosius followed a group of merchants taking their heavily laden wagons along the road from Kursk to Kiev, we catch a glimpse of the Rus' merchants who enabled Kiev's trade with other Rus' towns to flourish.[191] And, when the Prince of Kiev led his forces against the Polovtsians in order to protect the Greek route, we see how aware the political leaders of the city were of the need to keep goods flowing between Kiev and the Black Sea.[192] In conclusion, we need to integrate all the written evidence and numismatic data with the archaeological materials to create a new synthesis which examines in depth the flourishing of Kiev's trade between ca. 1100 and ca. 1240.

---

[191] "The Life of St. Theodosius," in G. P. Fedotov, comp. and ed., *A Treasury of Russian Spirituality* (New York, 1965), p. 21.

[192] *The Kievan Chronicle*, trans. and comm. Lisa L. Heinrich (Ann Arbor, 1982), pp. 286–290, (s.a. 1170).

Part II: The Seventeenth and Eighteenth Centuries

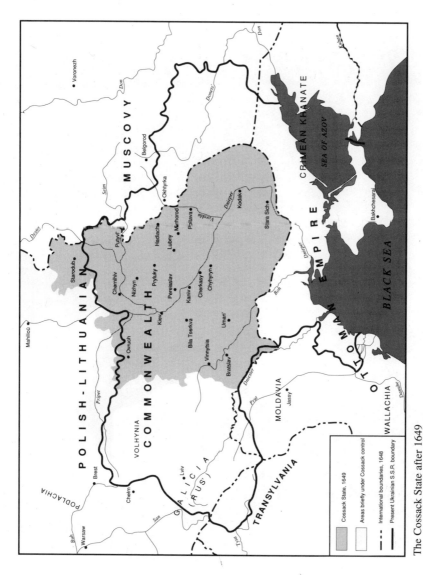

The Cossack State after 1649

(based on map in: Paul Robert Magocsi, *Ukraine: A Historical Atlas*, 3rd. rev. ed. [Toronto, 1987]; reprinted with permission from author)

CHAPTER FIVE

Cossack Ukraine and Baltic Trade 1600 – 1648: Some Observations on an Unresolved Issue

Stephen Velychenko

Between 1550 and 1700 Eastern Europe experienced a "second serf-dom"; that is to say, a period marked by peasant impoverishment, urban decline, and general economic regression.[1] Most historians see a relationship between this decline and agrarian export production, although they differ on the issue of whether export trade with Western Europe, which began in the middle of the sixteenth century, was the major cause of this "development of underdevelopment."[2] In the case of the Polish-Lithuanian Commonwealth, it is generally accepted that central Poland, the Western Ukraine (Red Ruś), the western part of the

---

[1] For discussion of the issue see L. Makkai, "Neo-Serfdom: Its Origins and Nature in East Central Europe," *Slavic Review* 34, no. 2 (June 1975):237 – 38; and W. Rusiński, "Some Remarks on the Differentiation of Agrarian Structure in East Central Europe, from the 16th to 18th Century," *Studia Historiae Oeconomicae* 13 (1978):83 – 96.

[2] M. M. Tsvibak, "Istoricheskaia teoriia Marksa i Engelsa i krepostnichestvo 'vtorogo izdaniia' v vostochnoi Evrope," in A. G. Prigozhin, ed., *Karl Marks i problemy istorii dokapitalisticheskikh formatsii* (Moscow, 1934), pp. 451 – 506; S. D. Skazkin, "Osnovnye problemy tak nazyvaemogo 'vtorogo izdaniia krepostnichestva' v srednei i vostochnoi Evrope," *Voprosy istorii*, 1958, no. 2, pp. 105 – 19; I. Wallerstein, *The Modern World System* (New York and London, 1974); R. Brenner, "The Origins of Capitalist Development: a Critique of Neo-Smithian Marxism," *New Left Review* 104 (July – August 1977):25 – 93; J. Topolski, "Sixteenth-Century Poland and the Turning Point in European Economic Development," in J. K. Fedorowicz, ed., *A Republic of Nobles* (Cambridge, 1982), pp. 79 – 90.

Volhynian palatinate, as well as western parts of present-day Belorussia and Lithuania, were all part of the Baltic trade system and affected by "neo-serfdom."[3] There is ambiguity, however, about the economic evolution of the central, or Cossack, Ukraine, that is, the Kievan, Bratslav, and the eastern part of the Volhynian palatinates. Whereas some historians dwell upon the misery and exploitation rampant in the central Ukraine before 1648, others draw attention to the vigorous growth that occurred in this region during the same period. There is a similar division of opinion among historians over the issue of whether the central Ukraine was influenced by Baltic trade and if so, to what extent.

Perhaps the first to have studied this subject was Wiktor Czermak who, in 1897, claimed that most of the grain exported through Gdańsk came from the central Ukraine. However, the article in which he made this claim was merely a summary of a more extensive work which apparently was not finished, and has remained unpublished. Since Czermak's essay has no footnotes, it is impossible to judge the validity of his assertion.[4] A few years later, Mykhailo Hrushevs'kyi argued that Baltic trade had a profound impact on Ukrainian economic development. He remarked that it was "only a matter of time" before export trade from early seventeenth-century central Ukraine would develop to the same degree that it had earlier in the Western Ukraine, and result in regression and serfdom.[5] In 1927, Andrii Iaroshevych argued indirectly in support of this position. In his monograph, he demonstrated that the presence of an agrarian capitalist lease system in the central Ukraine was a reflection of the fact that this region was

---

[3] For a discussion of regional differences and criticism of the assumption that the Polish-Lithuanian Commonwealth was a fundamentally homogenous entity see A. Kamiński, "Neo-Serfdom in Poland-Lithuania," *Slavic Review* 34, no. 2 (June 1975):253–68. See also A. Wyczański, "L'exploitation seigneuriale (Folwark) et l'exploitation paysanne. Subordination ou rivalité?" *Studia Historiae Oeconomicae* 17 (1983):6–14.

[4] W. Czermak, "Handel zbożowy Gdański w XVII w.," *Sprawozdania z czynności i posiedzeń Akademii Umiejętności* 5 (1898):9.

[5] M. Hrushevs'kyi, *Istoriia Ukrainy-Rusy*, vol. 6 (New York, 1956), p. 212. See also his *Dzherela do istorii Ukrainy-Rusy* (Lviv, 1895–1919), intro. and vol. 7, pp. 7–9; "Studii z ekonomichnoi istorii Ukrainy," *Literaturno-naukovyi vistnyk* 39, no. 7 (July 1907):60; 39, no. 8–9 (August-September 1907):35–37.

part of the western European market.[6] More recently, Maria Bogucka
and Viktor Romanovs'kyi have also subscribed to this view.[7] The
opposite point of view was expressed in 1902 by Adam Szelągowski,
who claimed that the central Ukraine was outside the sphere of the
Baltic trade system during the period in question. Stanisław Mielczarski, a contemporary Polish historian, also concluded that the central
Ukrainian lands were beyond the range of European markets. This
opinion was shared by Edward Lipiński, Witold Kula, and Jan
Malecki.[8]

Neither of these two opposed interpretations is based on what can
be considered sufficient evidence. Those who claimed that the
Ukraine was not part of the European Baltic trade system did so
ostensibly because they did not find more than one instance of a grain
shipment from the central Ukraine to Gdańsk! Hrushevs'kyi and,
later, Bogucka, fared somewhat better in this regard, and in support of
their claim each of them cited some ten instances of grain and potash
shipments from the central Ukraine to the Baltic. Romanovs'kyi gave
no particular examples at all, and merely refers to evidence available
in the Kiev archives, while Iaroshevych pointed out that the number of
sources on the subject was limited and that as far as he could determine, the lease system was only a secondary feature of the Ukrainian
economy.

A review of the relevant literature on the subject reveals that there
are about fifteen known instances of shipments of grain or potash sent
to Gdańsk from the central Ukraine—in some cases from towns as far

[6] A. I. Iaroshevych, "Kapitalistychna orenda na Ukraini za pol's'koi doby," *Zapysky sotsial'no-ekonomichnoho viddilu UAN* 5–6 (1927):250–53.

[7] M. Bogucka, *Handel zagraniczny Gdańska w pierwszej połowie XVII wieku*
(Wroclaw, Warsaw, Cracow, 1970), pp. 76–77; V. O. Romanovs'kyi (V. A.
Romanovskii), "Osnovnye problemy istorii feodalizma na levoberezhnoi Ukraine v
XVII–XVIII vv.," *Ezhegodnik po agrarnoi istorii vostochnoi Evropy, 1961 g.* (Riga,
1963), p. 185.

[8] A. Szelągowski, *Pieniądz i przewrót cen w XVI i XVII w Polsce* (Lviv, 1902),
p. 144; S. Mielczarski, *Rynek zbożowy na ziemach polskich* (Gdańsk, 1962), p. 106;
E. Lipiński, *Historia polskiej myśli społeczno-ekonomicznej do końca XVIII wieku*
(Wroclaw, Warsaw, Cracow, 1975), p. 244; J. Malecki, *Związki handlowe miast polskich z Gdańskiem w XVI i pierwszej połowie XVII wieku* (Wroclaw, Warsaw,
Cracow, 1968), pp. 7–8; W. Kula, *An Economic Theory of the Feudal System* (London, 1976), pp. 137, 162.

east as Uman', Kaniv, and Korsun'.[9] Obviously, on the basis of such a small body of empirical evidence, it is impossible to determine whether these shipments represented isolated instances, or a normal pattern of trade. In short, historians of Ukrainian-Baltic trade have not yet studied the economic relations between Western Europe and the southeastern part of the Commonwealth. They still have not determined how closely pre-1648 Cossack Ukraine was linked to the Baltic trade system, nor to what degree foreign trade influenced Ukrainian social and economic development, nor whether development in this part of Europe occurred because of, or in spite of, export trade. Consequently, whether or not pre-1648 Cossack Ukraine was part of the region affected by the ''second serfdom'' remains an open question. As was pointed out by the Polish historian Zenon Guldon, research is still needed on this subject.[10]

In the USSR, historians have almost totally ignored Ukrainian-Baltic trade and during the past sixty years their generalizations concerning its impact on the Ukraine have varied significantly. In histories of the Ukraine written before the Stalinist terror, it was explained that Baltic trade had reached the Dnieper lands and that foreign commerce had played a dual role in the region's socio-economic development. On the one hand, favorable conditions for agricultural exports stimulated Poland's eastern expansionism and led to increased exploitation. On the other hand, such commerce also created conditions in which new classes and social groups could develop, namely, urban burghers, hired laborers, and a yeoman-type peasantry such as the Cossacks. Furthermore, it was pointed out that small landholders and merchant-producers were harbingers of capital-

---

[9] For shipments other than the ones referred to by the historians mentioned in this paper, see I. Kryp''iakevych, *Bohdan Khmel'nyts'kyi* (Kiev, 1954), p. 20; O. Baranovich, *Ukraina nakanune osvoboditel'noi voiny serediny XVII veka* (Moscow, 1959), p. 59. There are two major published collections of sources relating to the central Ukraine: volumes 5, 6, 21, and 22 of A. Jabłonowski, *Źródła dziejowe* (Warsaw, 1877–1897), and pts. 6 and 7 of *Arkhiv Iugo-Zapadnoi Rossii*. In both, however, economic information concerns primarily Crown holdings. Historians still know little about the economic life of private villages and estates in the central Ukraine.

[10] Z. Guldon, *Z dziejów handlu Rzeczypospolitej w XVI–XVIII wieku* (Kielce, 1980), pp. 31–35.

ism, while conflict between these groups and the "feudal" gentry and magnates, was seen as a struggle over the rights of access to markets. Whereas direct and indirect Ukrainian participation in foreign trade was regarded as a vital precondition for capitalism, the monopoly of foreign trade by the gentry was seen as an impediment to internal economic development. It might be added that the Khmel'nyts'kyi revolt of 1648 may therefore be deemed "progressive' not only because it abolished "feudal" restraints on the Ukrainian economy, but also because it represented the forces of nascent agrarian capitalism.[11] This interpretation, however, was never elaborated upon in detail, nor was it supported by extensive research. Iaroshevych, meanwhile, demonstrated that a principal agent of international capitalist market forces in Cossack Ukraine before 1648 was none other than the Polish leaseholder, or *orendar*, a man whose sole interest was profit and increased production. The implications of this argument are significant for Marxists, since, if the Polish-controlled lease system is regarded as an element in early capitalist development, it becomes difficult to characterize peasant and Cossack resistance to it as "anti-feudal." Furthermore, such resistance could be "progressive" only if it were related to an early form of capitalism.[12] In any case, by approaching Ukrainian economic history with the assumption that Western trade and commerce were a major factor in explaining development, Soviet historians during the 1920s gave their readers much food for thought. But, unfortunately, their insights were not

[11] This interpretation was expounded by Matvii Iavors'kyi, *Narys istorii Ukrainy*, pt. 2 (Kiev, 1924), pp. 17, 69. See also his *Korotka istoriia Ukrainy*, published in six editions by 1928, and his *Istoriia Ukrainy v styslomu narysi*, 2d ed. (1928). Iavors'kyi's interpretation was modified in M. Redin et al., *Istoriia Ukrainy* (Kiev, 1932), pp. 58, 73–74, 92. Here Cossacks were not treated as "bourgeois," and less significance was attached to the role of urban burghers.

[12] Iaroshevych, "Kapitalystychna orenda," pp. 196–232. Implicitly, nascent Ukrainian capitalism was more "progressive" because it was Ukrainian and not foreign, but this line of thought was never developed. In 1953 and 1954, two leading East German historians clashed on the implications of treating demesne export production as a form of capitalism in the pages of *Zeitschrift für Geschichtswissenschaft*. The translation of both articles into Polish sparked off an equally lively debate in Poland. To my knowledge no similar debate has ever taken place in the Ukraine, although in 1965 Olena Kompan noted that peasant wars had to be pro-bourgeois even if they were anti-capitalist. See V. I. Shunkov et al., *Perekhod ot feodalizma k kapitalizmu v Rossii* (Moscow, 1969), p. 250.

followed up and studied in detail, as the theoretical principle that had generated them soon became politically unacceptable.

By 1941, Soviet histories of the Ukraine no longer pointed out that foreign trade and commerce played a positive role in Ukrainian development by stimulating the formation of a non-magnate dominated sphere of petty commodity production, though it was still admitted that these forces had caused Polish expansionism and led to increased exploitation in the Ukraine.[13] Thereafter, official Soviet historiography admits only that the central Ukraine was marginally affected by the Baltic export trade, and notes that the Ukraine was an important source of agricultural products. In general histories, the division of labor, handicraft production, urban growth, internal trade, and trade with Russia are now given more significance than the Ukraine's trade with the West as key factors in the country's history. Also, more attention is given to the negative consequences of export trade, particularly to the rise in exploitation, than to the development that it stimulated, while the link between foreign trade, development, and petty commodity production is usually ignored.[14] It is interesting to note in passing that, although no one knows how much Baltic grain originated in the Ukraine, Soviet historians frequently mention that the amount had to be significant. In the latest economic history of the Ukraine (part 4, chapter 4), R. D. Tolstov has taken this idea a step further and, without statistical evidence, speculated that a significant proportion of the grain exported from Gdańsk after 1583 must have come from the Ukraine because the rise in exports from that city happen to coincide with Polish expansion into the central Ukraine! He then wrote that a drop of "over 200 percent" in Polish exports after

---

[13] K. Huslystyi, *Narysy z istorii Ukrainy* (Kiev, 1941), pp. 91–92; S. M. Belousov et al., *Istoriia Ukrainy* (Kiev, 1941), pp. 68, 73. Between 1932 and 1941 there were no general histories of the Ukraine published in the USSR and very little of any kind of Ukrainian historical scholarship.

[14] O. K. Kasymenko et al., *Istoriia Ukrains'koi RSR*, vol. 1 (Kiev, 1953), pp. 126, 157; K. K. Dubyna et al., *Istoriia Ukrains'koi RSR*, vol. 1 (Kiev, 1967) pp. 122–23; I. Iu. Kondufor et al., *Istoriia Ukrains'koi RSR* vol. 1, pt. 2 (Kiev, 1979–1981), pp. 90, 152–59, 184–85. I. Boiko, in *Selianstvo Ukrainy v druhii polovyni XVI—pershii polovyni XVII st.* (Kiev, 1963), pp. 9, 34, 259, wrote that international markets had almost no impact on the central Ukraine, and that foreign export in general was not an important factor in Ukrainian development, yet he also regretted that "some historians" denied the influence of foreign trade.

1648 proved the importance of the Ukrainian contribution to the Baltic grain trade.[15]

At this point it is worth digressing for a moment to deal with the reasons for the interpretative shift summarized above, as well as the reasons for the lack of research concerning the question of trade relations between the Ukraine and Western Europe. As Soviet publications since the 1930s are supposed to follow a Marxist line, it is useful to begin by noting that Marxist theory postulates that social change is caused by internal contradictions, and not "external" forces such as trade. Consequently, since the 1930s, Soviet historians have been able to justify theoretically the relegation of foreign trade and commerce to a secondary place in their interpretation of Ukrainian history. But in volume 1 of *Das Kapital*, Marx wrote that "Modern capitalism started with world trade and the world markets." Later, in volume 3, he also pointed out that even though foreign trade in itself could not cause a transition from one mode of production to another—contrary to claims by Adam Smith, Henri Pirenne, and, most recently, Immanual Wallerstein—trade was an important agent of change, inasmuch as it gave production the character of "production for exchange value," and turned products "more and more into commodities."[16] Following

---

[15] T. I. Dereviankin, ed., *Istoriia narodnoho hospodarstva Ukrains'koi RSR*, vol. 1 (Kiev, 1983), p. 149. Such reasoning is quite unacceptable, even if Tolstov is given the benefit of the doubt, and it is assumed that all other factors were constant. Figures on the Polish grain trade indicate that the total amount of grain exported in 1648 was the same as in 1609 and 1611, and that in 1649 total exports were 99,808 *lasty* (1 *last* = 2.3 tons), the third greatest amount ever exported from Gdańsk. Conversely, in 1652 there was a drop in exports of 19,454 *lasty* as compared with the previous year's total. The difference was much larger than that between the 1648 and 1647 totals, and might have been caused by Khmel'nyts'kyi's prohibition of exports to Poland in 1651. In any case, we still do not know how much of the 1652 drop can be attributed to the central Ukraine. Between 1608 and 1648 the average total annual export of grain from Gdańsk was 77,333 *lasty*, while between 1648 and 1656, total annual average exports averaged 56,695 *lasty* yearly. This means a difference of 20,638 *lasty* between the pre-1648 and post-1648 figures. Thus according to Tolstov's reasoning, it would appear that roughly 25 percent of total Polish grain exports originated from the Ukraine, while the post-1648 drop would hardly come to 200 percent. See Bogucka, *Handel zagraniczny*, p. 38, and Cz. Biernat, "Statystyka obrotu zbożowego Gdańska od połowy XVII do 1795 r.," *Zapiski historyczne* 23, no. 1 (1957):126–27.

[16] See also the first three chapters of Karl Kautsky, *Agrarfrage* (Stuttgart, 1899) and chapters 27 and 29 of Rosa Luxemburg, *Accumulation of Capital* (London, 1951). It should be remembered that the young Marx shared Smith's optimism about the pro-

this line of thought, pre-Stalinist Ukrainian Marxist historians developed the idea that in early-modern central Ukraine, as in Western Europe, foreign trade and the commercialization it engendered were not only means or agents for the perpetuation of exploitation and subordination, but were also important factors contributing to the dissolution of feudalism, and the establishment of capitalist agriculture and of the preconditions for bourgeois development. From a Marxist point of view this was and is a tenable interpretation of sixteenth- and seventeenth-century Ukrainian economic history which, nevertheless, can be criticized if it reduces capitalism to commodity circulation. But by 1934 Stalin had made Marxism into a doctrine, and the Communist party's conception of Marxism became the only acceptable world view. Subsequently, the 1920s' interpretation of Ukrainian history became unacceptable and historians with "misconceptions" about the significance of commodity forms in feudalism became liable for prosecution under the criminal code. This ideological change can be related to Stalin's policies of forced industrial development and the building of "Socialism in One Country"—policies which called for an atmosphere of aroused passion and urgency, and a historiography to demonstrate how different, backward, and exploited the Russian Empire was in relation to Western Europe. It demanded the creation of a historical image that would highlight the achievements of the present by contrasting it with a deliberately exaggerated picture of past misery, which, whenever possible, was blamed on foreign forces.[17] This resulted in an essentially Russian nationalist, neo-Muscovite and Slavophile-inspired interpretation of the histories of the nations comprising the USSR, one which excluded the possibility

---

gressive nature of trade, and that it was Engels who noted that trade led to backwardness in Eastern Europe. Lenin gave no particular attention to pre-captialist economic history; whenever he did mention the subject, he agreed with Marx about the importance of commodity production and "merchant capitalism." See *Collected Works*, vol. 1 (Moscow, 1960) pp. 407, 427–29. But there is nothing in Lenin's writings to indicate similar agreement concerning the role of external commerce. In *The Development of Capitalism in Russia*, vol. 3 of *Collected Works* (Moscow, 1960), p. 39, he wrote: "Thus, the social division of labor is the basis of the *entire* [S.V.] process of the development of commodity economy and of capitalism."

[17] For a general discussion of party policy and historiography, see L. Tillett, *The Great Friendship: Soviet Historians on the Non-Russian Nationalities* (Chapel Hill, N.C., 1969); J. Barbar, *Soviet Historians in Crisis* (London, 1983), pp. 40–79.

that Western trade could have played a positive role in their economic development. Such an interpretation also stressed that all the nations of the USSR had been "feudal" for most of their existence, and relegated all pre-nineteenth-century capitalist elements in their past to a minor role in the overall historical process.[18] Trade with the West became significant only insofar as it could be shown to have contributed to regression and exploitation, while the emphasis that Soviet Marxist historians of the 1920s had placed on the development of commodity production in the Ukraine and its links to Western trade was replaced by an emphasis on the concomitant destitution and "feudal oppression."[19]

---

[18] Academic debate on theories of socioeconomic formations and transitions, as opposed to ritual polemics about "bourgeois nationalism" and pro-forma pleas for the comparative study of history, is the domain of Russian scholars. The only Ukrainian to make a major contribution to these debates, which took place between 1929 and 1934, and then again in the 1950s and 1960s, was V. O. Holobuts'kyi, "O nachale 'niskhodiashchei' stadii feodalnoi formatsii," *Voprosy istorii*, 1959, no. 9, pp. 123–37, and, "Sotsial'no-ekonomichni prychyny posylennia kripatstva v kraiinakh skhidnoi Evropy v XV–XVII st.," *Tezy dopovidei XVII naukovoi sesii Kyivs'koho instytutu narodnoho hospodarstva* (1965), pp. 126–28. These works were unavailable to me at the time of writing. The theoretical basis of the post-1934 Communist party line on historiography was formulated between 1929 and 1934. See A. G. Prigozhin, *Karl Marks i problemy sotsio-ekonomicheskikh formatsii* (Leningrad, 1933). Following the "de-stalinization" of 1956, the party has allowed historians to reconsider the theories of the 1920s, and to use them to a limited degree in their interpretations. See Shunkov, *Perekhod ot feodalizma*; S. D. Skazkin, ed., *Teoreticheskie i istoriograficheskie problemy genesisa kapitalizma* (Moscow, 1969). The ideas of Western Marxists on trade, early capitalist development, and related issues, are collected in R. Hilton, ed., *The Transition from Feudalism to Capitalism* (London, 1973). See also B. Hindess and P. Q. Hirst, *Pre-Capitalist Modes of Production* (London, 1975), pp. 260–308.

[19] After 1956, Soviet historians who took the Marxist historiography of the 1920s seriously became advocates of "early-capitalism." The Ukrainians belonging to this group broke with the prevailing practice of describing past socioeconomic relations solely as tales of misery and exploitation, and devoted more attention to the origins of capitalism and the development of commodity and market relations in the Ukraine. However, they did not link Ukrainian development with international trade, and did not identify any particular group as "progressive." See Dubyna, *Istoriia Ukrains'koi*, vol. 1, pp. 175–81; V. O. Holobuts'kyi, (Golobutskii), *Diplomaticheskaia istoriia osvoboditel'noi voiny Ukrainskogo naroda* (Kiev, 1962), pp. 50–56 and his *Ekonomichna istoriia Ukrains'koi RSR* (Kiev, 1970), pp. 70, 77, 97, 99, 101–102; V. A. Diadychenko et al., *Istoriia selianstva Ukrains'koi RSR*, vol. 1 (Kiev, 1967), pp.

To return to the main argument of this paper, it should be repeated that although there is some evidence of Baltic-central Ukrainian trade, its extent and impact has not been determined. Moreover, there is no reason to assume that this trade only had a negative impact, and only could have developed to the detriment of local burgher and peasant dealers. Royal Prussia, Pomerania, as well as colonial America, for example, exported agricultural products, yet did not experience a "development of underdevelopment." The question to be asked, therefore, is how, if at all, did Baltic trade affect existing commercial activity in a region where the gentry was not as successful as elsewhere in imposing its hegemony, and thus, unable to restrict the access of other estates to land, markets, and, most importantly, arms.[20] Did the distances involved, in fact, check the expansion of estates using serf labor for export production, or did this kind of development occur in the Cossack Ukraine between 1600 and 1648 at the same rate as it had a century earlier in the Western Ukraine? How were shipments of goods actually transported to Gdańsk? What was the scope

---

104–105, 118; M. Braichevs'kyi, "Perspektyvy doslidzhennia ukrains'kykh starozhytnostei XIV–XVII st.," *Seredni viky* 1 (1971):24–28, referred to seventeenth-century Ukrainian agrarian development as an example of "the American path." In an essay written in 1966, but never published in the USSR, he remarked that foreign trade had a profound influence on the early seventeenth-century Ukraine and linked it firmly with the West; "Pryiednannia chy voziednannia," in *Shyroke more Ukrainy* (Paris and Baltimore, 1972), p. 287. Opponents of the "early-capitalist" theory labeled it an ill-founded attempt to "backdate" capitalism that was aimed at raising the historical level of development of non-Russians "do urovnia tsentral'nykh raionov strany." N. Pavlenko said that Ukrainians were especially guilty of such backdating. See also Shunkov, *Perekhod ot feodalizma*, pp. 14–15, 266, 405; Skazkin, *Teoreticheskie*, pp. 200–201. Although "early-capitalism" still seems to be theoretically acceptable (L. V. Cherepnin, "Nekotorye voprosy istorii dokapitalisticheskikh formatsii v Rossii," *Kommunist*, 1975, no. 1, pp. 71–27), it is not to be found in the latest general and economic histories of the Ukraine.

[20] The right to bear arms was the prerogative of the nobility, as in theory their privileges were based upon their obligation to defend the realm. In 1526, 1582, and 1598, the Polish Sejm passed laws expressly forbidding anyone but the gentry to carry arms, yet in the Cossack Ukraine commoners were legally obliged to carry arms because of widespread military insecurity. Accordingly, the local populace could take advantage of this legal obligation and use their weapons in defense of their own interests. See Jabłonowski, *Źródła dziejowe*, vol. 5, intro., and pp. 40–42, 52, 60, 112; V. D. Otamanovskii, "Razvitie gorodskogo stroia na Ukraine v XIV–XVIII vv.," *Voprosy istorii*, 1958, no. 3, p. 134.

and scale of export trade from the Ukraine? Did estates export more than they produced by buying on local markets? And most importantly, was the central Ukraine a "peripheral" economic entity, or was it, together with the Western Ukraine and central Poland, an integral part of the European market? Who shipped what, how much, where, and how from the central Ukraine between 1600 and 1648? Only when these questions are answered will it be possible to determine whether the Cossack Ukraine experienced the "second serfdom," and if so, to what extent. The purpose of this paper, meanwhile, is not to provide answers, but only to point out the gaps in our knowledge and offer some guidelines for the much needed archival research.

International trade in wood, potash, tar, hemp, flax, and grain, was of particular importance in the past because, in the long run, it was these staples rather than luxury items that accounted for the major economic thrusts in European history. Before the coming of the railroad these products, which were either bulky or subject to spoilage, could be transported cheaply and quickly to sea ports only by river. The largest barge in the Commonwealth was called a *szkuta*. Manned by five or six men it could haul up to 70,000 kg in one load, while the smallest boat could haul up to 4,000 kg.[21] Wagons, by contrast, were limited to loads of 600 kg and were much slower. Pulled by two horses, the cargo could be transported an average of 30–35 km a day, while two oxen would haul it about 20–25 km daily, with a rest every third day. The differences between land and river transport were also dramatically reflected in the costs involved. Whereas land haulage could add anywhere between 4 to 125 percent to expenses, river transport added only 6–50 percent.[22] It has been calculated that under such conditions grain could be transported profitably by land for distances

---

[21] R. Rybarski, *Handel i polityka handlowa Polski w XVI stuleciu*, vol. 1 (Warsaw, 1958), p. 13. It has been calculated that 60–70 percent of the gentry who exported grain did not ship, on average, more than 3 *szkuta* (barges) a year. In order to produce one bargeload of grain, it was necessary to have approximately 700 hectares of land and a yield of at least 3:1. See Z. Iu. Kopysskii, "Rynochnye sviazy sel'skogo khoziaistva Belorussii XVI–pervoi poloviny XVII vv.," *Ezhegodnik po agrarnoi istorii vostochnoi Evropy, 1962 g.* (Minsk, 1964), p. 144.

[22] Rybarski, *Handel i polityka*, vol. 1, pp. 14–15.

of no more than 150 km (about 100 m).[23] Besides costs of transport, there were also expenses incurred at the toll stations along all the routes. On the 350 km route between Dolyna on the Dniester and Luts'k, for example, there were no less than twenty stations.[24] The gentry, of course, paid no tolls, while exemptions and privileges allowed some merchants to travel without paying duties some of the time. During the second half of the sixteenth century, between 4 and 17 percent of the merchant-owned grain which passed through the station at Wrocławek, passed toll-free. During the first half of the seventeenth century about 25 percent of marketed grain was traded by groups not belonging to the gentry, while between two-thirds and three-fourths of all grain that passed through the Warsaw station was not charged duty. Nonetheless, transport by groups other than gentry was restricted by the toll system which added anywhere between 10 to 50 percent to expenses.[25]

Considerations of distance, time, and costs, therefore, tied most long distance trade in staples to the major rivers and the towns situated along their banks. In the Commonwealth, Riga, Königsberg, and Elbląg, were the major international ports, but by far the biggest and most important trading center was Gdańsk. The city, located at the mouth of the Vistula, had at its disposal a vast network of rivers, including the San and the Buh.[26] Thanks to these rivers, Red Ruś and western Volhynia were directly linked to European markets by the end of the sixteenth century.

[23] Mielczarski, *Rynek zbożowy*, p. 67. For a more detailed discussion see his "Koszta transportu i ich wpływ na udział kupców w handlu zbożowym w Polsce XVI wieku," *Kwartalnik historyi kultury materialnej*, 1965, no. 2, pp. 269–96.

[24] Rybarski, *Handel i polityka*, vol. 1, pp. 296–303. Rybarski notes that Germany had more toll stations on its trade routes than did Poland (pp. 30–39).

[25] Ibid., vol. 2, p. 21; Bogucka, *Handel zagraniczny*, p. 81. It is estimated that 50 percent of the grain exported by the gentry belonged to the magnates. See H. Obuchowska-Pysior, *Handel wiślany w pierwszej połowie XVII wieku* (Wroclaw, 1964), p. 70.

[26] For Ukrainian trade routes see N. Rubinshtein, "Zapadnye puti torgovli Ukrainy-Rusi," *Visnyk Odes'koi komisii kraieznavstva pry UAN*, 1925, no. 2–3, pp. 120–34; S. Wysłouch, "Dawne drogi Polesia," *Ateneum Wilenskie* 12 (1937):162–204.

The territories drained by the Dnieper River lay outside the Vistula system. But because of the economic importance of bulk trade in staples to the Commonwealth, a number of projects were advanced in the late sixteenth and early seventeenth century to extend existing water routes and link the Dnieper by canal with the Baltic. The idea seems to have emerged for the first time in the middle of the sixteenth century when it was proposed to join the Dnieper to the Nieman via the Biarezina and the Villiia.[27] In 1618, the Polish writer Szymon Starowolski in his *Rada abo Pobudka na zniesienie Tatarów Perekopskich* outlined a plan to colonize the central and southern Ukraine, wherein he proposed that a canal be built to join the Dvina and the Biarezina rivers, a project that would have linked Kiev with Riga. The loss of Riga to Sweden in 1621 made his scheme unrealistic. Perhaps, in direct response to the loss of the Latvian city, a proposal was made in the Sejm that very same year to implement the earlier Biarezina-Nieman-Villiia plan.[28] As before, nothing came of the initiative, although the proposal was introduced again in the Sejm in 1631, after the Treaty of Altmark, when Poland was left with only two Baltic ports, Gdańsk and Königsberg. Władysław, then heir to the throne, took it upon himself to build the proposed canal at his own cost, and the Sejm gave him rights to all tolls until he had recouped his expenditures.[29] Finally, in 1636, Gdańsk merchants approached Stanisław Lubomirski, the *palatine* of Ruś, with a plan to join the Prypiat' and the Buh by building a canal via the Pina and Muchawiec rivers. Lubomirski asked the Sejm for funds and the project got as far as an initial survey of the proposed route.[30]

As is known, none of these ambitious plans were realized, and eastern Volhynia, Kiev, and Bratslav provinces remained without a canal link to the Baltic. But even so, the fifteen instances of export shipments (mentioned at the beginning of this paper), are an indication

[27] J. Piasecka, "Budowa kanałów na ziemach Rzeczypospolitej," *Kwartalnik historii nauki i techniki*, 1970, no. 2, p. 298.

[28] I. Baranowski, "Rzut oka na znaczenie Dniepru w dziejach gospodarczych Polski," *Przegląd historyczny* 3 (1916):278. The 1621 record of Sejm proceedings is unpublished and is in the Biblioteka Kórnicka, MS. 201.

[29] Baranowski, "Rzut oka," p. 278. The 1631 record of Sejm proceedings is unpublished and is in the Biblioteka Czartoryskich, MSS. 359, 123.

[30] Lipiński, *Historia Polskiej*, p. 243.

that bulk export trade in staples from the central Ukraine did occur, and obviously went along existing land and river routes despite the distance and difficulty involved. Because prices for wood products were high, and Ukrainian grain yields, which average 1:6 or 1:7 were higher than the Polish norm and thus made export profitable, bulk trade in these commodities was clearly worth the effort.[31]

Research on Ukrainian-Baltic trade could lead to important changes in our understanding of sixteenth- and seventeenth-century Ukrainian history. The main focus of any such research would be the records relating to the Commonwealth's three major river trade arteries: the Vistula-Buh-Prypiat' route, the Prypiat'-Nieman route, and the Dnieper-Dvina route. The most important sources would be the extant toll registers, although extant court and city registers of the towns situated along the river trade routes would also be relevant, as these frequently record litigation over export shipments.

The study of Ukrainian-Baltic trade could begin with the published registers of the Wrocławek toll station for the years 1537–1576 which would furnish the basis for estimating the Ukraine's contribution to the Gdańsk grain trade on the eve of Poland's expansion eastwards. In 1568, for example, 1,977 lasts of exported grain originated in Red Ruś. Given that the total export for that year was 62,472 lasts, this means that Ukrainian grain made up less than 1 percent of the total. In 1572 the Ukrainian share was even smaller, comprising only 522 lasts of a total of 45,031.[32] Examination of the city books and registers of Płock and Nur—two other major transit cities on the Buh-Vistula route—might permit similar estimates of the percentage of exports originating in the central Ukraine in later years[33] which, it should be noted, included wood products before 1600, but not grain.[34]

---

[31] I. Boiko, "Proizvoditel'nye sily v sel'skom khoziaistve Ukrainy v XVI–pervoi polovine XVII v.," *Ezhegodnik po agrarnoi istorii vostochnoi Evropy, 1961 g.*, p. 168. In Belorussia, where the average yield was 1:2 or 1:3, production for export was feasible only in the western parts of the country where there was direct access to a river route to the Baltic. M. Topolska, "Związki handlowe Białorusi wschodniej z Rygą," *Roczniki dziejów społecznych i gospodarczych* 29 (1968):14.

[32] Rybarski, *Handel i polityka*, vol. 1, p. 24; vol. 2, p. 18.

[33] Extant town records are held in the Archiwum Główny Aktów Dawnych in Warsaw. I have found no references to any extant toll registers from these towns.

[34] See Boiko, *Selianstvo Ukrainy*, pp. 208–34.

Another possible source of information about Ukrainian exports on the Buh-Vistula route are the Warsaw Customs registers for the years 1605 – 1651 which, thanks to meticulous clerks, contain data on gentry shipments between 1632 and 1651, even though these were not subject to duties. Insofar as the main regional Ukrainian river port was Ustyluh on the Buh near Horodło, the Warsaw registers would not have a record of goods sent from this town.[35] However, they might include reference to products shipped from another transit center for Ukrainian exports, Kazimierz Dolny. As the Warsaw registers also contain records of grain shipped by twenty-one magnate families as well as twenty-one individual magnates, many of whom had lands in the central Ukraine, a close examination of these files might also prove to be useful in tracing central Ukrainian staples.[36] It should also be noted that the town records of Kazimierz Dolny for the years 1616 – 1625 are to be found in the Lublin archives.

The Gdańsk archives provide yet another potential source of information on Ukrainian exports. Unfortunately, one particularly valuable collection, "300/24 handel," which held the records of the city's trade with its hinterland, was destroyed during World War II. However, copies of some of these contracts were entered into the registers of the deputy mayor; they contain the record of legal conflicts between merchants, exporters, and shippers as well as furnish evidence of trade between Gdańsk and the central Ukraine.[37] Information about Ukrainian goods might also be found in the "Missiva" collection, which was used by Malecki. It consists of sixty-four well-preserved books containing copies of the correspondence between the city council and its trading partners for the years 1526 – 1655. As Malecki's book is limited to a study of the contracts between Gdańsk and towns having the status of city, it might prove useful to re-examine these sources with an eye to Ukrainian trade. Similarly, because Malecki's work was limited to urban or burgher-controlled trade which

---

[35] The court records of Kholm—the neighboring capital—were published in 1896 in volume 23 of the *Akty izdavaemye Vilenskoi arkheografičeskoi komissii.*

[36] Obuchowska-Pysior, *Handel wiślany*, pp. 15, 148 – 49. The author paid no attention to the question of regionalization. Of the Royal Customs registers that were held in Warsaw, these books were the only ones to have survived the destruction of the city in 1944.

[37] Bogucka, *Handel zagraniczny*, p. 77.

accounted for only 25 percent of the Vistula trade, it might also be useful to re-examine his other sources for reference to gentry trade from the Ukraine. Another source that might prove useful is the *Glejty Żydowskie*—not only for Gdańsk, but other cities as well. These documents contain records of permission given to Jews to enter and trade in a given city and they include lists of goods and their place of origin. Malecki, for example, using the Gdańsk *Glejty* for the years 1641–1642, confirmed that western Volhynia was definitely integrated into the Baltic trade system.

Data on Ukrainian trade can also be found in the business records of a Scottish merchant, Samuel Edwards, whose headquarters were in Toruń. (The records are now part of the Toruń archives.) These records, which cover the years of 1645–1654, show that his agents in Zamość and Lublin traded with Volhynia and Podillia.[38] Edwards did not deal in staples, but the fact that his business records still exist indicates that the search for and examination of the records of other merchants—based along obvious Ukrainian trade routes—might be of value to historians of the Ukraine since these merchants could have served as intermediaries for Ukrainian goods.

Other sources of information untapped by historians studying the Ukraine and Baltic trade, are the records and registers of Brest and the towns along the Prypiat' River. This became a major Ukrainian trade route at the end of the fifteenth century, when the Lithuanian Grand Duke ordered Kievan merchants to stop using the traditional route via Luts'k and Kholm, and to ship their goods via Brest instead.[39] As a result, a major portion of Lithuanian and Ukrainian east-west trade was channeled through Pinsk and Mazyr. Later, toward the end of the sixteenth century, when the Kiev region still did not produce enough to feed its own towns, grain was shipped *eastward* along this route from Volhynia via the Prypiat' and either the Styr or Horyń rivers. What both these facts suggest is that the Prypiat', Styr/Horyń route was probably used for western trade during the seventeenth century, although to date, there is little evidence of any such traffic.[40] It is not

---

[38] J. Wojtowicz, "Toruńskie przedsiębiorstwo handlowe Samuela Edwardsa w XVII wieku," *Roczniki dziejów społecznych i gospodarczych* 14 (1953):210–53.

[39] Hrushevs'kyi, *Istoriia Ukrainy-Rusy*, 6:52–53.

[40] The Ostrozhsky estates, in the Stepan area in Volhynia, owned sixteen river barges for use on the Horyń. See Guldon, *Z dziejów handlu*, p. 33. Kopysskii noted

known if the toll registers for Pinsk and Mazyr still exist; however, the registers for Brest for 1583 and 1605 are in the Vilnius University Library.[41] As Brest could be reached by portage from the Prypiat', or by river from Ustyluh, a review of the town's registers, along with the town records of Luts'k—a major overland transit point—might indicate what was shipped westwards by land, and what was shipped via the Prypiat' and Styr or Horyń rivers. In passing, it should be remembered that land shipments via Luts'k could not have been made by private merchants or burghers from the central Ukraine, as the distance they would have had to travel to get to the Buh was well over the 150 km profitability limit. However, it was commercially feasible for a magnate to export goods along this route. Exempt from tolls and not obliged to pay for transport because he would use his serfs to do the work, the only limitations faced by a magnate sending goods to the Baltic ports by land was the number and carrying capacity of the wagons he could assemble.

Apart from the limited number of toll station registers that are to be found in present-day Belorussia, another problem faced by Western historians interested in Ukrainian-Baltic trade stems from the fact that Soviet scholars dealing with the economic history of Belorussia pay little attention to issues related to the Ukraine. For example, in an excellent study on Belorussian trade Kopysskii used the two known Brest registers, but he examined only the land trade and almost totally ignored issues pertaining to the Ukraine. Two years later, the Polish historian Zenon Guldon, using the 1583 register, (which was published in part in 1867), showed that in a two-month period almost 3,000 *lasty* of grain from Volhynia which were headed towards the Baltic had been shipped by river through Brest.[42] Clearly, if this example is anything to go by, there is ample information pertaining to

---

that Belorussians traded Ukrainian grain along the Prypiat' ("Rynochnye sviazy," p. 151).

[41] V. I. Meleshko, "Tamozhennye knigi kak istoricheskii istochnik," *Vestsi Akademii navuk Belaruskai SSR*, 1959, no. 4, pp. 154–57; and "Novye Belorusskie tamozhennye knigi pervoi poloviny XVII v.," *Istoricheskii arkhiv*, 1960, no. 4, pp. 202–203. The records of the Brest court are now held in the State Historical Archives in Minsk.

[42] Z. Iu. Kopysskii, "Iz istorii torgovykh sviazei gorodov Belorussii s gorodami Pol'shi," *Istoricheskie zapiski* 72 (1962):140–83. Guldon, *Z dziejów handlu*, p. 33.

Ukrainian economic history to be found in Belorussian documents.[43]

Besides the Buh and Prypiat' rivers, another possible Belorussian route between the central Ukraine and the Baltic lay along the Nieman, northern Sluch, and Biarezina rivers, on the way to Königsberg.[44] Shipments to this port could travel in either one of two ways. Either up the Biarezina and Svisłoch rivers to Minsk, or along the lower Prypiat' and northern Sluch rivers to Slutsk. In both cases a short portage was necessary to reach the Nieman. At first sight this seems to be an unlikely route; however, references to an export shipment to Königsberg made in 1605 from Chornobyl', as well as to Gdańsk merchants who traveled to the Cossack Ukraine without Polish permission after 1648, indicate that the Nieman and Biarezina rivers should definitely not be overlooked by researchers as possible routes for pre-1648 Ukrainian exports.[45] Another indication of the economic importance of this route for the Cossack Ukraine can be derived from Hetman Bohdan Khmel'nyts'kyi's policies toward Belorussia and Sweden between 1654 and 1657. Briefly, by 1655, Khmel'nyts'kyi's aims included the incorporation into the Hetmanate of part, if not all, of the palatinates of Brest-Litovsk, Novogrod, and Mstsislaŭ. Success would have given him control of, or at least toll free access to, the Prypiat', Biarezina and Nieman rivers. Furthermore, the Hetman's political legacy, the stillborn October 1657 treaty with Sweden, specified that the northwestern part of the Hetmanate was to include all of the Chelminsk and Płock palatinates, as well as

---

[43] For a discussion of extant archives, see Ia. D. Isaevich, ''Grodskie i zemskie akty vazhneishii istochnik po istorii agrarnykh otnoshenii v Rechi Pospolitoi v XVI–XVII vv.,'' *Ezhegodnik po agrarnoi istorii vostochnoi Evropy, 1961 g.*, pp. 90–99. Court and town records of the major Belorussian towns were published in *Istoriko-iuridicheskie materialy izvlechennye iz aktovykh knig gub. Vitebskoi i Mogilevskoi* (Vitsebsk, 1871–1893). See also *Akty izdavaemye Vilenskoi arkheograficheskoi komissiei* (Vilnius, 1865–1915).

[44] Although Klaipeda (Memel) was at the mouth of the Nieman, goods were not exported directly from this city but forwarded to Königsberg. The Prussian capital effectively dominated Klaipeda, and by 1619 was able to issue and enforce a decree forbidding the town to ship goods directly to Gdańsk.

[45] Kopysskii, ''Rynochnye sviazy,'' p. 143; Kryp''iakevych, *Bohdan Khmel'nyts'kyi*, pp. 292, 313–16.

the two western Belorussian provinces.[46] The Baltic orientation of these moves makes it reasonable to assume that one of the reasons for Kheml'nyts'kyi's plan to annex these non-Ukrainian and non-Orthodox territories was the desire to obtain free access to the Baltic via the Vistula and the Nieman for Ukrainian trade.

A study of pre-1648 exports along the Nieman-Königsberg route could begin with a search for references to Ukrainian goods in the toll registers of the following towns: Jurbarkas (1606, 1613), Kaunas (1600, 1601), and Hrodna (1600, 1605). They are in the Vilnius University Library. Although there are no known registers for Minsk or Slutsk, information on the commerce of these two towns and Vilnius might be found in the other registers and court records which are now part of the Belorussian and Lithuanian Central State Historical Archives.[47] Microfilm copies of the Königsberg customs registers for the years 1638, 1642, 1645, are now held in the Gdańsk Wojewódstwo Archives, while the originals, together with the rest of the city's extant archives, are in the Prussian privy State Archives in West Berlin.

Finally, a third possible river route for Ukrainian grain was along the Dvina and Lovat rivers. This was the northern part of the ancient "road from the Vikings to the Greeks," which linked Kiev to the eastern shores of the Baltic. During the period in question the Lovat was held by the Russians, but between 1562 and 1620 Lithuanian control of Riga allowed intermittent trade along the Dvina. The route was rendered inoperative from 1569 to 1579 when the Russians held Polatsk, and then again from 1601 to 1610 when the Swedes blockaded Riga. Although the city's export trade fell by 300 percent as a result of the blockade, 54 percent of east Baltic shipping still managed to pass through its harbors during those nine years. During the relatively peaceful years between 1610 and 1621, the total volume of eastern Baltic trade naturally increased substantially. It accounted for over 60 percent of the total Baltic trade in flax, hemp, and potash, and 5 percent of the total grain trade.[48] Historians have mentioned that

---

[46] Hrushevs'kyi, *Istoriia Ukrainy-Rusy,* 9:1270–1275; 10:65–70.

[47] See Isaevich, "Grodskie i zemskie akty." The 1601 Kaunas register was published in volume 14 of the *Akty izdavaemye Vilenskoi arkheograficheskoi komissiei.*

[48] Approximately 10–15 percent of this grain went through Riga. V. Doroshenko, "Eksport sel'skokhoziaistvennoi produksii vostochnoi Pribaltiki v 1562–1620 gg.," *Ezhegodnik po agrarnoi istorii vostochnoi Evropy, 1961 g.,* pp. 180–82 and "Eksport

the central and northern Ukraine were part of Riga's hinterland, but as yet no one has determined how much of Riga's goods originated there.[49] Research into this question could begin with an examination of the toll registers from three of the major transit towns—Polatsk (1616), Vitsebsk (1605), and Mahilioŭ (1612).[50] There are no known registers for the towns of Orsha and Shkłoŭ; to date, only two incomplete registers dating from 1591 and 1599 have been found from the Koknese (Kokenhusen) station near Riga (these are now in the Central Historical Archives in Moscow). The records of the Riga Commercial Court for the years 1613–1621 and the records of the Castle Court for the years 1581–1615 (both in the Latvian Central Historical Archives), could also prove to be helpful.[51] Admittedly, the Kiev-Riga route might not have been a favored one for early seventeenth-century exports originating in the central Ukraine. However, in 1605 Kostiantyn Ostrozhs'kyi and the Kiev gentry decided to support Sigismund III in his dynastic war against Sweden as well as in his Livonian war effort. Since the theater of both wars lay far away from the Ukraine, it is possible that one of the reasons for such a decision was the realization that Polish control over this northerly route was vital to their economic interests.[52]

Whereas some of the sources for studying the part that the central Ukrainian lands played in the Baltic trade can be found in Poland, important information is also to be found in Belorussian, Lithuanian,

Rygi na zachód w okresie przynależności do Rzeczpospolitej (1562–1620)," *Zapiski historyczne* 31, no. 1 (1966):7–44.

[49] V. Doroshenko, "Protokoly Rizhskogo torgovogo suda kak istochnik dlia izucheniia ekonomicheskikh sviazei Rigi s Russkimi, Belorusskimi i Litovskimi zemliamy v XVII v.," in Ia. P. Krastin et al., *Ekonomicheskie sviazy Pribaltiki s Rossiei* (Riga, 1968), pp. 118–21. See also A. Attman, *The Russian and Polish Markets in International Trade 1500–1650* (Goteborg, 1973), p. 48.

[50] The Polatsk and Mahilioŭ registers are in the Vilnius University Library, and the Vitsebsk register was published in 1883 in volume 1 of *Vitebskaia starina*.

[51] These might be among the microfilmed copies of the Riga records now held in the Herder Institute in Marburg, West Germany.

[52] H. Wisner, "Opinia szlachecka Rzeczypospolitej wobec polityki Szwedskiej Zygmunta III w latach 1587–1632," *Zapiski historyczne* 38, no. 2 (1973):21–22. Wisner does not address this question, but the Sejm records and letters that he used provide a convenient starting point for research.

Ukrainian, and other Soviet archives.[53] While Western and Polish scholars could conceivably undertake long-term projects to search through the Polish archives, the findings of such an endeavor would not be conclusive until they were matched by a similar undertaking based on access to Soviet archives. Will the Communist party ever give the support necessary for such an extensive research project? The answer depends on whether or not "perestroika" results in revision of two politically motivated assumptions: that Baltic trade played a negative role in Ukrainian economic history, and that Ukrainian ties with Russia were historically more important than ties with Europe.

[53] An annotated bibliography of articles and monographs with detailed descriptions of Soviet archival holdings may be found in P. K. Grimsted, *Archives and Manuscript Repositories in the USSR: Estonia, Latvia, Lithuania, and Belorussia* (Princeton, 1981).

CHAPTER SIX

Trade and Muscovite Economic Policy toward the Ukraine: The Movement of Cereal Grains during the Second Half of the Seventeenth Century

Carol B. Stevens

During the second half of the seventeenth century, the Muscovite government made a series of changes in its regulation of both internal and external trade. Changes in import tariffs on goods carried by foreigners began in 1646; in 1653 and 1667 further alterations led to a mild protectionism. Furthermore, internal customs duties were reformed and consolidated, which eased both the difficulties and expenses of long-distance trade inside of Muscovy. The emergence of a concrete policy regulating trade during this period is hardly surprising, as both internal and external customs receipts were a major fiscal resource for the state, and Muscovy in the second half of the seventeenth century was persistently in search of additional income.[1] There is little doubt that these national changes and other local experiments in trade regulation had an impact on Russian commerce.

---

[1] See, for example, J. Michael Hittle, *The Service City, State and Townsmen in Russia, 1600–1800* (Cambridge, Mass., 1979), pp. 69–72; K. V. Bazilevich, "Elementy merkantilizma v ekonomicheskoi politiki pravitel'stva Alekseia Mikhailovicha," *Uchenye zapiski Moskovskogo gosudarstvennogo universiteta* 41 (1940):3–34. Customs receipts represented about 20 percent of the Muscovite budget in 1680. P. N. Miliukov, *Gosudarstvennoe khoziaistvo Rossii v pervoi chetverti XVIII stoletiia i reforma Petra Velikogo*, 2d ed. (St. Petersburg, 1905), pp. 71–73.

Some trade goods, however, were occasionally of greater value to the Muscovite government when used for purposes other than promoting commercial development or contributing to higher customs receipts. Grain was frequently such a commodity; at times, it was used as a kind of salary payment to members of the Muscovite bureaucracy and the army, and the tsar held a monopoly on the export of grain to Western Europe.[2]

It is in this light that the following essay undertakes to explore the movement of grain over the border between Muscovy and its immediate western neighbor, the Ukrainian Hetmanate. During the second half of the century, there was a lively trade in cattle, cloth, furs, glass, and other items developing between the two areas. Among the entrepôts for these products were the south Russian border cities, particularly Putyvl' and Briansk, but also Khotmyshsk, Sevsk, and Kursk. Despite significant grain production both in the Ukraine and southern Muscovy, however, relatively little grain was traded across the border after the 1650s—either locally in times of shortage or famine, or for transshipment to more distant points where grain was more persistently in short supply. A few commentators have suggested, in passing, that the absence of such trade may be explained by phenomena such as "plentiful grain production" or the "absence of easy river routes" to transport such an unwieldy and voluminous product as grain.[3] These explanations are certainly plausible, but not universally applicable. The years of the "Ruin" in the Ukraine undercut crop production and must have accentuated demand for marketed cereal products; similarly, the late seventeenth century in Muscovy was punctuated by bad harvests, crop failures, and periodic

---

[2] Tsentral'nyi gosudarstvennyi arkhiv drevnykh aktov (hereafter TsGADA), fond 210 (Razriad), *Belgorodskii stol*, kniga 100, lists payments in furs, as well as in grain supplements. Also, see P. N. Petrov, "Rospis' raskhodov tsarstva Moskovskogo," *Zapiski otdeleniia russkoi i slavianskoi arkheologii Russkogo arkheologicheskogo obshchestva* 4 (1889):34; J. T. Fuhrman, *The Origins of Capitalism in Russia* (Chicago, 1972), p. 59.

[3] B. B. Kafengauz, *Ocherki vnutrennogo rynka Rossii v pervoi polovine XVIII veka* (Moscow, 1958), p. 289, reports the comments of Afanasii Shafonskii and M. M. Shcherbatov. M. V. Klochkov, *Naselenie Rossii pri Petre Velikom po perapisiam togo vremeni*, vol. 1 (St. Petersburg, 1911 –), p. 291, cites another document suggesting that internal Ukrainian grain trade in the early eighteenth century might have lured back the Ukrainian population.

price rises. Given a reasonably open border, some traffic across the frontier might have been expected, especially since the new, higher Muscovite customs tariffs were infrequently applied to goods entering from, or leaving for, the Ukraine.[4] Furthermore, though river routes certainly did not provide a convenient means for exporting anything from the Hetmanate into Muscovy, periodic Muscovite shipments downriver to Kiev clearly demonstrate that the obverse was not true.[5] The focus of this discussion, therefore, is to identify Muscovite policies which contributed to the low level of trade activity in grain between the southern Muscovite provinces and the Ukraine. Customs policies apart, there were at least three such practices: periodic attempts to restrain, if not eliminate, the export of grain through southern border towns, especially at mid-century; the character of the alcohol monopoly in Muscovy in the second half of the century; and, finally, uneven attempts to supply Russian armies and garrisons in the Ukraine, especially towards the end of the century. The latter two practices, particularly, absorbed some of the grain surpluses from each side of the frontier and moved them across the border, without that fact ever being reflected in market transactions.

Around the middle of the seventeenth century, a local trade in grain was apparently carried on with considerable freedom between the Polish Ukraine and southern Muscovite towns. The building of a fortified line across the Muscovite south after 1635 triggered a sudden, if not altogether voluntary, growth in the population of towns there. Belgorod, for example, gained some two hundred military households between 1626 and 1651; other towns grew as well, though not perhaps at the same rate.[6] Newly arrived Muscovite military personnel were

---

[4] Kafengauz's examination of customs books in border towns has led him to conclude that double taxes on imports were not often enforced against the Ukraine. My limited perusal of the material on trade between Muscovy and the Ukraine has certainly not contradicted that impression. Kafengauz, *Ocherki vnutrennogo rynka*, p. 21; C. B. Stevens, "The Politics of Food Supply: Grain and the State in Southern Russia," (Ph.D. diss., University of Michigan, 1985), p. 80.

[5] V. M. Vazhinskii, "Sbory zaprosnogo khleba v kontsa XVII veka dlia obezpecheniia krymskikh i azovskikh pokhodov," *Izvestiia Voronezhskogo pedagogicheskogo instituta* 153 (1975):24 – 25. These dispatches involved some overland carting, however. Ibid., p. 29.

[6] I. N. Miklashevskii, *K istorii khoziaistvennogo byta Moskovskogo gosudarstva*, pt. 1 (Moscow, 1894), pp. 103 – 109; V. P. Zagorovskii, *Belgorodskaia cherta*

not always able to provide for themselves from their own farmlands, whether because of the exigencies of their duties or the difficulties of opening new lands for cultivation. It is not surprising, then, that demand periodically rose for marketed grain. Ukrainians brought grain into Muscovy for local sale, or Muscovites crossed into "Lithuania," as Muscovite documents referred to it, in order to purchase foodstuffs. Within Muscovy, some of this trade took place outside fortress walls, segregated from Russian trade. Published customs books from selected years in the 1640s make this trade appear intermittent, or at least irregular; while Ukrainians were present at these marketplaces, far from all, or even most, of these traders were dealing in grain.[7]

There was no fixed direction in the flow of grain. In 1645 and again in 1648, the Ukraine suffered early frosts, drought, and locust infestation, resulting in crop shortages. Muscovite grain was carried across the border into the Polish Ukraine for sale; individual documents again show grain shipped in small amounts. In short, records from the 1640s suggest a local grain trade in both directions, paralleling a trade in sheepskin coats (*shuby*), fur, wax, and other products, and conducted at markets with a small turnover, dominated by winter sales and servitor-traders.[8] The chief restriction on the trade was the

---

(Voronezh, 1969), p. 141. Zagorovskii's figures for 1626, ibid., p. 27, argue that Belgorod grew by 370 servicemen. The building of new fortresses like Vol'nyi and Khotmyshsk meant a newly registered service population of over 1000 very close to the Hetmanate.

[7] AN SSSR, Institut russkogo iazyka, *Pamiatniki iuzhnovelikorusskogo narechiia. Tamozhennye knigi* (Moscow, 1982), Belgorod, pp. 7–18; Elets, pp. 75–80; Kursk, pp. 194–245; N. Ia. Novombergskii, *Ocherki vnutrennego upravleniia v Moskovskoi Rusi XVII stoletiia; prodovol'stvennoe stroenie*, 2 vols. (Tomsk and Moscow, 1914, 1959), vol. 1, nos. 41, 54; AN SSSR, *Vossoedinenie Ukrainy s Rossiei: Dokumenty i materialy*, 3 vols. (Moscow, 1954), vol. 1, nos. 240, 259, 268; Arkheograficheskaia komissiia, *Akty otnosiashchesia k istorii Iuzhnoi i Zapadnoi Rossii*, 15 vols. (St. Petersburg, 1862–1892), vol. 3, no. 141 (hereafter, *AIIuZR*).

[8] On trade, see, for example, *Vossoedinenie*, vol. 1, no. 244; Arcadius Kahan, "Natural Calamities and their Effect on Food Supply in Russia," *Jahrbücher für Geschichte Osteuropas* 16, no. 3 (September 1968); 371–72; V. S. Bakulin, "Torgovye oboroty na Belevskom rynke," *Trudy Moskovskogo gosudarstvennogo istoriko-arkhivnogo instituta* 21 (1965):296; V. A. Aleksandrov, "Streletskoe naselenie iuzhnykh gorodov Rossii v XVII veke," AN SSSR, *Novoe o proshlom nashei strany* (Moscow, 1967), pp. 246, 248.

repeated injunction against any Ukrainian attempts to introduce alcohol and tobacco.[9]

The rise in Hetman Bohdan Khmel'nyts'kyi's power and his declaration of autonomy did not apparently affect traders crossing the southern border. Repeated assurances were exchanged in 1648 and 1649 that traders should move freely across the frontier, providing they were armed with appropriate documents. Numerous "Lithuanians" apparently took advantage of the easy access to Muscovite grain markets during times of shortage. Some requested permission to purchase grain in Kursk; others appeared at Sevsk, Khotmyshsk, and Karpov. The military governor (voevoda) at Briansk reported that purchasers of grain were trying to avoid paying the appropriate customs duties.[10]

Very soon, however, a number of towns reported that "Lithuanian" purchases were creating shortfalls on local markets. The relatively large market at Putyvl' remained open to Ukrainian traders, provided they used the merchants' quarters (gostinnyi dvor) and paid their taxes. However, Khotmyshsk (a town with 887 service residents) reported that it would have difficulty in feeding its own population, if grain purchasers from across the frontier continued to buy up so much of the grain that was offered for sale locally. Briansk and Kozels'k limited cereal sales to local purchasers in 1650, and Kromy, too, preferred to hold onto its own grain supplies. Starvation was hardly at issue in the latter case, however; the extra purchases there threatened the supply of grain to the local distillery![11]

Orders to cease sales to foreigners might easily have had political and retaliatory motivation, as well as being motivated by need. Hetman Bohdan Khmel'nyts'kyi was negotiating with the Ottoman Empire in 1650, the year of many of these documents, and war seemed imminent. A similar decree from further north dating to 1650 states "za ikh mnogii nepravdy i grubosti im prodavat' ne dovedetsia" (for their great faithlessness and churlishness, one must not sell

---

[9] AIIuZR 3, no. 12; Dopolnenie, no. 127, for example.

[10] F. P. Shevchenko, Politychni ta ekonomichni zviazky Ukrainy z Rossiieiu v seredyni XVII st. (Kiev, 1969), pp. 385–86; Novombergskii, Ocherki vnutrennogo upravleniia, vol. 1, no. 46; AIIuZR 3, nos. 23, 36, 37, 79, 80.

[11] AIIuZR 3, nos. 36, 80; Novombergskii, Ocherki vnutrennogo upravleniia, vol. 2, nos. 383, 384; Shevchenko, Politychni ta ekonomichni zviazky, pp. 393, 396.

to them).[12] Khmel'nyts'kyi expressed a similar desire, a few years later, to resume the taxation of traders from Muscovy on a par with other foreigners.[13]

These considerations were not the only ones inspiring bans on grain export. Throughout the second half of the seventeenth century, most southern Russian towns, including those along the border, remained small and overwhelmingly military in population. Since most southern military personnel farmed their own, not overly productive, plots of land, it was a matter of military importance to Muscovy that food supplies should always be available to its southern garrisons. Many southern towns were shifting to new emergency food supply measures during the 1650s as the Belgorod fortified line reached completion. The new arrangements testify to the concern then felt by the southerners and the Muscovite government alike over this issue.[14] It is military interest which accounts at once for the intermittent character of the export bans, and explains their continuance into the next decades and even beyond the Peace of Andrusovo. For example, a decree to Orel in 1653 included grain in its tax schedule. Sevsk requested help in dealing with grain shortages in 1654; grain products were not even reaching the local marketplace, but were being bought up by Ukrainians in the villages of the province. In 1665, and again in 1669, the Komaritskii district (*volost'*) near Sevsk was reported to be selling its grain across the frontier to the Ukraine (*Malorossiskii goroda*), to the detriment of local military personnel. In 1665, the resulting trade ban included even Belgorod, an important military fortress which was considerably further from the Hetmanate than the other cities mentioned above. Another broad prohibition is recorded in the *Zapisnye knigi Moskovskogo stola* for 1664–1665; it forbade grain sales to the Ukraine in an effort to provide for the troops of the entire Belgorod and Sevsk districts. Without specific reference to the Ukraine, a simi-

---

[12] *AIIuZR* 3; Dopolnenie, pp. 111–12; quoted in Shevchenko, *Politychni ta ekonomichni zviazky*, p. 396.

[13] *AIIuZR* 3, no. 344. At least one Polish customs guard collected extra taxes despite official agreement to the contrary; *Vossoedinenie*, vol. 1, no. 260; Novombergskii, *Ocherki vnutrennogo upravleniia*, vol. 1, no. 591.

[14] Stevens, "Supply," p. 100.

lar ban occurred in the Kursk area some decades later.[15] Although military concerns provided a clear reason for these trade restraints, the Ukrainians in question were unfavorably impressed. Reported the governor of Sevsk: *"(oni) zlo shumiat"* (they are making an angry uproar).[16]

One should not infer from these descriptions that the border was perpetually closed to legal trade in grain; in fact, it was usually open. Nor should it be assumed that all of Muscovy's southern territories were exclusively populated by small subsistence farmers; a few provinces (particularly Orel, also Briansk, Belev, Putyvl', Sevsk, Mtsensk, Ryl'sk, and some Don towns) produced reliable trade surpluses by the 1670s which (except for the Don towns) mostly went northward for resale in Moscow.[17] However, since regular interruptions in trade were experienced even by the small-scale grain traders between southern Muscovy and the Hetmanate, transactions across the frontier must have seemed unreliable and hardly advantageous to the trader.

A second and parallel issue to be faced in considering the grain trade is that of the prices of rye and oats in Muscovy and the Ukraine. Although price data are scant in the extreme for the period, what little information is extant for the period prior to 1700 is extremely suggestive. The available materials are nothing more than occasional reports from military governors about the market price of grain at their own or nearby towns. What is particularly striking about those reports is the persistently low price of southern grain. Where available, prices from Ukrainian towns at the turn of the century are similar to those of southern Muscovy. Northern Russian towns which fed the Moscow markets had strikingly higher prices, sometimes twice, and often one-

---

[15] Novombergskii, *Ocherki vnutrennogo upravleniia*, vol. 1, nos. 14, 157, 177, 543, 592; vol. 2, no. 363; Arkheograficheskaia komissiia, *Russkaia istoricheskaia biblioteka*, vol. 11, *Zapisnaia kniga Moskovskogo stola* (St. Petersburg, 1889), p. 151; TsGADA, f. 210, *Belgorodskii stolbets*, 546, ll. 11–13, pp. 203–204. The years 1665–1668 were, of course, studded with the movement of Muscovite troops in and out of the Hetmanate.

[16] Novombergskii, *Ocherki vnutrennogo upravleniia*, vol. 1, no. 117.

[17] V. M. Vazhinskii, "Khlebnaia torgovlia na iuge Moskovskogo gosudarstva vo vtoroi polovine XVII veka," *Uchenye zapiski Moskovskogo oblastnogo pedagogicheskogo instituta im. N. K. Krupskoi* 127 (1963):8–23. The distribution of these cities has a great deal to do with their atypical landholding patterns. See also my "Supply," chap. 5.

and-one-half times as much.[18] If available recorded prices are at all representative, they offer a cogent reason why the grain trade should have run north-south rather than east-west, except for some limited local sales and in times of particular dearth.

For the most part, the grain trade from 1670 to the turn of the century did indeed run north and south. The Oka valley towns of Orel, Mtsensk, and Belev were a major source of grain for the Moscow area; Orel alone moved 7,733 tons in 1678. But little if any of this grain was drawn into Muscovite markets from the Ukraine.[19] The southern towns of the Seim-Desna basin, Putyvl', Ryl'sk, and Sevsk all had significant turnovers in grain (250–275 tons in the first two cases, 2,000 rubles-worth in the latter in 1670–1671), but grain purchases there were predominantly local. Since it was the center of a large military district, Sevsk had a captive market in its military personnel; Putyvl' had a resident population of virtually landless servitors who had been relocated when their lands were lost to Poland. Ukrainian purchasers and sellers sometimes appeared in these markets prior to 1670–1671. In the absence of later customs receipts from these cities, it is difficult to add anything, other than that the cities do not appear subsequently to have become transshipment points for grain going in either direction.[20] Nearby Kursk, a growing market town by the early 1700s, moved only 1,100 *chetverty* (119 tons) of grain in a year and merely 10 percent of that was of Ukrainian origin. Like most southern towns, Kursk's grain market had not prospered in the second half of the century. Briansk alone, the farthest north, had a persistent recorded grain trade with the Ukraine. Even there, the trade was limited, and there is no particular indication that cheap Ukrainian grain was being shipped to the pricier north-Muscovite markets in any

[18] V. N. Mironov, "Dvizhenie tsen na rzhi v Rossii v XVIII v.," in *Ezhegodnik po agrarnoi istorii vostochnoi Evropy* (1965):156–63; Stevens, "Supply," p. 223. This material was written before Mironov's book on grain prices in the late seventeenth through nineteenth century was available to me.

[19] Vazhinskii, "Khlebnaia torgovlia," pp. 1–16, 18–20; V. S. Bakulin, "Orel kak khlebnyi rynok vo vtoroi polovine XVIIv.," *Goroda feodal'noi Rossii* (Moscow, 1966), pp. 256–63, and also his "Torgovye oboroty," pp. 303–304.

[20] A. A. Novosel'skii, "Raspad sluzhilogo goroda," in AN SSSR, *Russkoe gosudarstvo v XVII v.* (Moscow, 1961), p. 246; Vazhinskii, "Khlebnaia torgovlia," pp. 16–19, 23; B. B. Kafengauz, "Ekonomicheskie sviazi Ukrainy i Rossii," in *Vossoedinenie*, vol. 2, pp. 422, 432; Aleksandrov, "Streletskoe naselenie," pp. 244, 248.

quantity. All grain sales totaled 3,000 rubles, but Ukrainians both bought and sold on a small scale. A Kievan made a single 100 ruble purchase in 1676; another Ukrainian sold a few rubles' worth. The situation was little changed by 1720, when equally small amounts changed hands. Other purchases taking place at Briansk were obscured by collective customs entries, which lumped grain, wax, and other items together.[21]

Whatever effect grain prices or periodic restrictions on export sales may have had on grain trade between southern Muscovy and the Hetmanate, another powerful disincentive existed to such traffic: the structure and regulation of alcohol sales on the eastern side of the border. The Muscovite government held a monopoly over the sale of alcoholic beverages within its own borders. Excise taxes imposed at the sales points were quite high, intended to capture a tidy profit for the national budget. Reforms in 1653 further limited the number of taverns (kruzhechnye dvory) where alcohol could be purchased. According to M. Ia. Volkhov, the reforms were intended to extend the government monopoly and increase government revenue from excise taxes. Much of the liquor sold at these taverns was manufactured from grain in nearby state-run distilleries. Given the high prices on alcohol set by the state, state-run stills were also highly lucrative, with profits that have been estimated as high as 100 percent; a more conservative estimate for vodka (dvoinoe vina) production alone is 35 percent.[22]

However lucrative these sales, the state alcohol production could not keep up with demand, especially as new distribution points opened after 1663. Furthermore, administering state-run stills proved a burdensome task. As a result, taverns began purchasing alcohol under contract from private distilleries during the second half of the seventeenth century. Despite this additional supply, alcohol prices

[21] Vazhinskii, "Khlebnaia torgovlia," pp. 18–20; Kafengauz, Ocherki vnutrennogo rynka, pp. 294, 296, 298, 315.

[22] M. Ia. Volkhov, Ocherki istorii promyslov Rossii, vtoraia polovina XVII-pervaia polovina XVIII veka, vinokurennoe proizvodstvo (Moscow, 1979), pp. 29–30, 36. The distillery at Voronezh produced vodka at 16 altyn, 4 dengi, a profit of slightly more than 35 percent. Also, see D. I. Bagalei, ed., "O prodazhnoi tsene vina v 1775 godu," Vremennik Imperatorskogo obshchestva istorii i drevnostei rossiiskikh 15 (1852):31–32.

remained high until the 1720s as demand continued to grow and the sales monopoly continued to pay the Russian government handsomely.

After mid-century, both southern Muscovy and the Hetmanate rapidly became important sources of privately distilled liquor. On both sides of the border, grain was apparently cheap, skilled labor was readily available, and there were few restrictions on alcohol production among small landholders. Even the fragmentary evidence available suggests that the trade in distilled alcohol from the Hetmanate into Muscovy was a lucrative and growing one. Government stills in Sevsk, Ryl'sk, and Putyvl' closed in the 1650s and 1660s under the influx of alcohol. The Briansk tavern sold mostly alcohol purchased from contractors, as well as a little the state still made. Another 2,000 pails of liquor were sold in the Briansk market, in addition to that bought by the tavern. Given profits as high as 28 kopeks (more than 100 percent) per pail, the local trade quickly became a longer distance one. Almost 69,000 pails of alcohol arrived in Moscow from the towns of the Left Bank alone during 1723.[23] The Left-Bank towns of Chernihiv and Nizhyn had more than 350 stills. It is not altogether certain that alcohol was easier to transport overland from the Ukraine than grain, but it was more lucrative, and traders did not have to worry at all about spoilage! All this activity was reflected in high excise payments.[24]

---

[23] Volkhov, *Ocherki istorii*, pp. 40–41, 45, 134–35; Kafengauz, *Ocherki vnutrennogo rynka*, p. 315. Southern Muscovy was also one of the few areas where domestic production continued legally on a wide scale after 1653. Government stills in Sloboda Ukraine were not even built in the seventeenth century. Ibid., pp. 33, 42. Volkhov, *Ocherki istorii*, p. 37, argues that the pre-payment contractors, in addition to demand, was what kept vodka prices high into the 1720s. Cf. I. Ditiatin, "Tsarskii tabak Moskovskogo gosudarstva," in his, *Stat'i po istorii Russkogo prava* (St. Petersburg, 1885), p. 480; I. T. Prizhkov, *Istoriia kabakov v Rossii v sviazi s istoriei Russkogo naroda* (St. Petersburg, 1868), p. 73.

[24] Kafengauz, *Ocherki vnutrennogo rynka*, p. 289. Southern districts' excise taxes represented three-fourths of the customs and excise totals from those areas in 1860, but the importance of alcohol was certainly not the only reason for that phenomenon. M. V. Dovnar-Zapol'skii, *Materialy dlia istorii biudzheta Razriadnogo prikaza* (Moscow, 1900), pp. 5–15.

Once the monopoly was in place, the Muscovite government's interest in the alcohol trade across the border focused on the collection of the customs duties. The regular customs tariff on alcohol (two *altyn* for each *chetvert'* of grain used in making the vodka) amounted to about a 12.5 percent tax on grain purchased for southern markets. Muscovy's efforts to collect it were not invariably crowned with success. Illegally imported alcohol, warned a decree of 1665, would be confiscated. The same threat was repeated in 1675, directed especially at the Ukraine. Special customs gates were even built in Sloboda Ukraine (the eastern Ukraine) to catch those trying to circumvent taxation by smuggling alcohol in from the south. It was, for all that, virtually an impossible task. The volumes of grain and alcohol involved in the transgressions that were uncovered are a clue to the size of the illegal traffic. Merchants from Starodub and Sosnytsia had about 50 pails of vodka stolen from them by "helpful" musketeers (*streltsy*) who escorted them from the border. More dramatically, the commander of a Ukrainian regiment wrote to reaffirm that merchants of his town would in future pass legally through customs—and would the military governor mind returning the 2,000 rubles' worth of liquor he had recently confiscated? With still greater aplomb, another official collected 10,000 *chetverty* (1,080 tons) of a grain tax in kind—and promptly sold it to a Ukrainian for the manufacture of alcohol.[25] Whether or not the duties were successfully collected, the scattered evidence of both legal and illegal trade strongly suggests that the Muscovite alcohol monopoly and its contracting system drew cereal grain off southern markets and thus probably detracted from local and long-distance transactions in that commodity.

Finally, the Muscovite military presence in the Hetmanate absorbed both Ukrainian and Muscovite grain supplies. Muscovite troops appeared in the Ukraine in considerable numbers after 1663. After 1666, supplies to maintain them were provided by the Muscovite government on an irregular basis. When supplies fell short, or failed to arrive at all, the troops were forced to depend on Ukrainian market resources. For example, as early as 1656–1657, some 2,000

---

[25] *AIIuZR* 3, nos. 3, 71; Novombergskii, *Ocherki vnutrennogo upravleniia*, vol. 1, no. 591. Paul Bushkovitch, *The Merchants of Muscovy, 1580–1650* (Cambridge, 1980), p. 190, fn. 6, suggests that Ukrainians supplied both grain and illegal liquor to Muscovite markets.

Muscovite army personnel arrived for duty in Ukrainian towns; with them from Muscovy came only 250 *chetverty* (27 tons) of grain, an amount adequate to maintain them, but not their horses, for slightly less than two weeks.[26]

When they became larger and permanent, these Muscovite garrisons made more serious demands. In the early years of the *Malorossiiskii prikaz*, these troops were supposed to be maintained by the Ukrainian towns where they were stationed. Kiev, with an urban population of about 1,200 households, was to have a Russian garrison of 5,000 men; Pereiaslav with 300 urban households, was to have 2,000 Russians, and the Chernihiv garrison, 1,200.[27] Muscovite efforts to supply troops regularly with food from within Muscovy did not begin until 1667. After an initial shipment of 688 tons to Kiev in 1665–1666, regular amounts (500–1,000 tons) of grain were set aside annually for shipment to the same destination from the Sevsk administrative district. Whenever possible, this volume was to be supplemented from the Belgorod district. Taxation in kind on south Russian landowners was intended to be a principal source of these shipments.[28]

To trace annual shipments to Kiev for each of the thirty-three years before the end of the century has not been possible. For the fourteen years for which records are available, the size of grain shipments varied from a low level of 6,739 *chetverty*, (728 tons) upward to 26,000 *chetverty* (over 2,800 tons). Only one amount, the largest, was adequate to maintain the garrison of 7,878 men that the Kievan fortress wanted. This was not as serious as it appears, however, as the garrison was rarely close to full strength. On eight occasions, when compared with the size of the resident garrison, the shipments recorded should have been adequate; on six they were not. Again, small shipments forced Muscovites to buy food on local markets. In

---

[26] Stevens, "Supply," pp. 203–204.

[27] K. A. Sofronenko, *Malorossiiskii prikaz Russkogo gosudarstva vtoroi poloviny XVII i nachala XVIII veka* (Moscow, 1960), pp. 165–71; V. A. Romanovskii, "Razvitie gorodov levoberezhnoi Ukrainy posle vossoedineniia s Rossiei," in *Vossoedinenie*, p. 400.

[28] TsGADA, fond 210; *Belgorodskaia kniga* 78, l. 245; ibid., 89, ll. 440–41; Vazhinskii, "Sbory zaprosnogo," pp. 24–25, and his, "Usilenie soldatskoi povinnosti v Rossii v XVII veka po materialam iuzhnykh uezdov," *Izvestiia Voronezhskogo gosudarstvennogo pedagogicheskogo instituta* 157 (1976):60.

1669 and 1670, calculations suggest that Russian troops were trying to purchase about 1,500 tons of extra grain near Kiev. These shortfalls were unpredictable. In 1673, 4,000 rubles appeared instead of the expected grain shipment. Other sums replaced or supplemented shipments in 1681, 1689, and 1697—in the first case a mere 1,000 rubles.[29] Such large and abrupt demands on Ukrainian grain supplies could not always be met. In 1670, hungry Muscovite troops reacted to the situation by deserting. The only supplies available to the Muscovite military commander there in 1673 proved to be so expensive that the 4,000 rubles available did not come close to provisioning the garrison. Such situations carried inherent military problems. In 1665, another Muscovite commander reported that Kievan merchants were selling goods to the enemy. Much though he would have liked to stop them, he feared that the merchants might retaliate by cutting off the Muscovite troops' own food supplies. When Muscovite campaign armies moved into the Hetmanate, as they did in 1665–1669 and in the mid–1670s, for example, their presence posed similar though less persistent strains on both troops and local supplies. It should be added that major campaigns were apparently a higher supply priority to the Muscovite army than the sustaining of regular garrisons.[30] Regardless of the military implications of these supply efforts, however, it seems reasonable to assume that persistent but irregular demands for marketed supplies in Kiev, as well as, periodically, in Nizhyn, Chernihiv, and Pereiaslav, provided an immediate, if unpredictable, market for local grain. Meanwhile, taxation in kind, to provide whatever supplies

[29] For the size of grain shipments and garrisons: Sofronenko, *Malorossiiskii prikaz*, pp. 165–71; *Simbirskii sbornik*, 2 vols. (Moscow, 1845, 1870), vol. 1, pt. 1, no. 28; vol. 1, *Malorossiiskie dela*, nos. 183, 186; A. A. Novosel'skii, "Dvortsovye krestiane Komaritskoi volosti vo vtoroi polovine XVII veka," in AN SSSR, *Voprosy istorii sel'skogo khoziaistva krestianstva i revoliutsionnogo dvizheniia v Rossii*, vol. 2 (Moscow, 1961), pp. 65–80; Novombergskii, *Ocherki vnutrennogo upravleniia*, vol. 1, nos. 120, 156, 313, 393, 394, 414, 460, 677, 678; Stevens, "Supply," pp. 203–204. Calculations of the adequacy of supplies are based on the norm of 3.29 *chetverty* per year per man, or three pounds of bread daily. Jeffrey Kaplow, *The Naming of Kings* (New York, 1972), p. 72.

[30] *Simbirskii sbornik*, vol. 1, *Malorossiiskie dela*, nos. 183, 186; Stevens, "Supply," pp. 75–77, 201. The commanders in 1673 and 1665 were Trubetskoi and Sheremetov, respectively.

Muscovy could muster for its garrisons, drained some surplus grain from the other side of the frontier.

In short, the limited character of Muscovite-Ukrainian trade in cereal grains can, I believe, be attributed partially to Muscovite policies vis-à-vis the Hetmanate. While periodic border bans on the trade provided a poor stimulus to local transactions at mid-century, later on, the profits from alcohol sales to the Muscovite monopoly and the military requirements of Muscovite troops in the Ukraine provided other outlets for surplus southern grains. Thus such economic integration as can be observed between Muscovy and the Ukraine in the latter half of the seventeenth century was not the result of trade in bulk cereal grains.

CHAPTER SEVEN

Petrine Mercantilist Economic Policies toward the Ukraine

Bohdan Krawchenko

Introduction

The focus of this paper is Peter I's (1672–1725) mercantilist economic policies towards the Ukraine. Since there is some debate as to whether Peter's economic reforms should be considered mercantilist,[1] our characterization requires some justification. Mercantilism—a body of policies and ideas which dominated Europe from the sixteenth to eighteenth centuries or roughly between the Middle Ages and the *laissez-faire* era—identified wealth with precious metals, advanced protectionism, export monopolies, balance of trade, exchange controls, the establishment of colonies, and the promotion of manufacture. During the mercantilist era the state, preoccupied with the exigencies of power, played a preponderant role in advancing economic development. Yet the economic policies and techniques of mercantilism were used for very different purposes in Europe, when compared to Russia. In Europe, mercantilism was a transitional era—a period of capital accumulation, changing social relations, with new conceptions of society coming to the fore.[2] In Europe the policies of the state served and enhanced certain vested social interests—those of tradesmen, merchants, and manufacturers. But in examining the

---

[1] See Alexander Gerschenkron, *Europe in the Russian Mirror: Four Lectures in Economic History* (London, 1970), pp. 62–96 .

[2] E. F. Heckscher, ''Mercantilism,'' *The Economic History Review* 7, no. 1 (November 1936): 44–54.

Petrine experience one could not possibly claim with Adam Smith that "the merchants and manufacturers have been far the principal architects . . . of the whole mercantile system."[3] Mercantilism in Russia served the interests of the state. One is tempted to agree with Plekhanov that in Russia "Peter carried to its extreme logical consequence the population's lack of rights vis-à-vis the state that is characteristic of Oriental despotism."[4] In a profound way Peter forced Russia further away from Europe and closer "towards the despotism of the Orient with their service states."[5] Peter's traditional Muscovite manner of tackling industrial development left the state stronger in relation to society: industry was established, but the entrepreneurial and commercial strata were stiffled. Russia's backwardness and unique sociopolitical heritage meant that unlike in Europe, mercantilism in Russia did not prepare the groundwork for modern industrial development. Russian mercantilism was therefore quite unique. Its specificity was the result of the underdevelopment of the Russian social formation.

Petrine mercantilist policies played a major role in extending the Russian socioeconomic system into the Ukraine. This process entailed tensions and conflict because the Ukrainian social formation in that period differed significantly from the Russian pattern. Social relations in the Ukraine, lacking Russia's patrimonial characteristics, were much more dynamic and progressive than in Russia. Serfdom was badly shattered as an institution because of the 1648 revolution, and the abundance of free land and a weak central authority—the Hetman state was unable to raise substantial surpluses to strengthen its apparatus of coercion precisely because of the emancipation of peasants—retarded the growth of onerous peasant obligations. The society had begun its entry into a money economy, there was much free labor, independent landholding, as well as relatively vibrant artisan, tradesmen, and merchant groups.[6] Of course the Ukrainian social

[3] Cited by Gerschenkron, *Europe*, p. 86.

[4] Georgii V. Plekhanov, "Peter the Great—An Oriental Despot," in M. Raeff, ed. *Peter the Great Changes Russia* (Lexington, Mass., 1972), p. 186.

[5] Gerschenkron, *Europe*, 95.

[6] O. O. Nesterenko, *Rozvytok promyslovosti na Ukraini*, vol. 1 (Kiev, 1959), pp. 32, 34; M. Ie. Slabchenko, *Orhanizatsiia hospodarstva Ukrainy vid khmel'nyshchyny do svitovoi viiny,* [sic] *Hospodarstvo Het'manshchyny XVII–XVIII stolittiv. Zemlevolodinnia ta formy sil's'koho hospodarstva* (Odessa, 1923), pp. 1–20.

formation—difficult to characterize because it was new and transitional—experienced social contradictions which have been amply analyzed in Soviet historiography.[7] But it was a social formation whose social and economic relations were much more characteristic of a central European pattern.[8] One of the principal and most devastating effects of Petrine mercantilism was to undermine permanently the main pillars of socioeconomic dynamism in Ukrainian society, especially those promoting the Ukraine's integration into Europe, namely the country's commercial strata.

Russia's backwardness dictated that only certain elements of the mercantilist approach to the economy would be employed. Thus, nowhere in Europe was such zeal shown for the establishment of state-appointed or state-licensed enterprises as in Russia. Yet, the Western preoccupation with foreign trade and precious metals appears to have played a very subordinate role in Russia. Foreign trade, which remained largely in foreign hands, did not even attract Peter's serious attention until the last years of his life.[9] Russia was simply too weak to organize foreign trade and commerce effectively and engage in beggar-my-neighbor trade relations with its European counterparts. But with respect to the Ukraine, a country which Russia through the presence of an army of occupation was in a position to dominate, these were precisely the policies which Russian authorities stressed. Predatory trade measures typical of mercantilist colonial practice and not state-directed economic development characterized Petrine mercantilism in the Ukraine. The Ukraine's experience within the system of Russian mercantilism was thus unique, a fact that has not been recognized in most Western and Soviet writing on the economic history of this period. Peter's policies towards manufacture are a case in point.

---

[7] See M. Iavors'kyi, *Istoriia Ukrainy v styslomu narysi* (Kharkiv, 1928), pp. 57–78; *Istoriia narodnoho hospodarstva Ukrains'koi RSR*, vol. 1 (Kiev, 1983), chap. 5.

[8] For an excellent discussion of characterizations of social formations, see Robert Brenner, "The Origins of Capitalist Development: A Critique of Neo-Smithian Marxism," *New Left Review* 105 (1977):22–96.

[9] Gerschenkron, *Europe*, p. 82.

Manufacture

In the first volume of the Soviet publication *Istoriia narodnoho hospodarstva Ukrains'koi RSR* it is affirmed that at the turn of the eighteenth century "favorable prospects opened up for the development of the reunited territories now that they were part of the Russian state" since "the more developed Russian economy exerted a positive influence on the economic development of the Ukraine."[10] The "new manufacturing era" which Peter inaugurated is given as proof of this positive development.[11] The Soviet Ukrainian encyclopedia, characterizing Petrine mercantilism as "progressive," noted that his policies "did much to enhance the development of manufacture" in the Ukraine.[12]

Indeed, at the time of his death, Peter left behind him some two hundred large industrial enterprises.[13] The Ukraine, however, was bypassed during this first industrialization drive since Peter neither established nor promoted the founding of manufactures in the Hetmanate. "State" industry, such as it emerged in the Ukraine in the eighteenth century, was a post-Petrine phenomenon.[14] After Peter's death, in time, some factories were founded in the Ukraine because of the strong personal influence of prominent Russian landowners who had obtained estates in the Ukraine—individuals such as Menshikov, Stroganov, Iusupov, and Rumiantsev.[15] It is they who eventually broke the "colonial blockade" of Ukrainian industry put in place by Peter.[16]

Peter's positive program of economic development in the Ukraine was limited to the establishment of a few large sheep and horse plantations, as well as some half-measures to improve the Ukraine's silk and

[10] *Istoriia narodnoho hospodarstva Ukrains'koi RSR*, p. 165.

[11] Ibid., p. 179.

[12] "Merkantylizm" in *Ukrains'ka radians'ka entsyklopediia*, vol. 9 (Kiev 1962), p. 66.

[13] L. Jay Oliva, *Russia in the Era of Peter the Great* (Englewood, N.J., 1969), p. 124.

[14] Oleksander Ohloblyn, *A History of Ukrainian Industry*, pt. 1, *Ocherki istorii ukrainskoi fabriky. Manufaktura v Getmanshchine* (Kiev, 1925; reprint, Munich, 1971), p. 46.

[15] Ibid., pp. 211–12.

[16] Ibid., p. 43.

tobacco industries.[17] These steps were taken in order to secure cheap raw materials essential for Russian manufacture and for the Russian army. Indeed, during Peter's administration many edicts (*ukazy*) were quite explicit about the fact that the Ukraine was to fulfill the function of a purely colonial economy.[18] It should be pointed out that Peter's efforts to establish agricultural enterprises in the Ukraine did not meet with success. The sheep plantations, for instance, were ill-conceived, poorly managed, and resented by the population who had to surrender a third of their sheep to establish them.[19] Not rooted in Ukrainian agricultural practice, these plantations experienced a succession of crises. Indeed, two years after Peter's death, in 1727, Hetman Danylo Apostol proposed that the plantations be disbanded,[20] as they eventually were.[21]

This is not to say that Peter was not concerned with the Ukraine's industries. On the contrary, in the second half of his reign, characterized by "manufacturing fever," the Ukraine's industries suffered many discriminatory measures designed to prevent them from becoming a serious competitor for the newly emerged Russian plants. Perhaps the most significant example in this regard was the Ukraine's chemical industry, one which according to a foreign contemporary was relatively well developed.[22] Potash production was undoubtedly the most significant component of this industry. In 1718 Peter prohibited the establishment of any new potash works (*budy* as they were called) in the Ukraine.[23] This measure limiting expansion, when combined with a ban subsequently imposed prohibiting the export of the Ukraine's potash to its established international markets, constricted potash production to satisfying purely local needs. In time, because of these restrictions, the indigenous potash industry lost its dominant

---

[17] M. E. Slabchenko, *Malorusskii polk v administrativnom otnoshenii* (Odessa, 1909), pp. 267–77.

[18] Ohloblyn, *Manufaktura v Getmanshchine*, p. 40.

[19] Slabchenko, *Malorusskii polk*, p. 272.

[20] Borys Krupnyts'kyi, *Het'man Danylo Apostol i ioho doba* (Augsburg, 1948) p. 139.

[21] Ibid., p. 140; Nesterenko, *Rozvytok promyslovosti*, vol. 1, p. 151.

[22] Volodymyr Sichynsky, *Ukraine in Foreign Comments and Descriptions from the VIth to XXth Century* (New York, 1953), p. 169.

[23] A. Lazarevskii, *Opisanie staroi Malorossii, Materialy dlia istorii zaseleniia, zemlevladeniia i upravleniia*, vol. 1 (Kiev, 1888), p. 108.

position even in the local market since it was unable to withstand competition from expanding potash works in Russia.[24]

Measures limiting or banning production were relatively infrequent, however, and were not the primary mechanism used to undermine the Ukraine's economy. Rather, that economy suffered because of steps taken by the Petrine administration to establish control over Ukrainian trade and commerce. Thus in the rest of the paper this is the aspect of Petrine policy which will be discussed.

Trade and Commerce

The last decades of the seventeenth century and the first decades of the eighteenth were characterized by a large and intensive expansion of trade in the Left-Bank Ukraine. A number of factors contributed towards this development. First, the Western European market had been starved of Ukrainian raw materials because of the disruption of commercial relations during the period of the "Ruin" and was anxious to resume trade. For similar reasons, the Ukrainian market, long denied access to Western European manufactured goods, showed a high demand for imports.[25] Second, because there was free trade with foreign countries, trade exchange could flourish and since Russian merchants did not enjoy a privileged position, Ukrainian merchants were the most active participants in this process.[26] Finally, the growth of a money economy, of merchant capital, and large-scale landholding in the Left-Bank Ukraine contributed towards an increase in production which necessitated the search for new Western markets.[27] This third point requires further elaboration.

The development of a money economy and the growing concentration of productive forces had already begun in the seventeenth century, during the rule of Hetmans Ivan Samoilovych and Ivan Mazepa,

---

[24] Ohloblyn, *Manufaktura v Gemanshchine*, p. 39. Ironically, the Russian potash industry was built largely using the expertise of Ukrainian master craftsmen from Kiev. See P. G. Liubomirov, *Ocherki po istorii russkoi promyshlennosti XVII, XVIII i nachalo XIX veka* (Moscow, 1947), p. 177n.

[25] Ohloblyn, *Manufaktura v Getmanshchine*, p. 32.

[26] O. S. Kompan, *Mista Ukrainy v druhii polovyni XVIII st.* (Kiev, 1963), pp. 98–99.

[27] Ivan Dzhydzhora, *Ukraina v pershii polovyni XVIII viku. Rozvidky i zamitky* (Kiev, 1930), p. 1.

and was a process particularly characteristic of the northern areas of the Hetmanate—the Starodub, Chernihiv, and, to some extent, the Nizhyn regiments. There, either through purchase or coercion, large estates, and with them many industrial concerns such as mills, distilleries, mines, and potash works, came into the hands of the leading representatives of the Cossack *starshyna* (officer class)—who were also active traders—and the burghers.[28] However, it was really in the post-Mazepist period, spurred by political factors, that the concentration of money and productive forces became a widespread phenomenon. After the Battle of Poltava and the terrible repression of Mazepa's followers, the *starshyna* and other elements of the Ukraine's upper classes found themselves in a precarious situation. They needed money desperately to purchase estates, mills, and other enterprises as a way of securing their material position.[29] The fact that Peter began to distribute estates in the Ukraine to his followers only hastened the Ukrainian upper classes' drive to accumulate wealth. Another factor which played a major role in developing a money economy were the massive payments in tax and in kind which were imposed on the Ukraine by Peter in order to sustain Russia's large permanent garrison left behind after the 1708–1709 events. It is true that the new burdens fell primarily on the shoulders of the peasantry, but increasingly the *starshyna* and other leading components of Ukrainian society also had to contribute. The need for money to meet these payments hastened the need for trade.[30] This is not to say that foreign trade began with Hetman Ivan Skoropads'kyi. On the contrary, the Ukraine had long established commercial relations with Western Europe. During the relative peace under Mazepa "merchant trade" was in a "flourishing state," as Bantysh-Kamenskii noted.[31] However, the new circumstances meant that notwithstanding the 1709 debacle, trade developed briskly, especially in the first half of Skoropads'kyi's rule, that is, up to around 1714, when Ukrainian trade received major blows from Petrine policies.

[28] Ohloblyn, *Manufaktura v Getmanshchine*, pp. 32–33.

[29] Nesterenko, *Rozvytok promyslovosti*, vol. 1, p. 211.

[30] Dzhydzhora, *Ukraina*, pp. 2–3.

[31] D. Bantysh-Kamenskii, *Materialy dlia otechestvennoi istorii*, vol. 2 (Moscow, 1859), p. 198.

Turning to an examination of Ukrainian trade it should be stressed that although the foundation of the Ukrainian and Russian economies in the eighteenth century was the same—namely, agriculture—"the products of the Ukrainian economy had already for a few centuries been known abroad ... [whereas] the Russian agricultural economy had only started on that path."[32] As an exporter and importer the Hetmanate represented a different economic profile from Russia and, indeed, had relatively few economic relations with its northern neighbor. The Hetmanate was closely tied to Austria, Germany, and Poland, which served as the chief markets for Ukrainian products, and exports from the Ukraine to other lands such as France and Holland also moved through these countries. Ukrainian exports went principally to Silesia (Breslau), Saxony, as well as to the Baltic ports of Gdańsk, Königsberg, and Riga—the latter became part of Russia in 1710.[33] Ukrainian exports consisted chiefly of oxen, leather (*iukhta*), bees wax, tallow, bacon, oil, bristles, rhubarb, wool, vodka (*horilka*), tobacco, anise, potash, tar, saltpeter (potassium nitrate), dried fish, corn, salt, and hemp.[34]

The paucity of data makes it difficult to establish the total value of Ukrainian exports or the relative importance of the commodities traded. Judging by the evidence it is probable that trade in oxen occupied a primary place, followed by hemp, tobacco, vodka, and grain.[35] Hemp, transported by waterway to Riga, was a rather important item. Reports suggest that trade was substantial. Thus, in the opinion of a Polish voevoda from Vitsebsk in 1710 more than one million rubles worth of Ukrainian goods had entered Poland that year.[36] Since this official possessed partial information, the real figure was undoubtedly higher. In 1708, to give a comparison which allows one to evaluate the significance of that figure, the total revenues of the Russian state amounted to 3.4 million rubles.[37] Given the evergrowing expansion of

[32] Ohloblyn, *Manufaktura v Getmanshchine*, p. 32.

[33] For a discussion of trade routes see I. Luchitskii, "K istorii torgovli v Malorossii XVIII v.," *Kievskaia starina* 45 (1894):155–58.

[34] Dmytro Doroshenko, *A Survey of Ukrainian History* (Winnipeg, 1975), p. 398.

[35] Lazarevskii, *Opisanie*, vol. 1, p. 108; vol. 2 (Kiev, 1893), pp. 189–90, 202.

[36] Dzhydzhora, *Ukraina*, p. 13.

[37] P. Miliukov, *Gosudarstvennoe khoziaistvo Rossii v pervoi chetverti XVIII stoletiia i reforma Petra velikogo* (St. Petersburg, 1905), p. 665.

the Russian state budget, it is easy to see why Peter cast a covetous eye on Ukrainian trade as a potential source of income.

Import was essential for export, especially during this period when there was a marked shortage of currency. Import facilitated exchange and acted as a substitute for the shortcomings of the monetary system. Dutch and English woolen cloth, linen, silk, handicrafts, scythes, saws, and arms are some of the import items which figure in the documents of that period.[38] We have no information about the total monetary value of imports, but, based on individual case studies, there is reason to believe that it was substantial. Thus, in 1704 the Kiev merchant Roman Iakymovych brought from Breslau nine wagons of saws and scythes valued at 15,000 Joachimsthalers (*iefymyky*) and in 1705 he imported 20,000 Joachimsthalers worth of goods.[39] (The official exchange rate was fifty kopeks for one Joachimsthaler; unofficially the rate was more than double that amount.) Evidence of close trading relations between the Hetmanate and foreign countries is the fact that this trade was based on mutual long-standing credit arrangements.

Trade in the Ukraine involved large layers of the population. Indicative of this is the fact that approximately 46 percent of the Left-Bank population in the latter half of the seventeenth century lived in towns, that is, roughly 450,000 people. Data on the state characteristics of the urban population reveal that over one-third was engaged in commerce, almost 10 percent as merchants. (Since these figures omit, for instance, the many Cossacks engaged in trade, they have to be revised upwards.) In contradistinction to the late eighteenth and nineteenth centuries, Ukrainians formed the overwhelming majority of the urban population.[40] Initially, the Cossacks, the *starshyna* in particular, were the most important merchants. As trade developed, a division of labor crystalized and merchants arose from among the burghers of

---

[38] Dzhydzhora, *Ukraina*, p. 15; Mikhail Sudienko, *Materialy dlia otechestvennoi istorii*, vol. 1, pt. 1 (Kiev, 1853), p. 62.

[39] Dzhydzhora, *Ukraina*, p. 16.

[40] See V. O. Romanovs'kyi, ed., *Perepysni knyhy 1666 roku* (Kiev, 1933), pp. iii–xi; Kompan, *Mista Ukrainy*, pp. 47–57, 106; A. I. Baranovich, *Ukraina nakanune osvoboditel'noi voiny serediny XVII v.* (Moscow, 1959), p. 139; B. B. Kafengauz, "Ekonomicheskie sviazi Ukrainy i Rossii v kontse XVII–nachale XVIII stoletiia," in *Vossoedinenie Ukrainy s Rossii 1654–1954. Sbornik statei* (Moscow, 1954), p. 422 and V. A. Romanovskii, "Razvitie gorodov levobereznoi Ukrainy posle vossoedineniia s Rossiei (vo vtoroi polovine XVII veka)," in ibid., p. 405.

Ukrainian towns to play a dominant role. Many tradesmen, peasants, and rank-and-file Cossacks were also involved in trade, carrying their produce to border towns to sell to merchants headed to foreign ports. Common Cossacks and peasants also made a living as carriers, freighting goods with their own carts and draft animals.[41]

Because Ukrainian trade was relatively lucrative, inevitably it came to the attention of Russian officials, especially when, as a consequence of Peter's reforms, Russian state finances experienced perennial crises. Although the tsar attempted to interfere with Ukrainian commerce before the Battle of Poltava, his efforts were largely unsuccessful because of the Hetmanate's autonomy. The Russian administrative structure in the Ukraine was weak and Hetmanate officials simply ignored edicts which they considered damaging to the economy. For instance, in 1703 an edict was issued which prohibited Ukrainian merchants from exporting hemp abroad and ordered them to trade with Russia instead. The Hetman administration paid no attention to this edict and trade with Riga and Breslau continued.[42] After Poltava, however, the situation changed. The Hetmanate's autonomy was restricted and there was now a large occupation army charged with enforcing Russia's regulations.

When we survey the numerous measures taken by the Petrine administration, it becomes apparent that not one was motivated by a desire to improve Ukrainian trade and industry. On the contrary, much effort went into undermining the Ukrainian economy. How can one square this with the other aspect of Peter's policy, namely, to integrate the hetmanate politically and economically into the Russian state? The fact of the matter is that despite Peter's integrationist drive, the Ukraine was considered a foreign, even hostile entity and economic policy reflected this perception. An excellent example of this thinking was Chancellor Osterman's suggestion that the Ukraine should be flooded with debased copper currency.[43] From a mercantilist point of view this meant treating the Ukraine as a completely foreign country to be exploited to the maximum. This was the framework within which Petrine policy towards Ukrainian trade operated. The specific measures which Peter took to control and exploit

---

[41] Doroshenko, *A Survey*, p. 397; Dzhydzhora, *Ukraina*, pp. 14–15.

[42] D. Bantysh-Kamenskii, *Istoriia Malorossii*, 3d ed. (Kiev, 1903), p. 592.

[43] Dzhydzhora, *Ukraina*, p. 30.

Ukrainian trade can be summarized in five points: 1) the redirection of Ukrainian trade towards Russian ports; 2) the placing of limits on private trade through the establishment of Russian monopolies; 3) the banning of the import of non-Russian goods; 4) the imposition of new customs duties; and 5) charging Russian organs of administration with the implementation of policy. We will examine more closely each of these points in turn.

Turning to the first point, namely, the redirection of Ukrainian trade, before we discuss what Peter's administration did concerning trade routes, what that administration failed to do is also significant for the purposes of our discussion. Trade routes through Poland were a life and death matter for Ukrainian merchants. Poland was never noted for its public order and during this period of upheavals, the safety of Ukrainian merchants and their goods emerged as a major concern. Customs officials in Poland were also notoriously unpredictable and ravenous.[44] A priori, one would have thought that when the Ukraine entered into the Russian orbit, the Ukraine would gain in terms of its trade relations with Poland. Russia, after all, was in a strong position to influence Polish policies. However, despite many pleas for intercession from both Ukrainian merchants and the hetman, the Russian administration continued to turn a deaf ear.[45] Even Skoropads'kyi's bribes of Russian residents in Poland did not move Russian officials to make representations on behalf of Ukrainian merchants.[46]

The first known example of attempts to redirect Ukrainian trade routes through bureaucratic means came with Peter's edict of 1701 ordering all Ukrainian merchants and traders to proceed with their goods only to the port of Azov and not to other towns. The annual fair established at Azov on Peter's name day was to be the only one permitted for trade purposes in the Ukraine.[47] Had this edict been enforced, it would have, in one blow, ruined the Ukrainian economy: the port of Azov led to nowhere. The Ukraine's vast network of fairs,

---

[44] See Dzhydzhora, *Ukraina*, pp. 17–25. For specific examples see Sudienko, *Materialy*, vol. 2 (Kiev, 1855), pp. 202–203.

[45] Dzhydzhora, *Ukraina*, p. 25.

[46] Sudienko, *Materialy*, vol. 2, pp. 405–406.

[47] *Polnoe sobranie zakonov Rossiiskoi imperii s 1693 goda* (hereafter *PSZ*), vol. 4 (Moscow, 1830), no. 1826.

far more extensive than that which existed in Russia,[48] would have collapsed. But the edict was so patently absurd and impossible to implement that it was ignored. Besides, Peter lost Azov under the terms of the 1711 Treaty of Pruth.

In 1701, coming on the heels of the Azov edict, was a new instruction whose consequences were longer lasting. Ukrainian merchants were ordered not to export hemp to Riga, but to direct their trade in that commodity to the artic port of Archangel.[49] Hemp was one of the most important commodities to be traded in terms of both the volume of trade and price, and, therefore, it also played a significant role in stimulating imports. It was also an item which was conveniently and easily transported overland to Biszęnkowice on the river Duna and then by boat to the closest port of Riga. To transport goods hundreds of additional kilometers through bogs and morasses to a port that was frozen for half the year would have meant financial suicide for Ukrainian merchants. Notwithstanding the fact that these merchants were absolved from paying port duties on hemp at Archangel, they risked non-compliance with the edict and made every effort to continue to send their goods to Riga via Biszęnkowice.[50] In 1711, the tsar formally allowed Ukrainian merchants to trade through Riga when that city was annexed by Russia.[51] However, the 1701 edict directing hemp to Archangel did much to create a climate of uncertainty and added enormous additional expense for the merchants who complied with the regulation.

The most dramatic and far-reaching measure regarding the redirection of Ukrainian trade routes was a 1714 *ukaz*. That edict had such an impact in the Hetmanate that fifty years later it would still figure in a memorandum to Catherine II written by the *starshyna* and nobility as an example of the violation of "Little Russia's rights," its right to "free trade" in particular.[52] The edict ordered merchants to use only Russian ports for the purposes of export. By then, the Ukraine's

---

[48] Nesterenko, *Rozvytok promyslovosti*, vol. 1, p. 114.

[49] Peter discusses this *ukaz* in *PSZ* vol. 5, no. 2768.

[50] Dzhydzhora, *Ukraina*, pp. 27–28.

[51] *PSZ*, vol. 5, no. 2768. See also Sudienko, *Materialy*, vol. 2, p. 202.

[52] "Proshenie malorossiiskogo shliakhetstva i starshin, vmeste s getmanom, o vozstanovlenii raznykh starinnykh prav Malorossii, podannoe Ekateriny II-i v 1764 godu," *Kievskaia starina* 6 (1883):338.

borders were encircled by Russian troops and the edict could be enforced. The following goods were affected: hemp, potash, leather (*iukhta*), pitch, bacon, wax, hemp oil, flax seed, bristles, glue, rhubarb, tar, and caviar. Violators of this regulation were to have their goods confiscated. Moreover, the merchants were prohibited from using the Biszęnkowice route (in Poland) to get to Riga (in Russia), but had to proceed through Russian territory.[53] Since Russian authorities knew that Ukrainian merchants, for whom Biszęnkowice was essential for their trade (see below), would resist the new measure, in 1715 a new regulation was issued making the hetman personally responsible for the merchants' behavior. This edict stipulated that all merchants from the Hetmanate, no matter where they resided, before proceeding to Riga, first had to go to Hlukhiv (the Hetmanate's capital) and have detailed inventories prepared for verification and certification by the hetman's administration. Without the proper documents they would not be allowed to cross the Ukrainian border.[54] The charge for the verification process, and the hundreds of additional kilometers added to the journey, entailed major new outlays of time and money. Despite the 1714 edict, it appears that many Ukrainian merchants took the risk and continued to use Biszęnkowice. In 1721 there came a new edict which strictly prohibited the Biszęnkowice route and out-lined in detail the new trade roads to be allowed: these were entirely within the boundaries of the Russian state, along the rivers Kasplia, Toroptsi, and Dvina, loading goods at Porichchia.[55] After this edict, it seems that few merchants were prepared to ignore the Russian administration's new strictures, which were enforced by a more formidable policing system than that which had previously existed.

This radical altering of Ukrainian trade routes did incalculable damage to that country's trade. The tsar's measures were introduced suddenly, without allowances being made for a transitional period, and they disoriented Ukrainian merchants. These merchants now had to travel along unfamiliar routes to unfamiliar ports where everything—storage, shipping arrangements, customers, and credit—had to be established anew. Since so much of Ukrainian trade had hitherto been based on long-established lines of credit, the sudden

[53] *PSZ*, vol. 5, no. 2793.
[54] Sudienko, *Materialy*, vol. 2, p. 65.
[55] *PSZ*, vol. 6, no. 3860.

dislocation of credit facilities ruined many. What was lost was not replaced in Russia, where commerce was still at a relatively primitive level of development. Accustomed to free trade and free competition, Ukrainian merchants were now plunged into an environment where commerce was strictly and bureaucratically controlled either by the state or by a few Russian merchant houses which had a privileged relationship to that state. Having little influence in Russia, Ukrainian merchants found themselves at the mercy of Russian interests. Tsarist regulations, moreover, kept constantly changing. Without an embassy in Petersburg, Ukrainian merchants often found out about the new laws when it was too late—at Russian border and customs posts—by which time their goods were subject to confiscation.[56] Peter had reoriented Ukrainian trade without having provided an elementary commercial infrastructure. Thus, in 1722 Ukrainian merchants complained to Hetman Skoropads'kyi that whereas at Biszenkowice there were proper storage facilities for hemp, and boats were readily available for transport to Riga, at the new location (on the river Kasplia) neither were to be seen.[57] Proper warehouses for hemp were not established until 1733.[58] Though merchants and Hetman Skoropads'kyi complained that the new regulations were ruining trade, the tsarist regime refused to alleviate the situation. The damage done to Ukrainian trade was of such proportions that Silesian towns experienced a decline. Indeed, it was only as a result of strong diplomatic representations from Austria, whose towns had been seriously affected by the rerouting of Ukrainian trade, that the tsarist administration in 1723 allowed some trade to resume through Poland.[59] This concession, however, was inconsequential since the bulk of commodities trade by Ukrainian merchants had by then been classified as state monopolies and taken out of the hands of private trade.

Ukrainian merchants had barely begun to establish trade under the new circumstances when they received an even more formidable blow. Russian commercial institutions and practices were now extended into the territory of the Hetmanate. The institutions and practices in question were: the Russian treasury's monopoly of trade

[56] Dzhydzhora, *Ukraina*, pp. 29, 35.
[57] Ibid., pp. 36–37.
[58] *PSZ*, vol. 8, no. 5982.
[59] Dzhydzhora, *Ukraina*, p. 78.

in a series of goods and commodities—the so-called *zapovednye tovary*; and the *gosti* (guests), that is, privileged Russian merchants who acted as the state's agents in collecting state revenues (customs duties and excises) and through whom the treasury traded in the *zapovednye tovary* or prohibited goods.

The practice of restricting private trade was long established in Russia. These state monopolies ruined many small and medium Russian merchants and only the *gosti* flourished—a fact admitted by Russian authorities themselves.[60] Nevertheless, the Russian state continued this policy, increasing the scope of the exclusive right of sale of goods in order to finance state expenditures. Initially, because of the Hetmanate's autonomy, Ukrainian merchants found themselves in an advantageous position relative to many of their Russian counterparts since in the Ukraine they could trade in goods which in Russia were monopolized by the state. Step by step this anomalous situation was removed. It was in 1714 that the whole panoply of *zapovednye tovary* was extended into the Ukraine. Interestingly, the Russian Senate queried Peter on the legality of this measure. The Senate wondered whether the "free people," meaning the residents of the Hetmanate, ought to have these restrictions imposed upon them. Peter retorted that he had in the past taken measures to regulate the Hetmanate's trade and would continue to do so in the future.[61] The list of prohibited goods was constantly extended between 1714 and 1719 until it covered virtually all items of Ukrainian trade. The following were affected: hemp, leather (*iukhta*), potash, pitch, bacon, wax, hemp oil, flax seed, tobacco, bristles, glue, tar, caviar, sheep skins and wool, rhubarb, saltpeter, gold, silver, silver coin, copper, and all foreign currency.[62]

These measures sounded the knell of Ukrainian merchants. To begin with, they caused chaos in the Ukrainian market as merchants and tradesmen, trying to second-guess which items would eventually be labelled "prohibited," off-loaded their stocks at greatly reduced

---

[60] *PSZ*, vol. 3, no. 1674.

[61] *PSZ*, vol. 5, no. 2768.

[62] *PSZ*, vol. 5, no. 2828; vol. 6, no. 3526; vol. 7, no. 4185; vol. 11, nos. 369, 406, 672, 673.

prices.[63] More importantly, merchants were now locked within the Russian state and it was only a matter of time before Russian *gosti* emerged as the dominant force in the Hetmanate's economy. Constricted in their choice of commercial partners, merchants in this monopolistic situation were at the mercy of powerful Russian figures. The ox trade, the pillar of Ukrainian commerce, was virtually ended when the indigenous population was forced to sell their cattle at bargain prices to agents of the Russian state. Powerful Russian figures in the Ukraine soon took advantage of the situation, this time for their personal enrichment.[64] Trade in hemp, another major item, was severely curtailed after Prince Alexandr Menshikov and others forced merchants and producers to sell them that commodity at half the normal price. Often, the Russian treasury simply refused to pay for the goods received. Payment in deficient goods and rotten produce became commonplace.[65] The ban on the export of currency also had fatal consequences since it meant that merchants could no longer cover their expenses for whatever foreign trade was allowed. (Although some of these currency restrictions were lifted in 1719, the lawlessness of border patrols—discussed below—meant that the problem remained an acute one.)[66] Skoropads'kyi, protesting tsarist policies, summarized the predicament of Ukrainian merchants rather succinctly when he noted that "merchants are now forced to give up their trade."[67] The number of merchant bankruptcies increased dramatically during the 1710s and 1720s and Skoropads'kyi's and Apostol's universals extending the period for the repayment of loans delayed, but could not reverse, the inevitable decline.[68]

Equally fatal for Ukrainian trade were the bans on imports. Between 1717 and 1719 stockings, needles, most woven goods, all woolen goods, all smooth cloth, worsted cloth, ribbon, gold and silver thread, all materials containing gold, silk, German brocade, chicory, cochineal paint, velvet, serviettes, table cloths, German salt, and

---

[63] Sudienko, *Materialy*, vol. 2, p. 59.

[64] Lazarevskii, *Opisanie*, vol. 2, pp. 201–202; Dzhydzhora, *Ukraina*, p. 10.

[65] Dzhydzhora, *Ukraina*, pp. 33, 41.

[66] D. Bantysh-Kamenskii, *Istochniki Malorossiiskoi istorii*, vol. 2 (Moscow, 1859), p. 282.

[67] Dzhydzhora, *Ukraina*, p. 36.

[68] See ibid., pp. 81–84; Sudienko, *Materialy*, vol. 1, pt. 1, p. 28; pt. 2, p. 67.

tobacco were affected.[69] Except for tobacco, which was plentiful in the Ukraine, the goods listed included the vast majority of items imported by Ukrainian merchants. This was Dzhydzhora's conclusion having compared the import restrictions with the list of items exported to Ukraine by Silesian merchants.[70] (As for tobacco, its export to Russia was at first prohibited; later it also joined the list of *zapovednye tovary*.)[71] The restrictions on imports were quite explicitly designed to protect Russian industries and trading companies. Thus, the 1719 edict which prohibited the import of needles stipulated that henceforth the item could only be purchased from the Riazan' enterprise of Sidor Tomilin and Pankrat Riumin.[72] The measure regarding wool and woolen cloth favored such Russian enterprises as Shchegolin's Moscow factory.[73] The ban on the import of silk and stockings was enacted to protect Petersburg merchants who themselves imported these goods from abroad.[74]

The import regulations liquidated at a stroke half the commercial operations of Ukrainian merchants. Ukrainian merchants, in effect, stopped being merchants in the proper sense of the word and became mere brokers of agricultural commodities. Having no choice other than to purchase manufactured wares from Russian traders, they were thus placed in a vulnerable, dependent position. Russian merchants obviously had the possibility of trading directly in these goods in the Ukraine since the demand for them remained. They could dispense with the Ukrainian merchants' mediating services, as they in fact increasingly did, and in time they displaced indigenous traders from their preeminent position in the Ukrainian domestic market.

Parallel to the measures regulating export and import, Russian authorities introduced new customs duties on the Hetmanate's frontiers. Hitherto in the Ukraine, under conditions of free trade, customs duties collected by the hetman's treasury were modest. According to long established practice, merchants paid import and export duties, called *inducta* and *evecta* respectively, and the tax rate was the same

---

[69] *PSZ*, vol. 5, nos. 3163, 3411; Slabchenko, *Malorusskii polk*, p. 257n.

[70] Dzhydzhora, *Ukraina*, p. 32.

[71] *PSZ*, vol. 1, no. 307; vol. 5, no. 1826.

[72] *PSZ*, vol. 5, no. 3411.

[73] Liubomirov, *Ocherki*, pp. 27–28.

[74] *PSZ*, vol. 5, no. 3163.

for both—2 percent *ad valorem*. In addition, merchants exporting through Poland paid a transit tax at customs houses in Poland. Foreign merchants importing goods to the Ukraine paid small duties at Ukrainian fairs.[75] But the situation changed radically following Poltava. In addition to established payments (*inducta* and *evecta*), the Russian state introduced special customs duties on the Ukrainian-Russian border which were collected by the Russian treasury. Having paid these, merchants also had to pay export duties for the same goods in Russian ports. The new Russian duties, which increased frequently, represented from 5 to 10 percent of the value of the goods. Moreover, payment had to be made in gold (*iefymky*). Imported goods brought into the Ukraine across the Russian border were also subjected to additional duties on that border ranging from 10 to 37 percent of the value of the goods.[76] The new customs duties were introduced at a time when general taxation in the Ukraine had increased sharply to pay the costs of maintaining the large Russian garrison and to sustain the thousands who labored in Russia on canals.[77] During the period of the Little Russian College the general tax levy increased from 45,527 rubles in 1722 to 414,342 rubles by 1724.[78] Friedrich Christian Weber, Braunschweig's ambassador to Peter's court from 1714–1720 wrote the following regarding Peter's policy of raising revenue in the Ukraine: "L'Ukraine n'est plus maintenant que l'ombre de ce qu'elle était autrefois."[79]

The reality was in fact much grimmer. Graft and corruption became the order of the day. The phenomenon was so widespread that tsarist investigators discovered that between 1722–1723 (the period of the Little Russian College), half of all revenues raised in the Ukraine was pocketed by Russian officials.[80] Traveling to Russian ports, the Ukrainian merchants had to run a veritable gauntlet of payments, not to speak of the countless bribes which had to be paid to

---

[75] "Proshenie," p. 338.

[76] Dzhydzhora, *Ukraina*, pp. 37–38.

[77] See Skoropads'kyi's protests regarding excessive taxation in the Ukraine in Nikolai Markevich, *Istoriia Malorossii*, vol. 2 (Moscow, 1842), pp. 511–21.

[78] P. Nechyporenko, "Pro proportsii ta ratsii na Het'manshchyni 1725–1750 rr.," *Zapysky istorychno-filolohichnoho viddilu Ukrains'koi Akademii nauk* 20 (1928):53.

[79] Friedrich Christian Weber, *Nouveaux Memoirs sur L'Etat Présent de la Grande Russie ou Moscovie*, vol. 1 (Paris, 1725), p. 82.

[80] Dzhydzhora, *Ukraina*, pp. 127–28.

have goods released from illegal seizures. The scourge of the Ukrainian trade were Russian border patrols who used every opportunity to fleece Ukrainian merchants. These patrols, for instance, introduced their own "soul tax," levying 10–50 kopeks on every individual who crossed the border. Thousands of rubles were thus collected annually by border authorities. These and similar ingenious taxes, it should be noted, were illegal, yet the Russian state did nothing to stop the practices. Having crossed the border into Russia, merchants were now confronted with numerous toll taxes, payments for obtaining clearance documents, etc. And all these payments had to be made in cash.[81] Small wonder then that normally staid merchants took to contraband trade, a trade that flourished across the Ukrainian-Polish border. But the rise of contraband trade provoked new reprisals. In 1721 customs farmers were installed on the Polish border with the Ukraine and were given sweeping authority, such as the right to confiscate the property of merchants who violated regulations.[82] These customs farmers used all possible pretexts to enrich themselves at the expense of Ukrainian traders.

The new duties and taxes stymied Ukrainian trade and also resulted in a further penetration of the Ukrainian market by Russians. To avoid paying double duties, Ukrainian merchants started hiring Russians to freight their goods and, thus, an important source of livelihood was lost to many Ukrainian townsmen and peasants. To survive the labyrinth of duties, payments, and bribes, Ukrainian merchants also started to engage Russian partners, further diminishing the role of the indigenous commercial strata. Since Russian traders were not subjected to the same tax burdens and duties as Ukrainians, many Russian merchants migrated to the Ukraine and started competing directly with the local population.[83]

Finally, Petrine policy undermined the Hetmanate's autonomy directly as responsibility for regulating the Ukrainian economy fell by and large into the hands of Russian officials. Each measure taken by the Petrine administration entailed the expansion of the Russian apparatus in the Ukraine. Petrine regulations were bad enough, but their impact was made substantially more devastating than the original

---

[81] Ibid., pp. 48–54.
[82] *PSZ*, vol. 6, no. 3731.
[83] Dzhydzhora, *Ukraina*, pp. 48–54; Sudienko, *Materialy*, vol. 1, pt. 2, pp. 15–17.

intent by the behavior of those charged with implementing them.

The first category of individuals which should be mentioned in this regard are the Russian notables who received the confiscated estates of Mazepa's followers. These individuals—such as Menshikov and Stroganov—became a power unto themselves within the Hetmanate. They avoided paying taxes and duties and launched themselves into the most lucrative sectors of the Ukrainian economy, namely, cattle and hemp. Claiming to hold monopolies from the tsar, they forced Ukrainian merchants to tear up their existing contracts and sell them their commodities at very reduced prices. They became, in short, powerful and unbeatable competitors for Ukrainian merchants.[84]

In the wake of the arrival of these powerful Russian figures, numerous Russian merchants and traders, from the Moscow and Kaluga provinces in particular, flocked to the Ukraine. Indeed, in this period the Ukraine was viewed as an Eldorado, a place where fortunes could be made easily and quickly by skulduggery. Documents of that period abound with complaints by Hetmanate officials of the behavior of these carpetbaggers.[85]

Ukrainian merchants and Hetmanate officials were powerless in the face of this situation because those charged with enforcing trade regulations were the troops of the Russian garrison, the border patrols in particular. For the troops, Ukrainian merchants were an evil to be barely tolerated. At various checkpoints these merchants and traders would be subjected to tedious searches, arbitrary confiscations and arrests, special payments, and general lawlessness. Contemporaries called this behavior "velikorossiiskoe obyknovenee," which they defined as a system in which it was impossible to distinguish the law from the lawlessness of officials.[86] Even such a major figure of the new Russian presence in the Ukraine as Sava Raguzinskii complained in 1712 that by not allowing trade across the Ukrainian border, Russian troops were ruining his concession as a customs farmer.[87] In 1720, to give another example, a Russian commandant refused to release from customs a massive shipment of salt, thereby creating a salt shortage in the Hetmanate. It took months of persistent efforts by

---

[84] Dzhydzhora, *Ukraina*, p. 42.

[85] Ibid., p. 43.

[86] Ibid., p. 54.

[87] Sudienko, *Materialy*, vol. 2, p. 420.

Skoropads'kyi and others to have the commodity released.[88] One can well imagine the fate of the goods of lesser mortals. Typical of the assuredness of the border patrol was the rude reply sent by a Russian border captain to Hetman Skoropads'kyi in response to the latter's complaints about unnecessary delays at the frontier.[89] In time, Russian troops recognized that they could use their privileged status to even better advantage. Thus, they themselves became traders: they paid no taxes or duties and had free access to border crossings.[90] They had, in short, a formidable competitive advantage over their Ukrainian counterparts.

Conclusion

Peter used mercantilist techniques to exploit the Ukrainian economy. While his fiscal objectives were met—the Russian treasury increased its revenues from the Ukraine, in the long run the Russian state destroyed a goose which laid golden eggs. As a result of Petrine policies, the Ukrainian economy declined sharply. This is what contemporaries tell us, and that much could be expected from his measures. Hopefully, further research in this much neglected field will supply us with some quantitative data which will enable us to gauge more precisely the scope of the downturn. The only data that we have found concern the urban population. It is a reasonable hypothesis that the size of the town population is related to economic prosperity. Comparing data of the seventeenth century with those of the late eighteenth, it is clear that throughout the eighteenth century a process of de-urbanization had occurred in the Left-Bank Ukraine.[91] Examining some individual towns we see, for example, that in 1654 Myrhorod had 817 households, but by 1767 only 147; Lokhvytsi declined from 523 to 163 households in the same period, and Poltava from 1333 to 600.[92] (If we multiply by five or six, we have some idea of what these figures mean in terms of the total population of the given

[88] Dzhydzhora, *Ukraina*, p. 52.

[89] Ibid.

[90] Sudienko, *Materialy*, vol. 1, pt. 2: pp. 15–17, 30–31.

[91] Compare data in Baranovich, *Ukraina*, p. 139, Kompan, *Mista*, pp. 72–73 with those in A. I. Dotsenko, "Heohrafichni osoblyvosti protsesiv urbanizatsii na Ukraini (XIX–XX st.)," *Ukrains'kyi istoryko-heohrafichnyi zbirnyk* 2 (1972):47.

[92] Slabchenko, *Hospodarstvo het'manshchyny*, vol. 1, p. 92.

towns.) Because important sectors of the urban economy were damaged, namely, trade, the town population dropped.

By undermining the economic position of the Ukrainian commercial groups, Petrine policies initiated a change in the national composition of these groups, as well as of the urban population. The changes which occurred in the Ukraine in this respect were profound. In 1711 the Danish envoy to Petersburg, Jul Just, had the following to say about the inhabitants of the Hetmanate: "They sell and buy all sorts of merchandise . . . and can choose whatever handicraft is to their liking and trade with whatever they want."[93] Half a century later (1786) Afanasii Shafonskii observed, "In a word, Little Russia both in terms of artisans and craftsmen is very poor . . . and all trade both large and small is in the hands of Russian merchants."[94] Accutely aware of the challenge posed to Ukrainian townsmen by privileged Russians, Hetman Apostol in 1727, two years after Peter's death, issued a universal instructing Russian soldiers, officers, and their families engaged in trade and commerce to cease their activities or have their property confiscated. He also ordered all Russian merchants and tradesmen without proper Hetmanate passports to leave the territory of the state and instructed that taxes were to be collected from all Russian residents who had hitherto avoided paying them.[95] But he lacked the wherewithall to enforce this law. The number of Russians in Ukraine increased from 40,000 in 1719 to 178,000 by 1782.[96] By the end of the eighteenth century Russian merchants had succeeded in their conquest of trade in the Left-Bank Ukraine; in their march to the south of the Ukraine, the question of competition was not even posed.[97] Thus, in the light of 1832 data, Russians represented 81 percent of the merchants in the province of Chernihiv and 63 percent in Poltava. Throughout the Ukraine there were no Ukrainians in the upper guild—those involved in foreign trade—only 15 percent in the

---

[93] Sichynsky, *Ukraine in Foreign Comments*, pp. 131–32.

[94] A. Shafonskii, *Chernigovskogo namestnichestva topograficheskoe opisanie* (Kiev, 1851), p. 21.

[95] Sudienko, *Materialy*, vol. 1, pt. 2, pp. 15–17.

[96] S. I. Bruk and V. M. Kabuzan, "Dinamika chislennosti i rasseleniia russkogo etnosa (1678–1917 gg.)," *Sovetskaia etnografiia*, 1982, no. 4, p. 17.

[97] N. Polons'ka-Vasylenko, *Zaselennia pivdennoi Ukrainy v polovyni XVIII st. (1734–1775)*, vol. 2 (Munich, 1960), p. 99.

second, and 26 percent in the third. What is indicative of the thoroughness of the conquest of the internal Ukrainian market was the fact that the third guild operated largely locally.[98] In short, Petrine policies played a large role in the "peasantization" of the Ukrainian social structure with all that this meant for the Ukrainians' subsequent national development.[99]

Peter's policies met with resistance in the Hetmanate. Skoropads'kyi and Apostol, themselves merchant-exporters and entrepreneurs, were remarkably forceful (given the Poltava defeat) on questions of trade and other matters pertaining to the Hetmanate's economy. The Hetmanate's budget depended on *inducta* and *evecta*, that is, revenues connected with trade, and merchants were major tax-payers. Thus, the question of trade was fundamental to the Hetmanate's autonomy and both Skoropads'kyi and Apostol under-stood this clearly.[100] Merchants as well saw the connection between the economic and the political, namely, that the economic policies were possible to introduce because the Hetmanate's autonomy had been eroded.[101]

As time went by, the economic measures introduced by Peter undermined the foundations of Ukrainian autonomy in a manner more effective than the tsar would have thought possible. Dzhydzhora in this connection gives an example of just one of the many unforeseen consequences of the 1714 edict banning the export of goods. To implement this measure the Russian administration installed border patrols. These patrols refused to recognize the merchants' passports issued by local magistrates or by the hetman's chancellery, despite Skoropads'kyi's vehement protests. Officials of Russian towns also did not acknowledge the validity of these documents. Merchants, of course, did not have the time or resources to redress this wrong. Instead, they took the logical step and went directly to the chancellery of the local Russian garrison administration and got them to issue passports, thus bypassing their own Hetmanate institutions. Without a

---

[98] Ohloblyn, *A History of Ukrainian Industry*, pt. 3, *Predkapitalisticheskaia fabrika* (Kiev, 1931; reprint, Munich, 1971), pp. 47–49.

[99] For a discussion of this question see Bohdan Krawchenko, *Social Change and National Consciousness in Twentieth-Century Ukraine* (London, 1985), chap. 1.

[100] Dzhydzhora, *Ukraina*, p. 75.

[101] Ibid., p. 74.

special edict to that effect, a decisive layer of the population learned that in matters most effecting their livelihood, the Hetmanate administration was not needed and could be dispensed with. One of the many essential ties that bound a people to their administration was thus broken.[102]

Petrine economic policies also began the transformation of the Ukrainian social formation into the Russian pattern, with the state suffocating society. In the petitions from individual merchants protesting Petrine measures, one heard "the pride of the European merchant" who expressed disbelief that authorities would treat commerce with such disdain and were prepared to ruin good trade so readily.[103] The hetman's state was after all organically tied to the leading social interests of that society—the *starshyna* and prominent merchants. The Russian state was the state's state. Under Peter, as civil society receded, this applied increasingly to the Ukraine as well.

[102] Ibid., pp. 93–94.
[103] Ibid., p. 46.

CHAPTER EIGHT

Ukrainian Grain and the Russian Market in the Late Eighteenth and Early Nineteenth Centuries

Robert E. Jones

Although the political and administrative integration of the Ukraine into the Russian Empire was completed during the last four decades of the eighteenth century, the Ukrainian economy remained separate and distinct in a number of important ways. The most important, and in many ways the most surprising, was the continuing absence of an integrated market for grain—an absence that persisted in spite of a growing demand for grain in central and northern Russia and a permanent and troublesome oversupply of grain in the Ukraine. To supplement meager harvests and to feed the burgeoning populations of Moscow and St. Petersburg surplus grain was brought into the areas outside the *chernozem* regions in ever increasing quantities from the Russian *chernozem* provinces south of Moscow and along the Volga.[1] At the same time, the existence of additional, untapped surpluses in the Ukraine presented the Russian government with an opportunity to increase the amount of grain on the market, raise its own revenue, and

---

[1] L. V. Seretinskii, "Pomeshchichiia votchina iaroslavskoi gubernii vo vtoroi polovine XVIII veka," *Uchenye zapiski iaroslavskogo gosudarstvennogo pedagogicheskogo instituta imini K. D. Ushinskogo* 25 (1858):482; R. E. Jones, "Getting the Goods to St. Petersburg: Water Transport from the Interior, 1703–1811," *Slavic Review* 43, no. 3 (October 1984):413–17.

improve Russia's balance of payments, if only those surpluses could be brought to market.

Within the regions outside the *chernozem* landlords abandoned cereal production, put their peasants on *obrok*, and encouraged them to find other means of employment. In principle some of those same lords deplored what they perceived as a growing trend toward the abandonment of agriculture and the separation of the peasant from his natural, god-given occupation. In her *Nakaz*, or Instruction, to the Legislative Commission of 1767 the Empress Catherine II criticized the growing use of *obrok* and urged the landlords to extract their dues in a manner that would not separate the peasant from his house and family so that the population might increase and agriculture might flourish.[2] Noticing the same trend, Prince M. M. Shcherbatov lamented the fact that agriculture in Russia was diminishing at a time when it should be thriving.[3] In practice, on the other hand, such people demonstrated a clear understanding of the economic forces that were beginning to reshape the economic geography of Russia in the 1760s. Catherine II put the peasants of the state and the crown on *obrok* and gave a high priority to the settlement and development of the steppe. Shcherbatov likewise put his peasants on *obrok* and sought to increase his revenues by engaging in activities other than agriculture. Among those activities was the purchase in the nearby town of Iaroslavl' of southern grain to be hauled up the Volga and resold at a profit in St. Petersburg.[4] In making such decisions Shcherbatov and the thousands of landlords (*pomeshchiki*) who ceased trying to grow grain in northern Russia faced up to the fact that it made no sense to cultivate cereals in regions outside the *chernozem*, where harvests were poor and uncertain, when grain could be brought in from the more fertile and productive regions of the south.[5]

---

[2] *Catherine the Great's Instruction (Nakaz) to the Legislative Commission, 1767*, ed. and trans. Paul Dukes (Newtonville, Mass., 1977), Articles 269–71, pp. 77–78.

[3] Seretinskii, "Pomeshchichiia votchina," p. 484.

[4] E. I. Indova, "Instruktsiia kniazia M. M. Shcherbatova prikazshchikam ego iaroslavskikh votchin (1758 g. s dobavleniiami po 1762 g.)," *Materialy po istorii sel'skogo khoziaistva i krest'ianstva SSSR*, vol. 6 (Moscow, 1965), p. 452.

[5] Seretinskii, "Pomeshchichiia votchina," p. 482.

A second source of demand for southern grain was the desire to export Russian grain through the Baltic to Europe. Peter the Great had banned grain exports from the Baltic ports in Russia (but not Livonia) in order to ensure his capital and the environs of an adequate supply of grain at a reasonable price.[6] In 1762, a combination of circumstances that included the recent death of the Empress Elizabeth and the near bankruptcy of the Russian government at the close of the Seven Years' War brought to the fore the issue of exporting Russian grain to Europe. In March 1762 the government of Peter III removed the restrictions on the export of grain.[7] After the coup d'état of 28 June 1762, the government of Catherine II suspended the new export policy. Catherine's Commission on Commerce argued for increased exports of agricultural products, including grains, to improve Russia's balance of trade, and the Russian Senate argued that higher grain prices resulting from increased exports would put more money in the hands of peasant taxpayers, reduce arrears, and increase the revenues of the state.[8] Catherine appreciated the logic of such arguments but remained unconvinced that higher prices would increase the supply of grain to St. Petersburg and northern Russia. She kept a close watch on grain prices in St. Petersburg and tied grain exports to those prices lest they disrupt the grain market in her capital. "The first thing," she asserted, "is to see that everyone has enough to eat."[9] When the capital received enough grain to ensure an adequate supply and fairly stable prices, she allowed grain exports from St. Petersburg and welcomed the benefits they brought to the Russian government and its subjects.[10]

Despite the existing and potential demand for cereals in northern Russia and at the Baltic ports, producers in the Ukraine found themselves with an unmarketable surplus of grain. After an abundant harvest in 1771, a French diplomat reported that "Piles of corn as big as

[6] *Ocherki istorii Leningrada*, vol. 1 (Moscow and Leningrad, 1955), p. 83.

[7] *Polnoe sobranie zakonov rossiiskoi imperii* (hereafter *PSZ*), 46 vols. (St. Petersburg, 1830), 1st ser., no. 11,489 (27 March 1762).

[8] Victor Kamendrowsky, "State and Economy in Catherinian Russia: the Dismantling of the Mercantile System of Peter the Great" (Ph.D. diss., University of North Carolina, 1982), p. 112.

[9] Quoted in ibid., p. 142.

[10] Ibid., p. 144. *PSZ*, 1st ser., no. 15,517 (22 September 1782).

houses, enough to feed all Europe, are again rotting in Podillia and Volhynia."[11] In 1784 a similar report informed the French government that grain was "at such a low price in the Ukraine that many landowners have abandoned its cultivation."[12] One of those landowners, L. N. Engel'gardt, later recalled that in the 1770s his father, a retired army colonel, had had to accept a job in the provincial bureaucracy in Belorussia because his estate in Malorossiia, as the Left-Bank Ukraine was then known, produced too little revenue to enable him to provide for his family and pay a debt of three thousand rubles that he owed to an aunt. Engel'gardt explained that "At that time the debt had not been repaid because incomes in the southern guberniias were practically insignificant; rye there sold for twenty-five kopecks a *chetvert'* and could not be sent elsewhere because there was no water transport and few distilleries."[13]

Contemporary writers on economic questions did not fail to observe the apparent contradiction between the surpluses and low prices for grain in Malorossiia and the growing demand and rising prices in the north. In 1786, after a careful study of the geography and economy of the region, Afanasii Shafons'kyi wrote a topographical description of the Chernihiv Vice-Regency in particular and of Malorossiia in general. He noted that the steppe of which those provinces were largely comprised produced six, eight, or even ten times more grain than the forest land to the north and that grain was so cheap in Malorossiia that the labor of cultivating it was almost unprofitable. The reason, he explained, was that Malorossiia was virtually surrounded by fertile areas abundantly supplied by their own harvests. The one exception he noted was Belorussia, where the inhabitants of Mahiliou province purchased grain from Malorossiia.[14]

Shcherbatov also commented on the fact that the large grain surpluses of the Ukraine did not reach the central regions of the empire,

[11] Quoted in Fernand Braudel, *Civilization and Capitalism*, vol. 1, *The Structures of Everyday Life* (New York, 1981), p. 188.

[12] Quoted in ibid., p. 188.

[13] L. N. Engel'gardt, *Zapiski 1766–1836* (Moscow, 1868), pp. 3–4.

[14] Afanasii Shafons'kyi (Shafonskii), *Chernigovskogo namestnichestva topograficheskoe opisanie s kratkim geograficheskim i istoricheskim opisaniem Maloi Rossii* (Kiev, 1851), pp. 16–15; M. M. Shcherbatov, *Neizdannye sochineniia* (Moscow, 1935).

much less the north. His explanation was the same as the one provided independently by Engel'gardt—the lack of water routes from
the Ukraine to Russia.[15]

The importance that Shcherbatov and Engel'gardt attached to the
absence of convenient water transport from the Ukraine to the north
may require some explanation. Overland transport by cart, wagon, or
sledge cost too much to be used over long distances for goods such as
grain whose weight and bulk were great in proportion to their prices.
Carts, wagons, and sledges were used for deliveries to local markets
and fairs and to wharves along the water routes, but on longer journeys the horses literally ate up the profits.[16] Before the coming of the
railroads, the transport of bulky goods over long distances meant
water transport.

In the eighteenth century there were three and only three water
routes that could be used to haul grain northward from the Ukraine,
and all of them imposed severe limitations on the quantities that could
be transported. Above Orsha and Dubrovna the upper Dnieper came
within thirty-five *versty* (1 *versta* = 0.66 mile) from the Luchesa
River, a tributary of the western Dvina. Shafons'kyi wrote that the
portage there was significant for the trade in hemp, which was loaded
on barges at the Poretskaia Wharf and shipped downstream to the port
at Riga.[17] Until 1774 grain moving down the western Dvina encountered an export duty when it crossed the border into Poland, and until
1782 it was subject to a 13 percent transit toll at the Livonian border

[15] M. M. Shcherbatov, *Neizdannye sochineniia* (Moscow, 1935), p. 7.

[16] On the need to supply St. Petersburg by water see John Perry, *The State of Russia
under the Present Czar* (London, 1716), pp. 40–41. Perry explained that a major lim-
itation on overland transport was "the very great Scarcity and Dearness of Forage for
Horses." In 1718 the Resident of the United Provinces wrote that Tver', Torzhok,
and Vyshnii Volochek were filled with goods waiting to be moved to St. Petersburg
by water and explained that they could not be moved overland because of the expense
of fodder and the poor condition of the roads. *Kratkii istoricheskii ocherk razvitiia i
deiatel'nosti vedomstva putei soobshcheniia za sto let ego sushchestvovaniia
1798–1898 gg.* (St. Petersburg, 1898), p. 3. On road conditions as a restraint on
overland transport, see M. A. Rakhmatulin, "Khlebnyi rynok i tseny v Rossii v pervoi
polovine XIX v.," in S. D. Skakin, ed., *Problemy genezisa kapitalizma* (Moscow,
1970), pp. 366–67.

[17] Shafons'kyi, *Chernigovskogo namestnichestva*, p. 19.

and to export duties at the port of Riga.[18] Even without those duties the cost of transportation, and especially of portage, made Ukrainian grain uncompetitive with the large quantities of cheaper grain that the Riga merchants could purchase in Poland and Livonia.

A second water route leading north from the Ukraine followed the Desna and its tributary the Seim. At a spot about nineteen miles north of the city of Kursk, the Toskar', a tributary of the Seim, came within five and one-half miles of the Ochka, a tributary of the Oka. That spot, on the hilly bank of the Toskar' River, served as the location of the Korennaia Fair, where Ukrainian goods entered the Russian economy and vice versa. The fair opened each year on the ninth Friday after Easter and lasted for two weeks. In addition to merchants from "Great and Little Russia," the fair attracted traders from Poland, Moldavia, Wallachia, Greece, and the Crimea, and in 1781 the total sales were estimated by a visiting member of the St. Petersburg Academy of Sciences at three million rubles.[19] More important for our purposes was the fact that the Korennaia Fair was a crucial link between the cycle of fairs held in the Ukraine and the major fairs in Russia, including the great Makar'evskaia Fair near Nizhnii Novgorod. The Soviet historian Kafengauz found that by value 64 percent of the goods brought to the fair in 1720 came from Malorossiia.[20] Those goods included cattle, sheep, cloth, books, hemp seed and hempseed oil, tobacco, and grain, but the quantities of grain were small. Kafengauz found, for example, that grain from the Ukraine shipped from the fair to Russia in 1726 amounted to one hundred *chetverty* of rye and forty-eight *chetverty* of wheat.[21]

The reasons grain played such an insignificant role in shipments from the Ukraine to the Korennaia Fair were the ones given by Shcherbatov and Shafons'kyi: the insufficiency of water transport and an abundance of cheap grain in the receiving region. The navigable Desna was a major highway for trade through the northern Ukraine

[18] Kamendrowsky, "State and Economy," p. 117; *PSZ*, 1st ser., no. 15,517 (22 September 1782).

[19] V. Zuev, *Puteshestvennye zapiski ot Peterburga do Khersona 1781–1782* (St. Petersburg, 1787), p. 145.

[20] B. B. Kafengauz, "Russko-ukrainskie torgovye sviazi," *Ocherki vnutrennogo rynka Rossii v pervoi polovine XVIII v.* (Moscow, 1958), p. 297.

[21] Ibid., p. 315.

and southern Russia, but the shallow Seim was navigable only during the spring flood, i.e., during the period immediately preceding the Korennaia Fair. Moreover, transporting grain to the region of Kursk, Orel, and Briansk was very nearly the East Slavic equivalent of carrying coals to Newcastle. Since the seventeenth century at least that region had been the dominant supplier of surplus grain for the Moscow market.[22] At the Korennaia Fair, as at Riga, the cost of growing and transporting Ukrainian grain usually exceeded the local costs of production in an area of considerable surplus.

The third water route from the Ukraine to the north followed the Desna to a point near the head of navigation from which goods could be portaged to the Ugra, a tributary of the Oka. After moving down the Ugra, goods could be hauled up its tributary, the Vora, and then portaged a short distance to the Gzhat', a tributary of the Volga. After 1722 boats loaded on the Gzhat' could carry grain and other goods to St. Petersburg without portage. In 1715 Peter I had ordered that the water route between the Volga and the head of navigation on the Gzhat' be improved for a distance of some seventy *versty* "so that boats with hemp and grain and other goods may pass."[23] In 1719 Peter established a trading wharf at the head of navigation on the Gzhat', at a village called Gzhatsk, in order "to increase commerce and the bringing of grain."[24]

Unlike the Poretskaia Wharf and the Korennaia Fair, Gzhatsk lay in an area of comparatively low fertility where Ukrainian grain enjoyed a considerable price advantage. The same was true of the entire region along the upper Volga, the Tvertsa, the Msta, and the Vokhov through which Ukrainian grain had to pass on its way from Gzhatsk to the markets and wharves of St. Petersburg. At the point where the Vora River joined the Ugra boats carrying grain from the Ukraine encountered boats hauling grain up the Ugra from the upper Oka. At Tver', where the Tvertsa River joined the Volga, boats from Gzhatsk carrying grain from the Ukraine and the upper Oka encountered boats moving upstream with grain from the middle Volga. Given the costs of

---

[22] V. M. Vazhinskii, "Khlebnaia torgovlia na iuge Moskovskogo gosudarstva vo vtoroi polovine XVII veka," *Uchënye zapiski Moskovskogo oblastnogo pedagogicheskogo instituta* 127 (1963):3–30.

[23] *PSZ*, 1st ser., no. 2,946 (28 October 1715).

[24] Ibid., no. 3,415 (11 November 1719).

transporting grain from the upper Oka or the middle Volga, grain from the Ukraine could certainly not be priced out of the market by grain from other sources, as often happened in Livonia or at the Korennaia Fair.

The first recorded shipments of grain from Gzhatsk arrived in St. Petersburg in 1721.[25] By the 1760s a number of Russian merchants were regularly engaged in transporting grain from the Ukraine to St. Petersburg. Although their grain came from several sources, the Tolchenovs, a family of grain merchants from the town of Dmitrov, organized yearly caravans of twelve or thirteen boats to transport grain from Gzhatsk to St. Petersburg.[26] In 1768 the governor of Novgorod guberniia informed Catherine II that merchants from the town of Rzhev on the upper Volga had raised two hundred thousand rubles to purchase grain and hemp in the Ukraine, and a petition from the merchants of Rzhev forwarded to the Senate in 1769 left no doubt that they had invested that money with the clear intention of selling those commodities in St. Petersburg.[27] Figures for the year 1777 show that in that year 464 boats from Gzhatsk and 121 from Rzhev arrived in St. Petersburg.[28] As Afanasii Shchekatov stated in the entry "Gzhatsk" in his geographical dictionary published in the first decade of the nineteenth century: "To Gzhatsk is brought a great quantity of iron and especially of grain and hemp from the Ukraine and from surrounding towns by merchants trading at the port of St. Petersburg."[29]

---

[25] M. Ia. Volkov, "Privoz khleba v raion Peterburga v 20-e gody XVIII v.," *Voprosy sotsial'no-ekonomicheskoi istorii i istochnikovedeniia perioda feodalizma v Rossii. Sbornik statei k 70 letiiu A. A. Novosel'skova* (Moscow, 1961), p. 124.

[26] A decree dated 22 May 1766 mentions a steward of the Tolchenovs moving twelve boats through the Vyshnii Volochek Canal between the Tvertsa and Msta rivers in 1765. *PSZ*, 1st ser., no. 12,656. An account of the Tolchenovs' role in the grain trade to St. Petersburg is given in N. I. Pavlenko, ed., *Zhurnal ili zapiski zhizni i priklichenii I. A. Tolchenova* (Moscow, 1974).

[27] Karl Blum, *Ein russischer Staatsmann. Des Grafen Jakob Johann Sievers Denkwürdigkeiten zur Geschichte Russlands*, 4 vols. (Leipzig and Heidelberg, 1857), vol. 1, p. 268. Communication from Sievers to the Senate, 16 November 1767, Tsentral'nyi gosudarstvennyi arkhiv drevnykh aktov (hereafter TsGADA), fond 248, delo 3716, p. 224.

[28] M. D. Chulkov, *Istoricheskoe opisanie rossiiskoi komertsii*, 7 vols. (St. Petersburg, 1781–1788), p. 638.

[29] Afanasii Shchekatov, *Slovar' geograficheskii gosudarstva rossiiskogo*, 7 vols. (Moscow, 1801–1809), p. 37.

Although merchants could make a profit by purchasing grain in the Ukraine and selling it in St. Petersburg, they could not respond to the demands of the market by increasing the amount of grain they transported. The waterways from the Desna to Tver' and from Tver' to St. Petersburg could carry only a limited number of boats in any given year. Improvements to the rivers and canals between Tver' and St. Petersburg in the last quarter of the eighteenth century had increased their carrying capacity from two thousand to four thousand a year, but a governmental study in 1802 cited the latter figure as the maximum number that could pass through those waterways in one year "under the best of conditions."[30] More important for our purposes were the limitations on transport imposed by the Gzhat' and Vazuza rivers leading from Gzhatsk to the upper Volga. Like the Seim, they were navigable only during the spring floods and could carry no more than five hundred boats a year at the very most. Since they moved downstream from Gzhatsk or Rzhev, the owners of those boats were invariably the first to arrive in Tver' with their cargoes and thus were the first to proceed through the system of rivers and canals to St. Petersburg, where they sold their grain for better prices than those who arrived later in the year. Under such conditions the trade in grain between Gzhatsk and St. Petersburg was profitable and regular but very restricted in comparison to both the actual demand and the potential supply.

To many Russians of the late eighteenth and early nineteenth centuries the obvious solution to the problem of agricultural surpluses in the *chernozem* regions lay in the improvement of transportation between those regions and the markets of the north. In 1763 Nikita Panin, the leading political figure of the 1760s, urged the government to create an infrastructure of roads and waterways to facilitate the marketing and export of Russia's agricultural surpluses.[31] Throughout the reign of Catherine II the broad outlines of Panin's proposal were filled in with specific proposals for improvements to the waterways from the south to the north. Most of them dealt either with improvements to

---

[30] D. Bakhturin, *Kratkoe opisanie vnutrennogo Rossiiskoi imperii vodokhodstva* (St. Petersburg, 1802), p. 6.

[31] M. N. Firsov, *Pravitel'stvo i obshchestvo v ikh otnosheniiakh k vneshnei torgovle Rossii v tsarstvovanie imperatritsy Ekateriny II* (Kazan, 1902), p. 53; David L. Ransel, *The Politics of Catherinian Russia* (New Haven, 1975), pp 147–48.

the existing system of waterways between Tver' and St. Petersburg or with the opening of alternative routes from the Volga to the Neva.

Several proposals for the improvement of waterways from south to north specifically addressed the possibility of moving Ukrainian surpluses to the port cities of St. Petersburg and Riga. In 1764 Jakob Sievers, the governor of the entire region through which goods had to be transported from the upper Volga to the capital, raised that possibility in a memorandum to the empress. He urged Catherine to take seriously a proposal that had recently been put forward by General L. M. Golonishev-Kutuzov for a canal that would link the source of the Volga at Lake Seliger with the Pola, a small river whose waters eventually reached St. Petersburg. He assured her that such a canal would improve abundance in the capital and "attach to it provinces that nature has put at a distance." Then Sievers went on to add a proposal of his own that the government create a direct water route from the Ukraine to St. Petersburg by linking the Desna with the Ugra and the Ugra with the Gzhat'. Through those canals, he argued, "The riches of the Ukraine will be brought to St. Petersburg. This canal [sic] will rival that of Louis XIV linking the Mediterranean with the Atlantic. Many lands and peoples will benefit from it."[32] In 1764 Sievers again called Golonishev-Kutuzov's proposal to Catherine's attention and reminded her that a canal between the Gzhat' and the Ugra would greatly facilitate the transport of Ukrainian grain and hemp to St. Petersburg.[33]

Although Sievers could see the potential economic consequences of his proposal for a direct water route from the Ukraine to the capital, he admittedly knew very little about hydroengineering and the practical difficulties his proposal entailed. The great problem with linking two small tributaries at a point near their headwaters lay not in digging the canal or building the locks but in keeping it filled with water. Canals linking the Desna with the Gzhat' would eliminate the need for expensive portages, but they would not raise the water level of the Gzhat'. As Sievers was to learn in making improvements to the waterways between Tver' and St. Petersburg, it was necessary to divert other rivers, build aqueducts, and drain lakes in order to operate the locks of such canals and to increase the flow of the rivers in the summertime.

[32] Sievers to Catherine, December 1764, TsGADA, fond 16, delo 785, p. 11.
[33] Blum, *Ein russischer Staatsmann*, vol. 1, p. 267.

Significantly, when he became Director of Water Communications for the entire Russian Empire in 1797, Sievers failed to revive his own proposals of 1764 and sought other ways of transporting goods from the Ukraine. Nevertheless, in 1804, a report on the Department of Water Communications proposed that Alexander I authorize construction of a canal between the Desna and the Oka "so that by such connections a certain amount of grain can be provided to St. Petersburg and Moscow from the fertile regions of the Ukraine." Like Sievers in 1764, however, the author of that report offered no evidence that such a project was feasible and conceded that the department had not yet made a study of the technical difficulties involved.[34]

The first partition of Poland aroused the Russian government's interest in linking the Dnieper to the port of Riga through the western Dvina. In 1778 and 1779 an engineer by the name of Gideras submitted detailed proposals for a canal between the two rivers, and the Senate sent General-Engineer Bauer to investigate. Intrigued but not persuaded by Bauer's report that the project was technically feasible, the Senate authorized Christian Truzson, a captain in the Corps of Engineers, to investigate further and make an estimate of the cost. In 1786 Truzson submitted one plan to link the Dnieper with the western Dvina at a cost of 3,990,785 rubles and another to link the Dnieper to the Lovat', a river whose waters eventually reached St. Petersburg by way of lake Il'men, for less than 6,000,000 rubles.[35] Since the government's total expenditures on public works including canals, roads, port facilities, and buildings totaled only 1,950,000 rubles in 1781 and 4,700,000 inflated rubles in 1796, the costs estimated in Truzson's report must have seemed prohibitive in 1786.[36] In any event the outbreak of the Second Russo-Turkish War in 1788 made them unthinkable.

Between 1770 and 1784 the Polish nobleman Prince Michael Ogiński opened a canal between the Shara, a tributary of the Nieman, and the Iatsel'd, a tributary of the Prypiat'. Constructed with limited

[34] Bakhturin, *Kratkoe opisanie*, p. 21.

[35] S. M. Zhitkov, *Istoricheskii obzor ustroistva i soderzhaniia vodnykh putei i portov v Rossii za stoletnii period 1798–1898* (St. Petersburg, 1900), pp. 30–32.

[36] Isabel de Madariaga, *Russia in the Age of Catherine the Great* (New Haven and London, 1981), p. 487. De Madariaga's figures are taken from the prerevolutionary Russian historian M. D. Chechulin, and she warns that they are not always reliable.

funds, it was of limited use until the Russian government recon-
structed it between 1799 and 1804, lengthening it to deepen the
draught and replacing the four original locks with eleven new ones.[37]

That undertaking reflected the new policy of the Russian government under Tsar Paul. Reversing his mother's policy on canals as on
virtually every other issue, the new monarch recalled Sievers to
government service, placed him in charge of the newly created
Department of Water Communications, and authorized unprecedented
sums for improvements to the waterways.[38] In addition to new canals
and other improvements to the waterways between the Volga and St.
Petersburg and the renovation of the Ogiński Canal, those projects
included a project submitted by Sievers in 1797 to join the Biarezina,
a tributary of the Dnieper, with the Ulla, a tributary of the Western
Dvina. Paul and Sievers gave the project high priority. Work began
in 1798 under Engineer-General De Witt and was completed on
schedule in 1805.[39] The report on the Department of Water Communications in 1802 stated that the aim of the so-called Biarezina Canal
was "the improvement of the commerce of the regions of Belorussia
and Malorossiia and in part of other southern regions."[40] The effect of
the Biarezina and Ogiński canals on the commerce of Belorussia and
the Ukraine remains to be studied. They must certainly have facilitated the export of hemp and the movement of salt from the Black Sea
regions to Belorussia and Poland, but evidence from the mid-
nineteenth century indicates that they did little or nothing to alleviate
the problem of excess grain production in the Ukraine.[41]

Catherine's failure to authorize and finance improvements to the
waterways has commonly been attributed to her involvement in
Russia's southward expansion and the wars with Turkey that resulted
from that expansion.[42] Yet that expansion and those wars were

---

[37] Zhitkov, *Istoricheskii obzor*, p. 35; D. Dubenskii, *Rassuzhdenie o vodianykh
soobshcheniakh v Rossii* (Moscow, 1825), p. 84.

[38] Robert E. Jones, *Provincial Development in Russia. Catherine II and Jacob Sievers* (New Brunswick, N.J., 1984), pp. 125–26; *Kratkii istoricheskii ocherk razvitiia i
deiatel'nosti vedomstva putei soobshcheniia*, p. 14.

[39] Zhitkov, *Istoricheskii obzor*, pp. 64–65.

[40] Bakhturin, *Kratkoe opisanie*, p. 15.

[41] See fns. 51, 52, and 53 below.

[42] Robert E. Jones, "Opposition to War and Expansion in Late Eighteenth Century
Russia," *Jahrbücher für Geschichte Osteuropas* 32 (1984):41–43.

intimately connected with the issue of marketing surplus Ukrainian grain. While Sievers and Paul wanted to move those surpluses to the ports and grain deficient regions of the north, Catherine sought to move them down the Dnieper to ports on the Black Sea. Instead of trying to alter the physical geography of southern Russia and Belorussia with canals, her policy was to alter the political geography of the entire Black Sea region by gaining ports and commercial rights on the Black Sea and right of passage through the Turkish Straits.

In 1768, at the very beginning of the First Russo-Turkish War, Catherine sent a scientific expedition under Academician J. A. Guldenstadt to explore the southern steppe. Guldenstadt returned to St. Petersburg on 20 December 1774, and just six days later he presented a formal paper to the Academy of Sciences on the subject of improving Russia's balance of payments by exporting the agricultural surpluses of the Ukraine and the Pontic steppe through the Black Sea.[43] By then Catherine had secured the basic goals of her southern policy with the Treaty of Kiuchuk-Kainardzhi in July 1774, and in 1775 she ordered the construction of a harbor at the mouth of the Dnieper.[44] The liman of the Dnieper, however, turned out to be too shallow for heavy laden, seagoing merchant vessels. Not until the peace of Iassy in January 1792 brought Russia the territory between the mouths of the southern Buh and the Dniester did Catherine find a suitable location for her long desired port on the Black Sea. On 24 May 1794 she approved a proposal for a harbor and city at Odessa. Significantly, when Paul authorized the creation of canals from the Volga and the Dnieper to the ports on the Baltic Sea, he simultaneously called a halt to the development of Odessa.[45] Exports of Ukrainian grain from Odessa began in earnest in the nineteenth century and soon proved that Guldenstadt and Catherine had made an accurate assessment of

---

[43] E. I. Druzhinina, "Znachenie russko-nemetskikh nauchnykh sviazei dlia khoziaistvennogo razvitiia iuzhnoi Ukrainy v kontse XVIII v.," *Mezhdunarodnye sviazi Rossii v XVII–XVIII vv.* (Moscow, 1966), pp. 225–32.

[44] Alan W. Fisher, *The Russian Annexation of the Crimea* (Cambridge, 1970), pp. 133–34.

[45] Zhitkov, *Istoricheskii obzor*, pp. 53–55. Paul later changed his mind in February 1800 in response to a plea from the inhabitants of Odessa.

their potential for improving Russia's balance of payments.[46] Those exports were much less successful, however, in reducing the grain surpluses of Malorossiia.

When Shafons'kyi wrote his topographical description of Malorossiia and the Chernihiv Vice-Regency in 1786 he saw the logical consequences of Catherine's southern policy. After describing the importance of the Dnieper as a trade route from earliest times to 1786, he added: "The acquisition of the Tauride oblast' and the opening of commerce on the Black Sea will no doubt open for the above mentioned guberniias a route along the Dnieper for supplying various products to wharves on the Black Sea and from there to the Mediterranean ..." On the preceding page Shafons'kyi had noted that the thirteen rapids of cataracts of the Dnieper and the large rocks present as far north as Kremenchuk "hinder navigation," but he had not realized the extent to which they could limit the use of the Dnieper as a commercial highway.[47]

In 1783 Potemkin had begun blasting a channel through the Dnieper Rapids in order to transport military supplies from his estates in southern Belorussia to the naval base at Kherson, but the work came to a halt with the outbreak of the Second Russo-Turkish war in 1787. In March 1796 Colonel-Engineer Francois Devolant submitted a proposal for completing the task. He had no doubt that it would succeed, "since the nature of the Dnieper Cataracts presents nothing that can prevent the government from taking effective measures for destroying those obstacles that make one of the most beautiful rivers in Russia *useless for commercial navigation*," and projected the cost as 4,782,885 rubles.[48] Sievers, who had seen the economic potential of such a waterway during a journey through the south in 1795, accepted Devolant's proposal in principle and the "cleaning" of the Dnieper Rapids began anew in 1798. In 1801 Sievers's successor, Count Kushelev obtained an appropriation of 40,000 rubles for continued

[46] Patricia Herlihy, "Russian Grain and Mediterranean Markets, 1774–1861," (Ph.D. diss., University of Pennsylvania, 1963), pp. 239–40.

[47] Shafons'kyi, *Chernigovskogo namestnichestva*, p. 5.

[48] Underlined in the original—R.E.J. "Remarques sur les cataractes du Dniepre jointent aux plans de nouvellement, faites par ordre de son excellence Monsieur le Grand-Maitre d'Artillerie." Tsentral'nyi gosudarstvennyi istoricheskii arkhiv, fond 155, delo 1, pp. 11–17.

work on the Dnieper Rapids, and the report on the Department of
Water Communications written in 1802 promised that by 1804 the
Dnieper would be open to navigation, "without which the Black Sea
will forever be of little importance to Russia. . . . Since the time that
Russia extended its sway over that sea all the difficulties of those obs-
tacles have made themselves all the more apparent."[49]

The author of that statement was wrong on both counts. In the first
place the "cleaning" of the Dnieper rapids failed to open that river to
extensive commercial navigation, and its use remained limited
throughout the first half of the nineteenth century.[50] In the second
place the Black Sea did acquire an enormous commercial importance
for Russia, and for the export of grain in particular, but that grain was
produced along the lower Dnieper as well as on the Buh, the Dniester,
the Don, and the Kuban'. It came, in other words, from Novorossiia
as opposed to Malorossiia. Those areas with easy access to the Black
Sea proved to be so enormously fertile that once they were settled they
once again presented the growers of Malorossiia with the dual problem of trying to ship surplus grain by inadequate and expensive means
into an area where grain was already abundant. Repeatedly the
growers pleaded with the imperial government for improved navigation along the Dnieper that would permit a reduction in the amount of
grain that was "rotting in the stacks in more than ten provinces," but
nothing helped until the building of the railroads in the latter half of
the century.[51] Thus, when a correspondent for a government trade
journal wrote an article on the condition of commerce in the Ukraine
in the early 1840s, he observed that "when presented with an average
harvest of 1:5, the growers of grain do not know where to sell the product of their labor."[52]

The evidence of price differentials between Malorossiia and other
regions supports the testimony of such observers. At the end of
February 1846 one *kul'* of rye flour cost 1.80 silver rubles in Kharkiv;
2.20 silver rubles in Poltava; 3.15 in Kiev; and 3.60 in Chernihiv.
Along the trade routes to the east, north, northwest, and south the

[49] *Kratkii istoricheskii ocherk razvitiia i deiatel'nosti vedomstva putei soobshcheniia*, p. 14; Bakhturin, *Kratkoe opisanie*, pp. 78–80.

[50] Rakhmatulin, "Khlebnyi rynok," p. 349.

[51] Ibid.

[52] Quoted in ibid., p. 348.

same quantity of rye flour sold for the following prices: 1.80 silver rubles in Kursk; 3.85 silver rubles in Gzhatsk and 4.40 in Tver'; 6.10 silver rubles in Smolensk and 6.80 silver rubles in Mahilioŭ; and 4.20 silver rubles in Kherson at the mouth of the Dnieper. The price was lowest in the southeast, where a *kul'* of rye flour cost 1.30 silver rubles in Tambov and 1.70 in Voronezh, and highest in the northwest, where a *kul'* of rye flour cost 8.10 silver rubles in Kovno and 9.00 in Pskov.[53] One cannot say for certain, but the price of grain in Malorossiia might have been lower still if growers had not already adjusted their sowings to match the anticipated demand.

Such differentials in the price of grain made it much less expensive for the imperial government to station the Russian army in the south than in the north. On the eve of the First Russo-Turkish War approximately 35,000 soldiers were billeted with the peasants and townsmen of Malorossiia.[54] In wartime that region was the base for the Russian armies operating to the south and southwest. During the Second Russo-Turkish War and following a drought in western and central Russia, the government imposed a tax in kind of two *chetveryky* of rye flour and one-and-a-half *garnetsi* of groats per male in the provinces of Kiev, Chernihiv, Novhorod Sivers'kyi, Kharkiv, Tambov, Voronezh, and Kursk. Such payments in kind were credited at a fixed price against tax arrears and future tax payments. Extended to other regions in 1794, the measure proved highly unpopular and was repealed in 1797, after which the government returned to purchasing grain at the market price.[55]

The one remaining use for surplus grain was conversion into alcohol. Not surprisingly, most of the empire's distilleries were located in regions were grain prices were at their lowest, i.e., in the *chernozem* regions of Russia and the Ukraine. Towards the end of the eighteenth century the four Russian guberniias of Penza, Riazan,

---

[53] Ibid., p. 343. In the nineteenth century a *kul'* was a unit of dry measure usually equivalent to 9 *pud* + 10 *funtiv* (360 lbs.) of rye or wheat and lesser weights of oats and lighter grains.

[54] John P. LeDonne, *Ruling Russia: Politics and Administration in the Age of Absolutism, 1762–1796* (Princeton, 1984), p. 310.

[55] Arcadius Kahan, *The Plow, the Hammer, and the Knout: An Economic History of Eighteenth Century Russia* (Chicago and London, 1985), p. 54, fns. 10, 11. 1 *chetveryk* = 26.24 liters; 1 *garnets'* = 3.27 liters.

Tambov, and Kaluga produced 1,657,000 *vedra* of vodka, or just about half of the 3,348,278 *vedra* produced in European Russia, excluding the Ukraine and the Baltic provinces. Yet in Malorossiia, the two guberniias of Kiev and Chernihiv alone produced a total of 1,184,000 *vedra*.[56] Vodka was not only higher in value than grain or flour, it was also much more compact and resistant to spoilage than the grain that had gone into making it and, therefore, it could be transported more easily by boat or even overland to consumers in Moscow and St. Petersburg and in army garrisons to the north and to the south. As Kahan has observed, distilling yielded monopoly profits to the nobility, tax revenues to the state, profits to grain merchants, and incomes to grain producers.[57]

Obviously the presence of surplus grain, limited markets, and low prices had their effects on the residents of Malorossiia. The landlords complained of low incomes and the low profitability of agriculture, but what of the peasants? The theory formulated by the Polish historian Witold Kula and accepted by Kahan as a general rule of thumb for the Russian Empire is that low grain prices meant high real incomes for peasants.[58] Catherine II was impressed by similar theories of the so-called "populationists," especially Johann von Justi and Joseph von Sonnenfels, who argued that low grain prices promoted the welfare of the people and the growth of the population, but she found it difficult to apply that theory consistently in her empire because low grain prices made it difficult for the peasants to pay their taxes.[59] It may be that a theory formulated for Poland and other lands where the demands of the state were relatively low does not hold true for the Russian Empire with its higher levels of taxation. A study of real incomes in Malorossiia in comparison to those in other parts of the empire is needed to illuminate the connection between grain prices and the welfare of the peasants.

Another theory that could be put to the test in Malorossiia is the hypothesis of the Polish historian Marian Małowist that rising grain prices and entry into the world grain market led Eastern European

[56] Ibid., p. 56. 1 *vedro* = 12.32 liters.

[57] Ibid.

[58] Ibid., p. 12. Witold Kula, *Teoria ekonomiczna ustroju feodalnego: Próba modelu* (Warsaw, 1962).

[59] Kamendrowsky, "State and Economy," pp. 48–56.

landowners to gain control of the land and of agricultural production and to reduce the peasants to serfs.[60] The evidence from Malorossiia in the eighteenth and early nineteenth centuries indicates that Malorossiia was at best a weak participant in any world market in grain before the middle of the nineteenth century, that sales outside the region accounted for only a small percentage of the total production of grain, and that landowners were constantly complaining that the cultivation of grain was unprofitable. The major cash crop of Malorossiia was not grain, but hemp, which is a garden crop rather than a field crop, and which cannot be grown on plantations in the way that many other crops can. In Malorossiia at any rate, the connection between participation in the world market and the development of serfdom or "neo-serfdom" seems much weaker than in places like Poland. Perhaps for the Ukraine and for Russia the correlation that should be made is between participation in the world market and the form that serfdom took: whether production for the market necessarily entailed *barshchina* as opposed to *obrok* as it tended to do in northern Russia after the middle of the eighteenth century. A close examination of the relationship between participation in the commercial production of grain and the development and characteristics of serfdom in Malorossiia would be a useful and appropriate test of such theories of serfdom. Obviously it lies beyond the limits of this paper.

What does seem clear is that the entire Ukraine remained outside the all-Russian market for grain until at least the second half of the nineteenth century. The lack of transportation from producers in the south to consumers in the north prevented the formation of a common market in grain. Growers with access to the major south flowing rivers sent their surplus grain to the Black Sea ports for export abroad, while those who did not have such access suffered and complained. The export of surplus Ukrainian grain was enormously important to the Russian Empire in helping to maintain the balance of trade but the only "integration" that can be spoken of in that sense was clearly not economic but financial.

[60] Małowist's views are set forth in the following works: *Studia z dziejów rzemiosła w okresie feudalismu w Zachodniej Europie w XIV i XV wieku* (Warsaw, 1954); "The Economic and Social Development of the Baltic Countries from the Fifteenth to the Seventeenth Centuries," *Economic History Review*, 2d ser., 12 (December 1959):177 – 89; *Croissance et regression en Europe XIVe – XVIIe siècles* (Paris, 1972).

Part III: The Nineteenth Century

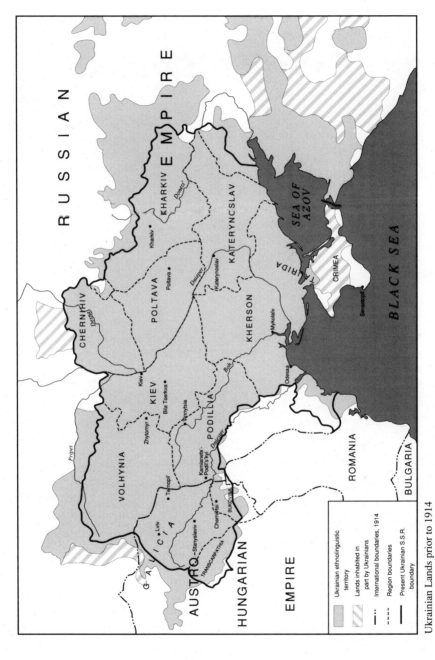

Ukrainian Lands prior to 1914
(based on map in: Paul Robert Magocsi, *Ukraine: A Historical Atlas*, 3rd. rev. ed. [Toronto, 1987]; reprinted with permission from author)

CHAPTER NINE

Population Change in the Ukraine in the Nineteenth Century

Ralph S. Clem

The nineteenth century witnessed major changes in the society and economy of the Ukraine, changes that were to have significant implications in later years. During this period, economic growth in the region, originally fueled by massive increases in agricultural production, was enhanced further by large-scale industrialization. Important in their own right, these economic trends also dramatically altered the size, distribution, and composition of the Ukraine's population; the argument could be made that the transformation so wrought was more profound and of greater consequence than any that has occurred before or since.

Economic development typically sets in motion various aspects of demographic change. In particular, population redistribution can be expected to take place both through inter- and intraregional migration and through urbanization. Migration generally acts as a mechanism to balance the supply of and demand for labor on a regional scale, while urbanization usually results from industrialization and the jobs created thereby which attract people to the cities. In many cases, these two forms of population redistribution occur jointly, as people move from rural areas in labor surplus regions to urban centers in regions where jobs are available.[1]

---

[1] Robert A. Lewis and Richard H. Rowland, *Population Redistribution in the USSR: Its Impact on Society, 1897–1977* (New York, 1979), pp. 3–12.

In any specific case, however, this general relationship between economic development and population change is likely to be modified by historical, cultural, and geographic factors. This is certainly true of the experience of the Russian Empire with modernization and its demographic concomitants, principally because the institution of serfdom restricted migration prior to 1861, and even after that date the vestiges of the servile system inhibited the movement of population.[2] Furthermore, within the tsarist state there were vast regional differences in the level of development—differences engendered by unique historical and political circumstances and by such basic considerations as natural resource endowment. The Ukraine, with its large territory and population and unparalleled combination of rich agricultural land and bountiful industrial mineral resources, was ideally situated for economic growth in the nineteenth century. As will be seen, the demographic impact of development in the Ukraine was considerably more far reaching than in virtually any other region of the empire.

Data and Methods

In attempting to investigate population change in the Ukraine in the nineteenth century, however, one encounters serious problems related to the availability and quality of demographic data. Prior to the first (and only) census of the Russian Empire in 1897, we have only partial statistical coverage of the population in the different censuses (*revizii*) and other, more fragmentary, sources; owing to their limited scope and reliability for demographic analysis, these figures can be used only in a generally descriptive way. Even with the 1897 enumeration, care must be taken to avoid pitfalls stemming from inadequacies of the data. Most importantly for our purposes, the 1897 census did not enumerate ethnic group identity per se, but rather collected information on the language and religious composition of the population.[3] Given the variation among and within ethnic groups in the Ukraine and elsewhere in the Russian Empire with regard to ethnic identity and language use and the fact that differences in the association of

[2] Geroid Tanquary Robinson, *Rural Russia Under the Old Regime* (Berkeley, 1969).

[3] Brian D. Silver, "The Ethnic and Language Dimensions in Russian and Soviet Censuses," in Ralph S. Clem, ed., *Research Guide to the Russian and Soviet Censuses* (Ithaca, N.Y., 1986), pp. 70–97.

these two variables are often correlated with demographic change (the very subject we wish to pursue here), it proved impossible to rely on the 1897 census for ethnic group population data. Accordingly, in this study data from the 1926 Soviet census were utilized to shed light on the ethnic composition of the Ukraine's population.

A second shortcoming of the 1897 census is the definition of "urban" employed in that enumeration; this is troublesome because the legal status criterion used in the census ruled out many centers which were clearly urban in size and function and included others which were just as clearly not.[4] To control for this problem, we adopted a consistent size-only criterion based on populations of fifteen thousand people or more, regardless of their legal standing as "official cities."

Finally, because the territory of the Ukraine has changed radically throughout the nineteenth and twentieth centuries, and because the internal political-administrative units of the region have also been altered repeatedly over the years, it was necessary to reorder data from the 1897 and 1926 censuses into a set of comparable units.[5] The spatial framework of analysis employed here is the territory of the Ukrainian SSR as it is constituted today, subdivided into its three main economic regions (the Donets'k-Dnieper region, the Southwest, and the South) and, for the 1926 data, subdivided further into the twenty-five oblasts. The economic regions are configured according to the 1959 census; the only change since 1959 has been the transfer of Kirovohrad oblast' from the Southwest to the Donets'k-Dnieper region. Because the Soviet Ukraine was truncated in 1926 compared to its present borders, it was also necessary to use data from the censuses of contiguous countries (mainly Poland) to round out the 1926 territory. This must be kept in mind when looking at figures for the western oblasts for 1926, where some population patterns are in a sense artificial because of subsequent border changes. In some

---

[4] Richard H. Rowland, "Migration and Urbanization Data in Russian and Soviet Censuses," in Ralph S. Clem, ed., *Research Guide to the Russian and Soviet Censuses* (Ithaca, N.Y., 1986), pp. 113–30.

[5] See Ralph S. Clem, "Estimating Regional Populations for the 1926 Soviet Census," *Soviet Studies* 29, no. 4 (October 1977):599–602; and J. William Leasure and Robert A. Lewis, *Population Changes in Russia and the USSR: A Set of Comparable Territorial Units* (San Diego, 1966).

instances, reference will be made to the group of nine guberniias which in 1897 closely approximated the territory of the Ukrainian SSR as it is now defined; here it will need to be recalled that about one-third of Chernihiv guberniia in 1897 is today outside of the Ukrainian Republic.[6]

Population Growth in the Ukraine
in the Nineteenth Century

Throughout the nineteenth century, an extraordinary rate of growth resulted in a rapid expansion of the Ukraine's population. According to Rashin, whose estimates are based on *reviziia* data, the nine guberniias of the Ukraine increased in population from 8.7 to 13.6 million between 1811 and 1863 (a 55 percent growth) and then to 23.4 million by 1897 (a 72 percent growth).[7] Over the same periods, the percentage growth for the guberniias of European Russia was 46 percent and 52 percent respectively, which means that the nine Ukrainian guberniias increased their share of the European Russian population from 21 percent in 1811 to 25 percent in 1897. Within the Ukraine, growth rates tended to be highest to the south throughout the nineteenth century, with Tavriia, Kherson, and Katerynoslav ranking close to the top of all guberniias in European Russia, while Poltava and Chernihiv in the northeastern Ukraine were among the lowest in the empire.[8]

This very rapid rate of population growth for the Ukraine was due to a combination of high natural increase (i.e., the excess of births over deaths) and a large volume of net in-migration. From the 1860s—which is the first period for which we have birth and death rates by guberniia for the Russian Empire—through the remainder of the nineteenth century, the rate of natural increase in the nine Ukrainian guberniias exceeded the national average, and often by a wide margin. For the period 1861 to 1913, all nine of the Ukrainian guberniias were in the top twenty in terms of natural increase among

---

[6] Leasure and Lewis, *Population Changes*, p. 4.

[7] A. G. Rashin, *Naselenie Rossii za 100 let* (Moscow, 1956), pp. 28 – 29, 44 – 45.

[8] Ibid., pp. 28 – 29, 44 – 45.

the fifty guberniias of European Russia, with Katerynoslav ranking number one and Tavriia number three overall.[9]

Interestingly, this much higher than average natural population growth, typically ranging from 1.5 to 2 percent per annum, owed more to a lower death rate than to exceedingly high fertility. That is, although the birth rate among the Ukrainian guberniias was certainly high by modern standards, compared to the rest of the empire it was not remarkably so. Death rates, on the other hand, were considerably lower in the Ukraine than in other areas of European Russia. Rashin reported the crude death rate for the Ukraine for the period 1867–1914 as 29.8/1000, as opposed to a figure of 33.7/1000 for all of European Russia.[10] To some extent, these rates were influenced by in-migration, which resulted in a higher than normal concentration of young adults in the population (migration tends to be selective of young adults), which in turn both increases the number of births and decreases the number of deaths relative to a population with a normal age distribution.

Yet, mortality conditions were no doubt more favorable in the Ukraine than in most other areas of the Russian Empire in the nineteenth century, as reflected in the much lower than average infant mortality rate in the former (infant mortality is a sensitive indicator of standards of living and, because it applies only to children of less than one year of age, is not biased by different age distributions).[11] The relatively low mortality rate in the Ukraine was probably due to a better and more stable supply of food in this region than elsewhere in the tsarist state.[12]

Although it is an extreme case, the example of Katerynoslav guberniia is interesting in connection with the point about high natural increase in the Ukraine. Over the quinquennium 1896–1900, the birth rate in this guberniia was reported as 55.2/1000 (near the upper limit of the biological capacity of people to reproduce) and the death rate as 25.8/1000, yielding a rate of natural increase of 29.4/1000, or almost 3 percent per annum compound growth. A population growing

[9] Ibid., pp. 54–59.

[10] Ibid., pp. 167–68.

[11] Frank Lorimer, *The Population of the Soviet Union: History and Prospects* (Geneva, 1946), pp. 80–83.

[12] M. V. Ptukha, *Smertnist' u Rossii i na Ukraina* (Kiev, 1926).

at that rate unchanged will double in size in twenty-three years. Such a demographic situation is similar to that in some developing countries today, where the well-known "population explosion" is taking place.[13]

Migration

Added to this high rate of natural increase was a major influx of migrants to the Ukraine, which in most cases easily offset the number of out-migrants to give the region overall a substantial net positive migration balance. For the most part, the migration patterns in the early nineteenth century are best viewed as a continuation of trends originating in the seventeenth and eighteenth centuries. Briefly, as the southern steppe came increasingly under the control of the tsarist state, the pattern of migration from the densely settled central Russian areas to the relatively sparsely inhabited frontier regions with superior agricultural resources accelerated. The flow of migrants to the south converged with that of Ukrainians from the Right Bank of the Dnieper. V. V. Pokshishevskii has estimated net migration to the forest steppe and the steppe during the seventeenth and eighteenth centuries at roughly 3.3 million, one million of which consisted of Ukrainians from the Right Bank. This movement involved a major redistribution of the Russian Empire's population, considering that at the end of the seventeenth century the population of the country was roughly between fifteen and sixteen million.[14]

In the first half of the nineteenth century, migration to the agricultural frontier continued, with net in-migration to the southern steppe estimated at about 2.6 million for the period 1800 to 1863; this movement slowed somewhat, but remained important, through the remainder of the nineteenth century.[15] In the latter part of the century, two new migration streams developed, one involving out-migration from the already densely populated areas of the northern Ukrainian steppe to the North Caucasus, Kazakhstan, and West Siberia, and the

---

[13] For a detailed discussion of fertility and its determinants in Russia, see Ansley J. Coale, Barbara Anderson, and Erna Harm, *Human Fertility in Russia since the Nineteenth Century* (Princeton, 1979).

[14] Lewis and Rowland, *Population Redistribution*, p. 47.

[15] V. V. Pokshishevskii, "Ocherki po zaseleniiu lesostepnykh i stepnykh raionov Russkoi ravniny," *Ekonomicheskaia geografiia SSR*, 1960, no. 5, pp. 3–68.

other bringing migrants to the developing mining and industrial centers of the eastern Ukraine.[16]

The 1897 census contained a question on place of birth; returns from this question can be used to estimate in-migration and to highlight the trends mentioned above. Considering as migrants those persons born in one guberniia but enumerated in another guberniia, it is possible to calculate in- and out-migration rates for each unit. Of the nine Ukrainian guberniias, the northern tier of Chernihiv, Poltava, and Kharkiv was an area of significant net out-migration in 1897, the southern zone of Tavriia, Katerynoslav, and Kherson was an area of major in-migration, and the western trio of Kiev, Volhynia, and Podillia was roughly in balance.[17] Taken together with the natural increase figures mentioned earlier, one can appreciate the internal variation within the Ukraine with regard to the growth of population. The South especially combined high natural increase with substantial net in-migration to achieve very rapid population growth, while much of the more moderate increase in Chernihiv, Poltava, and Kharkiv was siphoned off by out-migration in the late 1800s.

Migration is a highly complex phenomenon, and it is certainly beyond the scope of this paper to propose a definitive analysis of such a difficult subject. We can, however, point to several key causal factors as generating and directing migration streams to or from the Ukraine and other parts of the Russian Empire. First, we know that the propensity to migrate is influenced by the social and economic conditions obtaining in a given region. A shortage of agricultural land and non-agricultural jobs usually provides an impetus for out-migration; those most likely to move are young adults and those with marketable skills and better education. Barbara Anderson maintained that in addition to propelling people out of their native region, in the case of the Russian Empire in the nineteenth century, the characteristics of migrants also conditioned their choice of destinations. Thus, she demonstrated that migrants from areas of higher literacy and a more developed non-agricultural skill level dominated the streams to modernizing regions and to cities, while people with lower literacy

---

[16] Lorimer, *The Population of the Soviet Union*, pp. 24–28.

[17] Thomas Stanley Fedor, *Patterns of Urban Growth in the Russian Empire during the Nineteenth Century* (Chicago, 1975), pp. 33–34 [Department of Geography Research Paper, 163].

and mainly from a farming background tended to move to newer agricultural areas. In the tsarist empire this meant that the chronically
impoverished conditions in rural areas in central Russia led to both a
pressure for out-migration and a history of non-agricultural work (if
only temporary), which combined to direct people from that area to
cities and to regions of expanding mining and industry; the eastern
Ukraine was a prime destination for these migrants. At the same time,
migrants from the relatively better-off farming lands of the Ukraine,
with lower literacy and few non-agricultural skills, looked to areas of
new farming opportunities, such as Kazakhstan and West Siberia, as
population pressures mounted.[18]

By 1897, the distribution of population in the Ukraine had, in the
words of Frank Lorimer, "... become well adjusted to its natural
resources for agrarian economy."[19] Having achieved a population of
over twenty-nine million by 1897 (Table 9.1), the Ukraine was
overwhelmingly rural (only 10 percent of its population lived in
cities). The greatest concentration of people was in the Southwest,
where 60 percent of the population of the Ukraine lived on 48 percent
of its territory. In fact, population density in this region was the
highest in the Russian Empire outside of Poland and the Moscow
guberniia, with Kiev and Podillia guberniias (which are included in
the Southwest) exceeding sixty persons per square kilometer. By contrast, in the South densities ranged from fifteen to forty-five persons
per square kilometer, and in the Donets'k-Dnieper region from
twenty-five to sixty.[20]

Urbanization

In the latter part of the nineteenth century, another major shift in the
distribution of the Ukraine's population became evident: the growth of
industrial cities. Although historically there were a number of important urban centers in the Ukraine, in some cases dating back centuries,
the population, as mentioned earlier, was almost entirely rural. Other
than the obvious fact that most people in the Ukraine were engaged in

---

[18] Barbara A. Anderson, *Internal Migration during Modernization in Late
Nineteenth-Century Russia* (Princeton, 1980).

[19] Lorimer, *The Population of the Soviet Union*, p. 14.

[20] Ibid., pp. 15–16 and Plate 3.

Table 9.1

Total and Urban Population of Ukraine, 1897 and 1926

	Total		Urban[†]		Percent Urban	
	1897	1926	1897	1926	1897	1926
Ukrainian SSR*	29,164,233	37,950,800	3,023,468	4,917,613	10.4	12.9
*Donets'k-Dnieper Region**	7,846,363	11,967,756	828,645	1,707,980	10.5	14.3
Voroshylovhrad oblast'		1,326,269		142,809		10.8
Dnipropetrovs'k oblast'		1,750,183		332,293		19.0
Donets'k oblast'		1,583,405		300,197		19.0
Zaporizhzhia oblast'		960,145		107,441		11.2
Poltava oblast'		2,151,693		172,118		8.0
Sumy oblast'		1,812,398		183,794		10.1
Kharkiv oblast'		2,383,663		469,328		19.7
*Southwest Region**	17,558,515	21,610,377	1,340,346	2,179,621	7.6	10.1
Vinnytsia oblast'		2,545,045		135,945		5.3
Volhynia oblast'		941,182		83,605		8.9
Zhytomyr oblast'		1,620,894		132,291		8.2
Zakarpats'ka oblast'		697,145		83,344		12.0
Ivano-Frankivs'k oblast'		1,226,685		93,748		7.6
Kiev oblast'		2,503,500		593,399		23.7
Kirovohrad oblast'		1,397,282		101,603		7.3
Lviv oblast'		2,097,772		403,452		19.2
Rovno oblast'		893,657		38,662		4.3
Ternopil' oblast'		1,320,352		33,790		2.6
Khmel'nyts'kyi oblast'		1,805,585		97,247		5.4
Cherkasy oblast'		1,879,836		156,254		8.3
Chernihiv oblast'		1,911,766		118,239		6.2
Chernivtsi oblast'		769,676		108,042		14.0
*South Region**	3,759,355	4,372,667	854,477	1,030,012	22.7	23.6
Krym oblast'		713,823		278,628		39.0
Mykolaiv oblast'		1,081,381		158,179		14.6
Odessa oblast'		1,741,151		534,404		30.7
Kherson oblast'		836,306		58,801		7.0

Sources: 1897 figures from J. William Leasure and Robert A. Lewis, *Population Changes in Russia and the USSR: A Set of Comparable Territorial Units* (San Diego, 1966), pp. 27–28. For an explanation of 1926 figures, see R. S. Clem, "Estimating Regional Populations for the 1926 Soviet Census," *Soviet Studies* 29, no. 4 (October 1977): 599–602.

* Political-administrative boundaries as in the 1959 Soviet census.

† Definition of "urban" includes all centers with populations of 15,000 or more.

agriculture, the institution of serfdom hindered the process of urbanization in at least two ways: the majority of the rural population was legally bound to the land until 1861, and in many cases it remained bound de facto even after the Emancipation, and a disproportionately large share of factories—which normally would provide the economic base for urbanization—were located in rural areas to take advantage of inexpensive serf labor.[21] Most of the urban population in the Ukraine prior to the late nineteenth century consisted of those engaged in service occupations, merchants, handicraft workers, and military or government administrative personnel.[22] Periodic fairs were also economically important, particularly those held in Kiev, Kharkiv, Kremenchuk, Berdychiv, and Sumy.[23] Unlike Western Europe, therefore, manufacturing was not a major factor in the urban economy of the Ukraine during this period, and consequently a large city population could not be supported.

This situation, however, was to change dramatically and quickly in the last two decades of the nineteenth century with the advent of large-scale heavy industry in the eastern Ukraine. The development of the vast Donets'k Basin (Donbas) coal fields, linked by rail with the rich iron ore in the Kryvyi Rih deposits, together with infusions of foreign capital and technology, provided the basis for the rapid expansion of the iron and steel and associated metal-working industries. This in turn led to the growth of cities in Kharkiv, Kherson, and Katerynoslav guberniias as migrants moved to these areas to take jobs in the metallurgical centers.

From the data in Table 9.1 it can be seen that wide disparities existed in 1897 and 1926 in terms of the level of urbanization among the regions and oblasts of the Ukraine. In the South and in the industrial areas of the Donets'k-Dnieper region, the level of urbanization exceeded the national average (9.8 percent and 13.3 percent for 1897

---

[21] Olga Crisp, *Studies in the Russian Economy Before 1914* (New York, 1976), pp. 44–48; Fedor, *Patterns of Urban Growth*, pp. 54–79; Robert A. Lewis and Richard H. Rowland, "Urbanization in Russia and the USSR: 1897–1966," *Annals of the Association of American Geographers* 59 (1969):776–96; and Roger L. Thiede, "Urbanization and Industrialization in Pre-Revolutionary Russia," *The Professional Geographer* (February 1973):16–21.

[22] Fedor, *Patterns of Urban Growth*, p. 66; 30 percent of the population of Odessa, Kerch, and Tahanrih was composed of these service occupations.

[23] Ibid., pp. 55–56.

and 1926), whereas in most of the heavily populated Southwest the levels were quite low (excepting Kiev and Lviv oblasts). Over the period 1811 to 1914, nine of the top twenty cities in the Russian Empire ranked by percentage growth rates were in the Ukraine. The number one growth city at this time, Odessa, along with Symferopil', Mykolaiv, and Kherson in the South and the numbers seven and eight growth cities, Katerynoslav and Kharkiv from the Donets'k-Dnieper region, were illustrative of the rapid urban growth characteristic of the Ukraine. As a result, by 1914 four of the ten largest cities in the empire were in the Ukraine: Kiev (which had become the primate city for the entire Ukraine), Odessa, Kharkiv, and Katerynoslav.[24]

In most cases the percentage of in migrants within the urban population of the Ukraine was very high; in-migrants actually outnumbered locally born inhabitants in Odessa and Katerynoslav and came close to doing so in Tavriia, Kiev, and Kherson guberniias. Again, we can speculate that local rural-to-urban migration was not more numerous because conditions in agriculture were not unfavorable—relative to those elsewhere in the empire—in the Ukraine, and those who did move seemed to have been more inclined to migrate to new farming areas outside of the Ukraine. In the case of the Donbas, the four leading sources of in-migrants were Kharkiv, Kursk, Voronezh, and Orel guberniias, only one of which was an area with a traditional Ukrainian majority.[25]

Social and Political Implications of Population Trends

Because the Ukraine was a region of in-migration from other areas of the Russian Empire, by the time of the 1926 census some areas of the Ukrainian Republic were heavily non-Ukrainian in ethnic composition (Table 9.2). Within the Donets'k-Dnieper region there were major concentrations of ethnic Russians in the most industrialized areas; in Voroshylovhrad, Donets'k, Kharkiv, and Zaporizhzhia oblasts Russians accounted for roughly one-fifth to one-quarter of the total population and, more importantly, one-third to one-half of the urban population. In the South, Russians again were a major factor in the total

---

[24] Rashin, *Naselenie Rossii*, pp. 185–86.
[25] Anderson, *Internal Migration*, pp. 156–62.

Table 9.2

Ethnic Composition of the Total and Urban Population of Ukraine, 1926

	Ukrainians		Russians		Jews		Others	
	Total	Urban[†]	Total	Urban[†]	Total	Urban[†]	Total	Urban[†]
Ukrainian SSR*	72.4	36.7	8.4	23.6	6.3	24.3	12.9	15.4
*Donets'k-Dnieper Region**	78.9	49.4	14.6	30.8	2.9	15.0	3.6	4.8
Voroshylovhrad oblast'	70.0	42.5	26.5	47.8	1.1	4.4	2.4	5.3
Dnipropetrovs'k oblast'	82.9	46.8	8.9	26.5	5.1	20.8	3.1	5.9
Donets'k oblast'	61.4	35.9	25.6	49.8	2.2	7.2	10.8	7.1
Zaporizhzhia oblast'	66.7	39.2	18.3	34.3	3.4	19.2	11.6	7.3
Poltava oblast'	93.9	59.3	2.4	8.3	3.1	30.0	.6	2.4
Sumy oblast'	88.4	73.3	9.2	14.0	1.8	10.7	.6	2.0
Kharkiv oblast'	76.8	51.2	18.3	30.4	3.4	14.2	1.5	4.2
*Southwest Region**	74.8	35.5	2.6	9.2	7.8	31.9	14.8	23.4
Vinnytsia oblast'	87.5	47.4	1.7	7.9	7.6	36.2	3.2	8.5
Volhynia oblast'	61.1	10.5	.9	5.7	10.0	46.5	28.0	37.3
Zhytomyr oblast'	73.7	32.6	2.2	11.3	9.5	46.0	14.6	10.1
Zakarpats'ka oblast'	57.3	25.7	2.4	1.1	12.2	25.7	28.1	47.5
Ivano-Frankivs'k oblast'	68.7	12.9	0.0	0.0	7.3	23.1	24.0	64.0
Kiev oblast'	83.4	47.4	5.8	20.4	8.1	26.8	2.7	5.4
Kirovohrad oblast'	86.9	61.1	6.0	14.9	3.8	21.2	3.3	2.8
Lviv oblast'	47.5	12.1	0.0	0.0	12.2	32.6	40.3	55.3
Rovno oblast'	67.7	7.9	1.3	6.9	10.0	56.0	21.0	29.2
Ternopil' oblast'	51.0	8.1	.1	0.0	8.0	39.3	40.9	52.6
Khmel'nyts'kyi oblast'	81.9	47.1	1.2	5.2	7.9	40.0	9.0	7.7
Cherkasy oblast'	93.5	59.0	.8	4.3	.5	34.8	5.2	1.9
Chernihiv oblast'	90.0	64.3	6.8	13.9	2.5	20.1	.7	1.7
Chernivtsi oblast'	49.7	11.3	5.1	1.6	11.1	38.2	34.1	48.9
*South Region**	43.3	18.2	20.3	42.3	7.8	23.6	28.6	15.9
Krym oblast'	10.1	8.6	39.2	54.6	6.0	12.6	44.7	24.2
Mykolaiv oblast'	51.6	28.0	9.9	31.6	4.4	16.8	34.1	23.6
Odessa oblast'	39.1	18.4	19.4	39.7	12.2	31.3	29.3	10.6
Kherson oblast'	69.4	35.9	17.1	36.0	4.4	25.2	9.1	2.9

Source: R. S. Clem, ''Estimating Regional Populations for the 1926 Soviet Census,'' *Soviet Studies* 29, no. 4 (October 1977): 599–602.

* Political-administrative boundaries as in the 1959 Soviet census.

† Definition of ''urban'' includes all centers with populations of 15,000 or more.

and especially the urban populations. Only in the Southwest was the Russian presence unimportant numerically, except for Kiev where they formed about one-fifth of the urban population.[26]

The data in Table 9.2 also suggest the key role played by Jews in urban areas of the Ukraine; in fact, for the republic at large they out-numbered the Russians in cities. In the western oblasts, the large "other" population consisted mainly of Poles, but here it must be remembered that most of these areas were actually in Poland in 1926. In the South, the "other" group consisted primarily of Tatars, but also appreciable numbers of Romanians or Moldavians, Bulgarians, Greeks, and a host of smaller peoples.

The implications of demographic trends in the nineteenth century, especially migration, were to prove of lasting significance for the Ukraine. To a much larger extent than one might expect, the emerg-ing modern-urban sector of the Ukraine was preempted by non-Ukrainians, many of whom were in-migrants from other parts of the empire. In this sense, the political integration of the Ukraine within the tsarist state allowed for the migration of Russians to the new agri-cultural frontiers in the South and later to cities of the Donbas. Thus, the stage was set for even more dramatic change during the Soviet era as industrial and urban expansion accelerated. Ironically, the oppor-tunities available to ethnic Ukrainians in new farming areas in other parts of the empire drained off surplus population from rural areas in the Ukraine that otherwise might have provided the base for additional Ukrainian urbanization. Therefore, the simple fact that the Ukraine was an integral part of the vast, multiethnic Russian state militated against the full integration of Ukrainians into modern sectors of their ethnic homeland.

[26] Robert A. Lewis, Richard H. Rowland, and Ralph S. Clem, *Nationality and Population Change in Russia and the USSR: An Evaluation of Census Data, 1897–1970* (New York, 1976), pp. 129–91.

CHAPTER TEN

Industrial Development and the Expansion of Free Labor in the Ukraine during the First Half of the Nineteenth Century

Leonid Melnyk

In that part of the Ukraine which belonged to the Russian Empire the bulk of industry during the first half of the nineteenth century was either in the hands of the landlords or of the government. This condition prevailed also in other parts of the empire. During this period the share of industrial enterprises owned by merchants and prosperous townspeople increased significantly. Patrimonial enterprises based on serf labor could not compete with those owned by merchants based on free labor. After the reforms of 1861, landlords' establishments ceased to operate altogether. Therefore, capitalist enterprises—those owned by merchants and other urban dwellers—proved to be the more efficient.

In this paper these processes will be analyzed using the example of the industrial development in the Ukraine. Unlike central Russia, textile industries, particularly the cotton industry, were not well developed in the Ukraine. During the first half of the nineteenth century the two most important branches of industry were the food industry and the processing of animal products. The landlords maintained a dominant position in liquor distilling and sugar production, thereby preventing commercial capital from making significant inroads into these industries prior to the reforms. Rather, this capital was invested in urban industries. In the towns and cities, well-to-do merchants and other townspeople, ethnically Ukrainian, Russian, and Jewish, were founding many small tallowmaking, soapmaking, candlemaking, and tanning shops. A large number of dairies, wool scouring, brickmaking, and other types of businesses were predominantly operated by merchants, townspeople, and free peasants (Cossacks). These businesses usually supplied the local markets.

During the 1840s and 1850s, manufacturing expanded in such branches as leatherworking, tobacco, and wool scouring. In the growing cities of southern Ukraine—where merchants, many of whom were foreigners, were more influential—several relatively large enterprises were established. These included tallowmaking, tobacco processing, and rope making in Odessa and wool scouring and shipbuilding in Kherson and its environs.

Along with the development of the Black Sea shipping industry in the southern port cities, dock establishments and rope making shops flourished. These businesses utilized a significant number of freely hired workers who came from various parts of the Ukraine and Russia to work.

During the 1840s commercial capital began to penetrate into such an important branch of industry for that time as sugar production, which, until then, had been virtually monopolized by landlords. Merchants would start such businesses by leasing mills from landlords or by opening up their own. They also began to utilize such arrangements as extending credit to the landlord-sugar manufacturers or working as managers in sugar mills. Nonetheless, the proportion of commercial capitalists engaged in sugar production was still small prior to the reforms of 1861. The value of output of merchant-owned or merchant-leased mills was only 8.3 percent of the total value of the output of this industry.[1]

Commercial capital was relatively important in another branch of Ukrainian industry—wool textile production. In 1823 there were already forty-six capitalist wool processing shops and factories in the Ukraine which employed over two thousand workers. Because of the rather small market for this product, these establishments tended to be unstable; they expanded and contracted production and often went out of business.[2] During the period from 1830 to 1860 settlements of

---

[1] *Obzor razlichnykh otraslei manufakturnoi promyshlennosti Rossii*, vol. 1, Prilozhenie. *Vedomost' sveklosakharnykh zavodov* (St. Petersburg, 1864), pp. 5–78.

[2] O. O. Nesterenko, *Rozvytok promyslovosti na Ukraini*, vol. 1 (Kiev, 1959), pp. 183–99.

foreign textile workers and Russian merchants (Old Believers) began to appear in various towns in the Ukraine. They gave rise to the growth of such textile production centers as Dunaivtsi in Podillia, Radomyshl' in Volhynia, and Klyntsi in Chernihiv province. The wool industry developed particularly rapidly in Klyntsi, where from 1830 to 1860 the capital of enterprises grew almost fivefold. The products were sold widely and competed successfully with the products of the patrimonial enterprises.[3]

In general, in the period prior to the reforms, the proportion of capitalist-owned wool processing businesses increased steadily while many of the patrimonial enterprises decreased production or were shut down. By the end of the 1850s, twenty-two merchant-owned wool processing enterprises already accounted for close to 53 percent of the overall output of this industry in the Ukraine.[4]

By the end of the 1840s and particularly during the 1850s, mechanization, such as the use of steam-powered machines, was introduced rather intensively into the enterprises owned by the merchants. Technological progress was most evident in the southern Ukraine where steam-powered lumber mills were built. In Kiev province the merchants Iakhnenko and Symyrenko built a large steam-powered sugar mill. In Klyntsi merchant owners of wool processing plants introduced the first steam engines and mechanically operated spinning workshops.

Thus, prior to the reforms of 1861, capitalist enterprises in the Ukraine were concentrated in distinct locations amid many small or artisan as well as large patrimonial establishments. The areas of the greatest concentration of capitalist enterprises were the large cities (Kiev, Odessa, Kharkiv, Kherson) and towns (Klyntsi, Dunaivtsi, Horodyshche, Radomyshl'). The proportion of capitalist businesses relative to patrimonial businesses which utilized serf labor was small even by the end of the 1850s; the value of output of merchant-operated establishments was 8 to 9 million rubles a year while patrimonial enterprises at the time produced 36 to 38 million rubles worth

---

[3] F. Evgen'ev, "Sto let klintsovskoi sherstianoi promyshlennosti," *Klintsovskaia pechat'* (1925), pp. 42–45.

[4] T. I. Dereviankin, *Manufaktura na Ukraini v kintsi XVIII–pershii polovyni XIX st.* (Kiev, 1960), Addendum 6.

of goods (valued in 1850 rubles).[5] Capitalist enterprises, however, utilized more efficient production processes than their patrimonial counterparts. As a result, during the period following the 1861 reforms, by adopting a rapid pace of technological innovation, capitalist enterprises squeezed out the patrimonial manufacturing enterprises.

* * *

The starting point in the process of creating an industrial work force in the Ukraine has to be sought in the income and social stratification of the peasantry. This process grew in importance with the dismantling of the feudal serf system,

By the end of the 1830s in Chernihiv province alone, 15 thousand homeless peasants worked as domestic servants. In Poltava province out of 119 thousand homeless peasant families, 39 thousand were also landless. By the end of the 1840s up to 14 thousand peasants had neither their own land nor their own homesteads in this province. Permanently discharged soldiers, their wives and children were also a source of labor. Of the 3,400 discharged soldiers living in Kiev province in 1845, 1,100 worked as domestic servants and 342 as day laborers. In Kharkiv province 382 of the 4,000 retired soldiers were domestic servants. In some provinces of the Ukraine, one-third of the veterans were employed in various types of services.[6]

One of the results of the process of stratification of the peasants during the first half of the nineteenth century was the rise of wage labor. In the mid-1840s, close to 200 thousand state peasants alone were employed as wage laborers.[7] The largest proportion of wage laborers and seasonal workers came from the Left-Bank provinces: Poltava, Kharkiv, and Chernihiv. Almost one-third of the peasants who left their villages obtained passports for terms varying in length from half a year to up to three years. This indicates, in particular, that state peasants did not work on the land for long periods of time. One can assume that a significant proportion of these wage laborers sought employment either in the industrial or in the transportation sector.

[5] L. H. Melnyk, *Tekhnichnyi perevorot na Ukraini u XIX st.* (Kiev, 1972), p. 26.

[6] I. O. Hurzhii, *Zarodzhennia robitnychoho klasu Ukrainy* (Kiev, 1958), p. 26.

[7] L. H. Melnyk, *Do istorii robitnychoho klasu Ukrainy. Proletariat na pochatkovii stadii promyslovoho perevorotu* (Kiev, 1970), p. 8.

The general situation of wage-earning peasants in the Ukraine did not change appreciably during the 1850s. According to the very incomplete statistics available, the number of peasants who were away from the land at the end of the 1850s exceeded 200 thousand.[8] As in the previous decade, the largest number of wage earners came from the Ukraine's Left-Bank provinces.

The practice of leaving the land was particularly widespread among state peasants. During the 1850s in Kharkiv province these peasants obtained, on the average, sixty-eight thousand passports and tickets a year. The overwhelming majority, 90.4 percent, of the passports and tickets were given to state peasants.[9] As noted above, the main reason for the growth of wage labor was the impoverishment of the peasantry. In Tsarist Russia this social phenomenon was tantamount to [Marxian] primitive capital accumulation, insofar as the peasants were separated from their means of production. However, peasants did not become personally free; they remained bound either to the landlord or to the state. As early as the 1830s and 1840s the primary places of employment for peasants were in the manufacturing establishments. After the harvest many state peasants found employment in alcohol distilleries, sugar mills, and other manufacturing enterprises. In 1845, 3,500 peasants, 1,200 retired soldiers, 575 townspeople, 62 domestic servants, 72 free serfs, and 15 descendants of border guards came to Kiev to work. In the 1840s over 15 thousand men, mostly state peasants, came to Kharkiv for employment. Not infrequently, state peasants, behind in tax obligations, were sent by district authorities to work in sugar mills in order to repay their debts. In 1842, 500 indebted peasants from just one district of Pereiaslav province (Voitsekhivka) were sent to work in Bobryns'kyi's sugar mill.[10]

Thus, state peasants, deprived of land and other means of production, lived exclusively from the sale of their labor. The ranks of the industrial work force were also filled by townspeople, craftsmen, apprentices, and trainees. For example, in Odessa, of the 80 workers employed in Kovalivs'kyi's casting machine-building factory, 54 were residents of Odessa. Most of the workers employed in Kherson's

[8] I. M. Brover, *Ukraina na perelomi do promyslovoho kapitalizmu* (Kharkiv, 1933), p. 24.

[9] *Kharkovskii sbornik*, 1887, pp. 208–12.

[10] Hurzhii, *Zarodzhennia robitnychoho*, pp. 65–77, 90.

wool scouring establishments were either from Kherson or its environs. The 10 brickmaking firms in Kiev which belonged to merchants and affluent burghers employed free laborers, many of whom were poor townspeople.

State-owned enterprises, particularly military establishments, employed either state peasants or peasants recruited by the state. For example, as early as the end of the eighteenth century, 4 thousand state peasants were assigned to the Luhans'k foundry. By special decree, a portion of these workers were sent to work in mines during the 1820s. The predominant proportion of the workers in Kiev's Arsenal plant were apprentices, craftsmen, and trainees who had been recruited by the state. During the 1820s and 1830s this plant employed up to 700 craftsmen, including serfs recruited from patrimonial estates, soldiers' sons, and urban artisans. The state-owned Kiev Mezhyhirs'kyi earthenware plant primarily used serfs from the village of Petrivtsi for its labor force of more than 300 men.[11]

A sizable category of workers were serfs who worked in the enterprises of their landlords. Their number grew significantly during the second quarter of the nineteenth century, the period during which landlord-owned manufacturing enterprises flourished. These serf workers were completely bound to the landlords who transferred them from agricultural work to manufacturing establishments, where they fulfilled their corvée obligations. The literature of that period distinguishes three types of pre-proletariat cadres that were formed out of the serfs:

1) The landlord sent his serfs and servants away to a manufacturing enterprise owned by someone else in order to learn factory skills. The peasants were completely "removed" from the land, did not perform any agricultural duties, and by working in a factory became a "factory" class. Later, their children became workers. These peasant workers did not receive any wages other than food; their earnings went to the landlord who had sent them to the factory.

2) In the second type, half of the peasants worked for the landlord in his manufacturing establishment and the other half did agricultural work. The two groups changed places every week. The landlord

---

[11] *Istoriia robitnychoho klasu Ukrains'koi RSR*, vol. 1 (Kiev, 1967), p. 64; *'Arsenal' imeni V. I. Lenina* (Kiev, 1964), p. 16; Nesterenko, *Rozvytok promyslovosti*, pp. 299, 303.

benefited from this arrangement in two ways. First, this ensured that the work at the factory would be uninterrupted because a certain number of workers would be there every day. Secondly, the landlord did not have to bother with the peasants' upkeep since they retained a share of their farm output once the state and the village community received their shares. A contemporary observer noted the following: "In a word, factory work transformed the meaning of quitrent for the landlord to his advantage. Previously, he had received his quitrent irregularly. Factory income now provided him with twice as much."

3) A number of landlords who did not own their own manufacturing enterprises sent their serfs to work in nearby factories. One writer described this as follows:

> Fairly frequently, landlords sought ways of increasing their income by choosing promising boys from among their peasants (the majority of whom came from large families or were orphans) and sending them by contract to learn factory work for some length of time (usually for five or six years). The landlords provided the boys' upkeep, but did not have to pay for the training. Following the apprenticeship period, these craftsmen either remained in the factory or moved to another enterprise, but now worked for wages. However, the landlords themselves received the wages which were counted as quitrent.[12]

This is how the ranks of workers were formed out of the serfs. On the one hand, the workers were peasants who could be exploited more than ever before, while, on the other hand, these processes introduced a significant difference between the serf workers and the ordinary peasant serfs. Family status, specialization, qualifications, the division of labor, life away from the village and, most importantly, work in closed quarters with other workers, better literacy, and frequent group opposition to the exploitation by the managers were all factors that distinguished these workers from the peasants on the patrimonial estates.

Next, the formation of workers' cadres will be examined by focusing on one of the most important branches in Ukrainian industry during the 1840s and 1850s—namely, sugar production.

---

[12] *Zhurnal manufaktur i torgovli*, 1832, no. 6, pp. 86–87; S. Tomsinskii, "K voprosu o rabochykh kadrakh krepostnoi manufaktury XVIII v.," *Istoriia proletariata SSSR* 1/2(13/14) (1933):156–57.

During the 1840s three types of exploitation of workers could be found in the Ukrainian sugar mills: 1) serf labor in the small patrimonial mills; 2) quitrent-peasants, whose earnings counted towards their quitrent; and 3) hired labor (some mills employed free labor, while others hired landlord-owned peasants). Sometimes the work force in a mill consisted of a combination of these types. Peasants worked in a mill part of the time to fulfill their corvée obligations and, having done so, they would work for pay.

Up to the time of the emergence of "commercial" sugar mills, i.e., large establishments whose production was entirely determined by the market, serf labor predominated in this industry. "Even skilled workers," writes K. H. Voblyi, "were serfs who had learned their skills at the sugar mills of neighboring estates. Mills on estates with relatively small sugar beet fields and therefore a short production period, could manage without hiring outside labor."[13] Mills operated every day, while the peasants' corvée obligations required only three days' work per week. Additional days worked were then either counted toward the obligations of family members or the peasants received payment for the extra days.

As sugar mills grew in size, landlord owners began to employ free labor while continuing to use serfs. This mixed form of labor—serfs and wage earners combined—began to predominate in the sugar industry. At the beginning of the 1850s the proportion of hired labor grew significantly in the large "commercial" sugar mills, particularly in Kiev province. For example, on the Smila estates which belonged to Bobryns'kyi during the seasonal peak at the sugar mill, 180 thousand *chetverty* of sugar beets were processed annually (1 *chetvert'* = 0.108 tons). In the fall season alone 1,500 workers were needed per day in addition to the 4 thousand serfs. It was even necessary to hire up to 1,200 men from other provinces.[14]

State peasants were a source of freely hired labor—they did not have corvée obligations to fulfill and could therefore work for wages in manufacturing establishments. Landlord serfs who worked as tenant farmers also went to work in the sugar mills. Landlords who

[13] K. H. Voblyi, "Narysy z istorii rosiis'ko-ukrains'koi tsukrovoi promyslovosti," *Zbirnyk sotsial'no-ekonomichnoho viddilu VUAN*, vol. 1, pt. 2, no. 15 (Kiev, 1928), p. 9.

[14] Ibid.

operated these mills also hired peasants from other areas, even Russian and Belorussian provinces. These peasants were employed on the basis of contracts with their landlords for the duration of the fall – winter production season. Factory officials often made contractual arrangements with the peasant artels whose members came to the mills to work. At the Vil'shana sugar mill, for example, the labor force was made up of a peasant artel contracted for six months at 5.5 rubles per worker per month. Workers began and ended their work at designated times, they had to have their own clothes, and in the event of illness received no pay.[15]

The landlords also secured cadres of skilled labor by instituting apprenticeship programs. During the 1840s a number of sugar mill owners in the Podillia and Volhynia provinces took in serf children as apprentices. These boys from Ukrainian provinces received training in sugar production in the Vezhky plant owned by the landlord Shpakivs'kyi in Lithuania. Not infrequently, plant managers who hired foreign craftsmen required them to train the apprentice serfs in sugar processing work. By and large, at most mills, a work force was eventually fashioned out of skilled serf workers able to perform all the required tasks.

Landlord owners of sugar mills often bought serfs to work exclusively in the factories as "working people," thus severing their ties with the land. Such "peasants" were then completely drawn into the sphere of industrial work. The landlord Bobryns'kyi, for example, purchased one thousand serfs in Sumy district and put them to work as "factory people" in his mills. They received their own homes with garden plots, but no land allotments. They also received money wages and food.[16]

The labor force of serf workers also included indebted serfs who were sent by their masters to work in industry. The contracts drawn up between the landlords and the enterprise owners specified a certain number of such peasants to be sent to work. The peasants thus contracted were obliged to obey the factory management unconditionally and the factory's officials were given the same discretion in punishing these peasants as their masters had. These peasants were given passports valid for half a year and received monthly salaries and food.

---

[15] Ibid.

[16] *Statisticheskoe opisanie Kievskoi gubernii* (St. Petersburg, 1852), p. 81.

We shall now examine how the cadres of workers employed in the woolen and linen factories came to be formed. The patrimonial mills drew most of their labor from serfs belonging to the landlord/owner of the establishment. The serf workers were primarily peasants; the rest were the master's domestic servants and orphaned serfs. The composition of the workers employed in the patrimonial woolen enterprises in Kharkiv province is a typical example. At S. Bakhmetieva's woolen plant in the village of Nyzy in Sumy district, the workforce consisted of the following: 1 mechanic, 6 artisans, 8 apprentices, and 187 unskilled workers, all of whom were her serfs. A linen plant in the same village and owned by the same woman employed 1 craftsman and 20 unskilled workers, all serfs. Likewise, at the landlord V. Kondratiev's establishment in the same district, the craftsmen, apprentices, and all of the workers were serfs. A large cotton spinning mill located in Sumy district in the village of Vyshcha Syrovatka employed 700 craftsmen and unskilled laborers who were the serfs of the landlord/industrialist D. H. Rakhmanov. At the woolen factory in the village of Buimera in Lebedyn district, the 17 craftsmen, 210 unskilled men, and 198 unskilled women were the serfs of the landlord/industrialist I. V. Markov.[17]

In Chernihiv province the patrimonial woolen factories on the landlords' estates also employed serf labor. The only freely hired workers were either foreigners, townspeople, or peasants contracted from other landlords.

The capitalist enterprises by and large employed townspeople. In 1832 in Klyntsi, the center of capitalist woolen industry, 90 percent of the workers were urban dwellers. Only at the plant operated by Isaiev in the village of Novi Mezhyrychi were there 125 foreigners employed, i.e., 32.5 percent of all of the workers.[18] The merchants/owners of the enterprises in Klyntsi not only exploited the workers at the workplace but further exploited them by practicing the put-out system.

A characteristic of the formation of the pre-proletariat in the Ukraine was that in, addition to the Ukrainians recruited into its ranks, a significant proportion of Russian immigrants were employed. The

---

[17] State archives of Kharkiv oblast', f. z., Office of the Kharkiv Governor, op. 138, spr. 126, ark. 327, 328, 333, 388, 433, 514, 545, 546, 547.

[18] Dereviankin, *Manufaktura na Ukraini*, pp. 64–65.

inflow of Russians into the Ukrainian labor force occurred due to the emigration of artisans from Russian cities and the transfer by state officials of Russian workers to be employed in Ukrainian manufacturing establishments. Many sugar production workers, for example, were enlisted by commissioners from the central Russian provinces. A large number of peasants with quitrent obligations came to work in the Ukraine from these provinces. Russian craftsmen and skilled workers worked in the state-owned factories in the Ukraine. In 1840 at Ladomyrs'kyi's woolen factory in Novozubkiv district, Chernihiv province, there were 40 state and landlord peasants from Kaluga province. At the copper factory owned by the merchant A. Chernov in Nizhyn, the artisans were immigrant peasants, formerly serfs on church estates in Vladimir province. During the 1840s the leather-working enterprise run by the merchant Serebrennykov in Kiev employed 13 local residents, 8 retired military servicemen, and 25 landlord serfs from Russian provinces. During the 1850s most of the workers at the foundry owned by the Dekhtiarovs in Kiev were immigrants from Tula, Kaluga, Moscow, and Vladimir provinces. In the sugar mills of the Right-Bank Ukraine, state and landlord peasants were recruited from Belorussia and Orel and Smolensk provinces. In 1845 one-third of the artisans in Kiev were Russian immigrants.[19]

Thus, the main groups from which the pre-proletarian labor force in the Ukraine was formed consisted of: peasants deprived of their means of production (impoverished state peasants, landlord peasants on temporary leave from the land for a contracted period of time, and serfs "assigned" to factories); and impoverished urban artisans, townspeople, and village craftsmen. These groups acquired the requisite factory and technical skills and eventually became hired labor.

Industrial workers in the Ukraine prior to the reforms were characterized by their diversity, in particular, by the various degrees of dependence on the owners of the manufacturing establishments. In addition, even the townspeople who were hired workers in the capitalist establishments should not be confused with the industrial proletariat. They often had their own homes, plots of land, and their own workshops or tools at home. They were the forerunners of the proletariat.

---

[19] Hurzhii, *Zarodzhennia robitnychoho,* pp. 90–92; *Statisticheskoe opisanie,* p. 184.

As a result of the establishment of large manufacturing enterprises during the second quarter of the nineteenth century, a fairly sizable contingent of the pre-proletariat was formed in the Ukraine. By the end of the 1850s the number of workers employed in the sugar industry alone reached 45.5 thousand. According to I. O. Hurzhii, the total number of workers in all manufacturing establishments and workshops in the Ukraine prior to the 1861 reforms was about 135 thousand. During this period, of the 85 thousand workers who were engaged in industrial production, the largest proportion, 53.5 percent, worked in the sugar industry, 11.98 percent in woolen textiles, 5.5 percent in wool scouring, and 3.25 percent in brickmaking. The greatest concentration of sugar mill workers was in Kiev province (i.e., more than 62 percent of all sugar industry workers). Significant numbers of sugar mill workers could also be found in Chernihiv, Podillia, and Kharkiv provinces. The greatest concentration of woolen textile mill workers, 41 percent, was in Chernihiv province.[20]

In the first quarter of the nineteenth century the Ukraine was a region still characterized by patrimonial enterprises. Serf labor predominated in the industry of the Ukraine. The percentage of freely hired labor was much lower than in Russia proper. Serfs were still the main source of labor in such branches of industry as woolen textiles, metalworking, and iron forging—industries which were controlled for the most part by the landlords. Hired labor was primarily employed in the rope making, spinning, and candlemaking plants owned by merchants and other burghers. The importance of the latter enterprises for the total industrial output was, however, still insignificant.

During the second quarter of the nineteenth century the number of freely hired workers grew rapidly, while the number of serfs found in manufacturing decreased. In spite of the presence of substantial groups of serf workers in the sugar, woolen, linen, paper, and several other industries, the majority of workers, 54 percent, in Ukrainian manufacturing prior to the agricultural reforms were freely hired.[21]

The expansion of free labor in the main industrial branches in the Ukraine was linked with the beginnings of the industrial revolution in the Ukraine, i.e., the mechanization of production processes in the industrial enterprises. This is evident in the leading branch of

[20] Hurzhii, *Zarodzhennia robitnychoho*, pp. 97–98, 104.
[21] *Istoriia robitnychoho*, p. 69.

industry, the sugar industry. Technological change in the sugar industry involved the transition from a primitively organized production process that relied on manual labor ("fire powered" sugar mills) to mechanized processes ("steam powered"). The increased use of free labor was an integral part of this transition. The technology employed in the "fire powered" sugar plants was simple; most of it could be performed by serf workers. Hence, few skilled laborers (freely hired workers or serfs trained at other enterprises) were needed.

Serf labor proved to be inefficient at the "steam powered" sugar mills. As early as the 1840s and 1850s many landlord sugar producers (particularly on the Right Bank) were aware of the low level of productivity of serf labor and the resulting difficulties in rationalizing production. Furthermore, the serf workers retained a hostile attitude towards factory work, thereby reducing the efficiency of operations. Beginning with the 1840s, the formation of cadres of hired workers grew at an accelerated pace in the sugar industry. In the 1840s and 1850s, the sugar industry surpassed all other branches with respect to the utilization of hired labor. By the 1850s all aspects of production in the "commercial" sugar mills began to be carried out by hired workers.[22]

The degree of utilization of hired labor varied throughout the Ukraine. On the Right Bank, for example, there was a shortage of workers in the sugar industry. The rate of growth in this industry, particularly in Kiev province, exceeded the growth rate of available free labor. For this reason, many peasants were brought from Kursk, Kaluga, and other Russian provinces to work in the sugar mills. After the introduction of the "Inventories" in 1846 on the Right Bank, landowners/industrialists had to observe restrictions as to the employment in their sugar mills of peasants who had to meet their outstanding obligations. They were therefore compelled, for the most part, to make use of hired labor. Often, the owners employed peasants to work in the sugar mills by making agreements with village communes or with their landlords. In addition, some village communes forced indebted peasants to hire themselves out to the sugar plants in order to repay their tax arrears.

---

[22] Voblyi, "Narysy z istorii," pp. 34–35; B. V. Tikhonov, "Razvitie sveklosakharnoi promyshlennosti vo vtoroi polovine 40-kh i v 50-kh godakh XIX st. (K istorii nachala promyshlennogo perevorota)," *Istoricheskie zapiski* 62 (1958):152.

On the Left Bank, on the other hand, prior to the reforms, serf labor predominated in the sugar enterprises. According to one writer of that time, all the efforts of the owners of these mills "were geared toward reducing the amount of capital used in production as much as possible."[23]

The utilization of serf labor in the sugar industry on the Left Bank was the primary reason for the technological stagnation in this industry. The landlord mill owner sought ways of increasing profit not by technological improvements but by simplifying the production processes as much as possible in order to be able to exploit serf labor to the greatest extent possible. The simplicity of the equipment enabled the landlord to create cadres of skilled workers out of his serfs.

During the second quarter of the nineteenth century, the importance of hired labor grew in a less developed branch (relative to the sugar industry)—woolen textiles manufacturing. Although the woolen industry in the Ukraine, prior to the reforms, was based primarily on serf labor, as elsewhere in the empire, during the two decades preceding the 1861 reforms, the number of freely hired workers more than doubled. It must be emphasized, however, that the absolute majority of serf workers were employed in patrimonial woolen textile establishments, which ceased to operate, by and large, following the reforms. Free labor predominated in the capitalist enterprises, most of which continued to operate after the reforms, eventually becoming factories.

The use of free labor expanded concurrently with the ever-increasing number of larger establishments ("commercial" sugar mills and merchant-owned woolen textile enterprises). The availability of hired labor in turn ensured the continued development of these branches, facilitating the introduction of mechanized production processes.

Private manufacturing enterprises in the cities of southern Ukraine employed hired labor. Various immigrants—wage earners, poor peasants, and artisans—came to work in these businesses. For example, at the end of the 1850s Odessa alone increased its population by 10 thousand annually. Most sought employment in the rope-making,

---

[23] *Obzor razlichnykh* 1 (1862):43–44.

wool scouring, machinebuilding, and shipbuilding factories. The total number of industrial workers in all branches of industry reached 25 thousand in Katerynoslav province and 30 thousand in Kherson province. The ethnic composition of the pre-proletariat in the South was mixed. In addition to Ukrainians, and Russians, there were also Moldavians, Jews, Greeks, and Serbs.[24]

Thus, workers in the Ukraine in the 1840s and 1850s could be divided into two main groups: free labor and serfs. The majority of serf workers could be found in the woolen textile, alcohol distilling, sugar, linen, paper, saltpeter, and glass industries, in enterprises owned by the landlords. In many alcohol distilleries that were run by landlords and especially in the sugar mills, both serf and wage-earning labor were utilized. In enterprises—owned by merchants, townspeople, Cossacks, and state peasants—such as leatherworking, tallowmaking, candlemaking, soapmaking, tobacco, and wool scouring industries, hired labor was employed.[25] A characteristic feature of the second quarter of the nineteenth century was the gradual replacement of serf labor with free labor in all branches of industry due to technological change. This was particularly salient in the patrimonial enterprises of the leading branch of Ukrainian industry, the sugar industry.

---

[24] V. P. Vashchenko, ''Rozvytok kapitalistychnoi promyslovosti v mistakh Pivdnia Ukrainy,'' in *Pratsi Odes' koho derzhuniversytetu*, vol. 148, pt. 1, p. 198.

[25] Melnyk, *Do istorii robitnychoho*, p. 41.

CHAPTER ELEVEN

Development of the Ukrainian Economy, 1854 – 1917: The Imperial View

Martin C. Spechler *

It is understandable that most historians of the Ukrainian economy under Tsarist rule have adopted either a nationalist or a cosmopolitan view of the Ukraine's early industrialization. The cosmopolitan theory, associated with Adam Smith and the Manchester School, maintains that world development is best served by minimal intervention and free trade with the outside world. What is more, small trading units have the most to gain from openness because they can most easily specialize and improve their terms of trade. The cosmopolitan view, adopted widely by Western scholars but also by some early Ukrainian economists like Ivan Vernads'kyi (1821 – 1884) points with approval to the growing international role of the Ukraine as a supplier of wheat and other agricultural products and as an importer of agricultural machinery during the early twentieth century.[1] More broadly, the cosmopolitan view would credit the remarkable advances of the Ukrainian economy to its openness to foreign corporations, its increasing mercantile freedom for diverse ethnic groups, its remoteness from the dead hand of Russian bureaucracy, its commercialized agriculture, and its thriving port and commercial cities, such as Odessa and Kharkiv.

*The author wishes to thank Scott Seregny and the members of Indiana University Economic History Workshop for valuable comments and suggestions.
[1] M. E. Falkus, *The Industrialization of Russia 1700 – 1914* (London, 1972).

A contrary view, also well established in the historiography of the Ukraine (and other European latecomers) is the "national school," originated by the German Friedrich List in the middle of the nineteenth century.[2]

As is well known, List criticized Manchestrian liberal cosmopolitanism for neglecting the nation-building, mercantilist, and protectionist measures which he believed had established English supremacy. To overtake Britain, "the national school" called for a period of protectionism until indigenous industries could be made competitive.[3] Agriculture alone would be no basis for national progress.

In more recent times, populist writers, such as Immanuel Wallerstein and André Gunder-Frank, and several Latin American dependency theorists have made similar complaints against the metropolitan powers of our own day. Supposedly, the advanced capitalist powers have imposed their hegemony upon peripheral economies, such as Africa, Brazil, Poland, Russia, and the Ukraine.[4] According to these populists, peripheral economies have been forced to produce complementary raw materials, labor, and food for the metropolitan economies. Consequently, labor exploitation becomes more coercive and onerous. For the sake of their peoples, then, present-day dependencies are urged to throw off their bondage and to become more self-sufficient economically, technologically, culturally, and politically.

Economic nationalism can be derived from populism, as we have seen, or from Marxist-Leninist dialectic, as in the dogmas of Josef Stalin.[5] The national view is also compatible with fascist or even

---

[2] I. S. Koropeckyj, "Academic Economics in the Nineteenth-Century Ukraine," in I. S. Koropeckyj, ed. *Selected Contributions of Ukrainian Scholars to Economics* (Cambridge, Mass., 1984), pp. 163–222.

[3] Friedrich List, *National System of Political Economy* (New York, 1966).

[4] Immanuel Wallerstein, *The Modern World-System*, vol. 1 (New York, 1974), p. 139; André Gunder-Frank, *Capitalism and Underdevelopment in Latin America* (New York, 1967); idem, *Lumpenbourgeoisie and Lumpen-development* (New York, 1972).

[5] Marxists like V. I. Lenin sometimes embrace the cosmopolitan view, praising the progressive role of capitalism, and sometimes the rational view, when colonialism had ultimately to be overthrown to rationalize production.

liberal political orientations.[6] It can be radical or reformist.[7]

The national view is readily adopted, though often unconsciously and partially, by historians with strong sympathies and attachments to the Ukraine.[8] For them, economic thinking serves a very natural preference for preserving the rich cultural heritage of the Ukraine, even to reestablishing independence to this numerous and self-conscious European people.

The national view of Ukrainian economic development emphasizes the disadvantages of association with the Russian Empire and the outside capitalist world during early industrialization. Russian economic policy from Catherine II (1762–1796) and even before saw the Ukraine as a field of enrichment for Russians and sought to discriminate against indigenous enterprise. Excessive openness among part of the empire meant the best brains and the best profits would be skimmed off for luxurious consumption in the capitals and for bureaucratic and military waste. According to the national view, the Ukraine in the late nineteenth century could not protect its own industry and was thus condemned to produce wheat, coal, and other primary goods for the outside. The ethnic Ukrainian middle class was weakened and dispersed, while non-Ukrainians were preferred as middlemen and agents. Heavy taxes skimmed off the surplus without compensating government services.

Rather than expounding the cosmopolitan and national views of Ukrainian economic development, I wish to identify a third perspective and to apply it in a tentative way to Ukrainian developments. What I will call "the imperial view" draws on newer theories in political economy as well as upon findings of economic historians from countries comparable to the nineteenth-century Ukraine. The imperial view stresses potential advantages to a territorial unit, like the Ukraine, from existing within a hegemonic empire during early modern economic growth, provided that empire can be integrated

[6] Daniel Chirot and Thomas Hall, "World-System Theory," *American Review of Sociology* 8 (1982):81–106; R. Prebisch, "Commercial Policy in the Underdeveloped Countries," *American Economic Review* (May 1959):251–73.

[7] Robert Brenner, "The Origins of Capitalist Development: A Critique of Neo-Smithian Marxism," *New Left Review* 104 (July-August 1977):25–93.

[8] Konstantyn Kononenko, *Ukraine and Russia: A History of the Economic Relations Between Ukraine and Russia (1654–1917)* (Milwaukee, 1958).

commercially.[9] While the cosmopolitan view believes gains from trade come from maximum extension of the trading area—"division of labor is limited by the extent of the market," as Adam Smith taught—the imperial view sees some disadvantages from extreme openness. As we have learned from the neo-mercantilist theory of hegemony, an unregulated trade system tends to break down from pursuit of narrow self-interest.[10] Effective economic integration requires a dominant political power to enforce the rules of the game. The imperial hegemon also defends legitimate commercial interests at home and abroad, compensates losers for the consequences of efficient reallocations, builds interregional infrastructure, and serves as lender of last resort for temporary financial crises.[11] All these functions can be presented as public goods which no individual actor has sufficient material incentive to provide; if no one provides them, group members will fail to attain their joint optimum. The hegemon provides a social service to other group members; so long as the private rewards to the hegemonic leader do not exceed by too much the costs of undertaking it, its leadership will be accepted. Essentially, this is the theoretic justification of hegemony in the imperial view.

We may cite considerable, if dispersed, literature in political and economic history to defend the imperial view—namely, that empires have often served useful economic functions during early phases of economic development. Imperial hegemonies, of course, may not always be positive; they can overstay their historical welcome. They may also exploit their hegemonic position for pecuniary gain to the detriment of subordinate nations. Then hegemonic leadership becomes mere dominance.

Political historians since classical times have elaborated the theme of Pax Romana and Pax Britannica. But more recently George

---

[9] Simon Kuznets, *Modern Economic Growth* (New Haven, 1966), pp. 467, 472.

[10] Stephen Krasner, "State Power and the Structure of International Trade," *World Politics* 28, no. 3 (April, 1976):317–47; Robert Keohane, *After Hegemony: Cooperation and Discord in the World Political Economy* (Princeton, 1984).

[11] Charles P. Kindleberger, "Dominance and Leadership in the International Economy," *International Studies Quarterly*, June 1982, pp. 242–54.

Modelski,[12] Steven Krasner,[13] and others have pointed out the efflorescence of world trade and investment which has taken place during successive hegemonic periods led by Spain, England, and the United States. In Charles Kindleberger's analysis of the breakdown of the world economy in the 1920s and the 1930s, a crucial factor was the inability of Great Britain to exercise its role as world central banker together with the unwillingness of the United States to assume that hegemonic role.[14]

For understanding the Russian imperial role in the Ukraine, a more striking parallel is the experience of countries which played a subordinate role in other imperial systems. Normally, the national histories of countries constituent of the Hapsburg, British, Spanish, Turkish, Chinese, or Russian empires have been sharply critical of imperial policies as self-serving and exploitative. Such a stance is a natural response to frequent imperial attempts to subvert, co-opt, or suppress national cultures.

Nonetheless, some present-day scholars have arisen to challenge the national (or nationalistic) interpretations of their own economic past. Ivan Berend, the influential Hungarian economic historian, has pointed out the benefits to Hungary and Bohemia-Moravia from inclusion in the protected Austro-Hungarian market.[15] Railroads built for military and political purposes later promoted the economy, just as occurred in the Russian Empire. Riita Hjerppe has written that her native Finland benefited greatly from free access to the Russian market during the late nineteenth century. Finnish paper, cotton, furniture, metal and food processing industries expanded remarkably taking advantage of the high imperial tariffs of the last quarter of the nineteenth century. Russia provided loans for Finnish industry and exports.[16]

[12] George Modelski, "The Long Cycle of Global Politics and the Nation-State," *Comparative Studies in Society and History*, April 1978, pp. 214–38.

[13] Krasner, "State Power."

[14] Charles Kindleberger, *The World in Depression, 1929–1939* (Berkeley and Los Angeles, 1973).

[15] Ivan Berend, "Economic Dependence and Underdevelopment: A Case Study of Eastern Europe," *Mimeo*, 1985, p. 7.

[16] Riita Hjerppe, "Finland in the European Economy," *Mimeo*, 1985, pp. 115–28; Riita Hjerppe, Matti Peltonen, and Erkki Pihkala, "Investment in Finland, 1860–1979," *Scandinavian Economic History Review*, 1984, no. 1, 2, 3, p. 45.

Several Scandinavian countries and Ireland flourished on the basis of exports of dairy products, pork, iron and steel, and wood products to the open British market.[17] So did Australia and New Zealand, which were formally part of the empire. Whatever one may think of the pattern and motives of British overseas investment, Argentine and Canadian wheat and beef exporters similarly benefited from the thriving British market.[18] The United States has given Caribbean nations preferential access to the North American market.

Albert Hirschman showed that Nazi economic domination of its "informal empire" in southeast Europe brought substantial *short-term* advantages to Rumania, Yugoslavia, and Hungary.[19] Charles Kindleberger attributes Austria's outstanding postwar growth record to the open markets and monetary stability provided by West Germany.[20] All of these examples, to be sure, do not deny that on occasion an imperial power exploited a colonial area irrationally, meanly, and shortsightedly. Nonetheless, on many occasions, a self-confident imperial power with political and military priorities did promote the long-term economic development of subordinate national areas for the imperial welfare. In such cases, for the subject people as a whole, nationalism might be good politics, but would likely be bad economics.

Six Theses

We may elaborate the "imperial view" as six theses, which *may* apply to the Ukraine or to other large national areas imbedded in a multinational empire. I am not altogether convinced that on balance

[17] Alexander Gerschenkron, *Bread and Democracy in Germany* (New York, new edition, 1966), p. 33; Lennart Jöberg, "The Industrial Revolution in the Nordic Countries" in Carlo M. Cipolla, ed. *The Fontana Economic History of Europe*, vol. 4, pt. 2 (London, 1973), pp. 375–85; Cormac O'Grada, "The Irish Economy Before the Famine: Poverty and Progress," *Mimeo*, 1986.

[18] Richard E. Caves and Richard H. Holton, *The Canadian Economy, Prospect and Retrospect*, (Cambridge, Mass. 1959), p. 1912.

[19] Albert Hirschman, *National Power and the Structure of Foreign Trade* (Berkeley and Los Angeles, 1969); Martin C. Spechler and Alfred Tovias, "When Should Developing Countries Use Bilateral State Trading?," *World Development*, 1984, nos. 11/12, pp. 1077–86.

[20] Charles Kindleberger, *Europe's Post-War Growth: The Role of the Labor Supply* (Cambridge, Mass., 1970).

each one of the six theses applies to the Ukraine during the century before World War I. But there is some evidence that most do, and I will present some of that evidence in the next section. Furthermore, while no contemporary held all six theses, to my knowledge, some officials and economists held some of them in a rudimentary form. The construct "imperial view" may be seen as an antithesis of the "national view;" I would expect an eventual synthesis would include a dialectic resolution of the cosmopolitan, national, and imperial views of the economic development of national areas.

1) While nationalists have criticized alien decision-making as unjust in itself and certain to lead to exploitation, the imperial view holds that a *hegemon is necessary* to any stable international system based on exchange and long-term cooperation. Since the benefits provided by the hegemon are public goods—peace, free domestic trade, unified standards and laws, enforcement of long-distance contracts, prevention of chiseling, and so forth—elementary public choice theory predicts that peripheral entities will try and often succeed to obtain these benefits without sharing the costs—the famous free rider problem. So it has been for the British Empire,[21] so it is for the contemporary Soviet Empire.[22] Might one not say that the Roman Empire fell when the frontier areas failed to provide the taxes and soldiers to defend the empire as a whole against a common threat?

2) While social overhead capital—roads, railroads, ports, water control systems—is often built to suit the needs of the metropolitan center, as the national view maintains, the un-economic density and high up-front cost of these facilities benefit traders in the colonial areas. Russian, British, and Austrian railroads were often extended to

[21] Lance Davis and Robert A. Huttenback, "The Cost of Empire," in Roger L. Ranson, Richard Sutch, and Gary M. Walson, eds., *Explorations in the New Economic History* (New York, 1982), pp. 41–70; Lance Davis, "Mannon and the Pursuit of Empire: The Political Economy of British Imperialism, 1860–91," *Mimeo*, 1986.

[22] Martin C. Spechler, "Regional Developments in the U.S.S.R., 1958–1978," in *Soviet Economy in a Time of Change*, vol. 1 (Washington, D.C.: Joint Economic Committee, 1979), pp. 141–63; Michael Marrese and Jan Vanous, *Soviet Subsidization of Trade with Eastern Europe: A Soviet Perspective* (Berkeley, 1983); Padma Desai, "Is the Soviet Union Subsidizing Eastern Europe?," *European Economic Review* 29 (1985):1–10.

facilitate military access to Asia.[23] They hardly justified their early construction in economic benefits to the center. Infrastructure provided safe collateral for private loans to subordinate areas, since railroad, customs, and other use charges made extracting economic surplus easier for metropolitan investors. This does not mean no surplus remained at home, as the clamor for such investments amply proves.

3) Subordination to an empire usually has meant that the national economy is powerless to set protective tariffs or low exchange rates. Commercial and monetary policy is set by central authorities, presumably for their own benefit. It does not follow, though, that subordinate areas have no way to protect infant industry if that is desirable or that *imperial* protection had no benefits to peripheral national economies. Imperial protection often goes with imperial preference: free access to protected metropolitan markets can be turned to advantage if basic preconditions are sufficiently met. Preferential trade agreements always help the country receiving them, even if they divert trade of the granting partner.[24] A subordinate national area like Finland or Hungary can develop ''export'' specialties secure from outside (German) competition. Lower incomes and prices in the imperial currency give these areas protection far more effective and efficient in administrative terms than tariffs or quotas. Stories from many an empire of how local industry was ruined by floods of imports from elsewhere are easy to cite; they are equally easy to refute, since a region must generally export at least as much as it imports. Massive imports, if they exist, simply mean that exports have grown apace. The benefits from trade must also have grown.

If factors of production are mobile and wage rates flexible downwards, according to international trade theory, the national area need

[23] D. Spring, ''Railways and Economic Development in Turkestan Before 1917,'' in Leslie Symons and Colin White, eds., *Russian Transport* (London, 1975), pp. 46–74; Berend, ''Economic Dependence.''

[24] Jacob Viner, *The Customs Union Issue* (New York, 1950), pp. 41–48; R. G. Lipsey, ''The Theory of Customs Unions: Trade Diversion and Welfare,'' *Economica*, 24, no. 93 (February 1957):46.

not fear adopting a common currency—financial integration will be a benefit.[25]

4) While the peripheral national area is outside the circle of acquaintance and favoritism centered in the capital, as nationalists complain, lesser contact between center and periphery need not be entirely detrimental to the latter's development. It has often happened that the industry of the imperial capital declines or must be subsidized, owing to the inflated overhead and current costs there and the need to pay bribes. Enterprises in the center may be pressured to provide sinecures for influential people who simply wish to live in the abundant cultural life every imperial capital provides. Distributional coalitions, to use Olson's phrase,[26] form rapidly there, whether among guilds and trade unions or among industrialists favored by the metropolitan banks and government agencies. Peripheral industries are less sheltered from the unbroken wind of competition. Sclerosis from vested interests led to the decline of Venice, for example, and the rise of its hinterland.[27] Industries in Moscow were likewise disadvantaged to the advantage of Vladimir province and industrial centers further south.[28] Generally, in Russian areas, cities were not favorable to new industry.[29]

5) While a peripheral national area may lose mobile skills seeking the better opportunities and rich life in the metropolis—Myrdal's "backwash effects"[30]—there is another side to this familiar complaint, too. According to the imperial view, the return flow can be

[25] Peter B. Keven, "The Theory of Optimum Currency Areas: An Eclectic View," in R. A. Mundell and A. K. Swoboda, eds., *Monetary Problems of the International Economy* (Chicago, 1969), pp. 41–60; R. A. Mundell, "A Theory of Optimum Currency Areas," *American Economic Review* 51, no. 4 (September 1961):657–65.

[26] Mancur Olson, *The Rise and Decline of Nations* (New Haven, 1982), p. 44.

[27] Carlo Cipolla, ed., *The Economic Decline of Empires* (London, 1970).

[28] William L. Blackwell, *The Beginnings of Russian Industrialization 1800–1860* (Princeton, 1968).

[29] Thomas S. Fedor, *Patterns of Urban Growth in the Russian Empire during the Nineteenth Century* (Chicago, 1975) (Department of Geography Research Paper no. 163), p. 138; Olga Crisp, *Studies in the Russian Economy Before 1914* (London, 1976), p. 48; William L. Blackwell, "The Historical Geography of Industry in Russia," in James H. Bater and R. A. French, eds., *Studies in Russian Historical Geography* (London and New York, 1983), p. 416.

[30] Gunnar Myrdal, *Economic Theory and Under-Developed Regions* (London, 1957).

equally beneficial, though perhaps more troublesome at first acquaintance. Returnees and remittances from emigrants have been a major source of revenue for poor rural areas sending labor to the imperial center. What is more, peripheral areas often attract the rebels and misfits of traditional society—people who can prove themselves economically fitter by surviving on the frontier while also raising consumption expectations there. American, Australian, and Israeli frontier examples come to mind. J. K. Galbraith, an authority on Indian development, attributes the superior development of the Punjab region to the contribution of refugees after 1947.[31] In the Ukraine, Poles, Germans, Jews, and Ukrainians were often the engineers-managers of the newly established plants.[32] Russian and Polish landholders promoted the beet sugar industry, which flourished in the Ukraine despite an excise which favored the Baltic sugar refineries.[33]

6) While the national school argues that independence affords the possibility, even the potential, of doing better economically, this claim is better political rhetoric than realistic political economy. Whether an independent national elite would have promoted economic development is a matter which can only be judged by historical comparison. Many national elites who actually inherit rule from multinational empires find themselves left with substantial foreign elements. Often these non-natives are concentrated in trade or industry, since that is why they had come or had been brought to the periphery by the imperial authorities. Upon independence, demands for the ''nativization'' of trade and industry become irresistible to the new national elite frustrated by the usual difficulties of providing employment for its supporters. After independence, to cite some recent examples, several East African countries squeezed out their Indian trading classes. Algeria told its French teachers and administrators to return ''home.'' Ex-Portuguese colonies did likewise (and now regret it).

During the interwar period, independent Rumania turned on its Jewish and German urban classes, adversely affecting economic

---

[31] J. K. Galbraith, *The Nature of Mass Poverty* (Cambridge, Mass., 1979), chap. 8.

[32] Alfred Rieber, *Merchants and Entrepreneurs in Imperial Russia* (Chapel Hill, N.C., 1982); John McKay, *Pioneers for Profit* (Chicago, 1970), p. 91.

[33] Blackwell, *The Beginnings of Russian Industrialization*, pp. 69 – 70.

development in that agrarian nation.[34] Compared to newly independent Rumania, both Ottoman and Austrian empires had been more tolerant of Jews, Germans, and other minorities—not out of brotherly love or religious duty, but for what commercial people could do for modernizing those empires. Since Jews and Germans played similar roles in the Ukraine,[35] thus frustrating Ukrainian ambitions, would independence not also have been followed by vicious nativist persecutions? In 1876–1879 pogroms in several Ukrainian towns had devastated the property of Jewish artisans and small traders. The richer ones apparently still enjoyed the protection of the police. During 1918–1920, civil war strife had some anti-semitic coloration. Might this not have continued under conceivable home rule in the Ukraine?

The exchange of populations following disintegration of the great European empires after World War I added somewhat to the national homogeneity of European states, but it undoubtedly reduced the transnational flow of information, talent and new ideas. Although ideas may pass across national boundaries with exchange students, foreign language learning, multinational companies, and other modern devices for cultural integration, these are inadequate substitutes for heterogeneous populations. It has been observed that the fourteenth century saw a higher proportion of foreign students in European universities than exists today and a higher proportion of European elites who knew a single universal language (Latin). This was, needless to say, the legacy of the Holy Roman Empire and its later multinational successors.

The Imperial View Applied to the Ukraine

However plausible these parallel experiences may be, only detailed documentary and statistical study will provide confirmation that the six theses applied to the Ukraine[36] during the first sixty years of its industrialization.

---

[34] Joseph Rothschild, *East Central Europe Between the Two World Wars* (Seattle, 1974), p. 289.

[35] Arcadius Kahan, "Notes on Jewish Entrepreneurship in Tsarist Russia," in Gregory Guroff and Fred Carstersen, eds., *Entrepreneurship in Imperial Russia and the Soviet Union* (Princeton, 1983), pp. 104ff.

[36] Here taken to be the imperial provinces of Kiev, Chernihiv, Volhynia, Podillia, Poltava, Kherson, Katerynoslav, and Tavriia, which had a population of 23.4 million

As is well known, Russian imperial rule in the Ukraine began during the eighteenth century. Internal tariffs and road taxes were abolished in 1754. Settlement of serfs on the estates of Russian landlords and agricultural colonization by Germans, Jews, and others was the policy of Russian tsars from Peter the Great and Catherine II to Paul I and Nicholas I. After the 1831 Polish uprising, the government tried to settle Russian merchants, soldiers, and students in Kiev—with considerable success. Owing to restrictions on Ukrainian serfs before Emancipation, it was advantageous to bring Jewish artisans into an area which lacked craft industry. The Ukrainians were overwhelmingly agricultural peasants and remained so throughout the century.[37] "Fugitive" peasants swelled the in-migration of Russians, especially to the new Russian area in the east and eventually to the Donets' mining district. As a consequence of this in-migration, pacification, and high rates of natural increase, population density of the Ukraine rose forty times during the nineteenth century!

Between 1851 and 1897 the South was by far the fastest growing area of the empire, doubling its population in less than fifty years.[38] Migration also led to a mixed population, especially in the prosperous cities of Katerynoslav, Kherson, Mykolaiv, Sevastopil', and Odessa, begun as "Potëmkin villages" for Catherine's bemusement. Millions of Ukrainian peasants, on the other hand, went east to North Caucasus and Siberia in search of new lands rather than settle in cities closer to home. No wonder observers like Danielevski, in his *Fugitives in New Russia* (1860), compared the Ukraine to the American frontier. Mining cities like Iuzivka grew very rapidly, making many a peasant into a coal miner.

The development of the southern metallurgical area of the Donbas and Kryvyi Rih, once railroads had been extended latitudinally in the 1880s, is a familiar point of Russian economic history. But apparently

---

by the 1897 census. Seventy-three percent were Ukrainians, 12 percent Russians, 8 percent Jews, and 7 percent Germans, Poles, Tatars, Moldavians, and other nationalities. Around that time only about 13 percent of the population lived in cities. The Ukraine's urban population in 1897 was disproportionately non-Ukrainian (27 percent Jewish). See *Pervaia vseobshchaia perepis' naseleniia Rossiskoi imperii 1897 goda*, 89 vols. (St. Petersburg, 1897–1905).

[37] Hugh Seton-Watson, *The Russian Empire, 1801–1917* (Oxford, 1967), p. 667.

[38] Martin C. Spechler, "The Regional Concentration of Industry in Imperial Russia, 1854–1917," *Journal of European Economic History* 9, no. 2 (Fall 1980): Table 2.

the deconcentration of industrial activity was a basic trend throughout the nineteenth century. According to the figures assembled by Varzer and Kafengauz and reworked by the present author,[39] the share of the Ukraine in factory manufacturing output increased steadily from 9.4 percent of the European Empire in 1854 to 13.8 percent in 1887 and 21 percent by 1900. The Ukraine's share leveled off around 1908 at 22 percent. Owing to the nature of Ukrainian production, which included semi-finished materials of mining and agricultural origin, its share in value-added would have been even greater than in gross output.[40] The growth in the Ukraine's share of industrial production was largely at the expense of the Moscow area, since other peripheral areas also grew more than proportionately. Thus, scattered attempts to protect central industries had little effect. When one looks at the broader Russian Empire, excluding the Grand Duchy of Finland but including Asian and western provinces, the Ukraine's share also rises, though now also at the expense of Poland-Lithuania (an area of roughly equal population). The Ukraine's manufacturing share in 1897 somewhat exceeded its share of imperial population.

The manufacturing productivity of the Ukraine was high, with a gross output per worker two to four times the imperial average. Nominal incomes were high, too, while prices for basic foodstuffs and primitive housing were relatively low. In 1900, the average factory worker in the Ukraine earned 246 rubles—15 percent above the general imperial level.[41] Naturally, to import luxury items and capital goods was expensive, but such items would have been insignificant in the basket of wage goods purchased by workers of the Ukraine. How much such high real wages benefited Ukrainian peasants is a subject for future investigation. Some may have had to pass as Russians to obtain the benefits of progress.[42] In America's informal empire in Latin America, to cite a similar case, United States' investments have led to an increase in real wages for native workers.[43]

[39] Ibid., pp. 401ff.

[40] Spechler, "Regional Concentration of Industry," p. 422.

[41] Patricia Herlihy, "Ukrainian Cities in the Nineteenth Century," in Ivan Rudnytsky, ed., *Rethinking Ukrainian History* (Edmonton, Alberta, 1981), p. 148.

[42] Ibid., pp. 193, 146.

[43] Stanley Lebergott, "The Returns to U.S. Imperialism, 1890–1929," *Journal of Economic History* 40, no. 2 (June 1980):249.

Railroad building contributed enormously to the development of the Ukraine, owing to the natural limitations of water and land transport for grain, coal, and iron ore. Cheap transport established the superiority of Ukrainian pig-iron over the Urals, where water flows, labor supplies, and fuel were unreliable. An imperial network of railroads was also designed to take grain from the far south and southeast to the capitals and to the Baltic ports. Such long journeys had never before been practical—up the rivers and over the snow or through the mud. It seems doubtful that the Ukraine could have attracted foreign savings for these lines without imperial guarantees. French and Belgian capitalists seemed to prefer investing through St. Petersburg and Moscow banks. The monetary orthodoxy of the period of Vyshnegradskii and Witte, together with the warming diplomatic climate, encouraged this influx of capital and expertise.

Bridges and harbors were built with the often unintended consequence of promoting commerce.[44] Sanitary facilities constructed by the government in Kiev allowed considerable diversified growth in this "mother" of all Ukrainian cities, which had a quarter million inhabitants by 1837, though only 22 percent Ukrainian by nationality and a third by language.[45] Odessa, the Ukraine's largest city throughout the century, had relatively few Ukrainians, mostly humble in social status.[46]

The city of Luhans'k (latterly Voroshylovhrad), noted for its iron production, was established in 1795 by an imperial *ukaz* for the purpose of providing cannon and shot to the Russian navy on the Black Sea. For this purpose about three thousand Russian serfs and some 715,733 rubles were allocated. The city prospered, even though the armies it supplied in the Napoleonic and Crimean wars did not.[47] Later on, agricultural processing industries were added, as elsewhere. Luhans'k benefited particularly from Belgian and other foreign investment, but its reliance on manufacturing meant its rapid growth was especially discontinuous.

---

[44] Herlihy, "Ukrainian Cities," pp. 140, 151.

[45] Ibid., p. 148.

[46] Ibid., p. 149.

[47] W. E. D. Allen, *The Ukraine: A History* (Cambridge, 1941).

Up to the twentieth century, Ukrainian intellectuals apparently appreciated the boost the Russian Empire gave to their economic development. Mykhailo Drahomanov (died 1895), the well-known socialist and professor at Kiev University, laughed at suggestions that the Ukraine separate from the Russian Empire, citing common economic interests.[48] Though Austria-Hungary from its East Galician outpost tried to incite the Ukrainian population, it could find little support in the Ukrainian heartland, notwithstanding insensitive cultural Russification. Perhaps anti-Polish feeling was one reason. Despite growing nationalism on both sides of the border, Ukrainians did not call for separation from the empire in 1905–1906, as Poles and Caucasians did.[49] The nationalists' demands were mainly cultural.[50] It was not until later that most Ukrainians apparently began to feel that overall benefits from association with Russians no longer justified the psychic and material costs. For example, bureaucratic careers were often blocked to non-Russians. This gradual development is parallel to the experience of the Czechs in the Austro-Hungarian Empire. Only with the growth in urbanization and literacy in the national language did the Czechs begin to resist German hegemony.[51] Maybe it took the miseries of World War I and the Civil War to mobilize Ukrainian nationalism.

Returning to Other Views

The purpose of this paper has been to present reasoning and evidence that an "imperial view" does fit the evidence for the Ukraine in the sixty years before the First World War. The Russian Empire did provide a unified legal environment, social overhead capital before its commercial justification, and free access to Ukrainian goods such as sugar, wool, and grain. It furnished entrepreneurial capital to the Ukraine and maintained control, although foreign and domestic agents of many nationalities tried to succeed in this frontier area.

---

[48] Seton-Watson, *The Russian Empire*, p. 411.
[49] Allen, *The Ukraine*, p. 257.
[50] Seton-Watson, *The Russian Empire*, p. 608.
[51] Karl Deutsch, *Nationalism and Social Communication*, 2d ed. (Cambridge, Mass., 1966).

All this is not to deny points made by the cosmopolitan and national schools. For example, the tariff of 1822 against textile imports did lower Ukrainian terms of trade with Poland, which formerly sold textiles into its former hinterland. Without such trade diversion, farm machinery would have been cheaper and better in this prime agricultural area. On the other hand, a higher tariff on wool during the mid-century might have assisted Ukrainian sheep farmers in the Russian market, as Kharkiv interests repeatedly made clear.[52]

National-minded economists have also pointed out the apparently discriminatory impact of the Russian fiscal system. Because a substantial part of imperial taxes were excises on agricultural commodities, like sugar and vodka, or on commodities used by peasants, like kerosene and matches, it has been argued that tax collections substantially exceeded disbursements.[53] The evidence is dubious on two grounds. First, it seems to assume that all excises fall where they are collected, but modern public finance specialists usually believe that incidence of sugar and alcohol taxes would fall at least equally upon consumers. Secondly, the geographical benefit from spending on military, debt service, and railroad expenses is unclear in principle and highly controversial in practice. Until the basic data are exhumed from tsarist archives or inaccessible volumes and re-examined by modern standards of economics, this issue cannot be resolved to anyone's satisfaction. Much remains to be done before a disinterested, synthetic view can be presented.

---

[52] Kononenko, *Ukraine and Russia*, pp. 116–17.

[53] N. P. Iasnopol'skii, *O geograficheskom raspredelenii dokhodov i raskhodov Rossii*, 2 vols. (Kiev, 1890, 1897); M. Iavors'kyi, *Ukraina v epokhu kapitalizmu*, 3 vols. (Odessa, 1924), as cited in Kononenko, *Ukraine and Russia*, pp. 238–39.

CHAPTER TWELVE

Urbanization and the Ukrainian Economy in the Mid-Nineteenth Century

Boris P. Balan

This paper explores some aspects of the nature of the Ukrainian economy in the mid-nineteenth century, on the eve of the emancipation of the peasantry and the start of the rapid economic transformations which so greatly affected the Ukraine and the entire Russian Empire in the years leading to the revolution of 1917. In a broad sense, it attempts to gauge the degree to which the Ukrainian economy was integrated and the degree to which a recognizable, unitary economic system was developing in the region. While much research must be done before any definitive conclusions can be made regarding this very large issue, it seems to be both possible and desirable to offer at least some preliminary thoughts and data, if for no reason than to help develop a useful methodological approach to this issue. This paper will do this by examining the economic role and function of cities in the Ukraine and the relationship of Ukrainian urbanization to the economic development of the country. At the same time, some attention will be devoted to a comparison of the Ukrainian case to overall developments in the Russian Empire—considering both the uniqueness of the Ukrainian economy and its specific role in the much larger imperial economic system.

Following a short introduction, the paper will summarize the history of Ukrainian urbanization and briefly describe the regional pattern of urbanization that had emerged by the mid-nineteenth century. Next, the urban-rural nexus in the Ukraine will be explored, especially the development of commercial linkages between city and countryside. The next section will examine a crucial factor influencing these linkages, the fair system that dominated trade and commerce in the early nineteenth-century Ukraine, while the concluding part will examine the way in which these fairs influenced the nature of early Ukrainian industrialization.

With respect to the function of cities in the Ukrainian economy of the mid-nineteenth century, it appears that there are essentially two directions in which research can proceed. The first would attempt to uncover and evaluate the economic relationship between different cities (and by implication, different regions) of the country. It seems that it would be useful to study whether goods were being produced in one city and consumed in another; whether raw materials were extracted in one area to be processed in another region of the country; or whether goods were being imported into one city to be distributed through other cities and towns. This is essentially the approach outlined by Gilbert Rozman in his series of articles and monographs on comparative urbanization and political development.[1] In these works on Japan, China, the Russian Empire, and other countries, Rozman has developed an ambitious and far-reaching model of "urban networks" and "national marketing systems" in premodern or preindustrial societies. Concentrating on commercial relations between cities— something that can be judged by the functional differentiation and geographic distribution of cities—Rozman attempts to determine when more-or-less complete or integrated economic systems emerge within a given state. Naturally, in his view, this is a process that is closely linked to political developments, with the nature of a country's urban network clearly reflecting the political-administrative cohesiveness of the state.

This first approach I would term a horizontal one, focusing as it does on the relationship between cities across a given geographic region. Another manner of addressing the same question, but with a somewhat different emphasis, could be called a vertical approach. This, conceivably, would focus on the economic linkages between city and countryside and evaluate the role of cities within their immediate economic spheres as centers of local production, distribution, and con-

---

[1] See, for example, his *Urban Networks in Russia 1750–1800 and Premodern Periodization* (Princeton, 1976).

sumption.[2] Before turning to a larger discussion of the economic linkages between cities, it is imperative to examine this question more closely, and to understand the nature of cities and their economic role in their immediate settings. It is this approach, therefore, which is adopted in this paper and which will be developed in more detail as it applies to the Ukraine in its final preindustrial stage of development.

There are essentially two currents of thought in historiography and social science theory regarding the economic component of urban-rural relations in preindustrial societies.[3] The first stresses the antagonism between these two very different social systems. In this view, cities conquer and dominate the countryside both militarily and politically. Economically they consume resources (food, fuel, people) which are appropriated from the countryside. Because their production base is weak, they are seen to offer very little in return to rural inhabitants; therefore, cities are "parasites" in terms of their overall role in the society's economy. Their most important economic function is as commercial centers: they gather imports from near and far and distribute them to consumers, both in the countryside, but more importantly, in the cities themselves, where inhabitants generally enjoy a much higher standard of living. This antagonism is highlighted by the exclusiveness of urban society, a social system which is marked by protectionist artisan guilds, and which is culturally and socially isolated from the countryside. In summary, this approach argues that cities extract goods from the countryside to support their own privileged status, offering only rudimentary political, administrative, religious, or commercial services in return.[4]

A second approach, which has become popular in recent years, focuses on the economic interdependence of city and countryside. While recognizing that these are two distinct socioeconomic entities, this approach sees preindustrial cities as being fairly developed

---

[2] The best example of this approach is the work of Fernand Braudel, which will be discussed below.

[3] For a good review of the debate on the economic role of cities in preindustrial societies, see E. A. Wrigley, "Parasite or Stimulus: The Town in a Preindustrial Economy," in Philip Abrams and E. A. Wrigley, eds., *Towns in Societies: Essays in Economic History and Historical Sociology* (Cambridge, 1978).

[4] For the best example of this approach, see G. Sjoberg, *The Preindustrial City, Past and Present* (Glencoe, Ill., 1960).

economic entities which play an active role in larger regional economic systems. Cities extend both their political and economic reaches into the countryside, but on the whole the interrelationship is a mutually beneficial one. The implication of this is that cultural and social differences between city and countryside are less pronounced, mainly because of the spread of market relations and the greater involvement of rural producers in preindustrial production.

In order to understand this approach more fully, it is necessary to examine how some general features of urbanization are presented. In this view, cities arose in primitive societies to serve specific functions and satisfy very real needs. Thus, while it is possible to see cities as the very antithesis of the countryside, it is important to appreciate the close interdependence between city and country, and between city inhabitants and the vast majority of the population spread throughout villages, hamlets, and individual peasant households. In early history one of the first impetuses toward urbanization was the need for defense, something most easily provided by a contained and sheltered city complete with its walls and ramparts. Gradually cities acquired administrative functions, becoming both political and cultural centers. In all of these aspects cities were "above all else a set of institutions in the service of the countryside,"[5] providing security and political cohesion for the rest of the society.

At the same time, the growth of cities and towns was also a result of economic specialization, evidence of an emerging division of labor. While agriculture remained a rural activity, trade, commerce, and crafts were increasingly concentrated in and monopolized by cities. This differentiation was a consequence of the obvious benefits of concentration and specialization, namely, greater economic efficiency. In the end, therefore, cities usually combined a variety of functions: economic, military, political, social, and cultural, which were not available or could not easily be offered in small towns and villages, with their low population densities and subsistence lifestyle.

The crucial aspect of this functional differentiation was the resulting dynamic of integration which it initiated. With respect to the economy, Fernand Braudel has stated that the town "generalizes the

[5] Robert E. Dickinson, *The City Region in Western Europe* (London, 1967), p. 14.

market into a widespread phenomenon.''[6] By this he means that urban centers, by specializing their function into non-agrarian pursuits, became dependent upon the rural sector for food and other basic necessities (including even human resources), with the inevitable result being the creation of an exchange relationship mediated by the market mechanism. Therefore, the essential common characteristic shared by all towns is "the continuous dialogue with their rural surroundings, a prime necessity of everyday life."[7]

Many scholars who have adopted this approach admit that at the outset this relationship was very one-sided, with cities simply extracting from the countryside and offering little in return. This was reflected in the coercive nature of city-country relations. Over time, however, cities were able to replace this coercion with a more subtle economic-political domination based on the greater social and economic strength of urban centers. This not only allowed cities to extend their area of control and to improve their effectiveness, but also made the relationship considerably more beneficial for both parties, especially after the development of commerce and production in cities gave them more to offer in return. Thus, the market became the main mediator of city-country relations. Again, as Braudel has stated,

> there is no town without its villages, its scrap of rural life attached; no town that does not impose upon its hinterland the amenities of its market, the use of its shops, its weights and measures, its moneylenders, its lawyers, even its distractions. It has to dominate an empire, no matter how tiny, in order to exist.[8]

The Pattern of Ukrainian Urbanization

Before turning to a more detailed discussion of urban-rural relations in mid-nineteenth-century Ukraine, it is necessary to summarize the history and some of the important characteristics of Ukrainian urbanization. In general, the nature of urbanization in the early nineteenth century very much reflected the politically and economically unintegrated

---

[6] Fernand Braudel, *The Structures of Everyday Life: The Limits of the Possible* (New York, 1979), p. 481.

[7] Ibid.

[8] Ibid., pp. 481–82.

nature of the country. In fact, there were three easily identifiable patterns or traditions of urbanism in the territories that eventually came to constitute the modern Ukraine.

The core of the Ukrainian lands was the territories of the Hetmanate (especially Poltava and Chernihiv guberniias or provinces). This area had constituted a distinct part of the Russian Empire from the mid-seventeenth century, with a unique political and cultural order and social system. The next century, however, saw the gradual erosion of its semi-autonomous political system and the restructuring of the local society in line with the overall model of Russian society. This process involved a number of political changes (e.g., the introduction of the Provincial Reforms of the 1780s) and, importantly, the introduction and strengthening of serfdom in the area (at a time when this institution was already in decline in other parts of the empire).

Most cities in the seventeenth century had enjoyed some form of Magdeburg Law—granted either under Polish rule or by the hetman (in a few cases, by the tsar)—that had provided them the legal and political basis for a fairly independent existence. However, under the combined pressure of Russian merchants and officials, and the indifference toward the fate of the cities on the part of the military-agrarian Ukrainian elite (which the Cossack officers and nobles had become), the importance of Magdeburg Law declined steadily in the eighteenth century. When at the turn of the nineteenth century it was finally done away with in the region and the imperial laws governing cities were introduced, the city residents themselves could see little difference in their status.[9]

At this time cities were growing slowly. While there was a relatively high density of cities in the region, most remained quite small, and there was little differentiation between them in either size or function. Moreover, many smaller and mid-sized cities on the Left Bank

---

[9] For a description of the place of cities in the Hetmanate and the social and political integration of the Hetmanate into the Russian Empire, see Zenon E. Kohut, *Russian Centralism and Ukrainian Autonomy: Imperial Absorption of the Hetmanate, 1760s–1830s* (Cambridge, Mass., 1988). For a discussion of the indifference of the Cossack elite towards the plight of Ukrainian cities, and the subsequent decline in the economic significance and political autonomy of cities, see Pylyp Klymenko, "Misto i terytoriia na Ukraini za Hetmanshchyny," *Zapysky istorychno-filolohichnoho viddilu VUAN* 7–8 (1926):309–44.

were poorly differentiated from the villages around them. A common feature in the region was that many inhabitants of these cities and towns engaged in agricultural activities, working farmland either within the city limits or on adjacent fields. The urban population was increasingly Russian or Russified, but Ukrainian burghers formed a large minority, especially in the smaller cities of the region.

The Right Bank was the second major region of the Ukraine. It had only been acquired by the Russian Empire at the end of the eighteenth century, as a result of the partitions of Poland. For quite some time, however, the region remained more under the influence of Polish traditions and laws than Russian ones; on the whole, the Russian state simply was not powerful enough to do away with the local gentry (*szlachta*) who dominated politics in the region and who were the only people experienced in dealing with the peasantry. Some attempts to integrate the area into the empire were made in the 1830s and 1840s, following the first Polish rebellion, when the Provincial Reform was introduced and the old Lithuanian laws were replaced by the Russian legal code. For cities this meant the end of Magdeburg Law for the few royal cities (e.g., Luts'k) that had enjoyed this privilege.[10]

It is interesting to note, however, that many aspects of the Right-Bank urbanization pattern remained unaffected by Russian policies. One important and striking characteristic of urban development was the predominance and persistence of privately owned cities. Many cities in the region remained the private property, and under the direct control, of the Polish gentry throughout the first half of the nineteenth century. In Volhynia, for example, this included the following county capitals: Starokonstantyniv (population approximately 10,000), Dubno, Ostrih (population 7,000–8,000), and Rivne (5,000). In fact, the second largest city in the region, and probably the main commercial center at the time, Berdychiv, remained the private domain of the Radziwiłł family, even with a population of over 50,000 in 1860.

---

[10] For a good recent discussion of the integration of the Right Bank into the empire, see Edward Thaden, *Russia's Western Borderlands* (Princeton, 1984). For an overall discussion of cities in the area, see Volodymyr Antonovych, "O gorodakh iugo-zapadnoi Rossii po aktam 1432–1798," *Arkhiv Iugo-zapadnoi Rossii* (Kiev, 1870), and for a description of the underdevelopment of industry, see his "O promyshlennosti iugo-zapadnogo kraia v XVIII stoletiia," *Zapiski Iugo-zapadnogo otdela imp. russkogo obshchestva*, vol. 1 (Kiev, 1874), pp. 179–91.

Cities only came under the Russian Urban Statute of 1785 when they were confiscated or purchased by the state. A second characteristic of the urban pattern of the Right Bank was the presence of a very large number of small cities or towns (*mistechka*).[11] These too were mainly privately owned, and they were geared primarily towards serving the manorial economy. They were inhabited mostly by Jews who engaged in a variety of activities: commerce, crafts production, and even farming. Some became influential commercial centers, the sites of fairs and regular merchant gatherings, or important manufacturing centers. Most, however, remained impoverished little towns with a large number of petty merchants and artisans trying to eke out a living under very difficult circumstances.[12] For the purposes of tsarist administration, their inhabitants were all classified as belonging to the urban classes—something which helps to explain the high levels of urbanization in the area recorded in the censuses (*revizii*).

In general, there was a mixed urbanization pattern in the Right-Bank Ukraine. Urban densities ranged from fairly low in Volhynia to quite high in Podillia and Kiev guberniias. Growth rates also differed considerably: Volhynia in the first half of the century had one of the lowest growth rates in the entire Russian Empire, while Kiev guberniia's urban population grew rapidly. This was in great part due to the rapid growth of the city of Kiev itself, which reached a population of some 70,000 by the mid-century. This was primarily due to its importance as a cultural and religious center, and as a fairly important regional capital for the Russian state. As Patricia Herlihy has shown, as late as 1874 Kiev's population "was comprised chiefly of students, soldiers, monks, and bureaucrats."[13] Overall, the urban population

[11] I have provided the terms used in most Russian-language sources of the nineteenth century for the various types of settlements and social strata.

[12] For a good discussion of a number of small towns, see Pavel Ryndziunskii, *Gorodskoe grazhdanstvo v doreformennoi Rossii* (Moscow, 1958), pp. 306–10. This discussion is based on an extensive study of small towns in the Right-Bank Ukraine and other former Polish territories conducted by the statistician Petr Keppen for the Russian government in 1845–1846; unfortunately, it appears that this larger study was never published.

[13] Patricia Herlihy, "Ukrainian Cities in the Nineteenth Century," in Ivan L. Rudnytsky and John-Paul Himka, eds., *Rethinking Ukrainian History* (Edmonton, Alberta, 1981), p. 137.

was primarily Jewish and Polish, with small Russian and Ukrainian minorities.

The third region that comprised the Ukrainian territory was the steppe region (Kherson and Katerynoslav guberniias), acquired by Russia at the end of the eighteenth century.[14] However, unlike the Right Bank, this area had almost no prior urban tradition; for the most part, it had been largely unsettled or inhabited only by Tatars or the Zaporozhian Cossacks. In fact, this was one of the first areas where the Russian state attempted to impose an entirely new social order, without consideration for local traditions or practices. One aspect of this was Catherine's decree that the southern steppe was not to have serfdom; instead, it was to be settled by free peasants or colonists recruited abroad. As agriculture developed, however, some nobles began to transfer serfs from their northern estates to work on the large and prosperous frontier, thus establishing the practice of serfdom despite the official prohibitions.

A second feature of Russia's plan for the region was that cities were to be located, designated, and planned in accordance with the "systematic" laws and desires of the state. This was possible because of the lack of a strong local tradition of urbanization and historical privileges. The first major impetus for urbanization was the construction of naval ports, first on the Sea of Azov and then in Kherson and Mykolaiv. These were intended both for the Black Sea fleet, and for the international trade that Russia hoped to attract. Later, Odessa took on particular importance in this regard, becoming the largest and most important port in the south. In general, urbanization in the first half of the century was highly concentrated in these ports. Their importance as trading centers shaped their national composition, and Greeks, Italians, and other peoples experienced in Mediterranean trade came to dominate local life. The major industrial and mining centers that emerged in Katerynoslav and the Donbas in the second half of the

---

[14] For two general discussions of urbanization in this region, see Ryndziunskii, *Gorodskoe grazhdanstvo* and E. I. Druzhinina, *Iuzhnaia Ukraina v 1800–1825 gg.* (Moscow, 1970). In this paper we will not be treating the Crimea (Taurida gubernia) as an integral part of the Ukraine. This region's very unique history and culture, and its weak ties with the rest of the Ukrainian lands, make it very difficult to analyze in the context of Ukrainian history. The detail which would be needed to discuss its urban history is beyond the scope of this paper.

century were as yet unimportant. Katerynoslav itself had a population at the mid-century of only about 18,000.

By the mid-nineteenth century, most Ukrainian cities were governed under the 1785 Russian Urban Statute. This law essentially defined cities (*goroda*) as ruling places; settlements were granted urban charters because of their role as a capital, either of a county or a guberniia. Thus, each guberniia contained approximately ten to fifteen cities, one for each county. Meanwhile, the officially recognized urban strata comprised basically the two historic Russian urban groups: the merchants (*kuptsy*) and the burghers (*meshchany*; this stratum included a wide variety of people, such as petty merchants, guild artisans, and factory workers). As with all social classes in Russia, membership in both of these was largely hereditary. In these two cases membership brought certain privileges. Merchants were given the right to engage in commerce and were exempted from the poll tax, while burghers were allowed to practice their crafts, engage in petty trade, and avoid conscription. At the same time, membership entailed definite obligations; the two were to be largely self-governing and self-regulating, and they were to bear the main financial and administrative burden in the cities.[15]

While all of this may have been clear in theory, it was not so in practice. There are a number of peculiarities in Russian and particularly Ukrainian urban history which need to be considered during any discussion of the subject. This is especially true when one is using statistics from the period and attempting to measure the economic development and role of cities. These peculiarities may be summarized by the following:

1) Some settlements had city charters despite the fact that they had no official governing function. In Ukrainian guberniias this was often due to the shifting of guberniia and county borders at the turn of the nineteenth century which often left two former county capitals in a single county. Rather than simply take the urban charter away from

---

[15] The legal definitions of cities and urban classes are discussed in a number of sources, including Thomas Fedor, *Patterns of Urban Growth in the Russian Empire during the Nineteenth Century*, (Chicago; 1975); Rozman, *Urban Networks in Russia*; and especially Ryndziunskii, *Gorodskoe grazhdanstvo*. The best contemporary explanation of this rather complicated situation is in *Statisticheskie tablitsy rossiiskoi imperii za 1856 god*, vol. 2, pp. 65–110.

the city which was no longer the capital, the authorities began to refer to the settlements as *zashtatnye* or *bezuezdnye* (non-county) cities, inhabited, for the purposes of official statistics, by urban dwellers.

2) However, because of the basic agreement between city and governing place, many large settlements, even some with extremely vital economies, did not receive city charters, despite the fact that they may have been much more developed or economically significant than the legal cities. Thus, for the sake of official statistics, they remained villages inhabited by peasants. While for our period this does not constitute a major problem, it does become very significant for the second half of the nineteenth century, especially in the booming Donbas region where new settlements were being founded, gaining great economic importance very rapidly.

3) Some settlements had their inhabitants classified as belonging to urban strata despite the fact that the actual settlement was perhaps nothing more than a village in terms of economic significance and lifestyle (the small towns of the Right Bank and some *slobody* and *posady*—mostly former Cossack settlements or tax-exempt farming settlements established in the seventeenth century—of the Left Bank are the prime examples of this). This was primarily a result of the state's attempts to adjust to local traditions, especially Polish practices in the Right Bank, Belorussia, and Lithuania, where many small towns had been granted some form of urban status, either by the king or by local nobles.

4) Not all legally defined "urbanites" necessarily lived in cities. Merchants in particular, while they had to be officially registered in a city, often lived in villages in order to conduct their business.

5) Cities contained many inhabitants, especially peasants, who were not officially members of the urban strata, and who, therefore, would have appeared in censuses under different social categories. Thus, there was often a great discrepancy between the number of people belonging to the "urban strata" (*gorodskie soslovie*) and the actual population of cities.

6) There were individuals belonging to officially defined urban strata whose lifestyle and occupation were decidedly not urban. Most cities had at least some burghers who farmed small garden plots, kept orchards and livestock, etc. In some cities, even in relatively large ones in the Left Bank, it was often the case that almost the entire

population farmed for a living, raising extensive grain and other cash crops.

The Urban-Rural Nexus

One of the most striking features of Ukrainian development in the nineteenth century was the relative segregation of its cities and urban centers from the countryside. This section of the paper will examine the nature of the relationship between Ukrainian cities and their hinterlands, focusing primarily on economic questions. This relationship with the countryside will be compared with the situation in other parts of the empire.

Since one of the major consequences of urbanization and the establishment of an urban-rural exchange dynamic was the creation of a market economy, it is perhaps best to begin with some remarks regarding the growth of trade and commerce in early nineteenth-century Ukraine. The easiest way to start is to examine the social structure of the Ukraine, and especially statistics on the number of merchants, artisans, and other urban dwellers in the Ukrainian guberniias. The first source of data that we can consult regarding this question are the censuses, the regular tabulations of the population carried out for the purposes of taxation. The Soviet demographer Vladimir Kabuzan has standardized all of the data collected for the censuses, recalculating them on the basis of set territorial divisions and consistent definitions. According to his figures, the total male population of the eight guberniias that we are concerned with was approximately 5.7 million in 1857. Of these, some 9.4 percent were classified as belonging to the urban strata (the *meshchany* and *kuptsy*); 83 percent were peasants; and 7.6 percent belonged to other strata (nobles, priests, "foreigners"). The figures differed considerably by region. The most urbanized guberniias in the Ukraine, and among the most urbanized in the empire, were those of the Right Bank, where approximately 12.5 percent of the population belonged to the urban strata. This was mainly due to the large number of small towns. At the same time, only 78.6 percent of the population were peasants, and 8.9 percent were from other social strata (mostly the Polish nobility). The urban population of the steppe guberniias was also quite high, about 11 percent of the total, while that of the Left Bank was rather low, at 5.3 percent. As a whole, the figures for all of the Ukraine compare favorably with data for the rest of European Russia, where peasants

Table 12.1

Ukrainian Urban Strata, 1854

Guberniia	All Urban Classes	percentage of which *kuptsy*	percentage of which *meshchany*
Chernihiv	31,194	9.1	90.9
Kharkiv	21,165	11.2	88.8
Poltava	63,744	5.7	94.3
Left-Bank Ukraine	116,103	7.7	92.3
Volhynia	102,327	4.0	96.0
Podillia	105,191	6.6	93.4
Kiev	116,066	6.3	93.7
Right-Bank Ukraine	323,584	5.6	94.4
Katerynoslav	32,995	12.4	87.6
Kherson	72,868	8.4	91.6
Steppe region	105,821	9.7	90.3
Total	545,508	6.8	93.2

Source: Ryndziunskii, *Gorodskoe grazhdanstvo*, pp. 261, 297, 349.

numbered some 83 percent of the total population, urban dwellers 6.4 percent, and other strata 10 percent.[16]

At this point we are primarily concerned with the number and proportion of merchants in the urban strata as the best indicator of the generalization of market relations. Table 12.1, based on data collected by Ryndziunskii from sources similar to those used by Kabuzan, illustrates the situation in the mid-nineteenth century.

What this table shows—at least in comparison to the situation in the rest of European Russia—is the relative underdevelopment of

[16] Vladimir Kabuzan, *Izmeneniia v razmeshchenii naseleniia Rossii v XVIII— pervoi polovine XIX v. (Po materialam revizii)* (Moscow, 1971), pp. 167–78.

commerce in the Ukrainian guberniias. In the Ukraine merchants accounted for only 5.7 to 9.7 percent of the entire urban population. At that time, the figure for all of European Russia was 9.7 percent, almost double that of the Right Bank and 2 percent higher than in the Left Bank.[17] The backwardness of the Ukraine in this respect is considerably more noticeable when contrasted with specific regions of the empire. Even in the main agricultural regions—similar economically to much of the Ukraine—many guberniias had a considerably greater representation of merchants. For example, in Voronezh and Kursk, merchants accounted for over 14 percent of the urban classes; in Tambov, 13.7 percent; in Orlov, 12.4 percent; and in Riazan', 11.8 percent.[18] Even more striking is the contrast provided by the guberniias of the capital and central industrial regions. Here three guberniias counted over one-fifth of their urban populations as merchants: St. Petersburg, 20.3 percent; Moscow, 21.1 percent; and Vladimir, 24.3 percent; Tver's respective figure was 17.6 percent and Novgorod's was 16.3 percent. Even the least commercialized of these guberniias, Nizhegorod, counted 9.9 percent of its urban population as merchants, a figure higher than even the most advanced Ukrainian guberniia. Overall, in the eleven guberniias in this area there were 57,979 merchants, comprising 17.1 percent of the total urban population.[19]

Another indication of the backwardness of commerce is that the great majority of Ukrainian merchants traded only in small amounts. This is evidenced by their concentration in the third guild, which limited their commercial activities to local, often petty, retail trade. In 1858 there were some 10,941 individual merchants or combined merchant capital funds in the Ukrainian guberniias (of a total of 53,072 in all of European Russia). Of these, 10,440 were of the third, or lowest, category. Meanwhile, there were only 184 first guild merchants (merchants capitalized at over 15,000 rubles and allowed to engage in long-distance and international commerce), with 113 of these in Kherson, 26 in Kiev, 14 in Katerynoslav, 8 each in Volhynia, Poltava, and Kharkiv, 4 in Podillia, and 3 in Chernihiv. By comparison, 438 of the total 1,045 first guild merchants were in Moscow or St. Petersburg

---

[17] Ryndziunskii, *Gorodskoe grazhdanstvo*, p. 261.

[18] Ibid., p. 221.

[19] Ibid.

guberniias alone. Leaving out Kherson, there was an average of 10 first guild merchants per Ukrainian guberniia, as opposed to an average of 22 for European Russia.[20]

What these statistics fail to show is that the very character of trade and commerce seems to have been quite unique in Ukrainian cities, at least when compared to the situation in Russian cities. With regard to urban-rural commercial linkages, regularized and institutionalized trading patterns—predicated upon the dominance of urban centers—were slow to emerge. Quite simply, the Ukrainian city lagged in imposing the "amenities of its markets and the use of its shops" on the rural hinterland. In the nineteenth century it was still often the case that the market went to the peasants rather than the opposite. In Poltava guberniia, for example, relatively few merchants lived in the cities in which they were registered; rather, they resided permanently in villages and small towns, purchasing the peasants' production and, in turn, selling them manufactured goods.[21] Alfred Rieber has described commercial patterns and the role of Jewish merchants, particularly in the Right Bank, in the following way:

> Russian merchants engaged in commerce, traveled down from the north during the great annual fairs, and frequently discovered that Jewish merchants were their best customers, buying from the wholesalers and spreading out into the countryside to retail their purchases to the local population.[22]

The sight of peripatetic merchants, many of them barely making a living from their hard work, was a common one in mid-nineteenth-century Ukraine.

This sale of goods and collection of produce at the lowest level of the economy was actually part of a very large and complex commercial system which, for the most part, operated independently of the existing urban centers. In the 1850s Ivan Aksakov published a well-

---

[20] *Statisticheskie tablitsy ... za 1856 g.*, vol. 1, pp. 216–17.

[21] Nikolai Arandarenko, *Zapiski o poltavskoi gubernii*, vol. 2 (Poltava, 1850), p. 365.

[22] Alfred Rieber, *Merchants and Entrepreneurs in Imperial Russia* (Chapel Hill, N.C., 1982), pp. 57–58.

researched study of the Ukrainian fairs,[23] describing the "mechanism for the distribution of goods in the most remote rural small-holding and the collection therefrom of small quantities of produce whose value could only be realized if successfully accumulated into substantial quantity."[24] This system was necessitated by geographic conditions and the low population density which hindered the creation of central markets. "In this situation goods distribution, and collection of otherwise insignificant raw materials, was accomplished through the medium of petty rural markets, but also through the institution of roving rural peddler collectors."[25] Often, groups of traveling merchants would form, purchasing commercial goods on consignment and then spreading out into the countryside to sell them to consumers, in turn purchasing local crafts and agricultural produce.

We will return to examine this system of fairs in greater detail below. In the meantime, there are other simple means by which we can measure the role of cities as commercial centers for the countryside. The first is by considering the development of trade facilities in the cities themselves. Once again this is something which most historians consider to be an important indicator of the spread of a market economy. One Soviet Ukrainian historian points to the increase in the number of permanent stores (*magaziny*) in the Ukraine from 224 in 1825 to 803 in 1861 as an indisputable sign of progress.[26] Already in the late eighteenth century in the Left Bank various types of retail outlets in cities were offering a wide assortment of goods which were either produced locally, purchased at local fairs, or imported. These goods included primarily consumer items such as cloth and sugar, as well as some manufactured goods.[27] The pace of this commercial

---

[23] *Issledovanie o torgovle na ukrainskikh iarmarkakh* (St. Petersburg, 1854). Interestingly, this study was funded by an association of Moscow merchants.

[24] R. Gohstand, "The Geography of Trade in Nineteenth-Century Russia," in J. A. Bater and R. A. French, eds., *Studies in Russian Historical Geography*, vol. 2 (New York, 1983), p. 345.

[25] Ibid.

[26] V. Holobuts'kyi, *Ekonomichna istoriia Ukrains'koi RSR. Dozhovtnevyi period* (Kiev, 1970), p. 192. These figures refer only to permanent stores, and not the more numerous, but usually temporary, trading stalls.

[27] See V. Kulakovs'kyi, "Statsionarna torhivlia v mistakh livoberezhnoi Ukrainy v XVIII st.," *Istoriia narodnoho hospodarstva ta ekonomichnoi dumky Ukrains'koi RSR* 13 (1979):72–76.

development increased rapidly in the second half of the century, with Kiev, Kharkiv, and Kherson experiencing especially exceptional growth not only in the number of permanent retail outlets, but also in the total value of retail and wholesale trade.[28]

Closely related to the question of commerce is the state of industrial or crafts production in the Ukraine. By studying the number and distribution of artisans, craftsmen, and factory workers, we can gain a clearer image of urban economic life. Moreover, since many of the goods these individuals produced and the services they provided were consumed in the rural sector, this is a useful measure of the potential for urban-rural economic exchange. Naturally, it would be best also to examine data on local commerce and the value of trade at petty markets and bazaars for this purpose. Unfortunately, because this is a task beyond the scope of this paper, I will simply focus on some of the more readily available data and statistics.

Perhaps the best place to begin is with the figures on the total value of production by guberniia gathered by the Ministry of Finance. While these figures are in no way comprehensive, as the ministry generally did not regulate or collect data from small factories and shops, they are a useful indicator of the overall situation. In 1856 total production in European Russia was valued at about 222 million rubles. Of this, 116 million, or just over one-half of the total reported, was accounted for in just four guberniias: Moscow, 38 million; St. Petersburg, 37 million; Vladimir, 20 million, and Perm, 19 million. Kiev, the most industrialized Ukrainian guberniia, had some 9.5 million rubles of production; Kharkiv, 4.8 million; Kherson, 3.7 million; Chernihiv, 2.7 million; Katerynoslav, 2 million; Volhynia, 1.9 million; and Poltava, 1.5 million. In total, industrial production in the Ukrainian guberniias equaled about 26.1 million rubles, or 12 million less than Moscow guberniia alone.[29]

A further indication of economic underdevelopment, and especially the weakness of the urban-rural relationship in the Ukraine, is the extremely low number of artisans (*tsekhovie*) in Ukrainian cities. This is particularly revealing because it was precisely these individuals who were engaged in producing goods and providing services for

---

[28] See I. Hurzhii, *Ukraina v systemi vserosiis'koho rynku 60–90kh rokiv XIX st.* (Kiev, 1968), p. 102.

[29] *Statisticheskie tablitsy . . . za 1856 g.*, vol. 2, pp. 275–76.

Table 12.2

Artisans in Ukraine, 1858

Guberniia	Total	Guberniia	Total
Chernihiv	9,137	Podillia	7,452
Kharkiv	9,180	Kiev	14,586
Poltava	11,729	Katerynoslav	5,176
Volhynia	6,514	Kherson	9,607
TOTAL	70,237		

Source: O. O. Nesterenko, *Rozvytok promyslovosti na Ukraini*, vol. 1 (Kiev, 1959), p. 112.

local rural consumers. Table 12.2 gives some figures on the number of guild artisans in the Ukraine.

While at first glance these figures may seem to be quite high, comparison with all-Russian data quickly destroys this impression. In 1858, according to incomplete sources, there were already about 331,555 artisans in European Russia. Even more striking, however, is the fact that in St. Petersburg and Moscow guberniias alone there were about 83,000 artisans, more than in all of the Ukraine.[30] This, naturally, is something that did not escape the attention of contemporary observers. One detailed description of the economy of Poltava guberniia in the 1840s stated that:

> At this time, in comparison with the state of crafts in Russia, crafts in Poltava guberniia are insufficiently developed, even though—given the high population densities in many counties—they would be an appropriate form of activity for the inhabitants, especially those items needed for local industries and basic necessities.[31]

[30] William Blackwell, *The Beginnings of Russian Industrialization, 1800–1860* (Princeton, 1968), pp. 106–107.

[31] Arandarenko, *Zapiski o poltavskoi gubernii*, vol. 2, p. 356. It should be noted that Poltava in 1861 actually had the second highest number of artisans in the Ukraine, and that descriptions of many other Ukrainian gubernias would undoubtedly be even more negative.

Meanwhile, in Chernihiv guberniia, the state of manufacturing was described in the following way:

> Crafts production in Chernihiv guberniia is at a very unenviable level. The various industries and crafts are so poorly developed that their influence on the welfare of the inhabitants is almost unnoticeable. It is difficult to find any competent masters or any carpenters, tailors, cobblers, blacksmiths, etc., not only in the villages, but often in cities as well.[32]

Often this problem was only alleviated by the arrival of artisans from northern Russian guberniias who found it more profitable to travel hundreds of miles to practice their trades for a few months in Ukrainian cities than to remain in their native cities. This, it seems, was a rather widespread phenomenon, particularly in the Left Bank and steppe guberniias.[33] As one observer noted, however, this did have some negative consequences in the form of a drain of local capital to other regions, something that helped perpetuate the poverty of the Ukrainian regions.[34]

One particularly useful source of information on this subject, and in fact on all aspects of urban life in mid-nineteenth-century Ukraine, is an impressive two-volume report titled—*Ekonomicheskoe sostoianie gorodskikh poselenii evropeiskoi Rossii v 1861–1862 gg.*[35] Compiled by the Ministry of Internal Affairs on the basis of questionnaires completed by guberniia administrations, the books provide a comprehensive summary of the economic life of virtually all the cities of European Russia. In a standard form they give information on the geographic setting of each city, population (both the total number of inhabitants and the number and status of individuals registered in the city according to the censuses), and the state of local trade, crafts, and

---

[32] M. Domontovich, *Materiialy dlia geografii i statistiki Rossii. Chernigovskaia guberniia* (St. Petersburg, 1865), p. 365.

[33] It is specifically mentioned with regard to Chernihiv in ibid.; with regard to Poltava in Arandarenko, *Zapiski o poltavskoi gubernii*, vol. 2, p. 356; and with regard to the steppes in Ryndziunskii, *Gorodskoe grazhdanstvo*, p. 344.

[34] Arandarenko, *Zapiski o poltavskoi gubernii*, vol. 2, p. 356.

[35] Published in St. Petersburg in 1863, the volumes are organized by guberniia in alphabetical order, and each section is paginated separately; citations which follow, therefore, do not include page numbers.

industry. They also discuss some of the obstacles facing economic development, the presence or absence of agricultural activities within the city, and the condition of local finances and administration.

Unfortunately, it has not been possible to extract and analyze fully all of the data contained in these books. Even a survey, however, confirms the backwardness of commerce in Ukrainian cities. The description of virtually every city begins with the statement that "trade in the city is insignificant" (*nezamechatel'nyi*) or "unimportant" (*neznachitel'nyi*), usually confined to basic goods required by the local residents. This is confirmed especially by the underdevelopment of permanent commercial institutions and facilities. Trading stalls in most cities were said to barely meet the needs of the city residents. In Poltava guberniia, for example, in cities of less than five thousand inhabitants (of which there were six), there was only a total of 203 stalls (for an average of 35 per city), ranging from only 5 in Hlyns'k to 54 in Konstantynohrad. Meanwhile, in the seven cities of from five to ten thousand, the average number of stalls was approximately 63.[36]

On the whole these descriptions seem to be quite representative of the situation in much of the Ukraine. Another contemporary source, describing the economic development of Volhynia stated:

> In general, Volhynia guberniia belongs to that category of guberniias in which commercial activity has not achieved noticeable results . . . Still, trading in the cities and small towns, with few exceptions, is in the hands of Jews and although in the cities and small towns the variety of stalls is quite large, they are for the most part unimportant in terms of

---

[36] Unfortunately it is often difficult to arrive at precise averages, mainly because the figures frequently included a large number of stalls that were only used for a few weeks of the year during fairs and which should hardly be considered as permanent institutions. For example, in Romny there were 511 stalls, but the explanations state that only a few were used year-round, while of Poltava's 623 stalls only 130 functioned beyond the fairs. For the sake of this calculation I have simply not counted Romny's 511 but arbitrarily assigned it a figure of 63, the average for the rest of the guberniia's cities. Poltava, having a population of over ten thousand, was not included in the figure at all.

the number of quality of goods . . . crafts and various types of manufacturing are at a very low level of development.[37]

The situation in the Ukraine was especially backward when compared
with the more advanced Russian and Polish regions.[38] In both volume
and quality of goods being sold, retail trade seems to have been rather
underdeveloped in the small and medium-sized cities of the Ukraine.

With regard to the number of artisans and the level of production in
cities, these reports are equally critical. An almost random survey
reveals that in Kamianets'-Podil's'kyi, the largest city in Podillia,
"crafts are produced primarily for the needs of the city's residents"
while in Bratslav (population 5,024), also in Podillia, crafts production is "completely unimportant." Equally significant is the fact that
even when goods were produced in larger quantities, they were often
distributed to fairs and markets for sale and not sold in the city's
stalls. This was the case with Okhtyrka, the second largest city in
Kharkiv guberniia. Goods produced there worth some 50 thousand
rubles were mostly sold at other cities and the fairs in the region.
Similarly, the artisans of Berdychiv, one of the more economically
vital cities in the Ukraine at the time, sold most of their production to
petty traders who then distributed the goods throughout the countryside and at fairs both near and far. As with the collection of products
from the peasantry described above, these were cases where the
market went to the buyer.

This report is also interesting for what it says about the very quality
of urban life. As mentioned above, a common characteristics of
Ukrainian cities was their resemblance, in many ways, to simple villages. Scholars have often noted that legally registered "urbanites"
residing in officially recognized cities often farmed for a living. Thus,
for example, in the city of Olenka (population 3,359), Chernihiv
guberniia, 800 people cultivated grain alone. In addition, enough

[37] A. B. Bratchikov, *Materialy dlia issledovaniia volynskoi gubernii v statis-
ticheskom, etnograficheskom, sel'sko-khoziaistvennom i drugikh otnosheniiakh*, vol. 1
(Zhytomyr, 1868), p. 30.

[38] It is interesting to note just how little things had changed thirty years later. A
study of urban economies carried out in 1886 surveying many of the same issues came
to equally negative conclusions regarding the situation in Ukrainian cities. See Petr
V. Alabin, *Sbornik svedenii o nastoiashchem sostoianii gorodskogo khoziaistva v
glavneishikh gorodakh Rossii* (Samara, 1889).

vegetables were grown within the city to meet its needs; orchards were located within city limits; and 400 to 500 *pudy* of honey were produced annually in beehives in the city. In Slovians'k (population 10,225), Kharkiv guberniia, all 4,300 peasants living in the city farmed, as well as 153 families officially classified as *meshchany*. Even in Kiev 150 *meshchany* families farmed, either on their own land or on plots leased from the city, while an additional 700 *desiatiny* of land, parts of estates within the city, were under cultivation or used as pastures or orchards.[39]

In Volhynia guberniia typical cities were described by another contemporary source as comprising a series of concentric circles with Jewish merchants and *meshchany* concentrated in the city centers, the scene of a lively if somewhat impoverished commercial life. Surrounding the center was a ring of estates belonging to Polish nobles. The third and final ring, meanwhile,

> visually resembled the countryside. . . In simple wooden huts this is where the *meshchany*-peasants live with their usually small plots. . . Their main occupations are either crafts or grain farming or market gardening.[40]

The same seems to have been the case in the Left Bank as well. In Poltava guberniia, for example, in all the cities except Kremenchuk, "urban citizens, owning extensive lands, practice grain-farming and refrain from crafts and commerce."[41] The author of these words came to the conclusion that this not only slowed the provision of manufactured goods and services to the bulk of the population, but also retarded the growth of a large local market for agricultural goods which would have led to a rise in prices and, eventually, greater prosperity for all due to specialization and concentration. It must be noted that this phenomenon facilitated the self-sufficiency of many cities, further guaranteeing their economic isolation.

---

[39] All of these statistics come from the relevant sections of *Ekonomicheskoe sostoianie gorododskikh poselenii.*

[40] Bratchikov, *Materialy dlia issledovaniia volynskoi gubernii*, vol. 1, pp. 6–7.

[41] Arandarenko, *Zapiski o poltavskoi gubernii*, vol. 2, p. 356.

This economic isolation of cities was also evident in the guberniias of the steppe region, although there it took slightly different forms. In general, Katerynoslav, rather surprisingly given its incredible growth in the second half of the century, was perhaps one of the least developed guberniias in the Ukraine at the mid-century. As seen in Table 12.2, this guberniia had the fewest artisans of any Ukrainian guberniia, and the lack of local artisans was a pervasive problem throughout its early history.[42] Even the city of Katerynoslav itself was described in a letter by Vissarion Belinskii to his brother in 1846 as having long wide streets with some nice buildings, but its most memorable features were the peasants' mud and straw huts and the sight of pigs and piglets wandering on the streets with lame horses.[43]

In Kherson guberniia city-country relations faced a different problem which a simple statement on the number of artisans does not reveal. In this region three major activities were concentrated in the cities, none of which resulted in or reflected a strong relationship with the countryside. The first involved the processing of food goods for consumption in the cities themselves (flour and especially macaroni); the second, processing of goods for export (lard, wax, candles, etc.); and the third, service activities for the shipping industry (making of sails, shipbuilding, etc.). In Mykolaiv, Kherson, and Odessa most artisans and workers were occupied in these sectors and the cities had very little economic interchange with a rural sector. In Odessa in 1852 the total value of production for domestic markets was approximately one-eighth the value of production for export.[44] Odessa's economic segregation was further reinforced by a rather peculiar consequence of its status as a free port. For most of the early nineteenth century, in order to preserve its right to import manufactured goods free of duty, the city administration placed a tax on goods manufactured in the city for sale within the Russian Empire.[45] Obviously, the erection of a tariff border between the city and its "hinterland" seriously impeded the expansion of economic linkages, and,

---

[42] S. Ia. Borovoi, "Deiaki osoblyvosti promyslovoho rozvytku pivdennoi Ukrainy u doreformenyi period," *Istoriia narodnoho hospodarstva ta ekonomichnoi dumky Ukrains'koi RSR* 4–5 (1970):114.

[43] Cited in Hurzhii, *Ukraina v systemi vserosiis'koho rynku*, p. 10.

[44] Ryndziunskii, *Gorodskoe grazhdanstvo*, p. 360.

[45] Borovoi, "Deiaki osoblyvosti promyslovoho rozvytku," p. 115.

according to some historians, the economic development of the entire southern frontier.[46]

The Fair Network

In the mid-nineteenth century an extremely intricate system of fairs was in place covering virtually the entire country, especially the Left and Right Banks. Initially they arose in response to a variety of factors, including the expansive geography of the country, poor transportation linkages, and the unstable nature of the frontier. Under such conditions traveling merchants and fairs proved to be the most effective method for commercially integrating the area into the larger economy of the Empire. The impact of these fairs on the Ukrainian economy and the growth and development of cities was enormous.

This network of fairs emerged over a long period. Already in 1665 in the Left Bank there were 40 fairs operating on a regular basis. This number increased to 326 in the middle of the eighteenth century, and over 400 by the turn of the nineteenth century.[47] This rapid growth was matched in other parts of the country, and by 1820 some 2,000 fairs met regularly in the Ukraine, about one-half of the total of all fairs in the Russian Empire.[48] It is important to point out that these fairs retained their economic significance throughout the first half of the nineteenth century, even while the numbers and importance of similar fairs in Russia proper declined dramatically. In the 1850s there were still 425 fairs operating in Kharkiv guberniia and 372 in Poltava, compared to only 10 in Vladimir.[49]

Almost all fairs were held annually, usually coinciding with a feast date on the religious calendar from which they took their names. They were held in a variety of locales—cities, towns, suburbs, and villages—and lasted from one day to several weeks. A location often served as the site for as many as five or six separate fairs, each held at a different time of the year. The most common dates were late spring,

---

[46] See, in particular, ibid.

[47] V. M. Kulykovs'kyi, "Iarmarky i torhy v mistakh livoberezhnoi Ukrainy XVIII st.," *Istoriia narodnoho hospodarstva ta ekonomichnoi dumky Ukrains'koi RSR* 10 (1976):50. See also M. Volkov and Iu. Tikhonov, "Iarmarki Ukrainy v seredine XVIII v.," in *Istoricheskaia geografiia Rossii XVIII v.*, vol. 1 (Moscow, 1981).

[48] Rozman, *Urban Networks*, p. 213; Fedor, *Patterns of Urban Growth*, p. 55.

[49] Gohstand, "The Geography of Trade," p. 339.

summer, early fall, and mid-winter, as these were the easiest times to travel on the dirt roads and rivers that served as the main transportation arteries.

It is possible to divide the fairs into two types based on their size and character. Smaller fairs, usually lasting from a day to a week and involving a turnover of a few thousand or tens of thousands of rubles, generally served a retail function, attracting peasants and city residents from a relatively limited area. Large fairs, lasting for as long as three or four weeks and involving a turnover of hundreds of thousands or even millions of rubles, had a wholesale function, drawing merchants from a much larger area. The two types of fairs were interdependent and together formed a distinct network whereby the large wholesale fairs were actually the apex of a system in which lesser needs were served by a multitude of smaller fairs.[50]

Generally, the small fairs accomplished two tasks. First, they were the place where peasants and small estate owners sold their produce. In the Ukraine this included agricultural goods such as wheat (either as grain or bread), vegetables, alcohol, wax, livestock (especially horses, cattle, and sheep), wool, leather, and tobacco. In addition, peasants and city residents sold handicrafts and other items produced locally, such as baskets and linen. Second, small fairs serviced the needs of the local residents for goods brought from other parts of the empire or even imported from abroad. These included salt, small manufactured goods, and especially cloth and woolen products. In most instances merchants were the partners in these transactions, often purchasing the local goods at one fair and then returning later to the same site to sell the manufactured and imported goods. These small fairs often served as the main market for wares produced in local cities, something which is confirmed in the descriptions of trade patterns in the report—*Ekonomicheskoe sostoianie gorodskikh poselenii*.[51] These fairs were, in effect, the lowest nodal points in the entire commercial system.

Goods collected by merchants throughout the countryside were transported to the large fairs at the apex of the system. There they were sold in much larger lots to buyers from other parts of the

[50] Ibid., pp. 339–40.

[51] See also Ia. Zabelo, *Opyt issledovaniia ukrainskikh krestianskikh iarmarkov* (Poltava, 1892).

Ukraine, foreign countries, and especially north-central Russia. These fairs often had a specialized character and attracted similar goods from an extremely large area. Kharkiv—due to its strategic location vis-à-vis the industrial heartland near Moscow, the port of Odessa, the eastern reaches of the empire, and the entire Left Bank—became an especially important center in this regard. The Troits'kyi Fair in Kharkiv played a major role in the wool trade, with 1.7 million rubles worth of raw wool being sold there in 1861 alone (of total sales at the fair of some 2 million rubles). The Pokrovs'kyi Fair (1861 sales of 4 million rubles) was a major market for the sale of horses and cattle. The Khreshchens'kyi Fair also recorded horse sales of some 2 million rubles, although its product mix was more diverse. In all, total sales at the city's four fairs reached some 20 million rubles in 1861, with the Khreshchens'kyi leading at 12.5 million.[52]

It is interesting to trace the course of the goods sold in Kharkiv. In 1854 the local police registered 5,535 merchants who traded at the various fairs. Sixty percent of these merchants came from the Moscow-Vladimir region, and less than one-third from the Ukrainian guberniias. There were also eight from Austria and Prussia and fourteen from the Kingdom of Poland.[53] Much of the wool from the Troits'kyi Fair was purchased for processing in the factories of the Central Industrial Region, while the horses sold at the Khreshchens'kyi mainly went to the military.[54] Other goods sold at the fairs included livestock, honey, wax, wine (from the Crimea), and fruit. These were either purchased for consumption in the north, or, together with many of the horses and wool, taken to Riga, Odessa, or Warsaw for export.[55]

Another of the largest Ukrainian fairs was the Illins'kyi held at Romny until 1851 and then transferred to Poltava. Here too wool was a major commodity, with up to 100 thousand *pudy* (about 16 million kg.) being sold in 1846. Agricultural products traded there included hundreds of thousands of bushels of grain, destined mainly for guberniias to the north; fresh and preserved fruits which eventually made

---

[52] *Ekonomicheskoe sostoianie.*

[53] Blackwell, *The Beginnings of Russian Industrialization*, pp. 75–76.

[54] *Ekonomicheskoe sostoianie.*

[55] M. Slabchenko, *Materiialy do ekonomichno-sotsiial'noi istorii Ukrainy XIX st.* (Odessa, 1925), p. 231.

their way for consumption in Moscow, Kharkiv, and some cities of the Don region; and honey, wax, butter, and lard shipped to the ports on the Black Sea for consumption and export. In addition, rice, barley, and wheat made their way to guberniias to the west, while considerable quantities of sugar, either in a raw form or refined in small plants throughout the guberniia, were sold for use in Moscow and elsewhere. This fair was also important in the collection of peasant handicrafts from the Left Bank, including linen, sacks, and brushes. These goods were purchased by merchants from other guberniias. Finally, some of the textiles produced locally were sold at the Illins'kyi, mainly for shipment to Georgia and the Caucasus.[56] In addition to accumulating and marketing goods produced in the Ukrainian (and other southern) guberniias, the large fairs there also played a crucial role in the movement of goods into the country. Some, such as the Khreshchens'kyi, combined both of these functions. Of the total turnover of 9.7 million rubles in 1854, "the greatest part . . . consisted of a wide variety of cotton and woolen goods manufactured in Russia proper."[57] Sold there in 1861 were woolens, textiles, paper, and linen worth 4.5 million rubles; iron and copper worth 213,200 rubles; glass, ceramics, and earthenware worth 7,000 rubles; and dyes, wax, and candles worth 610,000 rubles.[58] In addition, leather, hats, books, coffee, tea, and sugar were traded in sizeable quantities.[59] Many of these goods were either produced in factories and workshops of the industrial regions near Moscow and St. Petersburg or in Poland (especially the textiles), or they were brought from more distant places—the iron from the Urals, and the tea, coffee, and luxury goods from other countries via the major seaports.[60]

The Illins'kyi Fair also involved trade in both directions, with large quantities of woolen, paper, silk, and fur goods being sold, particularly by Moscow-based merchants and industrialists.[61] The same was true for the Kontraktovyi Fair in Kiev, where "items from Russian factories find a sizeable market" and where local nobles and merchants

---

[56] Arandarenko, *Zapiski o poltavskoi gubernii*, vol. 2, pp. 361–62.
[57] Blackwell, *The Beginnings of Russian Industrialization*, p. 75.
[58] *Ekonomicheskoe sostoianie.*
[59] Ryndziunskii, *Gorodskoe grazhdanstvo*, p. 283.
[60] Ibid.
[61] *Ekonomicheskoe sostoianie.*

could sell goods from the region such as bread, sugar, and raw wool.[62] Somewhat different was the Khrestovozdvyzhens'kyi Fair in Krolevets', Chernihiv guberniia, which had total sales of 2.5 million rubles in 1861. This fair played only an insignificant role in the movement of goods out of the area, but it was a major distribution point for Russian manufactured goods, candles, and other "colonial" items, serving not only Chernihiv guberniia, but the entire Right Bank and Belorussia as well.[63]

These large fairs were frequented by the merchants and peddlers who purchased goods for resale, either at the small fairs or in the cities and villages of the Ukraine. This provided the final form of integration for the entire system, and the goods thus acquired filtered their way, over many months, to the lowest and most remote segments of the population. In some cases the fairs attracted peasants and *meshchany* who wished to avoid the middlemen and purchase the items they needed directly, but this was limited.

Overall, the fair system had a number of important consequences. In many ways it hindered urban growth because it provided an alternative forum for commercial exchanges. As has been noted, cities in most preindustrial societies were the centers of the commercial network and their markets dominated the surrounding countryside. In the Ukraine, the small fairs in particular displaced cities in this function. The peasantry's consumer needs were satisfied and the sale of their products was conducted outside the urban centers. In cases where the fairs were held in cities or towns the result was generally the same; while the cities experienced tremendous growth for a few days or weeks due to the influx of thousands of merchants and customers, such growth was only temporary. Even Kharkiv, the site of four major fairs, was largely unaffected by their activities, reverting after the closing of the fairs to a rather sleepy town of thirty thousand inhabitants. According to one historian, in Kharkiv, "as was the case in most cities with fairs, the buying and selling of the majority of goods had relatively little influence on the economy of the city itself."[64] To be sure, the situation changed somewhat in the second half of the century. Merchants often found it easier to store their goods in the city

[62] Ibid.

[63] Domontovich, *Chernigovskaia guberniia*, p. 406.

[64] Ryndziunskii, *Gorodskoe grazhdanstvo*, p. 282.

between fairs rather than move them from site to site, and they began to build permanent warehouses for this purpose. Furthermore, many began to settle in the cities and operate stores year-round, thus providing the base for a much more stable urban life. On the whole, however, it seems a little oversimplified to argue, as William Blackwell does, that "towns such as Kharkiv, which were the site of several fairs each year, were tending to become permanent urban markets."[65] For every such case it would be possible to find many others, for example, Poltava and Krolevets', which did not develop in the same way. Significantly, the continued importance of fairs in the Ukraine differed considerably from the situation in the north and west where permanent urban markets came to predominate as commercial centers much earlier.[66]

As the discussion of the commodity selection and character of the large fairs should suggest, a second and equally important result of the entire system was the effective integration of the Ukraine into the all-Russian economy. As historians such as Mykhailo Slabchenko have noted, over the course of the nineteenth century the Ukrainian guberniias essentially came to provide foodstuffs and raw materials for the empire while consuming finished goods from the north and west. This process was reinforced in 1822 when the introduction of tariffs "closed the doors of the Ukrainian market to foreign competition."[67] By the middle of the century large quantities of Russian-produced woolens, textiles, and other manufactured goods were exchanged at Ukrainian fairs for the foodstuffs needed to feed the large parts of the industrial heartland that were not agriculturally self-sufficient.[68] The "national marketing system" described by Rozman in his discussion of the urbanization pattern of the Russian Empire at the turn of the nineteenth century was basically extended into the Ukraine via the fair system.[69]

---

[65] Blackwell, *The Beginnings of Russian Industrialization*, p. 76.
[66] Gohstand, "The Geography of Trade," p. 339.
[67] Blackwell, *The Beginnings of Russian Industrialization*, p. 79.
[68] Ryndziunskii, *Gorodskoe grazhdanstvo*, p. 23.
[69] Rozman, *Urban Networks in Russia*.

Early Ukrainian Industrialization

The implications of the integration of the Ukraine into the imperial economy for the growth of cities were enormous. For a variety of reasons—the examination of which is beyond the scope of this paper—industrialization, and prior to that crafts production by artisans, had reached much higher levels of development in the guberniias of north and central Russia than in the Ukraine. In Moscow and St. Petersburg, and then in the regions surrounding these two cities (as well as in the Polish Kingdom), industry and manufacturing were well established by the beginning of the nineteenth century.[70] The fair system provided an effective mechanism for the distribution of goods produced in these areas into the Ukraine. Due to their superior quality and mostly lower prices resulting from economies of scale, Russian manufactured goods were able to undermine local production in the Ukraine, forcing out existing industries or preventing the establishment of new ones. This process went hand in hand with the takeover of the Ukrainian market by Russian merchants, and later by sales representatives of the factories themselves.[71]

In addition to simply retarding Ukrainian industrialization, it also influenced the character of those industries which did emerge. In the early nineteenth century most manufacturing in the Ukraine involved the processing of agricultural and other raw materials—activities that were most easily conducted near the sources of raw materials, either on estates or in villages, and not in the cities. This is evident from the data presented in Table 12.3, which lists the location of factories with sixteen or more workers for the years 1813–1814. The third group listed includes the Left- and Right-Bank guberniias, as well as other guberniias of the main agricultural regions.

---

[70] See William Blackwell, ''The Historical Geography of Industry in Russia during the Nineteenth Century,'' in James Bater and R. A. French, eds., *Russian Historical Geography*, vol. 2 (London, 1983).

[71] Slabchenko, *Materialy do ekonomichno-sotsial'noi istorii*, pp. 227–29.

Table 12.3

Location of Factories in the Russian Empire, 1813–1814

Region	Total Number of Factories	Percentage in Cities	Percentage in Villages
Agricultural and the East	327	30.0	70.0
The South and the Southeast	15	13.3	86.7
Capital provinces	292	57.9	42.1
Industrial provinces	295	52.4	47.6
The Baltic and Belorussia	53	22.6	77.4
The North and Siberia	36	69.4	30.6
Total	1,018	45.2	54.2

Source: Pavel Ryndziunskii, *Gorodskoe grazhdanstvo v doreformennoi Rossii* (Moscow, 1958), p. 34.

In fact, the situation was even worse than the given data imply. Of the 98 factories in cities of the agricultural region, 14 were actually located in small towns in Volhynia, Kiev, and Chernihiv guberniias, settlements that could hardly be considered cities. Additional statistics only reinforce this point. In 1813–1814, only three of the 55 cities of the Left Bank, and four of the 41 cities of the Right Bank had factories employing at least 16 workers. By comparison, forty of the 150 cities of the capital and central industrial regions had a total of 323 factories located in them, employing over 55 thousand workers.[72]

The rural nature of manufacturing remained a pervasive characteristic of Ukrainian economic development for many years. As late as the 1840s only some 27 percent of all factories identified in the country were in cities, while the value of their production accounted for just 28 percent of all production in the Ukraine. Table 12.4 provides a breakdown on the location of factories for each guberniia.

[72] Ryndziunskii, *Gorodskoe grazhdanstvo*, p. 39.

Table 12.4

Location of Factories in Selected Guberniias, 1845 – 1848

	Number of Factories	Total Value of Production	Number of Factories in Cities	Percentage of Urban Production
Podillia	488	126,438	52	4.7
Katerynoslav	260	1,103,223	69	41.5
Kharkiv	424	1,899,117	118	31.4
Kiev	484	5,118,739	97	14.0
Volhynia	334	744,704	72	12.2
Poltava	163	706,021	18	14.4
Chernihiv	194	1,572,187	52	5.2
Kherson	153	929,276	105	83.0
Total	2,500	13,337,645	583	21.6

Source: Nesterenko, *Rozvytok promyslovosti*, Appendix 1. The value of production is given in rubles. The figures for Kiev guberniia do not include 254 breweries and distilleries (total production of approximately 4.4 million rubles), for which locations were not given by Nesterenko. The overwhelming majority of these were no doubt located in the countryside, and their inclusion would have only reinforced the rural character of industry in the guberniia.

Related to the issue of the type and location of these industries was their seasonal nature. While precise figures are not readily available, many of these establishments only operated for a few months of the year. This was especially true of the many sugar beet refineries and alcohol distilleries which usually only functioned after the harvest and perhaps through the winter and early spring. It is not necessary to go into great detail to see that this certainly did little to encourage urbanization or steady urban growth rates. In this regard, many early industries in the Ukraine were only a complement to agricultural activities, and not a substitute.

In conclusion, it is quite clear that the Ukrainian economy, at least when examined through the prism of the function of cities, was not a particularly well-integrated economic system. The Ukrainian economy was not developing on the basis of local differentiation and economic specialization, where cities played a clearly defined role within a specific geographic entity. Rather, the functional differentiation that generally fueled urbanization in other societies was accompanied by a number of larger developments which resulted from the Ukraine's unique geographic location and political status. The territory's place in the larger imperial economic system mitigated the need for a locally contained specialization, and the region remained the agricultural hinterland for the urbanized heartland of the empire.

This in fact points to an interesting anomaly of Ukrainian economic development of the early nineteenth century. Despite the country's many disadvantages and overall backwardness in the eighteenth century, its economy did grow and develop considerably in the first half of the next century, particularly as evidenced by the expansion of modern commercial relations, the creation of a cash economy, and the overall rise in the standard of living (especially for rural dwellers). Significantly, however, this maturation occurred within the framework of the all-Russian economy. The crucial division of labor and economic function which signaled this process in most developing societies was accomplished primarily on the basis of a regional or geographic specialization rather than on the basis of local differentiation and urbanization. For the sake of argument, it appears that in developing countries that were largely isolated and independent, economic maturation usually saw the rise of local cities, local industries, and a local, self-contained division of labor. This was not the case for the Russian Empire, as there emerged an imperial division of labor, with industry being concentrated in the north and west and agriculture predominating in the south and east. Urban growth in the latter areas, therefore, was retarded, as cities lacked one of the basic purposes that fueled their growth in most modernizing societies.

CHAPTER THIRTEEN

The South Ukraine as an Economic Region in the Nineteenth Century

Patricia Herlihy

My purpose in this article is to examine the economic integration of the South Ukraine in the nineteenth century, and to review the commercial relationship of the region with other parts of the Ukraine, the Russian Empire, and the outside world. To do this, I must initially describe the region of our interest, characterize in general terms economic developments in our period, and state what I understand by the governing concept, "economic region."

In administrative terms, the South Ukraine consists of the three guberniias of Kherson, Katerynoslav, and Tavriia, or Taurida (the Crimea). (See Map 13.1.) These administrative borders enclose the core, but do not circumscribe the limits, of the economic region I examine.[1]

In ca. 1800, when our inquiry begins, this region had only recently been incorporated into the Russian Empire. In 1774 the Treaty of Kiuchuk-Kainardzhi with the Ottomans confirmed the imperial domination of the northern littoral of the Black Sea.[2] The lands which the

---

[1] As Holland Hunter stated in the volume reporting on the first of these conferences, "Defining the boundaries of the economy is . . . a basic political question—one that economists usually assume has been settled before their analysis begins." I. S. Koropeckyj, ed., *The Ukraine within the USSR: An Economic Balance Sheet* (New York, 1977), p. 4.

[2] E. I. Druzhinina, *Kiuchuk-Kainardzhiiskii mir: ego podgotovka i zakluchenie* (Moscow, 1955).

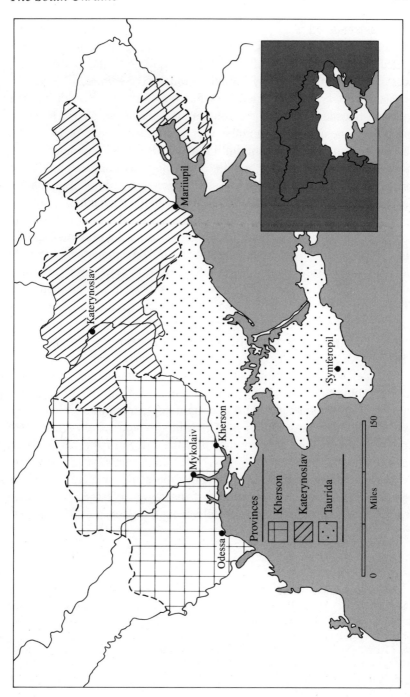

Map 13.1: The South Ukraine
(reprinted from Patricia Herlihy, *Odessa: A History, 1794–1914* [Cambridge, Mass., 1987])

Turks surrendered were predominantly chernozem steppe, very fertile but still very thinly settled. This "new Ukraine," as it is sometimes called, thus contrasted with the "old Ukraine" to the north, which was one of the most densely settled regions of the empire.

The new Ukraine remained very much a frontier region during the opening decades of the nineteenth century. For example, in Kherson guberniia, one out of seven males was in military service in 1827, and the ratio remained constant until the 1850s.[3] The population was, however, growing rapidly and the area of cultivation extending. A principal stimulus to growth was the opening of a voracious market for wheat in Western Europe, and for other products, such as wool and tallow, easily produced from animals raised on the South-Ukrainian steppes. The export of wheat to Western Europe first boomed during the Napoleonic Wars, but slackened in the immediate postwar decades, as western states imposed barriers ("corn laws") against wheat imports. But the abolition of the corn laws in western countries (from the 1840s), their soaring populations, industrialization and urbanization, sustained a steady growth in wheat exports, which continued over the second half of the century. Even the Crimean War (1853–1856) represented only a temporary interruption.

What exactly defines an economic region? I understand by the term a geographic area, in which local markets show similar price levels and price movements in regard to certain key commodities.[4] This area is "the whole of any region in which buyers and sellers are in such free intercourse with one another that the prices of the same goods tend to equality easily and quickly."[5] In other words, purchasers anywhere in the region pay approximately the same price for the same goods at the same time. Of course, if the region is large, "allowance must be made for the expense of delivering the goods to different pur-

---

[3] E. I. Druzhinina, *Iuzhnaia Ukraina v period krizisa feodalizma 1825–1860 gg.* (Moscow, 1981), p. 15. For statistics concerning the percentage of Ukrainians in the total population of the South Ukraine, see Myron Kordouba, *Le territoire et la population de l'Ukraine* (Berne, 1919), pp. 27–32, 73–94.

[4] Alfred Marshall, *Principles of Economics*, 8th ed. (New York and London, 1961), p. 324.

[5] Ibid., p. 324.

chasers.''[6] But if prices test the degree of regional integration, they are obviously not its cause. A high degree of regional integration requires the support of a substructure that facilitates the exchange of information and the transport of goods. Elements in the substructure are entrepôts or fairs, where both information and commodities are exchanged, and a suitably efficient system of communications and of transport. In an economically integrated region, goods move readily from areas of abundance to areas of scarcity. Goods are therefore distributed more evenly over space, and their prices everywhere tend to converge. Regional integration of this kind encourages specialization in production; the local areas produce what best they can on the basis of their differing factor endowments, and they use their surpluses to trade for their other needs.

It should, however, be noted that local markets may not be integrated to the same extent in regard to all commodities. The commodities most likely to be traded within the region are those that are widely consumed, are of predictable quality and are relatively durable. Cereals, wheat in particular, are often used in testing for the integration of markets.[7] Through a kind of "free rider" phenomenon, integration of regional markets in regard to one commodity aids integration in regard to others. Nonetheless, differences are likely to remain.

In examining the complex and changing economic situation of the South Ukraine in the nineteenth century, I shall first look at the substructure and then at the evidence of regional integration as revealed by prices. It must be admitted that the supporting data are not entirely satisfactory. My principal sources yielding price information are three. The first are the price schedules for rye, wheat and oats, published between the years 1846 and 1859 in the *Zhurnal* of the Ministry

[6] Ibid., p. 325.

[7] For the use of grain prices in the measuring of market integration, see R. W. Unger, "Integration of Baltic and Low Countries Grain Markets, 1400–1800," in J. M. van Winter, ed., *The Interactions of Amsterdam and Antwerp with the Baltic Region, 1400–1800* (Leiden, 1983), pp. 1–10. Unger uses wheat and rye prices to test for the emergence of an integrated cereal market in the Baltic region and the Low Countries. See also John Hurd II, "Railways and the Expansion of Markets in India, 1861–1921," *Explorations in Economic History* 12 (1975):263–88. Hurd uses wheat and rice prices to measure integration.

of Internal Affairs.[8] Unfortunately, the series given for the southern provinces contain many gaps. The first part of the series (up to 1856) gives prices by guberniia and the second (1856–1859) by city, thus impeding consistent analysis. The series is nonetheless valuable, and we also make use of official government publications to compile data for the last years of the nineteenth century.[9]

The second principal source is the prices collected by a Russian economist, Iuli Eduardovich Ianson, during a tour through the southern Ukraine in 1867 and 1868. He published the results of his research in 1870. Ianson studied markets both in the Odessa region and in the Crimea, and gathered price citations from a variety of private sources, chiefly account books kept by estate owners, merchants and millers.[10] His price series extends from 1860 to 1867.

Finally, in their study of the emergence of what they call an "All Russian agrarian market," I. D. Koval'chenko and L. V. Milov compiled much information about prices from the entire empire out of archival records and published data.[11] Unfortunately for our purposes, with rare exceptions they present the data in already processed form, chiefly through coefficients of correlation across guberniias. Moreover, the items used as the principal tests for integration are rye or rye flour and oats for the earlier period (to 1855). For the late nineteenth and early twentieth centuries (to 1914), they analyze the prices of draft

[8] *Zhurnal Ministerstva vnutrennykh del,* vols. 15–38 (St. Petersburg, 1846–1859).

[9] *Sbornik statistiko-ekonomicheskikh svedenii po sel'skonomu khoziaistvu Rossii i inostrannykh gosudarstv* (St. Petersburg, 1910–1912).

[10] Iu. Ianson, *Statisticheskoe issledovanie o khlebnoi torgovle v odesskom raione* (St. Petersburg, 1870), and his *Krim: ego khlebopashestvo i khlebnaia torgovliia* (St. Petersburg, 1870). For bibliography on grain and other prices, see T. F. Izmest'eva, "Istochniki po istorii tsen XIX—nachala XX veka," *Massovye istochniki po sotsial'no-ekonomicheskoi istorii Rossii perioda kapitalizma* (Moscow, 1979), pp. 381–411.

[11] I. D. Koval'chenko and L. V. Milov, *Vserossiiskii agrarnyi rynok XVIII-nachalo XX veka* (Moscow, 1974). See also Boris Mironov, "Le mouvement des prix des céréales en Russie du XVIIIe siècle au début du XXe siècle," *Annales: Economies, sociétés, civilisations* 41 (1986):217–51. Mironov's work appeared after I had finished my own research. His analysis, emphasizing the importance of the foreign demand for wheat, differs quite sharply from that of Koval'chenko and Milov, and both his method and conclusions, while referring to the entire empire, are very similar to my own analysis of cereal prices in the South Ukraine.

horses, cattle, and real estate, and also salaries. But they do not include in their analysis the prices of wheat.[12] Wheat prices are frequently cited in the series they exploit, at least from 1846, and wheat was a particularly important commodity of trade in chernozem regions. Their failure to consider this the most commercial of cereals is perplexing, in a book expressly devoted to the formation of the agrarian market. They do not explain why wheat was dropped or never included in the analysis. Why?

Although the book is not as useful for this study as it might have been, it nonetheless contains unique information not available outside of archives. I shall make much use of its data in this paper and shall also offer additional comment about its methods and content.

The Substructure

A. Fairs

It is well known that annual or seasonal fairs played a major role in the internal commerce of the Russian Empire.[13] For example, it was largely through fairs that the manufactures of the more industrialized, chiefly central guberniias were marketed in the predominantly agricultural regions, such as the Ukraine itself.[14] In the mid-nineteenth century, the value of Russian-made goods sold in Ukrainian fairs exceeded that of agricultural products purchased by Russian buyers, although the value of foreign manufactures allegedly exceeded that of

---

[12] Koval'chenko and Milov, *Vserossiiskii agrarnyi rynok*, p. 219, note that the most important commercial cereal at Zhytomyr, Kamianets'-Podil's'kyi, Poltava, Kharkiv, and Kiev was wheat, and that the export of wheat had been growing since the 1790s. The raising of wheat as a commercial crop in the chernozem regions in fact obstructed the development of the market for rye. "Only the powerful commercialization of wheat evidently overwhelmed the development of the market for rye." But should not this factor be given detailed examination in a study of the agrarian market?

[13] On fairs in the Russian Empire, see V. I. Denisov, *Iarmarki* (St. Petersburg, 1911); on Ukrainian fairs, see I. Aksakov, *Issledovanie o torgovle na Ukrainskikh iarmarkakh* (St. Petersburg, 1858); on fairs in the South Ukraine, see Druzhinina, *Iuzhnaia Ukraina*, pp. 177–80.

[14] Denisov, *Iarmarki*, p. 5. By 1910 there were some 2,200 fairs in the Ukraine, mostly minor ones of short duration.

the Russian by twenty times.[15] An economist writing in 1858 recognized the role fairs played in integrating markets when he stated, "There is no doubt that with the advent of the railroad from Moscow to the Black Sea all fairs along the route will diminish gradually, except perhaps the wool [fairs]."[16]

The principal Ukrainian fairs were at Kharkiv (some four major fairs a year, each lasting about a month), Poltava, Chernihiv, and Romny—all of which are in the northern Ukraine. The locally produced commodities traded at the fairs were primarily wheat, rye, millet, maize, animals, wool, tallow, sheepskins, and leather.[17] Because of its importance in foreign export, wheat enjoyed a special status.

In the southern Ukraine, however, fairs had only a limited importance. As shown on Map 13.2, the three southern guberniias contained only one important fair, that of Ielysavethrad (Kirovohrad). Its value of sales earned it tenth position among the eleven principal Ukrainian fairs.[18] The port cities (primarily Odessa) cast a shadow extending far into the hinterland, within which the fairs typical of the rest of the empire could not grow. Most purchases were made not at inland fairs but at the ports themselves. Or else, the purchasers at the ports went themselves or dispatched agents to buy these products, wheat especially, directly from the inland producers. Conversely too, the port cities were the foci by which foreign luxury products and manufactures were made available to inland purchasers.

In regions distant from the ports, agricultural commodities were purchased and gathered into large batches for shipment to Odessa. Principal towns serving this function were Kremenchuk and Katerynoslav (Dnipropetrovs'k) on the Dnieper River, and Mohyliv-on-the-Dniester. There were also other locales, not so much true markets as staging areas, where cereals were accumulated for shipment to the ports. Among the more important were Oleksandrivs'k (Zaporizhzhia) and Nykopil' on the Dnieper. Located just below the Dnieper rapids, Oleksandrivs'k and then Nykopil' gathered the wheat carried by land around the rapids and placed it on barges, to complete its

[15] Aksakov, *Issledovanie*, p. 47.

[16] Ibid., p. 47.

[17] I. O. Hurzhii, *Ukraina v systemi vserosiis'koho rynku 60–90kh rokiv XIX st.* (Kiev, 1968), p. 76.

[18] Aksakov, *Issledovanie*, p. 48.

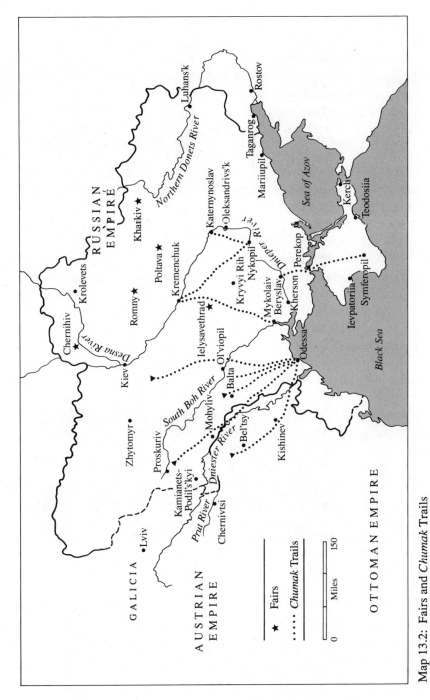

Map 13.2: Fairs and *Chumak* Trails
(reprinted from Patricia Herlihy, *Odessa: A History, 1794–1914* [Cambridge, Mass., 1987])

journey by water to the Black Sea ports. Of importance too was
Proskuriv (Khmel'nyts'kyi) in the basin of the Volhynian rivers; it
marked the northern limit of Odessa's region in the middle nineteenth
century.[19]

B. *Water Transport*

The importance of the ports for the inland economy indicates that very
early in the development of the region bulky commodities, such as
wheat, could be carried over considerable distances at acceptable
costs. The flat and treeless steppe was fairly easily traversed, both by
river boats and by carts.

The rivers emptying into the Black Sea were natural highways
across the steppe, but they were also very circuitous. Moreover, the
chief of them, the Dnieper, was also obstructed in its course by its
well-known series of rapids. Cargoes had to be unloaded and taken by
cart around them, and, as mentioned, Oleksandrivs'k marked the spot
where the river became navigable again. The Dnieper and the upper
Dniester largely defined the interior regions which could be served by
water transport.

Cabotage, or coastal shipping, played a role of considerable importance in linking together the Black Sea ports one with the others. For
example, between 1858 and 1867, the number of boat arrivals at the
port of Ievpatoriia in the Crimea averaged 355 per year, and the average yearly departures 347.[20] Approximately one-half of this coastal
trade out of the Crimea was with Odessa. The number of foreign ship
arrivals at the same port of Ievpatoriia was half as many. The port of
Kherson, at the mouth of the Boh, which eventually became Odessa's
great rival, was initially a satellite port, receiving and combining
smaller cargoes for transshipment to Odessa, the region's great
entrepôt for international commerce. In this function, it resembles
Oleksandrivs'k and Nykopil' on the Dnieper.

Unlike the ships in international trade, all those engaged in coastal
traffic were required by law to be of Russian ownership. Traffic on
the coastal waters intensified considerably in the nineteenth century.

---

[19] See Ianson, *Statisticheskoe issledovanie*, pp. i – iv.

[20] Ianson, *Krim*, Prilozhenie, no. 1.

Table 13.1

Arrivals of Cabotage Ships at Odessa, 1842 – 1892

Year	Arrivals
1842	431
1852	1209
1862	1365
1872	2777
1882	2693
1892	3401

Source: *Odessa, 1794 – 1894: Izdanie gorodskogo obshchestvennogo upravleniia k stoletiu goroda* (Odessa, 1895), p. 217.

Table 13.1 shows the number of arrivals of cabotage ships at the port of Odessa in the middle and late decades.

At first, most of the boats came from Kherson, but later, they also came from Akkerman (Bilhorod-Dnistrovs'kyi), Ochakiv, Mykolaiv, and Crimean ports, primarily Ievpatoriia. By the end of the nineteenth century, cabotage ships from Kherson carried grain, flour, wood, and coal; from Mariiupil', coal; from Akkerman, grain and wine; and from Ievpatoriia, salt. Like threads, these coastal voyages sewed together the region's maritime fringes.

C. The Chumaky

The vast inland region between the Dniester and Dnieper rivers was not adequately served by water transport, but it was the largest and most productive part of the economic region. To bring agricultural products to port required the use of great carts or wagons, pulled by oxen, and driven by teamsters known as *chumaky*. Their services remained important over the entire course of the nineteenth century. Map 13.2 shows the principal routes taken by the *chumaky* in the mid-part of the century. These routes show rather well the depth to which the pull of the ports extended into the hinterland. By 1870 five

major *chumaky* grain trails terminated in Odessa, only one in Mykolaiv, and none in Kherson. The *chumaky* routes originating in
Kremenchuk terminated in Beryslav and Nykopil'. Nykopil' was also
the chief terminus of the *chumaky* trail from Katerynoslav. Another
chumaky trail led to the Crimea; it was especially important for the
salt trade.

The range of the *chumaky* and their wagons is astounding, and is a
principal reason why fairs were not needed in the near vicinity of the
ports. For example, at the time of the Uspen'skyi Fair in Kharkiv
(August 15 to September 1 or later), the *chumaky* set forth from Kharkiv with empty carts for the Crimea; they purchased goods along the
way. If the weather was good (that is, dry) and if the *chumaky* gathered sufficient wares, they traveled on as far as Odessa and Bessarabia. There, they sold their goods and passed the winter. Early in the
spring those in the Crimea loaded up with salt and dried fish at
Perekop for the return trip. Some 100,000 wagons a year carried salt
from Perekop to Kharkiv. While horse-drawn wagons could move
winter and summer, the *chumaky* drove their oxen and carts only during summer, when the roads were dried out and the oxen could graze
on the growing grass. Each wagon could hold 40–50 *pudy* (ca.
1440–1800 pounds) of wheat. Its best speed was 30 *versty* (ca.
20 miles) per day and only 10 to 15 *versty* when the roads were
muddy. The oxen had to take shelter when it rained.[21] Since the grass
that the oxen consumed cost nothing and the *chumaky* slept in the
open air, this was a fairly economical method of land transport. But
the costs of moving wheat from hinterland to port remained high in
relative terms, as we shall see.

D. Railroads

Railroads came late into the South Ukraine, the first being constructed
in 1865 (from Balta to Odessa). Map 13.3 shows the railroads in the
Ukraine in 1906. It seems too that strategic rather than commercial
considerations dictated their routes. Some of the lines, however, followed the north-west, south-east direction of the Dniester and Boh
rivers, but more markedly, they paralleled the *chumaky* trails. The
length of the railroad lines increased in the South Ukraine (including

[21] Aksakov, *Issledovanie*, pp. 40–42.

the Don Military District) from 2,623 *versty* in 1870 to 4,789 in 1894. In 1880 trains brought in 79 percent of all grain to Odessa. The advent of the railroad significantly reduced the costs of shipping wheat to Odessa, as we shall see.

Nonetheless, the railroads did not replace the river barges, or even the *chumaky* carts, as the principal means of bringing cereals to port.[22] After 1880, the portion of wheat carried to port by train was actually declining. By 1892 the percentage of grain carried to Odessa by rail slipped to 32.2 percent.[23] This surprising trend partially resulted from high railroad tariffs (water transport was generally cheaper). Then too, contrary to all expectations, barges and carts could serve more economically the distant areas of cereal production, recently brought under cultivation.[24] It seems that, unlike the experience of India, the coming of railroads to the South Ukraine was not the decisive factor in integrating cereal markets within the region.[25]

The late construction and disappointing contribution of the railroads was one reason why the South Ukraine, in spite of growing exports, was unable to compete successfully against other world suppliers of wheat, the United States, Canada, Argentina, and others. In the late nineteenth century, beset by problems of transport and control of quality, the region progressively lost position among the world suppliers of wheat, to the United States, Canada, Argentina and other lands. Efficient inland transport in these latter countries gave them the competitive edge.

[22] As late as 1917 no grain reached Kherson as railway freight. Some grain was handled by carts, but more than 40 percent of all grain arriving at Kherson was shipped from the river port of Oleksandrivs'k. See Guy Michael, *Russian Experience, 1910–1917* (Privately published by Pauline Mc D. Michael, 1979), p. 142.

[23] V. A. Zolotov, *Khlebnyi eksport Rossii cherez porty Chernogo i Azovskogo morei v 60–90 gody XIX veka* (Rostov, 1966), p. 49.

[24] Ibid., p. 49. For details on the railroads in the south Ukraine, see A. M. Solov'eva, *Zheleznodorozhnyi transport Rossii vo vtoroi polovine XIX v.* (Moscow, 1975), pp. 90–93; and 188–92. See also *Istoriia narodnoho hospodarstva Ukrains'koi RSR*, Ekonomika dosotsialistychnykh formatsii, 1 (Kiev, 1983):265. For discussion of the inadequacies of railway transport to Odessa in this period, see Lewis Siegelbaum, "The Odessa Grain Trade: A Case Study in Urban Growth and Development in Tsarist Russia," *The Journal of European Economic History* 9, no. 1 (1980):129–30.

[25] John Hurd II, "Railways," pp. 263–88.

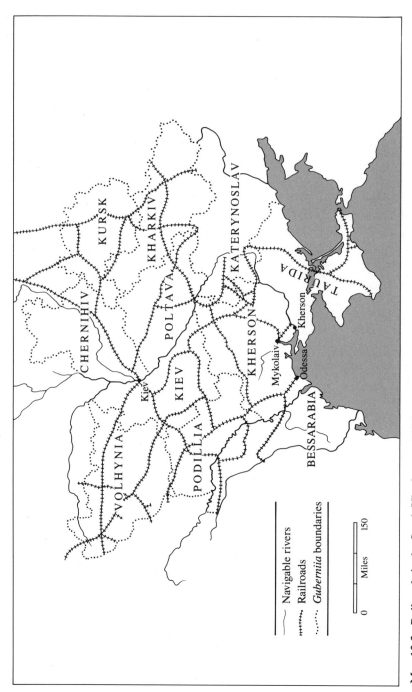

Map 13.3: Railroads in the South Ukraine, ca. 1907
(reprinted from Patricia Herlihy, *Odessa: A History, 1794–1914* [Cambridge, Mass., 1987])

The Integration of South-Ukrainian Markets

A. The Early Evidence, 1809–1819

The earlier price data available to us that include South-Ukrainian towns date from 1809 to 1819 and were published by Koval'chenko and Milov (Prilozhenie 3 and 4, with ten observations each, as the years 1812 and 1813 are combined). The two tables they provide cite prices by year for rye, rye flour, and for oats. I have taken their data for nine Ukrainian towns and, to gain added perspective, for one town located beyond the Ukraine's northern border, Mahilioŭ-on-the-Dnieper. Mahilioŭ was old-settled and densely settled, and lay outside the chernozem region. Its data help place the Ukrainian experience within a larger context.

The first schedule given by the Soviet authors mix together prices of rye (by *chetvert'*; 1 *chetvert'* = 0.108 tons) and of rye flour (by *kul'*; 1 *kul'* = 96.5 kg.). Although Koval'chenko and Milov do use this table to calculate coefficients of correlation, I did not think it worthwhile (nor did I have the data) to replicate the elaborate procedures by which they estimated the price of rye from that of rye flour.[26] Moreover, their resulting matrix of correlations gives some impossible values. In Table 28, the correlation of Arkhangel'sk with Chernihiv is .62, and of Chernihiv with Arkhangel'sk is .67; they should, of course, be the same. The correlation of Arkhangel'sk with Ufa is either .86 or .66, depending on what corner of the matrix one is reading. There are other indications of a rather careless proofreading. Given these difficulties, I decided not to examine the prices they give for rye and rye flour, nor the correlations derived from them.

The analysis here is thus limited to prices for oats—not an ideal commodity, as oats were less actively traded than other cereals. The average price for oats over the decade shows a large spread, ranging from 367 paper rubles per *chetvert'* at Kharkiv to 810 at Symferopil'. The schedules identify a region of very low prices in the northeast Ukraine (385.8 at Poltava, 364 at Kharkiv), though similar growing conditions in these close and contiguous provinces may be the principal reason. Two areas of high prices are found: in the Crimea (810.4

---

[26] *Vserossiiskii agrarnyi rynok*, pp. 71–72; the authors note that the procedure does not always yield satisfactory results.

Table 13.2

Correlation Matrix
Prices of Oats at Ukrainian and South-Russian Towns
1809–1819

	Katrv	Zhtmr	Km-Pd	Kiev	Mhl	Pltva	Smfpl	Khrkv	Khrsn	Chrnh
Katerynoslav		-.138	-.058	-.078	.745	.879	.649	.941	.384	.345
Zhytomyr	-.138		.849	.860	-.181	-.095	.347	-.243	.457	.128
Kamianets'-Podil's'kyi	-.058	.849		.833	-.074	-.134	.512	-.120	.553	.442
Kiev	.078	.860	.833		-.131	-.055	.410	-.166	.626	.381
Mahilioŭ	.745	-.181	-.074	-.131		.770	.752	.848	.137	.463
Poltava	.879	-.095	-.134	-.055	.770		.523	.914	.314	.338
Symferopil'	.649	.347	.512	.410	.752	.523		.648	.437	.552
Kharkiv	.941	-.243	-.120	-.166	.848	.914	.648		.226	.437
Kherson	.384	.457	.553	.626	.137	.314	.437	.226		.654
Chernihiv	.345	.128	.442	.381	.463	.338	.552	.437	.654	

Source: Based on prices cited in Koval'chenko and Milov, *Vserossiiskii agrarnyi rynok*, Prilozhenie 4.
Prices are in paper rubles per *chetvert'*.

rubles at Symferopil') and Mahilioŭ beyond the northern border (800.1 rubles). These are the only clearly delineated regions in these early years. Especially notable for our purposes are the big price differences in the three New-Russian towns (411.3 at Katerynoslav, 669.4 at Kherson, and 810.4 at Symferopil'). There was as yet no unified market for oats.

Table 13.2 gives the coefficients of correlations which we recalculated on the basis of the data supplied by Koval'chenko and Milov. The figures agree with their own results.

The number of negative correlations (12 out of 45, or more than a fourth) shows that the areas surveyed were still weakly integrated in the early nineteenth century. The correlations of Kherson with Katerynoslav (.384) and with Symferopil' (.437) are positive but very weak, showing little trade in oats in New Russia. Katerynoslav seems much more oriented toward Poltava (.879) and toward Kharkiv (.941), and to form part of a northeast Ukrainian sector marked by very low oat and perhaps wheat prices. There is, in sum, by 1809–1819 still no evidence that the southern Ukraine had coalesced as an economic region.

B. Midcentury

The next available set of data is the prices collected by the Ministry of Internal Affairs for rye, rye flour, wheat, oats, and hay, from August 1846 to September 1856.[27] The unit of observation was the guberniia,

---

[27] These data are also partially used by Koval'chenko and Milov; see their comments upon the quality of the reporting in ibid., pp. 75–76. But they omit, as we have mentioned, all the references to wheat prices, which were items of great interest to those who collected the data. Their methods also invite some criticisms. To establish the yearly price for rye and oats, they took the prices for the three spring months and for the three autumn months, and averaged them together, to arrive at a "spring-autumn" price, which they argue best represents the true value of the respective cereals for the given year. When spring or autumn prices were missing, as unfortunately is often the case, they substituted the prices from contiguous summer or winter months. The procedure effectively reduces the number of observations from the full forty-one (though this is rarely found) to only ten, one per year.

The chief criticisms that can be made about the procedure are two. First, it sacrifices data, as the observations for the summer and winter months enter only as substitutes, when they probably distort more than they supplement. The series is already very lacunous, and observations ought not to be wasted. Secondly, the wis-

and the intent was to collect prices twice every month. The complete series ought to have included forty-one observations, but no one of the southern guberniias I surveyed showed all citations. From Kherson, for example, there are only eleven citations for rye flour and for wheat, respectively. Moreover, the price series shows strong seasonal swings. Because the prices collected do not necessarily represent the same season of the year, correlations obviously become difficult.

I first calculated average prices for the three commodities for ten guberniias, eight in the Ukraine and two, Bessarabia and Mahiliou, just beyond its borders. I then matched prices of each guberniia with those of the other nine for each commodity, in order to determine which of the two areas showed the higher price. The highest possible score that a guberniia could attain was 27 (comparisons with nine other guberniias for three commodities). The comparisons identified two regions of consistently high prices and one in which they were quite low. The region of highest prices was Mahiliou, which scored 24 out of the possible 27. Only oats were slightly cheaper in Bessarabia, Tavriia, and Kherson. At Mahiliou the price of wheat was 43.5 percent higher than at Chernihiv just to its south, 43.3 percent higher than at Kiev, 47 percent above prices at Kharkiv and 52.6 percent above those of Poltava. Mahiliou with its large population and poor soil was clearly a region where food was very expensive. It stands very much apart from the other guberniias we included.

---

dom of averaging elements within a time series before analyzing the series as a whole is very questionable. It has the result of smoothing the variations from one element to another—smoothing out the very fluctuations that the coefficient is supposed to be measuring. The argument they advance for this dubious strategy is that they need to remove seasonal fluctuations. This they do, but what about the most powerful fluctuation of all—the abundance of the yearly harvests? In other words, a high correlation of yearly prices may show not integrated markets but the fact that the weather was the same, and harvests comparable over large areas of the empire.

For these reasons, I believed it necessary to use these observations, including, of course, those bearing upon wheat. The methods I used to adjust for seasonal fluctuations will be explained presently. The results of this effort to utilize the data were coefficients lower than those achieved by Koval'chenko and Milov. Still, researchers ought not to be beguiled by correlations in the .900s, and should not transform their data with that goal primarily in mind. Weak associations can be as interesting as strong.

By middle century, the second region of high cereal prices, on the other side of the Ukraine, had gained in visibility. It included Tavriia, which also scores 24 out of 27 but with much smaller differentials than those registered at Mahilioŭ; Bessarabia, with a score of 23; Kherson, with 19; and Podillia, with 15. These guberniias had ready access to ports and to the sea, and the influence of the ports seems apparent. For example, the price of wheat was 25.8 percent higher at Kherson than at Poltava; in Tavriia it was 34.6 percent higher. The period includes the record years of cereal exports from the Ukraine when crops failed in the West in 1846 and 1847. It is not unlikely that these areas close to the ports were responding to foreign demand and beginning to lure with high prices shipments of cereals from the deeper hinterland.

The averages also identify an area of very low cereal costs, the outlines of which we already saw in the early years of the century. The guberniias of low prices were Katerynoslav with a score of 10, Chernihiv (9), Kiev (8), Kharkiv (5), and Poltava (0). The price of oats, for example, was 1.87 rubles at Poltava, and 3.32 at Tavriia—almost double. The region of very cheap cereal prices now was extended to include the guberniias of Kiev and Chernihiv, which it did not clearly encompass in 1809–1819. The data, in sum, indicate much clearer differentiation of regions within the Ukraine and immediately beyond its borders.

I also calculated coefficients of correlation for the three sets of prices and the nine guberniias. Here, the different dates of the citations were a problem. To offset this, I inserted dummy values. When a citation was missing, I entered the closest previous true price into the series. But I did not want to manipulate the data too vigorously, and therefore did not calculate correlations for series in which out of the forty-one observations, fewer than twenty-one were real. Even so, the results were disappointing, particularly since at Kherson, the center of our interest, the citations for rye and for wheat were only eleven. Because the table is large and cumbersome, I do not reprint it here. Nonetheless, some conclusions seem appropriate.

The number of negative correlations for the ten guberniias collapse to only 12 out of the 234 calculated values—an indication that cereal prices in most places were responding to the same market forces. Given the need to insert dummy data, high correlations are not to be expected. Still, Kherson shows a reasonably strong correlation with

Bessarabia for oats (.760) and with Tavriia (.802), but slightly weaker with Katerynoslav (.671), weak with Kiev (.521); and almost no correlation with Kharkiv (.298) and Chernihiv (.270). This suggests that in the 1840s and 1850s, distance remained a powerful factor in obstructing the integration of markets.

From November 1856 the Ministry of Internal Affairs adopted cities, and no longer guberniias, as the units of observation, and continued to publish twice every month prices for rye flour, wheat, and oats. The practice was discontinued in September 1859. The complete series consists of seventeen citations. Again, however, gaps are frequent. For example, no prices at all are given for wheat at Kiev or Poltava. The short duration of the series and the strong seasonal fluctuation of prices also obstruct correlational analysis. On the other hand this set includes cities such as Odessa, Teodosiia, Berdians'k, Taganrog, and others, which are not represented in any earlier collection.

I selected sixteen Ukrainian cities, and also Kishinev in Bessarabia and Mahilioŭ-on-the-Dnieper, for analysis. As wheat was the most expensive and the most traded cereal, its prices are doubtlessly the best indicators of market structure. The average prices for wheat between November 1856 and September 1859 show a clear division into three groups or clusters. Wheat prices range from a low of 5.65 rubles per *chetvert'* at Kamianets'-Podil's'kyi to a high of 9.61 at Teodosiia in the Crimea. But no town shows a price in the range of 6 rubles, and only one, Berdians'k on the Sea of Azov, has a value between 8 and 9 rubles. We thus have clusters of cities showing cheap prices (less than 6 rubles), intermediate prices (7 rubles), and high prices (9 rubles).

To look first at the last cluster, Mahilioŭ (9.56 rubles per *chetvert'*) again emerges as a city with very high cereal costs. The other towns with high prices are all found on or close to the sea: Teodosiia (9.61) and Symferopil' (9.01) in the Crimea; Odessa (9.02); and perhaps Berdians'k (8.24). The cluster of cheapest markets includes Zhytomyr to the west of Kiev (5.83), Kamianets'-Podil's'kyi in Podillia (5.65), Kremenchuk (5.72), and Kharkiv (5.8). (Kiev and Poltava doubtlessly fall into this category, but for them wheat prices are not given.) These towns form a band distant from the sea. The third cluster of moderate-price markets consists of Kyshyniv in Bessarabia (7.21);

Balta in the Ukraine (7.34), a principal supplier to the Odessa market; Katerynoslav (7.66); and Rostov-on-the-Don (7.80). Two seaports are also found in this category, Kherson (7.66) and Taganrog (7.66). Most are inland cities but within moderate distances of ports. The two ports of Kherson and Taganrog still were not principal overseas shippers.

The novelty revealed in the data is the clear appearance of this intermediate tier of towns, which are showing the influence of the high prices for wheat offered on the seaboard but still sell their grain at a substantially lower price (approximately in the range of 7 rubles, as distinct from 9 at portside). Notable too is the reorientation of Katerynoslav, which earlier seemed turned toward the cheap-price zone of the deep hinterland, but now is fully in the zone of intermediate prices. The evidence, in sum, indicates that the pull of the ports was affecting ever more distant areas of the South Ukraine.

I calculated the coefficients of mutual correlation among all eighteen towns, which resulted in a huge table of nearly 900 cells. It confirmed some obvious expectations. Prices for wheat at Teodosiia show a high correlation with those at Symferopil' (.921) and also Kherson (.915). But the most surprising result was the low correlations registered by Odessa. Its strongest match was with Kishinev in Bessarabia (.780), a close supplier of its port. It registered comparable scores with nearby Balta (.731) and with Kamianets'-Podil's'kyi further along on the same *chumaky* trail (.726). It showed only moderately strong correlations with its sister ports of Rostov (.721), Teodosiia (.699), and Kherson (.664). None of these scores are very impressive. I take this to mean that the Odessa market was not primarily reflecting seasonal variations in cereal prices but the level of overseas demand. These variations still strongly affected prices at inland markets. The short duration of this series magnifies the importance of seasonal variations, and Odessa's prices seem less subject to them than those of inland cities.

C. The 1860s

We now can make use of the data collected by the economist Ianson, who exploited private sources and claimed that he spared no pains to assure its accuracy. The town of Mogilev which he included in his research is Mohyliv-on-the-Dniester, which falls within Odessa's region even as Mahiliou-on-the-Dnieper does not. Ianson's data also enlarges the number of Ukrainian towns that we can include in our analysis. Table 13.3 shows price movements at Odessa and at towns that were the principal inland suppliers to its port.

Table 13.3

Price in Rubles for a *Chetvert'* of Wheat
in the Odessa Region, 1860–1867

	Odessa	Nykopil'	Ielyzavethrad	Mohyliv	Bel'tsy	Proskuriv
1860	8.75	6.25	5.75	5.45	4.90	—
1861	8.50	5.50	5.25	5.40	4.70	—
1862	7.60	5.50	5.20	4.62	4.64	—
1863	7.25	6.00	5.90	4.15	5.20	—
1864	7.10	4.25	4.20	4.39	3.40	4.40
1865	7.68	7.20	4.80	6.00	5.90	3.80
1866	10.50	8.25	6.95	6.23	7.00	5.20
1867	11.75	11.00	8.00	8.52	10.00	8.40
Ave	8.64	6.74	5.75	5.59	5.71	5.45
Index	100	78	67	65	66	63

Source: Ianson, *Statisticheskoe issledovanie*, p. 277.

Table 13.3 shows that the wide divergence between the price of a *chetvert'* of wheat at portside and in the hinterland persisted through the 1860s. About one-third of its price at Odessa is attributable to transport costs. By this measure, the region remained weakly integrated in the 1860s. On the other hand, the movement of prices at all these observation points was becoming very close. Table 13.4 presents the correlations.

Table 13.4

Correlation Matrix:
Movements of Wheat Prices in Six Ukrainian Towns

	Odessa	Nykopil'	Ielyzavethrad	Mohyliv	Bel'tsy	Proskuriv
Odessa	—	.943	.978	.968	.923	.949
Nykopil'	.943	—	.949	.971	.995	.939
Ielyzavet-hrad	.978	.949	—	.931	.937	.956
Mohyliv	.968	.971	.931	—	.957	.953
Bel'tsy	.923	.995	.937	.957	—	.947
Proskuriv	.949	.939	.956	.953	.974	—

Source: Data in Table 13.3

In spite of the continuing large price differential between Odessa and the hinterland towns, the markets at all of them were responding to the same shifts in demand, radiating out of Odessa itself.

Table 13.4 measures the extension of Odessa's economic region into the hinterland. Its harbor also could take advantage of coastal shipping to extend its influence to other Black Sea ports. The indefatigable Ianson collected data from the Crimea, and this allows us to examine how well, in the 1860s, seacoast shipping, or cabotage, was integrating the coastal zones of the region. Table 13.5 shows monthly wheat prices at Teodosiia and Odessa from 1866 to 1868.

In all previous series, prices in the Crimea had surpassed those of Odessa. This was no longer the situation in 1866–1868. Moreover, correlations in prices between the two ports had not been noticeably strong in previous tests. Now, the high correlation of .968 shows that prices in both ports were moving very much to the same rhythm, which was doubtlessly set by overseas demand.

Table 13.6 shows price movements at Odessa and the second Crimean port of Ievpatoriia.

Table 13.5

Prices of Wheat at Teodosiia and Odessa,
Monthly Averages, 1866 – 1868

	Teodosiia	Odessa
1866 April	8.75	8.925
August	9.5	10.68
September	11.32	10.90
1867 July	9.0	11.00
August	10.0	11.56
September	11.0	12.87
November	11.5	12.94
December	12.12	11.12
1868 June	10.0	11.0
Average	10.35	11.22
Correlation	.968	

Source: Ianson, *Krim*, p. 70.

Table 13.6

Autumn Wheat Prices at Ievpatoriia and Odessa, 1863 – 1868

	Ievpatoriia	Odessa
1863	7.5	8.5
1864	6.5	8.25
1865	7.0	8.62
1866	8.5	12.25
1867	10.5	14.0
1868	9.5 (summer)	11.5
Average	8.25	10.52
Correlation	.984	

Source: Ianson, *Krim*, p. 70.

In effect, the comparison with Ievpatoriia supports the same conclusions as that with Teodosiia. The Crimea was no longer the area of the South Ukraine where wheat prices were highest. Odessa, riding the ever expanding demand of foreign purchasers, now claimed that distinction. But the price movements in the two ports show closer coordination than we found when we compared prices at Teodosiia and Odessa.

Table 13.7 compares the two Crimean ports of Ievpatoriia and Teodosiia, and extends the comparison to barley and oats.

Table 13.7

Indices of Autumn Cereal Prices
at Ievpatoriia and Teodosiia, 1865 – 1868

	Ievpatoriia			Teodosiia		
	Barley	Oats	Wheat	Barley	Oats	Wheat
1865	100	100	100	100	100	100
1866	142	125	121	138	166	135
1867	166	125	150	152	147	170
1868	150	161	125	180	166	156
Average	139.5	127.75	124	142.5	144.75	140.25
Correlation	.972	.972	.990			

Source: Ianson, *Krim*, p. 75.

The correlations are again very strong. The greater average costs of these cereals at Teodosiia primarily reflect the importance of the latter as an international exporter of grain.

The ports of the South Ukraine gained renown on international markets primarily through the sale of wheat. Wheat flour was a relatively new item of export in the 1860s. Table 13.8 shows how prices of flour compared at Odessa and Teodosiia.

Table 13.8

Prices of Wheat Flour at Teodosiia and Odessa, 1865 – 1867

	Teodosiia	Odessa
1865 Feb.	6.625	7.19
March	7.0	7.19
Nov.	6.75	8.16
1866 Feb.	6.875	8.12
May	7.25	8.60
Nov.	8.37	10.23
Dec.	9.0	9.86
1867 April	8.875	9.64
Oct.	8.75	10.9
Nov.	9.0	9.86
April	9.25	10.37
Average	7.97	9.13
Correlation .984		

Source: Ianson, *Krim*, p. 71.

Here, the price advantage that Odessa was offering is even more substantial than with wheat—again a change from the earlier pattern. But the correlation of the two price lists is again very high, confirming the strength of the ties between them and with their common overseas purchasers.

D. The Turn of the Century

Connected whether by *chumaky* trails, by railroad, or by barge or coastal vessel, the cities of the South Ukraine show clearly the primary characteristic of an integrated market already by the 1860s—the prices of the principal commodities show high correlations. But price levels also differed, reflecting the continuing high costs of transport. Table 13.9 shows us the pattern of wheat prices prevailing forty years later, at the turn of the nineteenth century, for the principal southern ports.

Table 13.9

Prices for a *Pud* of Winter Wheat, 1890 – 1909

	Rostov-on-the-Don	Taganrog	Mykolaiv	Odessa
1890 – 99	81.1	86.7	85.7	—
1900 – 04	84.4	88.4	88.4	102.0
1905	89.1	99.1	96.1	101.2
1906	94.9	95.1	90.9	95.2
1907	117.4	116.6	110.5	114.7
1908	136.4	129.0	125.6	132.8
1909	126.1	121.9	128.9	131.9
1910	109.1	108.1	97.8	110.7
Average	104.81	104.61	102.98	112.64
Index	93	93	92	100

Source: *Sbornik statistiko-ekonomicheskikh svedenii po sel'sknomu khoziaistvu Rossii i inostrannykh gosudarstv* (St. Petersburg, 1910 and 1912), pp. 336, 420.

Table 13.10

Correlation Matrix:
Wheat Prices

	Rostov-on-the-Don	Taganrog	Mykolaiv	Odessa
Rostov-on-the-Don	—	.996	.986	.984
Taganrog	.996	—	.976	.990
Mykolaiv	.986	.990	—	.994
Odessa	.984	.990	.994	—

Source: Preceding table.

Table 13.11 compares the three guberniias of New Russia and two immediate neighbors.

Table 13.11

Prices for a *Pud* of Winter Wheat, 1901 – 1910

	Bessarabia	Kherson	Tavriia	Katerynoslav	Don Cossack Territory
1901 – 05	75	77	85	77	78
1906	67	74	77	79	106
1907	123	128	128	124	117
1908	120	123	123	120	116
1909	126	108	118	109	97
1910	80	88	90	88	90
Average	98.5	99.67	103.5	99.5	100.67

Source: Same as Table 13.2, p. 432.

Table 13.12

Correlation Matrix
Prices of Winter Wheat, 1901 – 1910

	Bessarabia	Kherson	Tavriia	Katerynoslav	Don Cossack Territory
Bessarabia	—	.980	.989	.980	.890
Kherson	.980	—	.996	.998	.940
Tavriia	.989	.996	—	.997	.935
Katerynoslav	.980	.998	.997	—	.955
Don Cossack Territory	.890	.940	.935	.955	—

Source: Same as preceding table.

Price levels among these large regions had diminished to a maximum differential of 5 percent. And only the territory of the Don Cossacks shows less than maximum correlation in its price movements with its neighbors. The market for wheat in the South Ukraine was now strongly integrated.

Summary and Conclusion

Over the course of the nineteenth century, the South Ukraine gradually was integrated into a true economic region. The earliest data, dating from 1809 – 1819, show a region of high cereal prices beyond the Ukrainian border to the north, in the Belorussian guberniia of Mahilioŭ; one of very cheap prices in the northeast Ukraine (Kharkiv and Poltava); and again one of expensive prices in the extreme south, in the Crimea. Apart from the Crimea, the guberniias of the southern and western Ukraine fall into no consistent pattern and certainly did not form a unified market.

By the 1850s, this pattern had been modified but not erased. The southern littoral had become unified as a zone of high wheat prices, and an intermediate zone of moderately priced markets had coalesced just to its north, and just below the zone where prices remained very low. To the far north beyond the Ukrainian borders, the guberniia of Mahilioŭ retained its now traditional status as a zone of costly food. In creating this pattern, the burgeoning demand for wheat emanating from the ports seems to have played the crucial role. The influence of the ports is especially manifest in the inflationary effects it had on prices at Katerynoslav. Formerly oriented toward the cheap markets of the northeast Ukraine, Katerynoslav by the late 1850s had been drawn into the zone of moderately priced markets supplying the port cities.

By the 1860s, the more detailed data that become available show that for a large region extending inland from the sea as far as Proskuriv and Mohyliv-on-the-Dniester the movements of wheat prices were highly correlated. The same region of like price movements extended along the Black Sea coast and through the Crimea. Price levels, however, in the various towns show considerable differences, reflecting the continuing high cost of carrying the wheat from inland areas to the ports serving the international trade. By the turn of the century, these differences were much reduced. Still, some differential remained, and the territory of the Don Cossacks was not tightly joined economically with the other South-Ukrainian provinces. The systems of transport and communications uniting the region still left room for substantial improvements. Nonetheless, it should be apparent that the nineteenth century was a period of remarkable growth and change in the markets of the South Ukraine.

CHAPTER FOURTEEN

The East European Peasant Household and the Beginnings of Industry: East Galicia, 1786 – 1914*

Richard L. Rudolph

Introduction

The name "Galicia," and even more "East Galicia," in the nineteenth and early twentieth centuries was almost synonymous with the word poverty.* The name conjured up, and rightly so, the image of a destitute peasantry, living in an over-populated region with either dwarf holdings or no holdings at all. At the same time one thought of a class of large landholders dominating the region. One thought also of the diverse and complex relations between the ethnic groups, primarily the Poles, Ukrainians or Ruthenians, Jews, and Germans.[1] The expanding Polish state had taken over the area and while the elite had become Polonized, the vast majority of the enserfed peasantry on the *folwarks*, the large estates, were Ukrainians. In the last half of the

---

*East Galicia, as discussed in this study, refers to the area of Galicia prior to the dissolution of the Habsburg Monarchy roughly east of the San River. Today the area of former East Galicia, with the exception of the portions lying to the west of the San River, is part of the Ukrainian Soviet Socialist Republic. In many cases data for East Galicia alone were not available and therefore data for both West and East Galicia were used. If not specified, tables refer to Galicia as a whole.

[1] Until the beginning of the twentieth century the Ukrainians were referred to by themselves and others as "Ruthenians." In later years, the Poles often used this term rather than Ukrainians in efforts to discourage Ukrainian nationalist aspirations. With no intention to offend any nationalist sentimenets, both terms will be used here according to the historical context.

nineteenth century, for which we have data, the Ukrainians made up
almost two-thirds of the population of East Galicia and the Poles
about one-fourth.[2] The fact that the Poles were the lords and the
Ukrainians the peasants is noted in the Ukrainian saying, ''The Liakh
[Pole] is there to do the beating, and the peasant to do the suffering.''[3]
The lower economic level of the Ukrainians can be seen from the fact
that around 1910 the Polish minority paid 74 percent of the direct
taxes as compared with the Ukrainians who paid 26 percent.[4] The picture of East Galicia is not complete without the Jews, who in this
period made up some 12 to 14 percent of the inhabitants. The Jews
occupied an intermediary position between the landlords and the
peasants. They predominated in trade; they acted as factotums and
agents for the nobles; in some cases they leased the large estates.
While some Jews became wealthy, the ever increasing masses of Jews
were impoverished to an almost unbelievable degree. Indeed, the
peasants as a whole became pauperized to an extent not known elsewhere in the Habsburg Monarchy, or in most of Europe. To this mix
one adds the small number of German colonists, both agriculturalists
and rulers from the monarchy. After gaining the area in the partitions
of Poland, the Habsburgs made some attempts, particularly in the
eighteenth century, to improve conditions, but these were meager,
while attempts at large-scale industrialization in the latter part of the
nineteenth century also had limited success.

In spite of the bleak picture of the life and economy of East
Galicia—and the picture will probably get bleaker as we progress—
there are vital matters to detain us in the region. Most important, for
our purpose, is the examination of the reasons for the failure of
economic development in the area. Galician history is significant in
and of itself, but it is also a striking example of what is today seen as
an ''underdeveloped'' or ''late-developing'' economy. Like parts of
Asia or Latin America, we find in East Galicia a classic picture of vast
population growth, under-employment of labor in agriculture, and the
influx of industrial goods from abroad. An examination of the Gali-

---

[2] *Polish Encyclopaedia*, vol. 2 (Geneva, 1924), p. 530.

[3] Janusz Radziejowski, ''Ukrainians and Poles, The Shaping of Reciprocal Images
and Stereotypes,'' in *Acta Poloniae Historica* (Warsaw, 1984), p. 130.

[4] *Polish Encyclopaedia*, vol. 2, p. 550.

cian case may help to answer questions about the nature of economic development in general.

In speaking of the reasons for the limited development of the Galician economy there are generally two schools of thought. These are not so much differing points of view, nor are they mutually exclusive; they are rather differences of emphasis. On the one hand, there is the viewpoint which emphasizes external, or as economists would say, exogenous factors. According to this view the economic development of Galicia, as of all of Poland, was held back because of the semi-colonial nature of partitioned Poland.[5] Galicia is seen as being held back in its development by the Habsburgs, and utilized as a market for industrial goods from the western, more highly developed parts of the monarchy, as well as from Germany.[6] On the other hand, some writers stress internal factors, such as the archaic social structure, with a nobility holding anti-urban attitudes, the lack of a middle class, and the conservatism of the minds and practices of the peasants. One factor noted by many authors combines both points of view. They speak of the effect of the introduction of the railroads and of factory-produced goods on the internal market. As Helena Madurowicz-Urbańska has written,

> It is a sad paradox, marked by nineteenth-century Galician writers and statesmen, that the advance of the railroad undermined Galician industry, since the industry owed its existence to the lack of inexpensive means of transport. This paradox is the result of long years of neglect by the Austrian government. The expansion of the railroad network [1847—65 km; 1884—2,259 km; 1914—4,175 km] . . . caused lower-

---

[5] For a discussion of the different viewpoints see Witold Kula, *Historia gospodarcza Polski w dobie popowstaniowej 1864–1918* (Warsaw, 1947), pp. 60–63; Helena Madurowicz-Urbańska, "Die Industrie Galiziens im Rahmen der wirtschaftlichen Struktur der Donaumonarchie," in *Studia Austro-Polonica*, 1, Zeszyty naukowe universytetu Jagiellońskiego (Cracow, 1978), pp. 157–62; Franciszek Bujak, "Wirtschaftsgeschichte Galiziens," in Freie Vereinigung für staatswissenschaftliche Fortbildung in Wien, *Wirtschaftliche Zustände Galiziens in der Gegenwart* (Vienna and Leipzig, 1913), pp. 10, 16, 20; Mariusz Kulczykowski, "La désindustrialisation: problèmes de recherche sur l'example de la Galicie au XIXe siècle," in Pierre Deyon and Franklin Mendels, eds., *La protoindustrialisation: theorie et realité* (Budapest, 1982), pp. 15–19.

[6] Bujak, "Wirtschaftsgeschichte Galiziens," p. 12.

ing of transport costs and led to the downfall of a number of branches of production.[7]

She points out that earlier the high transport costs were "a sort of protective tariff for manufacture in agriculture areas."[8] These views are similar to those expressed by other noted economic historians, such as Franciszek Bujak, Witold Kula, and Mariusz Kulczykowski.[9] The paradox of the expanding railroads bringing about less industrialization is heightened by the arguments put forth that the Habsburgs held back development by a policy of holding back the expansion of railroads in the area.[10]

*   *   *

The effect of the railroads again points up the similarity of this region to many others around the world. In particular, and most important, it underlines the importance of the region as a primarily peasant area, beginning to form a base of manufacture, and then succumbing to the competition of large-scale industry from outside the region. What was taking place in Galicia appears to have been a process repeated in many areas, a process that has come to be called "de-industrialization." The idea of de-industrialization is that in many of the colonial countries or regions what took place was not stagnation, but the interruption of a process of nascent industrialization, which was cut off and became, instead, a process of devolution.

Recent studies of industrialization have usually regarded the process as a long and gradual one, rather than one of sudden industrial spurts or revolutions. The term "proto-industrialization" has come to be adopted to denote the stage at which cottage industry and peasant by-employment begins to produce for wider and wider markets and wherein gradually networks of trade, and skilled traders, and larger manufacturing centers are established. In some regions the population grows precipitously as the non-agricultural sidelines of the peasants

[7] Madurowicz-Urbańska, "Industrie Galiziens," p. 171.

[8] Ibid.

[9] Bujak, "Wirtschaftsgeschichte Galiziens," p. 16; Kula, *Historia gospodarcza*, pp. 62ff.; Kulczykowski, "La désindustrialisation," p. 23.

[10] Bujak, "Wirtschaftsgeschichte Galiziens," p. 15.

permit the support of larger numbers of the peasant population. In a number of cases the proto-industrialization serves as the beginning of large-scale industrialization. In others, overwhelmed by the inflow of goods from already industrialized areas, or hampered by a variety of conditions internally, perhaps economic, political or social, the process reaches a dead end, and "de-industrialization" sets in. With de-industrialization, the population in the agricultural and proto-industrial regions grows, but instead of becoming workers in industry or handicraft producers, the population becomes a mass of underemployed impoverished dwellers on the land, or else migrates to the cities where no work is available. Thus, one finds the increasing poverty of the typical underdeveloped regions.[11]

In the growing literature on this process of beginning industrialization, increasing attention has been given to the exact role of the peasant household and peasant family. In East Galicia there was a predominantly agricultural society, but we have already heard the economic historians cited earlier mention industry as well. Rather than address all the questions as to the reasons for the laggard development of East Galicia, this study will deal primarily with the internal factors, questions of the internal economic development of the region. In so doing, the study will center on several of the primary questions relating to the relationship of the peasant household and family to nascent industrialization.

The basic question to be asked is whether the nature of the peasant household and family structure had something to do with the specific pattern of economic development in East Galicia. In other words, did the particular nature of the agricultural and family structure play a major role in hindering economic development? To deal with the major question, we shall look at a set of interrelated questions: 1) What were the various external influences upon the structure of the

[11] There is a vast literature on the theme of proto-industrialization. For a survey of recent ideas see Franklin Mendels, "Protoindustrialization: Theory and Reality. General Report," in *Eighth International Economic History Congress, Budapest, 1982, "A" Themes* (Budapest, 1982). On de-industrialization see Charles Tilly, "Flows of Capital and Forms of Industry in Europe, 1500–1900," in Deyon and Mendels, eds., *La proto-industrialisation*, and Maurice Lévy-Leboyer, *Les banques européennes et l'industrialisation internationale dans la première moitié du XIXe siècle* (Paris, 1964), pp. 183–88.

peasant family? 2) What role did marriage and inheritance patterns play on the economics of the peasant household? 3) What factors influenced peasant economic strategies? 4) Finally, what was the relationship between these factors (family structure, inheritance, economic strategies) upon beginning industrialization?

Agriculture, Industry, and Population, 1786–1914

1. *Agriculture*

A well-informed German gentleman, J. G. Kohl, traveling in East Galicia around 1840, wrote the following:

> The enserfdom of the peasant is still as strong here as elsewhere in Poland. Herr Dupin had made a map representing the enlightenment in France, on which the uneducated and uncultivated areas were shaded-in darkly, while the more cultured areas were lighter and the enlightened areas were completely bright. If one were to draw a similar map of serfdom in Poland, one would have to make the entire land pitch black, without any light marks. To be sure, here and there several nuances of black would appear. . . . In Galicia, and particularly in Ruthenian [East] Galicia there might be a bit of weak lighter areas.[12]

It is within this historical context of "black" serfdom that one must see the roots of the Galician peasant problem of the nineteenth and twentieth centuries. Speaking of the eighteenth century, Bujak wrote that "The status of the economic life of Galicia can be characterized as a strong throwback to the economic relations of the Middle Ages."[13]

It appears that in the main the serf estates divided the arable land fairly evenly between the peasants' portion and the lord's demesne, although the lord held the forests and pastures, which under serfdom could be partially used by the peasants.[14] At the same time the peasant

---

[12] J. G. Kohl, *Reisen im Inneren von Russland und Polen* (Dresden and Leipzig, 1841), p. 56.

[13] Bujak, "Wirtschaftsgeschichte Galiziens," p. 10.

[14] Jean Rutkowski, "Le régime agraire en Pologne au XVIIIe siècle," *Revue d'histoire économique et sociale*, 1927, no. 1, p. 67.

was free to deal with agriculture as he chose upon his own holding.[15] From the Middle Ages until the time of the enserfment of the peasantry the landholdings of the peasantry seemed to be fairly equal.[16] This may well have reflected their origins in a communal system of agriculture which some authors have seen as an ubiquitous development in the Middle Ages as population pressure forced peasants to consolidate their individual holdings and then divide them into two or three fields to be rotated biennially or triennially between crops and fallow.[17] Some of these peasant communes were still to be found in East Galicia in the nineteenth century.[18] In the course of time, however, the land came to be divided by the peasant households, or to be parceled out differentially by the lords upon a death in a peasant family, so that eventually the holdings were of different sizes. By the eighteenth century there were clear and distinct gradations in the size of peasant holdings. Some peasants had significant holdings, others were cotters, and some held no land at all.

In practice the lands of the lord (dominical) and that of the peasants (rustical) were often not divided into separate areas; the land was worked together. This gave rise to great difficulties following both the Josephine patent of 1786 and the liberation of the serfs in 1848; for the next hundred years numerous problems arose as to the land ownership of particular parcels of land.[19]

The obligations of the peasants to the lord were many and varied, but an almost universal practice was that of labor services (*robot* or *panszczyzna*) which were due from almost every peasant. The larger households furnished labor with transport animals (*robota ciągła*) while the smaller peasants furnished manual labor (*robota ręczna*).[20] In common practice two manual labor days were equivalent to one

---

[15] Ibid.

[16] Rutkowski, 'Le régime agraire," p. 79.

[17] Jerome Blum, "The European Village as Community: Origins and Functions," *Agricultural History* 45 (July 1971):160, 170; Roman Rosdolsky, "Die ostgalizische Dorfgemeinschaft und ihre Auflösung," *Vierteljahrschrift für Sozial- und Wirtschaftsgeschichte* 41 (1954):97–145.

[18] Rosdolsky, "Die ostgalizische Dorfgemeinschaft," p. 103, passim.

[19] Ludwig von Mises, "Die Entwicklung des gutsherrlichbäuerlichen Verhältnisses in Galizien (1772–1848)," *Wiener Staatswissenschaftliche Studien* (1902):95.

[20] Ibid., pp. 61–63.

transport service day.[21] The *robot* furnished the lords with great quantities of labor. In 1772 there were some 221,482 householders furnishing 30,000,000 *robot* days per year and in 1847 there were 334,367 householders furnishing almost 38,000,000 *robot* days.[22] It was possible for a householder to substitute a family member or servant for the person owing *robot*.[23] The peasants worked on the manorial fields at times four to five and even six days a week, while contributing various portions of their produce as tributes or taxes.[24] It has been estimated that even into the nineteenth century the average peasant in East Galicia was able to retain for his own use only 25 to 30 percent of his income.[25]

When Austria took over the area, the government under Emperor Joseph II attempted to improve the laggard production on the estates. The heart of the Josephine policy was to help develop a business class and the peasantry at the expense of the nobility. After conducting studies of the condition of the land and peasants in Galicia, the Josephine reforms were introduced. By the Robot Patent of 16 June 1786, the *robot* was not ended but was reduced somewhat. The nobles argued that if the peasants held land, they would be lazy, and therefore would be unproductive. The royal response was that the peasants were lazy because they did not have their own land, and thus in 1787 decrees were introduced permitting them to hold land.[26] The landowner and peasant were to work out their landholding rights between them and the peasants could buy land through voluntary agreements and be freed of various obligations. As has been said so many times concerning the Josephine reforms of various types, these reforms, too, bore little fruit. After Galician agriculture was ignored for many years, the bloody peasant uprisings in Galicia in 1846 and the revolution of 1848 led the government to make further concessions The major change in agriculture came with the *Grundentlastung* of 1848, when the peasants

---

[21] Ibid.

[22] Ibid., p. 98.

[23] Ibid., pp. 25f.

[24] Roman Rosdolsky, ''The Distribution of the Agrarian Product in Feudalism,'' *Journal of Economic History* 11, no. 3 (Summer 1951): 254–55.

[25] Ibid., p. 256; Alan S. Milward and S. B. Saul, *The Economic Development of Continental Europe, 1780–1870* (Totowa, N.J., 1973), p. 64.

[26] Von Mises, ''Entwicklung,'' pp. 61–63.

were to be freed of the *robot*. This settlement took longer to institute in Galicia than elsewhere in the monarchy, with the result that it took until March of 1857 for it to be completed.

After 1848 with the opportunity for peasants to devote more time for their own land, more production might have been expected, but available estimates show that this did not seem to be the case. (See Table 14.1.) Until the 1880s agricultural production remained relatively stable, and in per capita terms even decreased. This was so for several reasons. First of all, the agriculture of Galicia in general was plagued by two major problems. First, there was a trend toward the fragmentation of peasant holdings as the population grew. This tendency reached major proportions as parents divided land for their successors. The number of holdings in Galicia in 1820 was 527,740; the number rose to 584,625 in 1857 and to over a million in 1902, over a ninety percent increase.[27] This figure is in part misleading, because it reflects the practice of parcelling out agricultural holdings to various family members, rather than necessarily denoting division of the sum of holdings of individual peasants. Nevertheless, there was a clear tendency for the individual peasants, even summing up their holdings, to have smaller total areas under their control. The *morcellement* as the French call it, or fragmentation of the size of holdings, reached extreme proportions in the area. This practice grew out of a combination of legal practices and peasant traditions. Secondly, aside from the limited sizes of land holdings, there was also a great problem with respect to the entanglement of various parcels with each other. As mentioned above, it had often been difficult to establish which land was held by the lord or by other peasants. In addition, land was often held in various fields in different locations, often in long strips. As a result, agricultural practice was further held back when the peasant was forced to work in many different scattered areas. Huge areas of land were wasted as borders on the various strips, while the practice remaining from earlier times of farming in strips led to an almost ludicrous narrowness to an individual's holdings.[28] It was said in one area that if a dog lay on one peasant's strip of land, his tail would be on the

---

[27] *Polish Encyclopaedia*, vol. 3 (1922), p. 249.
[28] Ibid.

property of another peasant and his nose on the land of a third.[29] The problem has been described well by a Polish economist:

> One peasant's property consists on the average of twenty to thirty separate lots. They are sometimes four to five miles away from farm buildings or extend in strips of a few yards wide over a length of a kilometer if not more. The mere loss resulting from the unproductive edges may be computed at 250,000 to 371,000 acres, worth anything from 30.8 to 46.3 million dollars. The difficulty of reaching enclosed lots often gives rise to the necessity of passing over neighboring properties, with the result that intensive cultivation is almost impossible.[30]

As a consequence of the parceling and extreme entanglement of land, there was an increasing number of law suits concerning property holdings. To these law suits were also added large numbers of suits owing to the fact that after 1848 the landholders refused to give up their rights to pastures and forest land, which had been used earlier by the peasants. Thus, the newly independent peasant suffered for want of pasture or forest usage.[31] Between 1870 and 1880 there were 32,000 cases brought to the court concerning contested rights to forest and pasture land.[32]

For many years economists theorized that free peasants would be more productive than the serfs. As described above, however, some institutional factors may hamper the growth of agriculture among a free peasantry. In the case of the East Galician peasantry this was most surely the case. In addition to the practices of dividing the land among heirs, a number of other factors held back production. Agricultural data are always difficult to work with, and even today the sophisticated methods of calculating national income run into a stone wall when attempting to estimate the farmer's own consumption of foodstuffs for his family and feed for livestock. Nevertheless, the overall production data and the fact that the holdings were so small lend credence to the belief that the farmers did not farm more inten-

---

[29] Stefan Kieniewicz, *The Emancipation of the Polish Peasantry* (Chicago and London, 1969), p. 204.

[30] Bujak, "Wirtschaftsgeschichte Galiziens," p. 17; von Mises, "Entwicklung," p. 98.

[31] Bujak, "Wirtschaftsgeschichte Galiziens," p. 17.

[32] Idem.

Table 14.1

Galician Agricultural Production, 1789–1913
(1830/50 = 100)

Year	Wheat 1,000 tons	%	Corn 1,000 tons	%	Potatoes 1,000 tons	%	Flax 1,000 tons
1789	1,258						
1830/50	1,307	100	21.9	100	1,221.5	100	14.3 (1841)
1851	1,253	96	8.8	40	1,337.2	109	
1857	948	73	10.4	22	1,159.1	95	
1869/75	1,460	112	55.5	253	1,716.7	140	
1876/85	1,563	119	83.5	381	2,636.9	216	13.6 (1880)
1886/95	1,650	126	98.7	451	3,423.4	280	9.6 (1890)
1895/1904	1,682	131	83.6	382	4,273.9	350	7.6 (1900)
1904/13	2,479	180	83.8	383	5,832.5	477	7.9 (1904/13)

Source: Roman Sandgruber, *Österreichische Agrarstatistik, 1750–1918* (Munich, 1978).

sively or extensively than before. Above all, the dis-economies of scale of the smaller holdings as compared with the large estates of former times acted as a hindrance to greater agricultural production. In addition, contemporary accounts describe the degree to which the peasant did not choose to work on the large estates.[33] Although such accounts speak of the refusal of the peasant to work on the estates, even for wages, and bemoan the shortage of labor, there are not enough data to verify this. It is probably true that the newly liberated peasant had what economists call a backward bending supply curve, i.e., less labor was furnished as income increased or in this case as a living could be eked out on his own land and he had the satisfaction of working for himself. Still, the unemployed, or underemployed peasant population grew extensively and worked on the estates whenever they could, as can be observed from other sources. There is also the question as to the relative wages offered by the estates, at particular points of time in the nineteenth century. Until we have more studies it is difficult to evaluate the degree to which peasants refrained from working on the estates, but this remains an important question.

Another factor which does not lend itself to ready quantitative analysis is the effect of alcohol on the production of the peasant. Both contemporaries and historians remark upon the degree to which the peasantry was hampered by the high level of alcoholism in the nineteenth century. In the 1840s the German traveler, Kohl, remarked on the extensive drunkenness to be seen in East Galicia, and noted that the Ukrainian peasants were known "to be thrifty and parsimonious up to the point where liquor consumption was concerned."[34] A contemporary estimated that the Poles in the middle of the nineteenth century consumed some 3.25 gallons of distilled liquor per capita; official data in the Austrian Monarchy show alcohol consumption in mid-century to be 2.4 gallons per capita per year in the western lands of the monarchy, the German and Slavic parts. This could be contrasted with the mid-1960s when alcohol consumption was not 2.5 gallons, but only 2.5 quarts per capita per annum in Poland![35] On the large estates of East Galicia the major source of income was often

---

[33] Idem.

[34] Kohl, *Reisen*, pp. 34ff.

[35] Jerome Blum, *The End of the Old Order in Rural Europe* (Princeton, 1978), p. 48.

distilling, which became even more lucrative with the so-called propi-
nation or monopoly given to the large estateholders until 1890.[36] Even
well into the twentieth century the landlords often paid their workers
in scrip which could be redeemed for liquor at the landlord-owned and
Jewish-run inns. It has been maintained that the importance of
alcohol production in Galicia had much to do with the occupation of
Galicia by the Austrians. According to this view it was in the interests
of the landed proprietors to have unlimited beer and brandy consumption because the estates had lost their northern export markets, and
exports to the south were out of the question because of the difficulties
of transport. Thus the surplus of grain was used to make liquor for
peasant consumption.[37] After the depression of 1873 churches took
the lead in establishing a temperance movement which apparently had
some success.[38] The entire problem of the nature of alcoholism and its
effects in history is a major one, and deserves more study. Although
work has begun in this field for America, which evidently suffered a
similar problem in the mid-nineteenth century, there are not yet, to my
knowledge, like studies in Poland.[39] Bujak, however, has noted the
degree to which pervasive alcoholism caused the peasants to neglect
their holdings.[40]

The level of technique in agriculture tended to remain low
throughout the period we are discussing. In East Galicia in the
eighteenth century the primary crops were wheat, corn, and potatoes,
with potatoes far in the lead. In the early nineteenth century wheat
gave way to corn, for fodder and distilling, and the potato became the
mainstay of the peasant's diet.[41] It was under Joseph II that efforts
were made to improve agriculture in the region, and it is from this
time that one notes the presence of German colonists and the introduction of clover and the potato. The potato rapidly became vital in the

---

[36] *Polish Encyclopaedia*, vol. 3, p. 238.

[37] Wladyslaw Rusiński, "Veränderungen in der Struktur und ökonomischen Lage
der polnischen Bauernschaft an der Wende vom 18. zum 19. Jahrhundert," in Dan
Berindei et al., eds., *Der Bauer Mittel- und Osteuropas im Sozio-Ökonomischen Wan-
del des 18. und 19. Jahrhunderts* (Cologne and Vienna, 1973), p. 90.

[38] *Polish Encyclopaedia*, vol. 3, p. 240.

[39] W. J. Rorabaugh, *The Alcoholic Republic* (New York, 1979).

[40] Bujak, "Wirtschaftsgeschichte Galiziens," p. 17.

[41] Kula, *Historia gospodarcza*, p. 67; Bujak, "Wirtschaftsgeschichte Galiziens,"
p. 8.

diet of the people; it is estimated that because of its use the Galician population increased by over 39 percent between 1810 and 1846.[42] Writing in mid-century, Kohl remarks that "the potato is increasingly popular, and in no part of Poland, Posen [Poznań] excepted, is the root so much eaten as in Galicia."[43] In 1847 and 1848 came the potato blight and famine, but the potato continued to be the staple.

On the large estates the emphasis was on grain production, but even on the large estates the period after 1848 was difficult. The large estates were short of capital for any technological innovations, and suffered particularly in the post-1848 period because the paperwork involving estimates for the payment for the loss of peasant services was not completed until 1857. Thus for a number of years the estates were left without the draft horses furnished by the peasants as well as, in many cases, the peasant labor itself. The estates could not afford to buy cattle, tools, or implements and pay wages at the same time, and there was no credit institution to furnish capital on good terms. One author wrote in 1912 that apart from the problems and the "disastrous influence exercised later on by the distressing delays in the reconstruction of properties [reunion of scattered lots], . . . the state of anarchy that prevailed concerning the use of communal lands, the different servitudes that still encumbered certain properties, and the lack of restraint in the parceling-out of small farms, added also to the difficulties of the situation. The evils, therefore, from which Galician agriculture and rural property are still suffering at the present time are due to the incapacity and clumsiness with which agrarian reforms were carried out."[44]

In the 1880s a rise in various forms of agricultural production is noticeable. An important addition at that time was the lowly pig, which became a vital element in the small farm peasant economy. The number of pigs went from around 675,000 in 1850 to over a million by 1900 and to almost two million in 1910.[45] By the turn of the century the combination of livestock, potatoes, and either some form of handicraft or remittances from emigrants or migrant laborers, sup-

---

[42] Bujak, "Wirtschaftsgeschichte Galiziens," pp. 10, 11, 14.

[43] Kohl, *Reisen*, p. 57.

[44] *Polish Encyclopaedia*, vol. 3, p. 255.

[45] Sandgruber, *Österreichische Agrarstatistik*, p. 207.

ported a vast semi-landless population.[46] In East Galicia fruit growing was widely practiced but because of the poor business practices and lack of transport the western areas obtained their fruit from Hungary or the Tirol.

While the smallholders concentrated on livestock, on the large estates changes also took place in the last third of the century. First the competition of Austrian wool devastated the raising of sheep in Galicia, and from the 1880s on the competition of inexpensive American grains undercut the Galician producers. In East Galicia some of the producers concentrated on sugar beets and sugar refining, but with little success in comparison to the widely developed industry in the western part of the monarchy, particularly in the Bohemian Crownlands. While the monopoly on distilling disappeared in 1890, subsidies to the industry made it a profitable, and for many estates *the only profitable*, source of income.[47] Prior to 1848, a major source of support for many estates was the practice of using the peasant services for various types of manufacture, such as textiles, construction, mining, and glass or paper making. It is not clear to what extent this disappeared after 1848 but some sources speak of the reticence of landowners to use wage-labor in their factories and suggest that the practice died out.[48]

2. Industry

East Galicia is a classic example of what has come to be called proto-industrialization. In the early part of the nineteenth century we already see the beginnings of manufacture on the large estates and production of various goods by the peasantry. I have argued else-

---

[46] Stella Hryniuk has recently published a revisionist approach to the whole nature of agriculture in East Galicia, arguing that the poverty and backwardness of the East Galician peasant may be a myth because the peasants did introduce new techniques in agriculture and particularly engaged in the production of livestock and of such crops as did not appear in the national statistics. She argues that this "unrecorded economy," beginning in the last several decades of the nineteenth century, made the agricultural sector profitable. Stella Hryniuk, "Peasant Agriculture in East Galicia in the Late Nineteenth Century," *Slavonic and East European Review* 63 (April 1985): 228–43.

[47] *Polish Encyclopaedia*, vol. 3, pp. 256–58.

[48] Ibid.

where, with respect to Russian economic development, that it may well be the case that the serf system itself promotes the beginnings of industrialization.[49] Briefly recapitulated, the hypothesis is that both landlords distant from and near to markets promote the non-agricultural activities of the peasants. If the large landholder is distant from the market, he wishes to husband his capital, and therefore, produces as many goods as possible on the estate for the consumption of the peasants and his own family. If the market is near, the desire is to promote manufacture of goods by the unpaid laborers in order to utilize income from such goods to satisfy his own demands of varying sorts. This theory, it might be added, had its origins in the work of a Polish economic historian, Witold Kula, which described the desire of Polish lords for autarky on their estates.[50] In another connection I have also discussed the origins of industry on the large serf estates in Bohemia and Moravia.[51] In Galicia the same development appears to have taken place. Most notably, already in the eighteenth century the major form of by-employment of the peasants was the production of textiles. In fact every village tenant was obliged to produce a given quantity of yarn or cloth from flax and wool provided by the estate, and the estate sold the surplus left over after covering its own needs. The peasants also manufactured coarse cloth for the estate and for sale or export.[52] Peasant labor was also used for other forms of manufacture: lumber, wooden utensils and tools, tar, potash and timber—all were based on the vast forests of the landed proprietors. Glassworks, iron furnaces, and papermills were founded as well in East Galicia.[53] For the most part these were run by the *robot* labor of the peasants, and in some cases they were managed by small contractors who paid a sum for the wood taken from the forest. Peasants were also engaged in making pottery, locks, leather goods, and various other branches of cottage industry. The main hallmark for the theoreticians dealing with

---

[49] Richard L. Rudolph, "Agricultural Structure and Proto-Industrialization in Russia: Economic Development with Unfree Labor," *Journal of Economic History* 45, no. 1 (March 1985):47–69.

[50] Cf. Witold Kula, *Teoria ekonomiczna ustroju feudalnego* (Warsaw, 1983).

[51] Richard L. Rudolph, "Social Structure and the Beginning of Austrian Economic Growth," *East Central Europe/L'Europe du Centre-Est* 7, no. 2 (1980):207–24.

[52] *Polish Encyclopaedia*, vol. 3, p. 237, and Bujak, "Wirtschaftsgeschichte Galiziens," p. 8.

[53] *Polish Encyclopaedia*, vol. 2, pp. 237ff.

proto-industrialization which designated the difference between common peasant production and the beginnings of a wider scale development is the degree to which such production is made for the market as opposed to purely domestic consumption. In the case of most of the activities discussed here, the only one which fits the description of production for a broader market, at least until 1848, was the production of textiles.

Before 1848 in general, industry of any sort was poorly developed in the region. In 1852, for example, there were only twenty steam engines in all of Galicia.[54] In 1852, there were only sixty-four kilometers of railroad track; only in 1862 did a line reach all the way to Lviv; and not until 1869 did a line reach the eastern borders of Galicia.[55] There is no way in which one could speak of an industrial revolution in Galicia. In the early nineteenth century, in the whole territory there were only forty small iron mills, utilizing poor iron ore, primarily for Hungary; there were twenty glass mills and twelve papermills; and from 1823 to 1845 eighteen small sugar refineries, all of which failed after a short time.[56]

In the period after 1848 the situation improved to some extent, but not in any breathtaking fashion. Until the end of the monarchy Galicia had a poorly developed coal industry; from 1870 to 1907 production increased from 0.2 to 1.4 million tons, but this was not even enough to cover domestic demand.[57] Under the reigns of Maria Theresa and Joseph II there were helpful attempts to promote industry, but after 1815 nothing was done. From 1815, in fact, until the 1850s, there appears to have been a steady decline ''reaching catastrophic proportions in the 1850s.'' At the end of the 1870s there was again some upward movement.[58] From the 1880s there was a rather large upswing in line with the conjuncture in the rest of the monarchy. In particular, from 1890 on there was sharp growth in several branches. A key element, of course, was the petroleum industry.[59] The great

---

[54] Bujak, ''Wirtschaftsgeschichte Galiziens,'' p. 15.

[55] Ibid.

[56] Ibid., p. 21.

[57] Madurowicz-Urbańska, ''Industrie Galiziens,'' p. 162.

[58] Ibid., p. 159.

[59] Cf. Janusz Bar, Andrzej Burzyński, Helena Madurowicz-Urbańska, and Krzysztof Zamorski, ''Le problème de la protoindustrialisation dans l'industrie pétrolière en Galicie—La Pologne autrichienne au XIXe siècle,'' in Deyon and Men-

upswing in petroleum production was, however, accompanied by declining world prices. From 1902 to 1911, there was almost a doubling in the value of production of the mines and mills in Galicia.[60] The sugar industry had some success in the nineteenth century but after the 1880s it decayed.[61]

The key element in the industrial structure of Galicia in the latter half of the nineteenth century until the end of the monarchy was light industry. The predominant force in industry, in fact, was still the proto-industrial peasant producer. Indeed, the most striking element in Galician industrial development is that it is primarily based on the smallest of scales. Even the petroleum industry, which one might think of as a highly organized central business, was in actuality made up, like most of the other branches in Galicia, of small producers. In 1907, for example, there was a total of 344 firms with a total labor force of 5,930, or an average of 17 workers per firm.[62] The entire industry was based on the landed estates. In Galicia, the landowners held the mineral rights and it was the landed proprietor who became the capitalist. The available labor was purely seasonal and was supplied by local peasants to supplement their income or by landless workers in the localities.[63] Several historians have recently argued that this industry differs sharply from normal proto-industrial activities in that it makes no impact on normal peasant family life.[64]

For industry as a whole the tiny enterprise predominated. Bujak worked with the industrial census of 1902 and remarked that "the poverty of Galician commerce is revealed in the number of enterprises that have only one employee. Such small firms make up two-thirds of all the firms and employ 30 percent of all industrial workers."[65] Further, 73 percent of the workers worked in firms of less than five employees.[66] With very few exceptions, almost every industrial branch was based on numerous miniscule producers. The data above

---

dels, eds., *La protoindustrialisation*.

[60] Madurowicz-Urbańska, "Industrie Galiziens," p. 166.

[61] Ibid., p. 163.

[62] Ibid., p. 167.

[63] Bar et al., "Le problème de la protoindustrialisation."

[64] Ibid.

[65] Franciszek Bujak, *Galicya*, vol. 1 (Lviv and Warsaw, 1908), p. 264.

[66] Ibid., p. 266.

pertain to all of Galicia, and data specifically for East Galicia are lacking, but conditions held equally in both areas; if anything, the size of enterprise was smaller in the east where only 30 percent of the industrial workers were to be found.[67]

As in most areas involved in the beginnings of industrialization, textiles appeared to play a leading role. The textile industry, as we have seen, was rooted in the large estate system and it continued to grow in the nineteenth century. Although we do not have enough studies to make any definitive judgments, it seems that there was a qualitative change from the earlier cottage industry in the beginnings of manufacture in this branch. Mariusz Kulczykowski has made several excellent studies of the proto-industrial textile industry of Galicia, centered in Andrychów. This region does not lie exactly within the purview of this study, but it is worthwhile looking at for a few moments. First of all, early theories of proto-industrialization maintained that manufacture began to come about as different regions specialized and as each built up a symbiotic relationship with the other. Thus, one area, generally poor in agricultural land, would expand its production of cottage-industry items such as textiles, handicraft, metalwork, and the like, and then sell these to well-located agricultural regions, which in turn would increase their own specialization in agriculture. In the process, it was noted that population density increased sharply in proto-industrial regions as the poor peasants could increase their family size because of the manufacture conducted at first in the home and later in small manufactories. Further studies maintained that it was not only in regions with poor land that such proto-industrial activities might take place, but they were also to be found in regions with short growing seasons or with gender-differentiated labor patterns, or within the same regions with such gender or time differences. It could be argued further that such proto-industrial activity could take place within the same household where there were enough family members to divide labor between agricultural and proto-industrial activities. That this was often the case in Galicia will be discussed later.

[67] Madurowicz-Urbańska, "Industrie Galiziens," p. 164.

* * *

What we find in Galicia is something of all three cases: the sharpest division was between East and West Galicia. In the west, particularly in the foothill regions of the mountains, one saw a rise in both textile production and population density, while the more agricultural regions of the east had less highly developed proto-industrial activities. That is to say, the cottage industry was ubiquitous, but did not reach the scale in the east that it apparently did in the west. It is in this context that one can understand our German traveler's being perplexed by the phenomenon and writing, "It is remarkable and wondrous that the density of the population and the fertility of the soil in different regions is in an inverse relationship, and that when one goes from east to west the soil gets worse and the population grows more dense."[68] Thus, one finds the most extensive developments of cottage industry producing for the market, or proto-industrialization, in the western areas of Galicia. Yet, one also finds such production throughout all of Galicia. The full extent of this cottage industry, based on peasant labor for the most part, has been discussed at some length by historians.[69] The pattern in Western Europe and in other parts of Poland, such as Łódz, had been for the transformation from cottage industry to small manufacturing firms to large-scale factories; and for the most part as the economy grew many aspects of the production process were still subcontracted to petty cottage industries, which continued to grow for some time, until they were gradually overwhelmed by the complete industrialization of their tasks. In Galicia, however, what we see is an expansion of the productive units of small scale; there is horizontal movement (expansion of the number of producers) but not

[68] Kohl, *Reisen*, p. 197.

[69] Jan Rutkowski, *Historia gospodarcza polski*, vol. 2 (Poznań, 1950), pp. 260–66; Bujak, *Galicya*, vol. 2, pp. 295–97, 488–49, passim; Bujak, "Wirtschaftsgeschichte Galiziens," pp. 8, 13; Mariusz Kulczykowski, "Le travail de manufacture dans les familles paysannes au XVIIIe siècle," Instituto Internazionale di Storia Economica, *Forme de evoluzione del lavoro in Europa: Secoli XIII/XVIII* (Prato, 1981), typescript; Kulczykowski, "Industrie paysanne et formation du marché national en Pologne au XVIIIe siècle," *Annales*, 24 (January–February 1969):61–69; Kulczykowski, *Andrychowski ośrodek płócienniczy w XVIII i XIX wieku* (Wrocław, 1982); Kulczykowski, *Chłopskie tkactwo bawełniane w ośrodku andrychowskim w XIX wieku* (Wrocław, 1976).

vertical movement (concentration of manufacture and technological growth). Attempts to build larger factories were overwhelmed by the competition from the peasant producers. The reasons for this were several and will be discussed in our analysis of the peasant economy.

Before doing that, however, it is necessary to note one other vital element in the economic landscape of East Galicia, and that is the role of the bourgeoisie, the middle class so often spoken of as the key to industrialization. In fact, several authors have argued that it was precisely the absence of a developed middle class with adequate capital that acted as a major obstacle to the development of large-scale industry. For the most part in East Galicia there was not what one distinguishes as a middle class in Western Europe. The reasons for this lie in the social structure which the nineteenth century inherited from the earlier times. From the fifteenth and sixteenth centuries the Polish nobility had received the right to hold peasants on the land and they had also legislated their own right to command all trade. As a result of this, there came the decline of the middle classes and of the cities, which to a great extent were made up of Germans and Jews. It became the practice of the nobility to maintain a strata of Jewish agents and helpers, themselves often in a semi-serf position, subject to the whims of their lords. This strata of the Jews became the rental agents, merchants, rent collectors, money lenders, and innkeepers with the tasks of lending the lord's money or selling the lord's liquor. As the Polish nobility moved into the area of East Galicia, many nobles established large estates and carried over the practice of utilizing their Jewish agents. Many of the Jews became managers of the estates for absentee landowners and ran the estates on the *arenda* system whereby various activities were farmed out, primarily to their fellow Jews, such as the clearing and selling of timber, trade in cattle, distilling, marketing of various products, and the like. As these Jews moved into the area so did their Jewish compatriots, often the impoverished artisans and craftsmen who had made up a goodly portion of the early city populations. In the course of the eighteenth and nineteenth centuries these people came to be an important part of the economic life of East Galicia and made up what could be called the middle class. With easy access to other Jews in other towns, with their tradition of literacy in a primarily illiterate peasant area, and with their general state of detachment from the land (by law for the most part), they became ideal candidates for middlemen between both peasant producers and nobles and the market. It should be noted that above all their lack of land and need of sustenance made for a strong impetus to engage in any activity which would sustain them.[70]

The small towns which developed with a small Christian middle class for the most part dealt with liquor, the keeping of inns, while the growing Jewish population engaged in business activities of every sort. As proto-industrial activities grew, and later as foreign goods came into the area, the Jews became the middlemen, extraordinaire. At the same time, Jewish population increased manifold. From the time of their freedom in 1848, in particular, the population increased sharply. In 1831, they made up 5.6 percent of the population in Galicia, in 1869, some 10.6 percent, and in 1890, some 11.6 percent.[71] As the population of East Galicia grew in great numbers the Jewish population grew apace, slightly declining at the beginning of the 1900s. Around 1890 the Jewish population of East Galicia reached almost 14 percent and declined to 12.5 percent in 1910.[72] The Jewish population had been ubiquitous since the incursions of the Poles in the seventeenth century and by the mid-nineteenth century, although some Jews became wealthy lessees of the great latifundia, most of the Jews were in an impoverished state, living in small market towns, the famous "Luftmenschen," living on air, from truck farming, petty trade, financial intermediation, and the charity of their fellow Jews. The conditions of the Jewish masses have been described by many people. Sometimes living six people in a small room, taking turns using the bed, the poverty was overwhelming. Kohl, in the 1840s, wrote that "there is no question that many cattle in Switzerland are better housed than these hundreds of thousands of the poor and impoverished Jews of Poland."[73]

---

[70] Cf. Nachum Gross, ed., *Economic History of the Jews* (New York, 1975), pp. 113–18, 125–28 et passim; Arcadius Kahan, "Notes on Jewish Entrepreneurship in Tsarist Russia," in Gregory Guroff and Fred V. Carstrensen, eds., *Entrepreneurship in Imperial Russia and the Soviet Union* (Princeton, 1983); Adam Skierko, "The Jews in Poland," *Polish Encyclopaedia*, vol. 2.

[71] Bujak, "Wirtschaftsgeschichte Galiziens," p. 16.

[72] *Polish Encyclopaedia*, vol. 2, p. 69.

[73] Kohl, *Reisen*, pp. 130ff. Also see Wolfgang Häusler, *Das Galizische Judentum in der Habsburgermonarchie* (Munich, 1979).

In Western Europe the middle classes were made up of people of various origins and various occupations; they played the role of marketers for peasant produce, or "factors," and eventually set up factories. In East Galicia, however, the intermediaries between the poor peasant makers of textiles and the market were either small peasants or the masses of poor Jewish dealers. By the turn of the century, the Jews in East Galicia made up over 94 percent of the commercial class. Neither of these groups had capital or the kind of outlook which moved them to do more than eke out a living on the margins of society. Thus, in effect, any efforts to build bigger and better factories could be undercut by the competition of the swarms of cheap peasant products sold by substinance-level merchants. As we said earlier, it is this "middle class" which is often seen as a key factor in the low capital and technological level of Galician industry. As Bujak put it, the key to the lack of growth of industry after 1848 was

> the lack of intelligent people with capital who could and wanted to organize industry on a capitalist basis. All the people who dealt with the textile industry in Galicia were uneducated and fundless peasants and Jews, who in the decisive moment lacked the ability to move; large-scale industrial enterprises were for the most part the property of large landholders.[74]

3. *Population*

Before dealing directly with the peasant household, it is necessary to see the household in the aggregated demographic setting. It can be seen from Tables 14.2 and 14.3 that the population of Galicia as a whole more than doubled in the nineteenth century, with the population growth remaining relatively slow from the end of the eighteenth century to the middle of the nineteenth century. From that point the process accelerates and the area goes from a population of 4.5 million to a little over 8 million in 1910. (See Table 14.2.) While we do not have separate data going back that far for East Galicia, we can see that population in that area increased from 3.45 million in 1869 to 5.3 million in 1910. (See Table 14.3.) In the thirty-year period from 1880 to

[74] Bujak, "Wirtschaftsgeschichte Galiziens," pp. 9, 16; cf. Madurowicz-Urbańska, "Industrie Galiziens," p. 172.

1910 the population of East Galicia grew by almost 40 percent, while that of West Galicia grew by some 27 percent. (See Table 14.3.) The overall index of growth in Table 14.3 shows that the growth rate did not differ a great deal from that of the western half of the monarchy, but the mere figures conceal the reality. In fact, this growth rate alone was quite different in its effects in the western areas with their economic upswing at the time than it was for the eastern sections where the economic advance was much less.[75] Further, the growth rates do not reveal the extent to which there was out-migration of the population. Between 1880 and 1910 some 843,880 people are noted as having emigrated.[76] If we consider that the population had reached eight million in 1910 this means that almost 10 percent of the population had emigrated in this period! One could only conjecture that the population, at the rate of growth current at that time, would have been very much larger had the migrants stayed behind. From the 1880s on we begin to see mass out-migration, which reached mass proportions with the beginnings of "migration fever" in the 1890s with the children of peasants either moving to other countries or parts of the empire or else migrating as a whole seasonally for work.[77]

If we examine the general demographic data we see that what was taking place in Galicia in the latter part of the nineteenth century was what has come to be called the demographic transition, a phase gone through by the various nations in the eighteenth and nineteenth centuries in Europe. The hallmarks of the transition were a decrease in the death rate followed by a decrease in the birth rate. In the gap of time between falling death rates and the decisions of the population to decrease births, there comes a sharp growth in population. The data for the death rate in Galicia shows a rate of 33.22 per thousand in 1829 and one of 23.26 in 1913, or a drop of ten points. In the same period the birth rate fell only slightly, although it did fall from 38.72 in 1829 to 36.06 in 1913, or a 2.6 point fall. In some areas the birth rate remained very high even in the early 1900s. Data for 1901 – 1910

---

[75] Bujak, "Wirtschaftsgeschichte Galiziens," p. 16.

[76] Leon Biegeleisen, *Przewód spadkowo—opiekuńczy a ustrój własności chłopskiej* (Lviv, 1914), p. 5.

[77] The Polish emigration rate was higher than that of the Ukrainians. Jan Rutkowski, *Historia gospodarcza*, vol. 2, p. 233.

Table 14.2

Population of Galicia, 1792–1910

Year	Population	Index (1851 = 100)
1792	3,504,600[a]	76.9
1820	3,893,445	85.5
1830	4,484,146	98.4
1840	4,797,243	105.3
1851	4,555,477	100.0
1860	4,855,919	106.6
1870	5,487,419	120.4
1880	5,965,323	130.9
1890	6,607,816	145.0
1900	7,315,939	160.6
1910	8,022,126	176.1

[a]excludes Cracow.

Source: 1792–1840, *Statistiche Tafeln, 1825–1845; 1851–1910, Österreichisches Statistisches Handbuch*, 1882–1910.

show that in thirty-five of the districts of East Galicia the birth rate was higher than the national average, reaching 40 to 50 per thousand in some areas.[78] However, the death rate was also higher in East than in West Galicia.[79]

[78] Calculated from data in *Tafeln zur Statistik der Österreichischen Monarchie* (Vienna, 1829–1865); *Statistisches Jahrbuch* (Vienna, 1872–1881); and *Österreichisches Statistisches Handbuch für die im Reichsrat Vertretenen Königreiche und Länder* (Vienna, 1882–1918).

[79] *Polish Encyclopaedia*, vol. 2, pp. 271, 326.

Table 14.3

Population of East and West Galicia

| | East Galicia | | West Galicia | | Austrian Total | |
Year	Population	Index*	Population	Index	Population	Index
1869	3,450,195	90.0			20,394,980	92.1
1880	3.834,707	100.0	2,103,754	100.0	22,144,244	100.0
1890	4,293,573	111.9	2,285,262	108.6	23,895,413	107.9
1900	4,796,875	125.1	2,487,828	118.2	26,150,708	118.1
1910	5,317,158	139.0	2,666,991	126.8	28,571,934	129.0

*1880 = 100.

Sources: West Galicia: *Polish Encyclopaedia*, 2:507; East Galicia: *Polish Encyclopaedia*, 2:530; Austria: Birgit Bolognese-Leuchtenmüller, *Bevölkerungsentwicklung und Berufsstruktur, Gesundheits-und Fürsorgewesen in Österreich, 1750–1918* (Vienna, 1978), pt. 2, p. 1.

The population generally was located in the countryside; in 1900 over 82 percent of the Galician population was listed as rural.[80] At the same time, the density of population in the countryside became great, higher than in any other area of the monarchy, and in fact higher than in any other area of Europe. While at the time of the partitions there had been already a population density of 32 per square kilometer, the density reached 102 per square kilometer by 1914.[81] What all these figures demonstrate is that although there was a major increase in the production of foodstuffs, there was an even greater growth in population. While an almost quadrupling of the population since the partitions could be supported by the land, the margin appears to have been almost reached by the end of the nineteenth century with vast rural over-population on miniscule holdings.

[80] Biegeleisen, *Przewód*, p. 5.
[81] Madurowicz-Urbańska, "Industrie Galiziens," p. 158.

The Peasant Household and Economy

1. Strategies of the Peasant Household

In his study of the inheritance practices of the Galician peasant, K. Kowalski wrote that to understand the customs "first and foremost one has to know the peasant soul, his way of thinking, the point of view from which he is best accustomed to operate, and to calculate the things that matter to him most."[82] It is precisely our contention here that it is within this peasant soul, as it views the parameters of its field of action, that the choices are made which determine the fate of the much larger economy of which we have been speaking. In other words, the peasant is faced with certain choices, delimited by the constraints of the legal structure and the economic conditions of the moment. Within these limitations, these parameters, the peasant acts with certain goals in mind. His means of confronting the world, his instrument of operation is his family—or better, his household economy. By utilizing the members of his family he may obtain his goals, or at least attempt to do so.

The hypothesis we are putting forth here is that the peasant has two primary goals: first, the maintenance and expansion of his property for his family and for future generations; secondly, the welfare of his family at given stages in the life cycle of the family. This welfare is defined by economic constraints at some periods and by traditions, particularly inheritance patterns, at others. What is crucial is that a tension emerges between these two goals. The aim of expanding property comes into conflict with immediate economic needs at one stage of the family life cycle, and with traditional inheritance patterns at another stage. The manner in which the peasant family copes with this tension in turn affects the manner in which the peasant household interacts with the outside world. In this way we begin with a view of the nature of peasant strategies and go on to evaluate the effects of such strategies on economic growth and the beginnings of industrialization.

---

[82] Karol Kowalski, "Prawne zwyczaje w zakresie wyposażenia dzieci i dziedziczenia oraz sprawa podzielności małych gospodarstw wiejskich w byłym zaborze austrijackim," in Karol Kowalski, Stefan M. Grzybowski, Konstanty Grzybowski, and Rudolf Karpiniec, *Zwyczaje spadkowe włościan w Polsce*, pt. 1, *Zwyczaje spadkowe włościan w województwach południowych* (Warsaw, 1928), p. 5.

The internalized lessons from his culture over the generations have made the peasant feel that at all costs he must hold on to the land; it is the source of his sustenance, his security in old age, and his status in the community. He has also internalized the view that the family comes above all else; he must provide for his family and hold them together as an entity. A. V. Chayanov has posited that the chief motive force of the peasant's activity is provided by the needs of the family at different stages in the life cycle of that family.[83] We agree with this hypothesis and point out that the strategies of the peasant change according to the stages in the family life cycle.

We would go even further, though, and argue that not only are the needs of the family at an immediate time operating on the peasant's decisions, but he must weigh these against future costs or benefits. It has been argued that a key goal of the family is maximization of the holdings and income of the family. In their classic study of the Polish peasant, Thomas and Znaniecki have noted the chief aims of the peasant family. They wrote that "under the old family system the normal tendency of the peasant was to have as many goods as possible pass from a lower to a higher economic category, to turn all property into land and as much as possible of income into property."[84] The second item on their list is worth noting—the idea of turning as much property into land as possible. The peasant is not interested in leaving the land, and in our Galician case is often desirous of having his children continue to work the land. A Polish peasant writes to his son in America in 1913: "We are very glad that you keep so much poultry and a pig; it is as if you had a farm. When you learn to keep poultry and pigs, and when your children grow up, then you will go to a farm."[85] In the Galician context we are describing it was obviously imperative that the children be brought up to be peasants, continuers of the family holdings and traditions, not only because of the views inherent in peasant thought but because of the lack of almost any alternatives. An exception was the sending of some children abroad, but this was often done as a strategy to hold the rest of the family

---

[83] A. V. Chayanov, *The Theory of Peasant Economy* (Homewood, Ill., 1966), pp. xxiii, 53ff.

[84] William I. Thomas and Florian Znaniecki, *The Polish Peasant in Europe and America*, vol. 4 (New York, 1920), p. 12.

[85] Ibid., vol. 1, p. 390.

together. When a peasant wanted to pay off some children in goods or money in order to maintain his holding at its current size after his death, the children balked at the practice and preferred land.[86] Even in the 1970s in Galicia children of peasants were quite reluctant to lose their ties to the land.[87]

If we go along with our working hypothesis that the primary goals of the peasant family are the maintenance and expansion of the family land and the welfare of the family, as defined by both economic need and inheritance patterns, then one can immediately see that a tension can arise between these two goals. This cannot be stressed any too strongly, because this tension is at the heart of the peasant strategies in Galicia as we see them. As we have said, the peasant goals are a constant, imbued over generations into the peasant's mentality. At the same time, there are the other variables at work: economic, legal, and institutional constraints. These may change or they may remain static, but in any case they delimit the peasant's room to maneuver. In everyday life the peasant is faced with the problem, on the one hand, of feeding his family and at the same time providing for its future welfare. The way in which the peasant deals with the tension between present and future needs is very much like that described by A. V. Chayanov and Theodor Shanin for Russia, but with a distinct Polish variation. Chayanov and Shanin noted that the peasants adjust the size of their holdings according to the life cycle of the peasant family.[88] This, of course, is obvious in the Russian experience where the land was periodically repartitioned as new work units, new couples were added to the family. The same kind of repartition quite possibly took place when the peasants of Poland first pooled their holdings and began to work the land together. We have already spoken of the communal system with its repartitional tenure which was common in the later Middle Ages. At the time we are discussing here, however, the communal work had been generally dropped, except on the large

---

[86] Kowalski, "Prawne zwyczaje," p. 64.

[87] Lucjan Kocik, "A Note on the Custom of 'Paying Off' on Family Farms in Poland," in Norman Long, ed., *Family and Work in Rural Societies: Perspectives on Non-Wage Labour* (London and New York, 1984), pp. 136ff.

[88] Cf. Chayanov, *Theory of Peasant Economy*, pp. 245ff. and Theodor Shanin, *The Awkward Class* (Oxford, 1972), pp. 115–21.

estates, but the same strategy appears to have taken place. The Polish peasant, too, adjusted his holdings to his family's size.

*   *   *

The tension we speak of worked in the following way. It was in the peasant's interest to expand his holdings and to gain as much income as possible. It was also imperative to have a number of children: children would help run the farm in the short run and in the long run would be his and his wife's sole source of support. As the children came of age the problem became one of providing sustenance for them in their own lives. It became necessary to establish the children on their own holdings or to provide the girls with dowries. In this case it often became necessary to either give land away to the children or to sell it. The problem was, then, how to maintain and even enlarge the family holding and at the same time provide for the total family entity in the future. The usual solution to this problem was for the peasant householder in his early years to accrue as much property as possible and then to let go of his acquisitions in later life. Stefan Kieniewicz has described the peasant's family life cycle as follows:

> When he came of age, the son of a villager received from his parents two to three acres of land, and his wife's dowry was another acre or two. By means of hard labor, thrift, and outside work, he managed to purchase more land, and then he inherited still more after the death of his parents and in-laws. His holding attained the maximum size when he was nearing fifty. Now his children were growing up and he felt obliged to 'write off' some acres for them before he died. He began his career as a smallholder; he was a middle-sized owner for a short time; he died as a smallholder. And most probably he would leave each of his children a little less land than he had inherited himself.[89]

The peasant strategy, then, was indeed to adjust the land size to his family life cycle. The description by Kieniewicz leaves a bit out, particularly as to the Galician regions, and we must now examine the particularities of that region, the manner in which the peasant strategy was carried out, and the effects on the entire community.

---

[89] Kieniewicz, *The Emancipation of the Polish Peasantry*, p. 212.

2. Peasant Household in East Galicia

The pattern of peasant life differed in Galicia from that of other parts of Poland and it may be that this fact offers a key to understanding the particular and laggard nature of industrialization in Galicia. A combination of laws and peasant customs combined to lock the peasant economy and thus, the economy of all Galicia into a low level of development.

The most blatant difference between Galicia and other regions in Poland was the small size of the average landholding. From 1819 to 1901 there took place a process whereby the average size of holding declined markedly, to say the least. In 1819 about 27 percent of all holdings were under two hectares; by 1901, over 40 percent of all holdings were this small size (about five acres). In the same period, 1819 to 1901, holdings from two to five hectares increased from 25 percent to over 37 percent of all holdings. (See Table 14.4.) What this meant was that roughly 80 percent of all holdings were under five hectares (or twelve acres).[90] A major cause of this is to be found in the legal structure of the various areas of Poland. In the Russian-occupied area the normal size of holding for an estate could not by law be under six *morgs* (a *morg* being 1.4 acres). In the Prussian area there was strict enforcement of the concept of *Erbhof*; large estates were to be transferred from generation to generation. In Galicia, on the other hand, both peasant customs and, for a time, the law worked to fragment the holdings.[91]

In other areas of partitioned Poland there tended to be a polarization in the size of estates over time, with the growth of both a number of very small holdings and larger consolidated holdings. In Galicia, however, the pattern was not one of consolidation or of polarization; as the data for the size of holdings reveals, there was only a tendency for the increase of very small holdings, either too small to farm or barely marginal. The size of peasant holdings tended to become equalized as the large estates found themselves in difficulty toward the latter part of the century and began to sell off parcels to the peasants. Although in Galicia from 1848 to 1868 a law was enacted to enforce

[90] Biegeleisen, *Przewód*, pp. 25f.
[91] Danuta Markowska, *Rodzina w społeczności wiejskiej—ciągłość i zmiana* (Warsaw, 1976), p. 23.

Table 14.4

Size of Peasant Landholdings in Galicia

	1819	1859	1882	1901
Size of Holding:	*Percentage of Holdings:*			
Under 2 hectares	27.4	35.4	59.6	42.2
2 – 5	24.9	24.66	24.35	37.4
5 – 10	26.2	23.67	11.9	15.1
10 – 20	14.36	11.65	3.0	3.7
20 – 50	6.48	4.32	1.0	0.8

Source: Leon Biegeleisen, *Przewód spadkowo—opiekunczy a ustrój własności chłopskiej* (Lviv, 1914), p. 2.

primogeniture with the land going to the oldest son, the law was ignored and was finally repealed.[92]

There were five different civil law codes operating in Poland with respect to laws of property, marriage and inheritance.[93] In actual fact, however, it is quite necessary to distinguish between law, customs and actual practices. In most cases, the law, unless strictly enforced, was secondary to peasant customs, and these in turn varied from region to region. In practice the individual peasants appear to have followed the regional usages. It is probably no accident that most Polish works dealing with inheritance have in the title the term "inheritance customs" rather than "inheritance laws."

Data on the exact nature of the peasant family are sparse. From what little we know it appears that although one hears of large extended patriarchal families in some of the mountainous regions, like the *zadruga* of the south Slavs, for the most part we are dealing with

[92] Ibid., p. 22; Kowalski, "Prawne zwyczaje," pp. 68–71, 77.

[93] Markowska, *Rodzina*, p. 22; Arthur R. Nitzburg, "Polish Systems of Inheritance," *The Polish Review* 12 (Winter 1967):12.

either multi-generational (stem) families or nuclear families.[94] Among the Ukrainians, as among the Russians, the practice upon marriage was generally to bring the bride into the wider circle of the family. Among the Poles, however, each newly married couple tended to establish their own living quarters and their own new families.[95] With respect to the general inheritance patterns of the two groups, however, there appears to have been no difference.[96]

Much has been written of the so-called European marriage pattern, or more properly the northwest European pattern, in which the average age of marriage was over twenty-three for women and twenty-six for men, and in which a high proportion of the population never married. In Galicia, however, this pattern was not followed by any means. What one finds here is the "eastern European marriage pattern." In 1828 over 44 percent of the men and 72 percent of the women married before the age of twenty-four. At the same time, 48 percent of the women married before the age of twenty. The rates fluctuated throughout the century and generally went up, especially for men; in 1903, 18 percent of the men married before the age of twenty-four as did 60 percent of the women, with roughly 30 percent of the women marrying under the age of twenty.[97]

Wincenty Styś has made an excellent study of twenty peasant villages in Galicia in the period from 1787 to 1931.[98] In the course of these studies he has provided some extremely useful data and hypotheses. Styś has demonstrated fairly conclusively for the data for this area, as well as from a larger number of regions, that there was higher fertility on large holdings than on small ones. An exception to this were the holdings of peasants with little or no land who were able to work on large estates or supplement their income through cottage industry or handicraft, i.e., our typical proto-industrial case.[99] In effect, the peasants with larger holdings assumed that they could have

---

[94] Cf. Kohl, *Reisen*, p. 34.

[95] Thomas and Znaniecki, *The Polish Peasant*, vol. 4, p. 27.

[96] Kowalski, "Prawne zwyczaje," 65.

[97] See fn. 78.

[98] See Wincenty Styś, *Współzależność rozwoju rodziny chłopskiej i jej gospodarstwa* (Wrocław, 1959); idem, *Rozdrabnianie gruntów chłopskich w byłym zaborze austriackim od roku 1787 do 1931* (Lviv, 1934); idem, *Wpływ uprzemysłowienia na ustrój rolny* (Lviv, 1936).

[99] Styś, *Współzależność rozwoju rodziny chłopskiej*, pp. 530ff.

more children. As the children grew up and were provided with land, the size of the average holdings decreased. Thus, one saw something of a self-regulating process whereby, as in the description given earlier of the average peasant's life course, the peasant family kept returning to a small holding.

Styś enumerates the average size of families in his villages at the beginning of the 1900s. Mortality appeared much higher for landless peasants, who generally had 2.89 children surviving; peasants with holdings from about one-half to five hectares ranged from an average of 4 to 5.46 children, while peasant holdings of five to ten hectares averaged 6.28 to 7.92 children; peasants with holdings over ten hectares had an average of 9 or 10 children.[100] (See Tables 14.5 and 14.6).

All of the children had to be provided for and the holding kept intact. The vehicle for doing this was the pattern of inheritance, and because of the importance of passing on the land, on the one hand, and providing for numerous children, on the other, the inheritance system took on great importance. The system of inheritance, in fact, was one of the most important, if not the most important means by which the peasant directed his family's fortunes.

3. *Inheritance Patterns*

In 1868 the Sejm enacted a law protecting the right of peasants freely to divide their land, thus honoring the traditional custom and practice of the Galician peasantry.[101] As we have already seen, the system of partible inheritance was a major cause of the perpetual fragmentation of the peasant holdings.

The extent of these holdings is shown in Tables 14.4 and 14.7. From the peasant's point of view the division was perfectly logical. As Bujak wrote:

> Since at least the end of the eighteenth century the peasantry in general has profited in full from the free division of their land and it is neces-sary to recognize that at the present time the peasantry does profit from it, because they must keep their children at home to help them [the

---

[100] Ibid., p. 535.
[101] Bujak, *Galicya*, vol. 1, p. 251.

Table 14.5
Model Illustrating the Artificial Increase of Average Fertility
Due to Fragmentation of Holdings and Spread of Birth Control

Year	Average Size of Farm in Hectares	Groups of Farms According to their Size in Hectares							All	Specification
		0–1	1–2	2–3	3–4	4–5	5–7	7–10		
1880	3.41	3	8	13	12	6	5	3	50	Mothers
		6.32	6.32	6.32	6.32	6.32	6.32	6.32	6.32	Average Fertility
		18.96	50.56	82.16	75.84	37.92	31.60	18.96	316.00	Number of Children
1890	3.14	4	9	14	11	6	4	2	50	Mothers
		5.47	5.47	5.47	5.47	5.47	5.47	5.47	5.47	Average Fertility
		21.88	49.23	76.58	60.17	32.82	21.88	10.94	273.50	Number of Children
1900	2.85	5	10	15	11	5	3	1	50	Mothers
		3.95	3.95	3.95	3.95	3.95	3.95	3.95	3.95	Average Fertility
		19.75	39.50	59.25	43.45	19.75	11.85	3.95	197.50	Number of Children
All	3.13	12	27	42	34	17	12	6	150	Mothers
		5.05	5.16	5.10	5.28	5.32	5.44	5.64	5.25	Average Fertility
		60.59	139.29	217.99	179.46	90.49	65.33	33.85	787.00	Number of Children
Average Birth-year of Women		1891.7	1890.7	1890.5	1889.7	1889.4	1888.3	1886.7	1890.0	

Source: Wincenty Styś, *Współzależność rozwoju rodziny chłopskiej i jej gospodarstwa* (Wrocław, 1959), p. 534.

Table 14.6
Fertility of Mothers Born between 1855–1880

No.	Specification	Landless	Size of Peasant Farms in Hectares										Total
			0–0.5	0.5–1	1–2	2–3	3–4	4–5	5–7	7–10	10–15	Over 15	
1.	Number of Mothers	9	13	23	47	53	10	13	18	13	1	1	201
2.	Ave. Year of Birth	1872	1875	1875	1876	1875	1875	1873	1875	1874	1875	1876	1875
3.	Ave. Age at Marriage (Years)	31	25	25	25	24	23	23	22	20	23	18	24
4.	Ave. Period of Potential Fertility (Years)	14	20	20	20	21	22	22	23	25	22	27	21
5.	Ave. Period of Actual Fertility (Years)	9	15	15	17	18	19	19	20	23	16	29	18
6.	Actual Fertility as Percentage of Potential Fertility	66.4	75.3	76.8	86.2	82.1	88.6	86.4	88.0	91.6	72.7	107.4	83.7
7.	Ave. Age of Mother at Birth of Last Child	40	40	40	42	41	42	42	42	43	39	47	41
8.	Ave. No. of Children Born	3.89	5.46	5.30	6.10	6.57	6.40	7.54	7.83	9.08	9.00	10.00	6.48
9.	Ave. No. of Children Deceased	1.00	1.31	1.22	1.21	1.57	1.00	2.08	1.55	1.16	—	2.00	1.37
10.	Ave. No. of Children Surviving	2.89	4.15	4.08	4.89	5.00	5.40	5.46	6.28	7.92	9.00	8.00	5.11
11.	Child Mortality per 1000	257	239	230	199	238	156	275	200	127	—	200	212
12.	Ave. No. of Children Born per Year of Potential Fertility	0.28	0.27	0.26	0.30	0.31	0.29	0.34	0.35	0.37	0.41	0.37	0.31
13.	Ave. No. of Children Born per Year of Actual Fertility	0.43	0.36	0.34	0.35	0.37	0.33	0.40	0.39	0.40	0.56	0.34	0.37

Source: Styś, *Współzależność rozwoju rodziny*, p. 535.

movement to the cities does not halt in the slightest the growth of the agricultural population] and the peasants profit from their help on the land until they come of age when the peasant must provide them with certain land to which they have already earned the right through their labor. In a word there is no other means to provide a living; it is not possible for the peasant to endow one of his children to the disadvantage of another.[102]

The basis of the laws and of peasant practice was to ensure that the children would have agricultural land. In some areas there was a tendency to favor either the son or daughter, generally based on whether it was wished to continue patrilineal or matrilineal control over the property. In one village, rather than letting land leave the male line, it was passed on to brothers and to daughters, but the normal practice was to pass the land on to the eldest son.[103] Although there was partible inheritance the strong tendency was to try and keep the land together. In practice this was not always possible because it was felt that the peasant must be fair to all his children.

If the peasant had children who were not yet of age the practice was to divide the land and property equally among them. If some of them were of age the peasant made every effort to make sure that the land was held by one child, usually the eldest son, and the other children were "paid off," either in parcels of land or in property. In some regions, particularly among the German population, the practice widely seen in central and northern Europe was used. At a given age the parents would retire and hand the land over to the eldest son; commonly, this took place at the time that the son married. The son then arranged for the care of the parents for the rest of their lives and made arrangements to "pay off" his siblings. In cases where there was no will the court generally made one of the children, again usually the eldest son, the executor who would gain the holding and pay off his siblings.[104]

[102] Ibid., vol. 1, p. 497.
[103] Kowalski, "Prawne zwyczaje," pp. 60–62.
[104] Ibid., pp. 61–64.

Table 14.7

Relative Size of Peasant Holdings in 1902 (percentage)

Size of Holding in Hectares	Galicia	West Galicia	East Galicia
up to 0.5	6.9	7.4	6.5
0.5 – 1	12.4	11.7	12.6
1 – 2	23.3	22.5	23.5
2 – 5	37.5	37.5	37.2
5 – 10	15.0	15.5	14.4
10 – 20	3.85	4.0	3.7
20 – 50	0.8	0.85	0.7
50 – 100	0.25	0.28	0.2
100+	0.52	0.59	0.34

Source: Bujak, *Galicya*, 3:245.

The practice of contracting with the parents to give them food, a bit of land to work and housing was often a bitter pill for the peasant couple to take, but custom forced them to do it. The peasants went to the notary to legalize the contract and it was said that the father went to the notary on wings but returned crawling in the mud. The shock of having to give up control of the holding is shown poignantly in a letter from a peasant to his absent children. The peasant had just given over the holding to a son. He wrote:

> So, dear children, work and economize as much as you can for your old age, because old people suffer misery. May our Lord God make you happy and bless you with your children; and don't forget us, *but speak to us as long as we are alive.*[105]

What we have described here sounds quite logical and rational, but in practice the peasant did not necessarily make such rational calculations. In giving the land away, for example, it was rare that the

[105] Thomas and Znaniecki, *The Polish Peasant*, vol. 1, p. 393 (my emphasis).

peasant would estimate its worth. The same was true for the many small parcels of land which were used to pay off children. The result was that there were a great many quarrels and lawsuits about the inheritance settlements.[106]

The peasant felt very strongly, again through the iron guidance of custom, that he must deal equitably with his children. This practice is still engrained in country life in Poland. In his study of peasant attitudes and practices in present-day Galicia, Lucjan Kocik, a Polish sociologist writing in 1981, noted that "At the present, since farms below 8 ha cannot legally be subdivided, the custom of paying off has become the major form of regulating intra-familial obligations, despite the fact that the practice is actually legally forbidden."[107]

The Peasant Household and the Overall Economy

The peasant family sought more income and more property so that it could both maintain the landed holding intact and pay off the children who did not remain on the land. To do this, the family adopted what might be called a strategy of diversification.[108] The family utilized its members in a number of ways to bring in needed income; various members of the family might be sent out to work seasonally in Prussia, to work on neighboring estates, to sell livestock, to work with handicraft or textile making. In short, the family was widely utilized in a number of activities, some of which were and some not of an agricultural nature. Toward the end of the century, of course, income was obtained on a vast scale from emigrants' remittances. Some 42 percent of holdings had people working on other holdings.[109]

This was a traditional approach by the peasant family, as is described by Kohl:

---

[106] Cf. ibid., vol. 4, pp. 14ff; Bujak, *Galicya*, vol. 1, p. 199.

[107] Kocik, "A Note on the Custom of 'Paying Off'," p. 136.

[108] See Richard L. Rudolph, "Family Structure and Proto-Industrialization in Russia," *Journal of Economic History* 40, no. 1 (March 1980):115.

[109] Tibor Kolossa, "Statistische Untersuchung der sozialen Struktur der Agrarbevölkerung in den Ländern der österreichisch-ungarischen Monarchie (um 1900)," in *Die Agrarfrage in der Österreichisch-Ungarischen Monarchie 1900–1918* (Bucharest, 1965), p. 166.

With more or less variations, one finds the [patriarchal family] among the Ruthenians. The father holds the sceptre of the family; everything is guided by him, even the activities of the women. He divides the work according to the abilities of his son and step-daughter; his most capable son inherits the household. Everyone obeys his orders, and his mere appearance is enough to cut off the activities of the family. One son must take care of trading the livestock, a second work as a carter in distant regions, and if there are more sons at hand, these must either work or trade with ironware or in other ways earn their way. One daughter helps the mother with the housework, while others work with the spindle, weave or spin linen for sale.[110]

In this manner the peasant family interacted with the economy at large and it was in this manner that proto-industrialization took place. Furthermore, this diversification permitted a larger population to exist than otherwise would have on the land available. What is striking, and indeed almost astonishing, is that by the practice of adjusting the size of the land to the family needs at various stages of the family life cycle and by utilizing family labor outside the holding, the Galician peasant population on the land remained remarkably stable! If we compare the size of the population from 1890 to 1910 with the percentage active in agriculture this is evident. (See Table 14.8.) What we find is that although the general population increased from 6.6 million to 8 million, the number actively engaged in agriculture only went up from 5.1 million to 5.8 million! At the same time, Bujak lists the land held by the peasants as 4.5 million hectares in 1852 and 4.9 million in 1889, again a striking stability.[111] If one adds to this the fact that the average size of holdings tended to remain relatively stable, although the parceling increased as bits of land were bought and sold, it is clear that the peasant system was much more static than is apparent at first glance. The peasant had a strategy for keeping holdings intact, meeting family needs—and the system worked.

[110] Kohl, *Reisen*, p. 34.
[111] Bujak, *Galicya*, 253.

Table 14.8

Stability of the Galician Agricultural Population

Year	Population (millions)	Percentage Actively engaged in Agriculture	Population in culture (millions)
1890	6.6	77.2	5.1
1900	7.3	76.6	5.6
1910	8.0	73.0	5.8

Source: Kolossa, "Statistische Untersuchung," pp. 137, 139.

With respect to the effect of this policy on the economy at large, it meant that a low level, non-expanding economy was maintained. The large population on the land kept purchasing power at a minimum and kept repeating the cycle. Instead of consolidating larger holdings and building up the technology, the capital that was obtained and the land that was gained was dissipated anew with each succeeding generation. The result of the ability of the peasant household to exploit itself, so to speak, meant that it could readily meet the competition of factory production of many items. Kulczykowski argued that the peasant handicraft and cottage methods of production had distinct advantages over factory production The factories needed fresh capital, new technology and technological expertise, and good markets. The peasant, on the other hand, did not need capital, had long experience with low level techniques, and could operate in local and traditional markets.[112] There is, indeed, an analogous situation here to that of Russia where the factory system in the eighteenth century had great difficulty in competition with peasant producers.[113]

[112] Kulczykowski, *Chłopskie tkactwo bawełniane*, p. 150.
[113] M. I. Tugan-Baranovskii, *Russkaia fabrika v proshlom i nastoiashchem* (Moscow, 1922), p. 166.

Kulczykowski remarks that "market demand also played a considerable role in the maintenance of peasant weaving centers duing the period when all of the features of de-industrialization were manifest. As long as there were areas of poor communication in Europe, which were not reached by factory products and where a consumer market with a traditional structure of needs and tastes existed, peasant weaving centers had their own, although increasingly limited, ready markets."[114]

Kulczykowski also notes something that is profoundly important—the manner in which the peasant-based industry holds back industrialization. He argues that:

> since the weaving centers were almost always located in over-populated areas, they were characterized by a large and ever-increasing supply of cheap labor. Thus, dispersed weaving without capital investment in machines and buildings brought high profits. The surplus and low cost of labour conditioned the mode of production. The maintenance of family production by the same factors led to a total cessation of technical progress in the field of weaving. The thought of technical changes in peasant family production was totally alien to the peasant weaver.[115]

It would be helpful to compare the Galician case with that of China where historians ask a similar question as to the reason for the lack of movement from handicraft and cottage industry on to manufacture. For China, too, it has been argued that the answer lies partly in the family-centered peasant holding wherein the rising population is absorbed by the family itself, working on its small holdings with zero marginal productivity rather than leaving the land. Kang Chao, in discussing the laggard nature of early Chinese growth, has argued that there is an important difference between family production and a small manufactory. The family production techniques hold back innovation while the beginning manufactories, what he calls "handicraft factories," promote industrialization:

---

[114] Mariusz Kulczykowski, "The Genesis and Historical Significance of Domestic Manufacture in Central and Eastern Europe" (typescript), p. 14.
[115] Ibid., p. 13.

Scale economy is another important factor. This is definitely in favor of handicraft factories over family production for many goods. Handicraft factories can practice division of labor, use more productive techniques and equipment, and can more effectively train workers for better skill. Unless the benefits of scale economies are offset by high transportation cost, family production tends to shy away from those production lines. . . . Handicraft factories are usually more dynamic in the sense that they have the potential to breed new technology. [In the case of family production] the most unfortunate thing is that the existence of a large quantity of redundant labor has the tendency to dispel a production institution that is most dynamic and viable for breeding new technology in the pre-industrialization framework. The existence of redundant labor can also resist the importation of advanced technology from outside. Therefore, over-population in a country would inevitably delay the process of industrialization.[116]

What one sees, indeed, in East Galicia is just such a case in which labor reaches a point where its marginal productivity is zero and where such labor undercuts the building of factories and furnishes a limited market for industrial goods in general. The working hypothesis offered here is that the mentality of the peasant household was basically responsible for holding back the industrialization of Galicia. The peasant family worked toward its goals with a set of strategies. These included adjusting the land to the size of the family through what was, in effect, partible inheritance and the utilization of family members in various cottage industry and by-employment endeavours. These strategies were in turn shaped by custom and tradition as these influenced the way in which the family faced the economic realities—too little land and little non-agricultural employment. The family did succeed in fulfilling its goals, but the methods used worked against any improvement in productivity. The peasant family, then, was the unwitting architect of its own poverty.

East Galicia, then, appears to fit the description of "de-industrialization," as developed in the literature on early industrialization. De-industrialization is proto-industrialization without concentration. It is the process of the multiplication of small producers horizontally, so to speak, rather than vertically. Small producers expand until

---

[116] K. Chao, "Textile Production in Traditional China," in Deyon and Mendels, eds., *La protoindustrialisation*, p. 3.

the point where more efficient producers in other areas drive them from the market; this process often leaves the region less industrial than it was before the process of proto-industrialization began.[117]

This brief essay can in no way do justice to a picture of the economic development in the region. This excursion may, however, invoke some fascinating questions for further research. The inheritance patterns of the other regions of Poland and the Ukraine must be examined to evaluate their influence on cottage production and industrialization. Furthermore, years of research on industrialization in various countries has made us aware of the great variety of paths toward industrialization. In the various cases when one human resource is lacking another seems to appear as a functional substitute. In one place we find peasant cottage industry as a source of expansion, in another middlemen and bourgeois entrepreneurs, and in others either serfs themselves or nobles step in. What is intriguing in Galicia is that neither the peasants, nor the Jews, *qua* middle-class, nor the nobles fulfilled this role. Finally, although a great deal of stress is given in this essay to peasant family strategies, it would be unreasonable to assume a mono-causal view of these strategies as the only hindrances to growth; in point of fact, the strategies must be viewed first and foremost within the framework of the so-called real sector of the economy. What, indeed, were the causes of the economic parameters within which the peasant family was limited in its room to maneuver? The discussion here may point to the key role of the peasant household in economic development in the region. In this light, East Galicia may be seen, not as an economic backwater, but as a vitally rich area for the examination of the unfolding of the life of the peasant family in its complex interaction between custom and economic reality.

[117] Tilly, "Flows of Capital and Forms of Industry," p. 15.

Index

List of Contributors

Boris P. Balan
Encyclopedia of Ukraine
University of Toronto
Toronto, Ontario

Ralph S. Clem
Department of International Relations
Florida International University
Miami, Florida

Peter B. Golden
Department of History
Rutgers University
Newark, New Jersey

Patricia Herlihy
Department of History
Brown University
Providence, Rhode Island

Robert E. Jones
Department of History
University of Massachusetts – Amherst
Amherst, Massachusetts

Daniel H. Kaiser
Department of History
Grinnell College
Grinnell, Iowa

I. S. Koropeckyj
Department of Economics
Temple University
Philadelphia, Pennsylvania

Bohdan Krawchenko
Canadian Institute of Ukrainian Studies
University of Alberta
Edmonton, Alberta

Leonid Melnyk
Department of History
Kiev State University
Kiev, Ukrainian SSR

Thomas S. Noonan
Department of History
University of Minnesota
Minneapolis, Minnesota

Richard L. Rudolph
Department of History
University of Minnesota
Minneapolis, Minnesota

Martin C. Spechler
Department of Economics
Indiana University—Purdue University at Indianapolis
Indianapolis, Indiana

Carol B. Stevens
Department of History
Colgate University
Hamilton, New York

Stephen Velychenko
Chair of Ukrainian Studies
University of Toronto

 **Harvard Ukrainian Research Institute**
Selected Publications

The Ukrainian Economy: Achievements, Problems, Challenges. Ed. by I. S. Koropeckyj. Harvard Series in Ukrainian Studies. Clothbound, ISBN 0-916458-51-2. Paperback, ISBN 0-916458-57-1. 1992.

Selected Contributions of Ukrainian Scholars to Economics. Ed. by I. S. Koropeckyj. Harvard Ukrainian Research Institute, Sources and Documents Series. Clothbound, ISBN 0-916458-10-5. 1984.

Republic vs. Autocracy. Poland-Lithuanian and Russia, 1686–1697. Andrzej S. Kamiński. Harvard Series in Ukrainian Studies. Clothbound, ISBN 0-916458-45-8. Paperback 916458-49-0. 1993.

The Lords' Jews. Magnate-Jewish Relations in the Polish-Lithuanian Commonwealth during the 18th Century. M. J. Rosman. Harvard Series in Ukrainian Studies (Copublished with the Center for Jewish Studies, Harvard University, Texts and Studies Series). 2nd printing. Clothbound, ISBN 0-916458-18-0. Paperback, ISBN 0-916458-47-4. 1991.

Meletij Smotryc'kyj. David A. Frick. Harvard Series in Ukrainian Studies. Clothbound, ISBN 0-916458-55-5. Paperback, ISBN 0-916458-60-1. 1994.

A Description of Ukraine. Guillaume le Vasseur, Sieur de Beauplan. Translated, annotated, and with an introduction by Andrew B. Pernal and Dennis F. Essar. Harvard Series in Ukrainian Studies. Clothbound set, ISBN 0-916458-44-X. (Set includes text and separate mapcase with 28 reproductions of Beauplan's maps and 1 modern guide map.) 1993.

To receive a free catalogue of all Harvard Ukrainian Research Institute publications (including the journal *Harvard Ukrainian Studies*) please write, fax, or call to:

HURI Publications
1583 Massachusetts Avenue
Cambridge, MA 02138
USA
tel. 617-495-3692 fax. 617-495-8097